A Bird To

CW00385750

Travels of a B

Robert Duncan

(some names and locations have been changed)

Printed in Poland

First Printing, 2019

ISBN 9781794166356

Littlehouse Publications 2019

Curlew Croft, Keiss, Scotland

Rob Duncan is a retired College Lecturer. Having grown up in the far North of Scotland, he moved to Edinburgh to study Zoology, where he also picked up the bug for motorbikes. He first worked as an Animal Behaviour researcher in Cambridge and went on to spend 30 years lecturing, teaching and running science courses for adults. He has followed a life-long passion for birding, both in the UK and across the world. Rob is now a full-time carer for his wife. This is his first book.

Front cover: El Portalet Pass, Pyrenees.
Rear cover: White & Dalmatian Pelicans over Danube Delta

For Anne, Claire & Iain

With thanks to Claire & Iain for making my trip possible, and for help & encouragement in writing this book. Thanks also to John Smart, Amy Barker and Marten Cieluch for proof reading parts of the text.
Special thanks to Amy for the cover design, and everyone at Littlehouse Publications for putting up with me while writing this book.

CONTENTS

Prologue

The first mention of a bike trip in my diary appeared three years before I embarked on the trip which forms the bulk of this book. I had just turned 51. Up until that point, the diary was full of angst and narcissistic bleating; a foreboding of things to come, constantly aware that time was running out. In another life, I had promised myself that I would ride a big motorbike through the South of France to Nice (the route on which I had met my wife). In 30 years that hadn't happened – not even a germ of it. I could also count roughly how many springs there were left for the birding that I wanted to "get around to someday": a classic, but very specific bucket list. There were finite chances to see the mass migration of birds of prey across the Straits of Gibraltar, to visit the ancient marshes and forests of Poland, and to sail the Southern Ocean in search of Albatross. There were particular bird species that I always assumed I'd track down one day: Lammergeier, a rare, bone-cracking vulture; Black Woodpecker, the elusive, dagger-billed bird of cool European forests; and at least three "common" species of Albatross, waiting to be found across the oceans of the world.

My wife, Anne, has Multiple Sclerosis. We had lived with it since her diagnosis, but now, over 30 years on, it was impacting on daily life: her legs had gradually stopped working and she became reliant on a wheelchair – and on me. The twenty or so birding seasons I could see ahead of me might be reduced to just a few. I'm not sure it was a healthy way to look at life, but at least it was grounded in reality. Time *was* running out – it is running out for everybody. Perhaps some people don't see this until it's too late, but my diary betrays a panicked dawning: I knew I'd do none of those things unless I got on with it, pronto.

Chapter 1 – Bikes

It is Edinburgh, 1977. I'm a twenty-year-old Zoology student, buzzing around the city on a little blue Suzuki 120 motorcycle, for which the only qualifications are a provisional licence and plastic L plates. I ride from my one-bed tenement flat in Easter Road to lectures at Kings Buildings on the southern fringes of the city. The little bike also takes me to my summer job in the St James Centre shopping mall, right in the middle of town, close to Princes Street and it's famous gardens, surveyed grimly from above by the even more famous Edinburgh Castle; happy days in a beautiful and grand city.

The affordable freedom of riding the little Suzuki around these ancient cobbled streets, gives me the bug for bikes and I plan to buy my next, bigger one, saving my double time Sunday earnings from the shopping centre job. I also read Jack Kerouac's "On The Road" and a magazine article about a mountain route from Grenoble to Nice, allegedly a driver's paradise. My youthful plans now include a life dream to ride a big BMW motorbike down that road, in emulation of Kerouac's spirit.

*

I leant the bike in a slow curve across the road, through a sheet of running water and into a stony lay-by. In the space of just 60 miles, I had already pulled in twice for a boost of caffeine and a warm up. This time I stopped because I just couldn't go on – not even to the next café. Soaked, dripping, tired and cold, with my damaged back aching, and many miles still to ride in this relentless rain, I cried into my helmet. Even that, I did only half-heartedly. Two bikers rode past, waving. Disguised in my motorcycle gear, I don't suppose I looked the way I felt: defeated by circumstance, pain and loneliness. Normally the cheery half salute from fellow bikers would lift my spirits, but I waved indifferently and didn't even look up (I knew the bikes were Harleys – I could tell by the deep throb of the engines and the low slung outline of the bikes as they slipped by).

It was early May and I had been riding for four weeks through good weather and bad, but lately, day after day, it had rained – and rained very hard. I wasn't to know, but this was the worst period of rain and flooding in central and Eastern Europe for over fifteen years. I had set out from Portsmouth on the ferry to Santander with my motorcycle all set up for touring, and now I was in northern Romania, heading for the border with Hungary. I had arrived at this dismal Romanian lay-by through a series of life-changing events, which began thirty years earlier in 1970s Edinburgh. Ultimately, at the age of 53, they led me to set off from Suffolk on a motorcycle journey around Europe in a quest to find the continent's most enigmatic and elusive bird species.

A catalyst to the whole bike trip idea was "Long Way Round", an epic motorcycle circumnavigation by Ewan McGregor and Charley Boorman. This adventure was lavishly serialised on television the same year, which I caught on a re-run some time later, after it had already become passé in biker circles. For me it coincided with those restless revelations about the sands of time-and it lit a fire under me.

McGregor is, of course, even better known as a Hollywood superstar (Trainspotting, Star Wars, Big Fish, Salmon Fishing In The Yemen and many more) while Boorman, less well known for his acting, is son of the famous John Boorman, film director, producer and scriptwriter (Point Blank, Deliverance, Excalibur, Hope and Glory). With that background, small wonder they were able to turn their bike ride around the world into a major television/DVD series. And a wonderful thing it is too. I loved it and it was important in pushing me on with my plans. In fact, it advanced those plans by three years. After watching the series, I could find no good reason to wait – and every good reason to get on with it as soon as possible: it put the bit between my teeth.

This is not the place to do a re-run or summary of Long Way Round, but I do want to dispel one clichéd assumption that lots of people have made: I did not embark on my trip as a copy-cat of what they did. They were an inspiration and I watched and re-watched the whole TV series to get pointers and to keep up the momentum – but my challenge was very different to theirs and my dreams were anchored in my own past.

To be honest, Long Way Round is sometimes sneered at in the purist world of biker adventure travel. There are insane individuals who have crossed the most difficult terrain on Earth on motorcycles, with no support, film crew, doctor or even a riding companion. I think they're mad, but then again, I was to be on my own as well; a novice, covering huge distances and not always that close to civilisation. Charley and Ewan did us all a favour: they made us see that such things are worth trying and that they can be done. I thank them for their inspiration[1].

Long Way Round reminded me very powerfully of my intention, many years before in Edinburgh, to ride a big bike down through France. It made me realise that I could resurrect that youthful exuberance and tap into it. As I watched Ewan and Charley goof their way round the world, it set me free and I decided to combine the bike trip with my birding ambitions: the "Biking Birder" was born!

I had to consider so many things: I was a novice, I didn't even own a bike, I had no licence and I was well into my fifties. It had been over thirty years since I had been on a bike (riding round Edinburgh on my beloved 120cc Suzuki Bloop[2]) and now, no longer a presumptuously hopeful twenty-year-old, if I was to finally realise my dream, I had to face all the training and testing on a big brute of a bike. Unlike those Edinburgh days in the 70s, you could no longer just stick up L plates and ride off. Even for my wee Suzuki (or today's equivalent), you now have

[1]I even e-mailed Charley Boorman about my trip. Charley wrote a really uplifting, simple reply wishing me all the best. That was the real catalyst from Long Way Round. Thank you Charley.

[2]Known as the Bloop, from its 100cc predecessor's acronym of "B100P". I always thought that was quite cute and am delighted after all these years to get it into print somewhere.

to complete a one day Compulsory Basic Training (CBT) and you still need those L plates. After this you can then do an intensive training course to ride "big" bikes (anything over 125 cc, but generally 400cc or more).

I also had a full-time job, a severely disabled wife and two kids (by this stage my daughter, Claire, was in the middle of a vet degree and son, Iain, was doing A-levels). In no way would I be doing a Long Way Round – this would be more like .The the Hard Way!

The prospective bike trip changed my life; it gave me a new focus. I carried on more or less as normal at work (still chasing my tail, but caring less), at home and with friends, but I felt as if I was on auto-pilot; as if I was watching myself go through the motions, while the real me concentrated on the trip. I had to make a big effort not to become consumed by it. Looking back, I'm sure people noticed and many probably got bored with my obsession. I think I went around telling everybody about it. I even announced to my line manager at work that I'd need some special leave:

"Fred, I need some time off to do this."

"How much time?" he asked, suspiciously.

I told him.

"TWO MONTHS!? I doubt if that's on, but I'll ask the powers that be. It would be unpaid, of course, and depends if we can get someone to cover. The days of sabbatical leave have gone mate, sorry."

Fred was more of a friend than a colleague so I told him how I felt.

"Well Fred, you may as well know, if it comes to it, I'll resign in order to do this trip."

Was I mad? Probably – but it felt liberating to tell him. I'd had this sense of reckless liberation once before, and it had proven dangerous. That one had led to all sorts of kamikaze, self-destructive acts... but that's another story.

My big bike trip was no longer just a pipe dream or panicky words in a diary, but I may not have had the courage to see it through had I not felt an unshakeable belief that I had to do this or my life wouldn't be worth living.

I planned hard, starting with a rash booking for the CBT course in the middle of winter. One February day in freezing cold rain, at the age of 51, I re-acquainted myself with riding a motorcycle: a little 125cc training school bike – and I found it surprisingly tough. To be out there on a bitter winter morning, struggling with this recalcitrant machine, something certainly must have changed in my life! By April, it had warmed up a bit and I booked five days of intensive – and expensive – "big bike" training.

I decided to stick with the outfit that ran the CBT course: Perfect Motorcycle Tuition (PMT!), run by the instructor, Steve. Steve was a very big guy – overweight actually (a lot of bikers seem to be huge) – and he had a worrying slowness to him, which was nevertheless somehow calming. He followed us, dwarfing his big Yamaha Bandit (while my feet hardly touched the ground on my bike) and he delivered his radio instructions in a breathy, disconnected, rather bored voice. I guess it all became a little formulaic for him after a while, but the real reason for his apparent disengagement only became clear after I finished the training and sat my test.

I got on fine for the first couple of days, riding round in the safety of a school playground, but once we were out on the streets and getting on to the trickier stuff I started having problems.

"Steve, I can't do it," I said one day, "if I fail, it will be because of this."

Try as I might, I just could not get the slow U-turn with a big bike. Dejection crept in and my spirits fell. And bloody Nemi, my twenty-something training companion, could turn his Suzuki GS500, no trouble – the confidence of youth. As if to rub it in, Steve made him do it over and over, to be sure he could repeat it. Terrific for Nemi, but I had to just stand and watch, getting even more dejected. I finally dropped the heavy Honda CB500 by trying too hard. The sound of a big bike, even slowly crashing to the ground, is very unpleasant; it only emphasised my failure. On top of that, the bike fell on my foot – that's how I know how heavy a Honda CB500 is. I didn't tell anyone – but it bloody hurt!

"Do it again, Duncan," said Steve (he often mixed up my first and last names).

"Don't look down, look ahead, where you want to go. Look at that white van up there and the bike will follow."

Finally, I got it – sort of. But I couldn't reliably repeat the manoeuvre: a slow, deliberate 180 degree turn from one kerb to the other in a fairly narrow road. To this day, manoeuvring a big bike at walking pace is an anxious thing for me. Steve had made it clear that I would fail the test if I couldn't do this U-turn in one go, under control and with feet off the ground. No pressure then.

I borrowed a small Yamaha 125cc bike for the weekend from PMT. I practised the damn U-turn over and over. He had told me to keep my head up and look where I wanted to go and "the bike would follow". This seemed so improbable that I had to overcome every instinct to look down at the front wheel (which was, after all, the thing that turned – wasn't it?). After a while, blow me, it worked. I could whip that little bike round a treat. All I need to do now was transfer my new skill to the big 500. That worked too, but it was still hit or miss. I was going to fail.

Riding a bike is so different to driving a car. It's a much more physical experience and some operations are almost the opposite of those in a car. For a start, you change gear with your left foot; first gear is down on the lever, and the other five gears are up, through neutral, with your toe. If you ever see a biker at traffic lights fannying around with his left foot, instead of taking off, he'll be a novice, trying to find neutral. Then there are the indicators: on most bikes (apart from BMWs), they are just weird. There is a tiny little button next to your left thumb as you hold the clutch grip: pull it left and the left indicators flash, push it to the right and... well, you get the idea. But that's not the weird bit. It's that the indicators stay on after you turn – no one has invented a self-cancelling indicator for a bike[3]. You can be riding along (concentrating on all the other weird stuff you have to do to stay alive on a bike) with your previous turn signal winking away, confusing the hell out of everyone else on the road. I did that a lot. I was *definitely* going to fail.

Finally, the day came. I had completed my five days of intensive "big bike" training with Steve. Time was up and he took Nemi and me the fifteen miles to the Aylesbury test centre... on a dual carriageway... in a strong head-wind... at over 70 mph! I'd rarely gone over 50 during training and I arrived at the test centre, a nervous wreck (maybe that was why Steve called his school, PMT!). I failed.

As it turned out, it wasn't the dreaded U-turn that got me, but nearly everything else. I blame the weasel I had for an examiner and Steve for taking us to the test centre at warp speed on a bloody motorway! And... well, to be honest, I wasn't ready, so I made two or three major cock-ups all by myself. This big bike test was not easy, especially at my age. By the way, Nemi failed as well – the examiner really *was* a weasel!

Bike training itself had also been a weird experience. Steve rode behind us, sometimes delivering an impressive train of instructions as he watched us ride ahead: in the wrong lanes, going too fast, too slow, the wrong way or just generally cocking everything up.

PMT as an outfit hadn't exactly filled me with confidence, but I'd chosen them for the initial CBT training on the basis of convenience and price. They were just moving office when I signed up for the five-day, "big bike" course and their new room was a disorganised mess, but I had got used to Steve and could cope with his style. It wasn't until after my training, when I was about to buy the old Honda CB500 from him (yes, the one I had dropped on my foot doing the U-turns), that I learned he was

---

[3]Not totally true! There are a few bikes and conversion kits you can get and I believe that most Harleys come with self-cancelling indicators. Trouble is, they can't work the way a car does – by linking to the steering wheel. Those that do exist, work on distance travelled or time delay; I'll leave it to the reader to ponder the technical and safety issues of that one.

narcoleptic (prone to falling asleep in the middle of activities) – *a narcoleptic motorcycle instructor!?*Not long after my own training, he – allegedly – fell asleep while out with students, and rode into the back of one of them. I did wonder why he sometimes sounded drunk over the radio headsets in our helmets. But I liked Steve and I hope his PMT has somehow managed to keep going.

I paid Steve another £100 for a day's intensive training and a re-test. This time it was at a test centre in Pinner, closer to home, and the examiner was so different: calm, encouraging, smiling and basically a nice bloke (unlike the weasel). I set off from the centre on the re-test and – I know this is a huge cliché – I felt "at one" with the bike. I really did. I felt it was with me, not against me. I belonged on the bike and, for a change, it liked me... I passed!

By autumn of that year, I still had no bike – lots of plans, but no bike. I really needed to practice riding and, since passing my test, I had lost a summer of decent weather by messing about on eBay, looking for a suitable bike, but finding nothing. I wanted an interim machine to practice on, not the one I'd take on a proper trip. That was still going to be a BMW (yes, yes, just like Long Way Round, I know) or some other touring model. I tried eBay again and was led a fruitless dance by Dave-the-Kiwi, who was supposedly selling a nice BMW 650 Strada, all set up and ready for touring. It never materialised and to this day I wonder what scam Dave was trying to pull. Whatever it was, I must have been too cautious to get sucked into it – or maybe I just missed a damn good deal.

I went on the annual pilgrimage to our little croft house in the far North of Scotland – minus bike. Even here, a mere seven miles from John O' Groats, bikes seemed to be everywhere[4]. Every second bloke I talked to owned a bike. Why had I not noticed this before? It deflated me a bit. What I was doing didn't

[4]It should have been obvious to me that this part of Scotland was a magnet for bikers; Land's End to John O' Groats and all that, plus the coast road from Inverness to Caithness must be one of the best biking roads in the UK – and now there is the North Coast (NC) 500 around the top of Scotland.

seem the least bit special any more: every Tom, Dick, and Harry had a bike... AND they all went on trips abroad. I had to really keep hold of what made my plans important – to me at least.

I considered lots of models: Kawasaki, Suzuki, BMW, Honda and gradually fixed on buying a Honda CB500, like the one I had learned on. I spent hours on eBay again, but the searches were hopeless. If I got close to buying one, I got beaten in the auction or a deal was struck somehow and the seller removed it before I even got a chance (good old eBay!). Even the purchase of the PMT bike fell through when Steve had his narcoleptic accident. Finally, out of frustration, I contacted some dealers.

"Oh, a CB500, they're like gold dust, mate." said one.

Tell me something I don't know!

"See, all the couriers love them 'cos they're so reliable."

Finally, one of those "domino" events occurred, where one chance remark or incident ends up changing everything. I phoned Robotech, a small local bike dealer and got into a long conversation with a guy called Bill. I never met Bill, but he is responsible for the bike I eventually took round Europe. It started badly. He only confirmed what I already knew: decent CB500s were "like gold dust, mate", but he seemed keen to help a floundering novice. After a lot of advice and chat, Bill rounded off the conversation.

"Tell you what, try Honda in Chiswick, " he said, "they're a big outfit, but they only take in good bikes. Ask for Guy. He's been there a while. Tell him I sent you and he'll see you all right."

I phoned Chiswick Honda and asked for Guy. Miraculously, he happened to have a CB500 I could look at.

Chiswick Honda is a big flash car showroom, which also specialises in bikes. The place looks like a spaceport. The building is a wedge-shaped glass and steel clone of any number of modern structures you see in Britain these days, especially in car-showroom-land. It is the sort of place where they make sure all the dirty bits (like mechanics, black with oil) are kept well out of sight. The customer only sees the sparkling new bikes, the sales staff in their cute red polo tops, the pretty, made-up girl at the large, curved reception desk and – the final clincher for me – a coffee and pastries bar!

I approached Spaceport Reception Terminal, gave my name and asked for Guy. He was with a customer, but wouldn't be very long. I had a complimentary coffee and croissant (of course) then wandered round looking at all the shiny new bikes, mostly Honda, but a few others as well. Bikes like these are so sexy: raw power, glamour and hi-tech engineering just drips off them (I was really getting back into bikes!). As I strolled around, I noticed an interesting machine parked against the wall of a curving staircase that went up to Spaceport Control Centre. It was a big Honda, all silver and new – except that it wasn't new. At four years old, it only had 1600 miles on the clock and looked like it had never been ridden. Apart from heat discolouration on the exhaust, there was no sign that it had done even those paltry 1600 miles. It was way too big and heavy for me and, at two and a half grand for a temporary machine to practice on, was over my budget anyway – but it looked lovely.

"Hello, sorry to keep you waiting, " came a voice from behind me: it was Guy in his bright red polo top with a "Honda" wing logo embroidered on his left shoulder. He was very clean cut, short like me, but stocky and maybe a little younger. From his confident air, he was clearly one of the senior salesmen. We shook hands and, by way of introduction, I pretended to know Bill from Robotech. Guy seemed fairly neutral about my acquaintance with Bill, but it did seem to smooth things along a bit.

"You wanted to see the CB500? We've just got it in," he said, leading me across a courtyard to a new looking, corrugated metal outbuilding. It was a black motorcycle; identical to the one I had learned on, bar the colour. I had a good look. It was worn, but sound.

"We won't bother doing anything with it," said Guy "took it as a trade-in, but it's too old for the showroom. We'll just auction it off. If you want it, you can take it as seen, no guarantee, but give you a good price on it."

I was hesitant. It was showing its age and that would be fine if I was getting an eBay bargain, but not if I was paying a dealer's profit. It was also at the top of my budget at £1500 and, without a warranty, I couldn't see the advantage of buying from a dealer. He saw my hesitation and, like the good salesman he was, he spotted an opening.

"Listen, if you're not sure, let me show you something else – much better for you." I had told him about my proposed trip. Maybe that had been a mistake since he now knew what might catch my imagination.

Back in Spaceport, he led me over to... that big silver Honda!

"I saw this," I said immediately, "it's lovely, but way too big for me. I'm not ready for that."

I was genuinely intimidated by the thing and didn't hide my apprehension. But Guy must have seen this a million times: novice biker scared of his first big bike. He ignored me.

"Want to have a test ride?" he said. I was speechless at first, but then protested: the price, the size, the weight, I only wanted a cheap first bike; something I could drop on my foot and not get too upset.

"Just take her round the block. If you don't like it, that's fine."

You can maybe guess the rest. Still very nervous, I swung my leg over the seat, very aware that I needed to clear that huge petrol tank – it was all so unfamiliar to this new boy. After an all too brief run-down of the controls from Alex, Guy's assistant, I started it up and rode off as if I was on Steve's old CB500. But oh how smooth, how silky smooth, this was. Why had I been so impressed by that rattling box of nails that I learned on? And the size/weight problem? Didn't even feel it! I was sold, completely and utterly sold. The budget went out of the window! I even found myself thinking: "Who knows, this bike, with its 1600 miles, might even do for the trip."

A week later, I went to pick the bike up from Spaceport Honda. I took a train from Harrow & Wealdstone station to Gunnersbury and walked self-consciously out into Chiswick High Road, clutching my Arai helmet like a cherished old friend. I had my bike jacket on and carried a rucksack with bike boots, trousers and gloves.

On the train, I had been reading "Running With The Moon" by Johnny Bealby, an excellent tale of bike travel down through Africa. With this in my mind and being there, all ready to ride, I had an overwhelming urge to get the bike and ride off on my trip right there and then. Under those circumstances, that felt right.

Having previously come by car straight off the M4, Gunnersbury Station was unfamiliar and Spaceport Honda was nowhere in sight. I asked for directions.

"Dunno mate, I'm not from round here."

Why is it that the first person you ask is never a local? Is there some sort of magnetic attraction between people who don't know where they are? Do I subconsciously pick out those who are in the same position – i.e. lost? Do other people do that, or is it just me? Next, I deliberately chose someone who looked familiar with his surroundings: I approached a bloke leaning against a concrete pillar, reading a free newspaper.

"Dunno mate. I don't live here."

But it's Honda Spaceport! Somebody must know it for God's sake. Then:

"Hang on, I think I know the place – looks like a big spaceport? Straight up here, head for the M4 flyover, you can't miss it."

A few more coffees and a couple of pastries later, I was the very proud owner of a near-as-damn-it new Honda CBF600. Apart from an administrative hiccup over the true mileage and identity of the bike (for a while, the paperwork seemed not to agree), it was plain sailing. Throwing caution to the wind, I had added another £200 for a centre-stand and a rear luggage box, and I bought a massive chain lock in the Spaceport Accessories Bay.

I rode off down Chiswick High road, the M4 swishing above me until I came to the post office where I needed to put road tax on the bike. The whole ritual of parking a bike, getting off it, locking things in the top box and removing helmet and gloves was so unfamiliar, I felt self-consciously gauche as if the whole world was watching me. And the bike was so heavy! At anything below walking speed, gravity seemed to suddenly switch on (away from the Spaceport perhaps!). It was like moving a bullock. It almost had a mind of its own. And that weight! This was going to take some getting used to.

Riding home was a joy though. Nothing can quite compare to the feeling of zipping along on your first big bike. The power is awesome. It could do 0 to 60mph in about four seconds – comparable with many large sports cars. The first time I gave that a real try, I almost lost hold of it. The bike leapt ahead before I was ready. Even though I was (supposedly) in control, nothing prepared me for the sheer grunt and snap as the engine shot the bike forward. That gave me a little scare! I rode the rest of the way home a bit more sedately.

Chapter 2 – Birds

As part of our third-year Zoology course at Kings Buildings, Professor Roger Short, a hotshot academic, visits us to talk about reproductive biology in cows and sheep. At the end of his lecture, he offers one of us a chance to work on something which has intrigued him, but which he has had no time to follow up: a project training sniffer dogs to detect oestrus in cows. Oestrus is the exact time when a cow is able to conceive. Spotting it is a major task for farmers so they can either mate the cows with a bull or decide to get the artificial insemination man in – which could be an expensive waste of time if you get it wrong.

"Let Aubrey know after the lecture if you are interested," says Roger Short to the group as he packs up.

I am definitely interested. I'd always been into dogs, and reproductive biology is my favourite area of study. I love it all and am happy as a pig in the proverbial. In Scotland, you start a degree a year earlier than in England so it takes four years. I am glad to have another year to come; these are and were the best years of my life. Working hard, loving my course – a bit of a geek I suppose – I am immersed in it all. I speak to Aubrey Manning, our professor of Zoology and he arranges an appointment for me to see Roger Short. I assume loads of my fellow students will also be trying for this chance to get a foot in the door of biological research with one of the "big men". We know Roger Short's reputation: he is head of his research unit within the university and has written one of the textbooks we are using. It would be a real coup to get this placement.

*

You may be reading this as a bike trip travelogue and I hope it gives you some joy, but there is, you may have gathered, another side to this tale; I am in fact, much more birder than biker.

Trouble is, the term "biker" conjures up a certain image, a stereotype, which I believe your average true biker is quite happy to cultivate: they are rough, they are tough – strong silent types. Bikers don't wash... or eat... or feel pain. They are fearless. They wear leathers (all the time). They congregate in great masses at greasy spoons to out-do each other, then they scream around country roads, frightening animals and small children (especially at weekends in North Wales). Some, or all, of that stereotype may be true, but almost none of it is true of me or most of the bikers I know (except the washing bit!). My mentality and approach to life belong more with the typical birding clan than with petrol-head bikers.

In the birding world the tendency to classify, group and name birds seems to extend to the participants: you slot into a sort of hierarchy. This has been admirably set out in the Little Black Bird Book by Bill Oddie, the famous, but grumpy television celebrity birder. It goes as follows: "twitchers" are very serious, fanatical birdwatchers who travel the length of the country (and further) to see a new bird and who really know their stuff (or claim to); if you are serious, but less fanatical, you may be a "birder" and may or may not really know your stuff; then there are "birdwatchers" – dedicated people who generally keep an eye on their local birds, keeping detailed records, whether the birds are common or not; weekend softies who only go to RSPB reserves to find birds and who patiently work out the difference between Green and Wood Sandpiper, but never remember it for next time, are called "dudes" (they also wear their binocular straps way too long and dress up in some expensive, must-have uniform associated with outdoor hobbies); and finally, "robin-strokers" – little old ladies who just think birds are lovely. I suspect that last one is Bill Oddie's invention, but it makes me laugh. As for me, I'm definitely a second-rate birder and like most of those, I'm also a closet twitcher – a new or rare bird always gets the heart rate up just a bit.

Most people rise up the hierarchy, starting as plain old bird watchers (or maybe even dudes), turning into birders when they get some detailed knowledge and experience and can tell birds from just their flight or song. Nearly every birder I know has morphed into the twitcher at some time or other. A mad few get hooked so badly they remain manic twitchers for many years, losing friends, jobs, girlfriends or even wives in the process. Such people have become famous, even legendary in birding circles. Most of us eventually see the folly of this lifestyle and stop rushing off for the next new bird (or "Tick" on "The List"[5]). Nowadays, I keep an eye on my local patch, contribute to national surveys, visit the better places to see good (or even "twitchable"!) birds at the right time of year and, if I can manage it, I go abroad – because, quite simply they have more and better birds there. We have lost so much in this country and – somewhat sadly – that may have been the single most important reason for choosing a birding trip around Europe.

Birding has also become extremely hi-tech over the years, although it started on the humble landline network in the seventies and eighties, the hub being a single telephone in a B&B called Nancy's in Cley on the North Norfolk coast. To birders of a certain age, the thought of Nancy's will bring a nostalgic tear to the eye. You could phone there almost any time of day and some gruff birder would answer. People would phone in rare bird sightings ("the gen") from anywhere in Britain and if you were there when the phone rang, you jotted it all down in a scruffy ring notebook next to someone's egg and chips, or alternatively, you read out to the caller whatever gen had been phoned in that day.

Nancy has long since hung up her frying pans and, of course, it has now all changed. First, there were pagers, then e-mail, then newsgroups and finally the Power of The Internet. You can now subscribe to highly commercial, web-based bird information services (owned or run by some of the original

---

[5]"The List" is another classifying/grouping/collecting phenomenon associated with birding, which I have to admit, shares characteristics with train and plane spotting. A new bird on The List is a "Tick", The List is usually those birds seen in Britain or Britain & Ireland (The UK List), but it can also be birds seen anywhere in the world (the Life List, on which a new bird is a "lifer"). There is the Garden List, the Local Patch List, the County List and the Year List. Some perverts even have a TV/Film List – don't ask. I have a Bike Trip List... of course I do!

Nancy's café twitchers, by the way) and receive alerts of rare birds within minutes, sometimes seconds, of them being seen, anywhere in the country. The gen comes in via your e mail or even your mobile (which can have the inevitable bird "apps" loaded for maximum cool nerd-appeal) so you can down tools, job, girlfriend, or wife and hare off after the bird in question, in the hope that it won't have legged/winged it before you get there.

Then there is all the gear. I find the clothing and "accessories" mind-numbingly boring and anyway this isn't the place to be discussing the finer points of Gore-Tex or folding chairs, but the optical side of things is seductively rich in geeky lure and I had to investigate very carefully what gear I could carry on a bike (oh the hardship!). Like Hi-Fi (for which I'd also had a penchant in the distant past – in common with many blokes of my age, I suspect), birding has a plethora of highly technical gadgets for seeing birds at their best: binoculars, monoculars, telescopes, tripods, clamps, eyepieces, straps, cases and – new on the block – "digiscoping".

Here, I must declare myself a non-photographer. Another sect in the birding world seems to have developed in recent years (leaving old farts like me behind): the amateur nature photographer. With huge – enormous – lenses that really belong behind the goal at a football match, these people manage to take stunning photos of rare (or beautiful) birds and post them on all sorts of Internet sites from Facebook and photo sharing sites to personal blogs and the bird information services mentioned earlier. I see the appeal, I really do, but I can't quite justify lugging around three grand worth of optical gear to spend hours on a photo when there are so many birds to see – and, if you're a serious birder, you need to carry binoculars and telescope as well. Digiscoping on the other hand, appeals much more. It involves attaching a small digital camera to your telescope and taking the picture – effectively using the 'scope as a big lens. Proper photographers will snort derisively, but it is a good compromise and did me just fine for record shots on my sojourns around Europe.

Binoculars and telescopes are obviously another rich seam for techy geek-ness. It can be all talk of roof prisms, lens coatings, light dispersion, eyepieces and close focusing. Are your "bins" 8's or 10's (magnification)? Which are best in low light, in woodland or for sea-watching? Is your telescope the "ED" version with lens coatings that add on another (yes, another!) £400 to the price tag? And is it made by Nikon or Zeiss or – flavour of the month at the time of writing – Swarovski?

As with Hi-Fi decades earlier, I was into some of this optical nerdity. In the mid-80s, I eventually blew £1000 on a pair of binoculars – the best in the world at the time. In my defence, I still have them and didn't fall into the trap of constantly upgrading. My best-in-the-world Leica 10 x 40 "Red Spots" are now old, way behind the times (even I have to admit the new generation optics are so much better) and probably in need of a good service, but I love them – and they've gone with me everywhere.

Like most people interested in birds and in watching them, I also like to know about the places they live in – or should be living in, i.e. their habitats. To quote Prince Philip: "I'm no tree-hugger", but I care deeply about the state of our natural habitats, especially in Europe, where it is still possible to visit pristine and ancient wild places without doing them too much damage. In my days as a college lecturer, I would take reluctant groups of students (mostly city kids from Edmonton or Haringey) to any nature reserve, field course, or bird ringing demonstration that I could; if birding could be bolted on, so much the better. The students thought I was an eccentric nut – more and more as the decades rolled on. By the end of the nineties, I had cut out the bird ringing visits and became reluctant to even admit an interest in birds to the street-wise, hip-hop youth that populated my groups. It was strange to witness this minor cultural change and more than a little sad to think that the up-coming urban generation seemed further from developing an environmental conscience than ever before.

The idea of a bike trip to Europe without visiting such wild places was unthinkable. Likewise, I couldn't ignore the mouth-watering bird species available as I travelled, any more than I could go out without my Red Spots; the concept of birding with a motorbike just followed on. Trouble was, I had no idea if anyone had tried this before. Might there be a newsgroup or Facebook group of biking birders out there somewhere? Surely someone would have given it a go? I Googled and browsed, searched and linked, but came up with only one person – in the whole world – who had specifically chosen to do what I was planning. For that alone, he is worthy of mention: his name is Robert Tymistra and he lives in Canada. I contacted Robert by e-mail and the simple act of dialogue with a like-minded soul did wonders for my sense of momentum. He also had a refreshing approach. For a start, he was instrumental in helping me settle on which bike to use on the trip. He had done some birding in North America on his BMW F650, a relatively small bike compared to the 1200cc monsters that McGregor & Boorman rode on Long Way Round. When I queried his bike as perhaps a little underpowered for major touring, he replied that it had plenty off-road capability for him and, "Anyway, what's the rush?". He was right, of course, and that sentiment informed a lot of my planning and indeed the ethos for the whole trip from then on.[6]

Apart from this transatlantic contact across the Interweb, there was nothing and no one else. I posted little adverts on birding websites, newsgroups and message boards, but aside from some good luck wishes and a few birders who also had motorcycles, nothing concrete. It was even worse when trawling biker sites and magazines. The term "bird" only brought up web images of biker-babes and semi-nude models draped across fearsome looking motorcycles next to fat, greasy geezers with Hell's Angels logos all over them and their machines. In terms of the image of women in biking circles, it sailed very close to

---

[6]Thanks, Robert and I hope you manage your adventure from North to South America.

the wind. To be honest, it was verging on soft porn. Titillating though that might have been, I got cheesed off with the sexual innuendo behind "birds and bikes" or even just "birding" ("oh you mean the feathered variety, nod-nod, wink-wink" – oh how original, how funny!), I gave up quickly on that avenue of "research".

I was on my own then. In a small way, the concept of birding around Europe on a motorcycle was going to be genuinely ground-breaking. My mission now was to see if it would be feasible or sensible... or even an enjoyable experience.

At this point, having bored all my friends rigid with it all, my best friend and birding buddy John, declared that he was planning a permanent return from New Zealand to the UK. He said he would like to join me on the trip. At first, I felt a bit lukewarm; this was my baby, after all, my adventure to see if biking and birding would work together. I wasn't sure I was ready to share, but John announced that he'd also developed an interest in bikes and had already done his first bit of the training. I began to warm to the idea of having a touring companion, especially one who would be as keen on getting to the birds as I was.

Part of my initial hesitation with John was about the route; I didn't want to change it. I had more or less fixed on starting at Gibraltar in April, for the mass migration, as thousands of birds become squeezed into a narrow corridor to cross the strait between wintering quarters in eastern and southern Africa and breeding grounds in Europe. My finishing point was going to be Lithuania, where I wanted to end with a visit to an old friend's grave. John suggested other possibilities, and a dialogue began by e-mail from one side of the globe to the other. To an old fogey like me, it felt amazing to be doing this at a distance of 12 000 miles and it felt good to have someone else's input – I had me a touring, birding and biking buddy, and my best friend to boot.

The main issues with using a bike as opposed to a car were keeping the expensive optics safe and secure, carrying all the other gear, and getting to bird sites over potentially difficult terrain. Most birders will recognise that good birds are very often in out of the way places where even a 4x4 vehicle might struggle, so I had to think carefully. I still had my sights set on a BMW – probably the new big brother to Robert Tymistra's 650, an off-road 850cc machine which was confusingly called the GS650 (why BMW, why?).

Meantime, I was riding my Honda 600 to work nearly every day and in nearly all weathers (apart from ice). It started badly when, mere days after acquiring it, I dropped the bulky, heavy bike as I pushed it out of the carport, scratching the engine casing and busting the clutch lever of my lovely, nearly-new motorcycle. Soon after this, I dropped it again, this time in the car park at work. Pushing it off its centre-stand, I lost the balance point. Over it went – and when a big bike decides to go – it goes! In fact, in trying to stop it, I got pulled over and fell right on top of the thing. More than that, it tapped a scooter standing next to it, which fell onto another scooter, which collapsed onto an adjacent car. All in all, that lot cost me £250 in repairs to my work colleagues' scooters and it bruised my self-confidence no end. It was an extremely low point and I almost gave up on the trip altogether: if I couldn't manage the bike getting out of the house and a car park, what chance would I have riding it across Europe?

But these things are sent to try us so I stuck with it and, of course, I still had all the pleasure and anticipation of planning my bird route. It kept me happily off the streets for nearly a year and I found it all so much easier than the biking side of things. I knew precious little about bikes and touring – a real novice – but I knew about birds, about where and when to see them and I already had all the guidebooks I needed. I bought a stack of maps from Stanfords Map Shop, a wonderful place with every and any map you could wish for, and I found a couple of online websites for plotting a detailed route. Getting engrossed in that world of fantasy-soon-to-become-reality became one of the most satisfying aspects of the whole thing. Most people will recognise the pleasure of anticipating and planning a holiday; multiply that by a hundred and you'll get some idea of how good it was to be consumed by this project for months on end. Even now, when I look back on all that, it provides almost as much satisfaction as memories of the trip itself.

I got hold of bird trip reports[7] for most of the areas I hoped to visit and spent hours analysing them to work out a route that would take in the best sites and see the main species. As I researched this nature reserve and that national park, this bird species and that bird organisation, a route seemed to slowly and naturally unfold. Like a lengthening snake, it grew across my map of Europe, which I had stuck on the wall in our little box bedroom/study. I spent many happy moments gazing at this map and pondering. I was determined to see more of the magical area of Spain called Extremadura, in which sits the glorious Monfrague National Park where I had already spent short family holidays and sampled the rich bird life. This meant my starting point was fixed: Portsmouth for the ferry to Santander in Northern Spain. I also wanted to see the Millau Viaduct, the "Bridge in The Clouds" in southern France and, for biking, the spaghetti hairpins of the Transfagarasan Pass in Central Romania, thought by some to be the best driving road in the world. My final destination after abandoning all birding was to be, bizarrely enough, a grave-yard in Kaunas, Lithuania: I wanted to visit the last resting place of a dear friend, Wilma and meet her sister, Alma for the first time. There seemed to be a two-ferry option of returning from there via Northern Germany and Denmark to Harwich, a mere 40 miles from our new home in Suffolk. The route was falling into place.

The rest came to me as I dug around site guides, websites and maps, lost in bird-finding reverie. Some places were already legendary, having for many years been on my wish-list of "places to see before I die": the Danube Delta, the Hortobagy

---

[7]The Bird Trip Report is a slightly obscure and heart-warming aspect of the birding world; it is common practice for birders to produce a report of the places and birds seen on their trips. There is even a register of these reports compiled by a man called Steve Whitehouse (now online) and they are (or were) available free; a superb and immensely helpful resource for someone like me, planning such a journey – thank you Steve and trip-reporters, one and all. If you are wondering how to get hold of my trip report – you're holding it!

Wetlands in Hungary, the Camargue in France, the Straits of Gibraltar, the Burgas Wetlands in Bulgaria and Biebrza Marshes in Poland. As I immersed myself in their riches and lore, reading guidebooks, bird books and web information, these places determined where I would be taking the bike, rather than where would be good for riding, but I didn't care – hell, I wasn't even a proper biker. Little was I to know how much that would test me.

As it all unfolded, I settled on a few places where I needed to spend some time and where I might need some local gen or even a guide. The Extremadura region of Spain was a hotspot for me so I booked accommodation near Trujillo. To maximise my chances of seeing Lammergeier in the Pyrenees, I booked a couple of nights at the Boletas Bird Watching Centre near Huesca in north-east Spain, I arranged a couple of days guided birding in Bulgaria, four days on a "Floating Hotel" on the Danube Delta and a few days near the Hortobagy Wetlands in Hungary. God bless the Internet and e-mail for making all this possible with relative ease from a comfortable room at home. Back in the day, this would all have been long and difficult to arrange.

A rather lovely example of this was the communication I had with Alina of Ibis Tours in Tulcea, Romania. I started by contacting Gerard Gorman, the author of *"Birding in Eastern Europe"* (*the* birding guidebook at the time for this area). Gerard wasn't free to guide me on the dates when I would be in Romania, but he recommended Ibis Tours – and Daniel Petrescu in particular. I e-mailed the Ibis Tours office and had a look on their website; talk about whetting the appetite! Daniel's superb photographs adorned the site with a clear emphasis on bird life, but also accompanied by beautiful, exotic landscapes and views of the Danube Delta. My e-mail outlined plans and tentative dates for a stop in Romania. A reply came back swiftly:-

From: IBIS TOURS
To: ROBERT DUNCAN
Subject: Răspuns: Birding guide Romania/Bulgaria

Dear Robert,
I hope this program will be on your wish:
I think you do not need transport by car because you will
come alone with motorcycle.
We suggest the following program with accommodation on
Floating Hotel:
First day will be staying on Floating Hotel with a group
from British.
The second day after breakfast you go in the Danube Delta
with Floating Hotel.
Days three you will explore the Danube Delta with the same
accommodation.
Fourth day will explore the Danube Delta with a smaller
boat on the way back to Tulcea, check out.
A price calculation for you with this program is of 300 Euro,
and includes: accommodation on the Floating Hotel; 3
meals/day; transport on water; specialist guide; local
assistance.
Waiting and your opinion on this proposal.
Best regards,
Alina Mitea
IBIS TOURS

The subsequent exchange of emails (and the posting of
money via international bank transfer) made the whole thing
seem very real. The idea of a Floating Hotel on the Danube
Delta with Daniel Petrescu as a guide was a dream come true
and Alina seemed so "can do", that I felt things were really
happening. I also felt that I had got to know Alina a little – she
had been intrigued by the mention of a bike and a few more
trivial emails flew back and forth. I couldn't wait to arrive at
this distant, foreign place with fabulous birds, a Floating Hotel
and a girl called Alina to meet me. As often happens, I had a
picture of her in my mind and I was keen to see if I was right.

The same sort of helpful and encouraging mail exchanges
took place to book the other guides in Spain, Bulgaria and

Hungary. As arrangements fell into place, the trip began to take shape. Apart from the ferry out to Santander, these were to be the only places I pre-booked. They only accounted for eleven days of the whole seven weeks; the rest, excitingly, was to be worked out as I travelled.

I planned to camp as often as possible. I can't exactly explain why, other than lack of experience. I wanted to have the flexibility to pitch a tent in the middle of nowhere (naïve) and to save some money on potentially expensive hotel bills (wrong). With this in mind, I spent considerable time and energy getting to grips with the world of camping. After a steep, Internet-enabled learning curve, I procured tent, sleeping bag, camping stove and sleeping mat – all extra lightweight and/or small for carrying on the bike and all another world to me. Here I must extol the virtues of good ol' eBay: I got most of this equipment, and advice to go with it, from what they like to call "the eBay community", the nebulous citizenship of eBayland to which I now belonged. Nearly every purchase was sound and at a good price. I had no idea if "this camping thing" (as I later called it on the dictaphone – also from eBay!), was going to work for me, but I was to find out soon enough.

Even more exciting for a birder type was the choice and purchase of optical equipment. I was like a kid in a sweetie shop! I already had my Red Spots, but needed to finally ditch my ancient draw-tube telescope and heavy tripod. My telescope had been a second-hand job, which at the time in the mid-eighties, was a well-known model and standard issue in the birding world (an Optolyth 30x75 for any old nerds out there). This heavy, bulky stuff had to go; I needed something light and small enough to fit inside a bike pannier, and there was only one place to get it: Birdfair!

The British Birdfair is the biggest event of its kind in Europe, maybe in the world. It is a testament to the love we Brits have for wildlife and the importance we place on it. The fair is a rambling collection of huge tents, marquees, Portaloos and food outlets, all set in fields right on the edge of Rutland Water Nature Reserve near Oakham in the Midlands. It takes place annually at the end of August and, from all over the world, it attracts birding holiday companies, bird guides, artists, photographers, optical and clothing companies, birding publishers and magazines, and a raft of other birding-related outfits. This, in turn, attracts a huge audience of birders, TV celebrities and guest speakers.

My interest at the fair was to buy my optics for the trip and to feel out some magazines about commissioning an article on my journey. I also hoped to get some sponsorship, advertising revenue or just publicity. I had set up a website to raise some funds for charity on the back of my trip and thought a deal might be struck with some of the companies. I ear-marked these and hunted them down at the fair, trying to convince them to sponsor me, with some publicity for them as a carrot; perhaps a sticker or something on the bike. I got no takers. I got very little from bike companies or shops and I learned that you have to be very pushy to get that sort of thing organised. I had also left it too late to make contacts and convince people to back me with anything concrete. I did, however, get a positive response about writing an article: "Bird Watching", the first popular bird watching magazine in the UK, said they would be interested, as did their main rival, "Birdwatch".

I wandered around the rest of the fair, meeting friends and acquaintances and chatting to the various stallholders until I came across the optical marquees. Hoping to get some part-exchange for my old Optolyth 'scope, I was after a good deal on a new, lightweight telescope and tripod. The only deal I could find was on a Nikon telescope selling for £70 off the already discounted Fair price – because it was pink! I did hesitate over the colour and it is to this day a source of mischievous derision among my birding friends but, for the purposes of my bike trip, I didn't care. It was still a fabulous Nikon ED50 'scope; compact and light, but with beautifully clear optics, courtesy of its light-dispersing lens coatings and crisp zoom eyepiece.

Bike luggage like the panniers (cases you clip onto a frame on the bike), top box and tank bag, had also to be researched, chosen and purchased. I needed the right metal rack to fit all this onto the bike and I had a host of other associated bits and pieces to buy, not least a proper screen to keep the buffeting air off me as I rode along on the faster roads.

The rest of the trip was up to me while on the road. Looking at the line on my map, which now snaked around Spain, across the Pyrenees, through southern France and Italy then hairpinned through the whole of Eastern Europe (with a question mark over a flying visit into Turkey), I couldn't see how I would fit it all in. I had no start date, but I reckoned I could just about have seven weeks away from home, work and family. Try as I might, I couldn't make it all fit; I needed either another week or I had to cut out one major destination. In the end, I ditched Gibraltar and the Coto Donana in the far south-west of Spain. The birders among you may be shouting at me;

"NOOOO! How can you miss out the Donana? And Gib. for migration? What about all those Honey Buzzards, eagles and storks flying cross from Morocco?".

Well, I'd been to both before; Donana was terrific, but very recent, and Gib' was a washed out disaster – twice! (I only saw one forlorn Yellow-legged Gull in the torrential rain). All the other places on my route were going to be new to me and deserved inclusion much more. By dropping these two sites, I gained five precious days for covering the miles, for contingency in case of disasters and, hopefully, for staying a while longer at some places to make sure I could find the key birds on my target list.

Yes, another list had emerged: the "Target List" for the trip. I've already mentioned some of these species: those that I've wanted to track down for many years. I've been salivating over some of them since my early birding days, but others came to me only as I researched the trip. An example of the former is the already mentioned, Lammergeier; I've wanted one of those for years! The name alone sets it apart[8]. It is a type of vulture but,

[8]The name Lammergeier, from German, means "lamb hawk" from the belief that they killed lambs. In fact, they are well known as bone-cracking scavengers, but are as closely related to hawks as to other vultures, hence their unique and rather more appealing appearance. Their Latin name, *Gypaetus barbatus* means Bearded Vulture

where other species are named Black Vulture, Griffon Vulture or Egyptian Vulture, Lammergeier is just Lammergeier (check that spelling!). Just the name conjures up far away, inaccessible places and a sense of mystery (well, it does to most bird fanatics).

Lammergeiers look different too: much more like an eagle than a vulture, they have a feathered head and neck while other vultures look scraggy and ugly with bare skin around neck and face. The tail of a Lammergeier is an unusual diamond shape and very distinctive in flight, along with their fairly bright orangey underparts, pale head and black wings. These birds are also huge, even compared to other vultures; quite a sight, if you get the chance. In Europe at least, Lammergeiers inhabit out-of-the-way, mountainous places, and the Spanish Pyrenees has nearly all of Western Europe's population (only 80-100 breeding pairs, and declining).

Finally, these creatures have a glorious way of eating. Having found a carcass, usually after other more numerous vultures have stripped it, Lammergeiers will pick up large bones and fly powerfully aloft. From a considerable height they drop the bone onto a favourite rock until it shatters. The big bird will then descend rapidly, but gracefully to eat the rich marrow and pieces of bone – whole! Unfortunately, none of this was likely to be seen by me: you need to set out a carcass at a favoured location way up in the mountains and be there at the crack of dawn. This would need time, contacts and planning that I couldn't sort out on a trip like mine.

Conversely, a bird that I had very little knowledge of, but which went on the Target List purely as a result of researching the route, was Masked Shrike. I love the whole shrike family. They are like miniature birds of prey: rapacious, usually boldly marked and pretty much out in the open with showy flight, feeding and perching behaviour. Their habit of impaling their prey (anything from a bee to a lizard) on a "larder" of thorns or barbed wire has earned them the gruesome generic name of Butcher Bird. Despite this, all shrikes are attractive birds and I

because they have small tufts where a moustache might be.

always give them more than a second glance. We no longer have shrikes regularly breeding in the UK since the demise to extinction of Red-backed Shrike in the late 1980s. Perhaps I like them so much because of that and because I was lucky (or unlucky?) enough to see the last breeding pair in Britain in 1987. They returned for the last time in 1988. Thankfully, since then, a few pairs have returned to breed in this country for the first time in over twenty years at a secret and protected site in Dartmoor[9]. We regularly get another species, Great Grey Shrike, mainly in winter in ones and twos, but shrikes as a whole are absent from our shores. Europe, on the other hand, abounds with them: Red-backed, Woodchat (gorgeous and common), Great Grey, Lesser Grey and... Masked Shrike. I'm not sure why it is called Masked because all common European shrikes have a black mask across their eyes, but it is a distinctive bird with lots of bold black and white plumage and rust-coloured underparts. Outside Greece (where I had no plans to visit on this trip), Masked Shrike is very rare as a breeding bird. The only country I had a hope of connecting with one was in Bulgaria and only in one particular place. It had to go on the list!

Other species were included on my Target List because they were rare or elusive. Many of these were essentially Asian birds on the extreme western edges of their ranges. These included Paddyfield Warbler and Pied Wheatear, both of which are Asian species present on the west coast of the Black Sea in Bulgaria and Romania – but nowhere else in Europe.

There were other, equally exciting and enigmatic target birds such as Black Woodpecker (and other woodpeckers that we don't have in the UK, especially Three-toed), Pin-tailed and Black-bellied Sandgrouse, Great and Little Bustard, Spanish Imperial Eagle, Azure-winged Magpie, Wallcreeper, Imperial Eagle, Levant Sparrowhawk, Red-footed Falcon, Great White

---

[9]At that time, the last pair of Red-backed shrikes in the UK bred at St Helen's picnic site, Santon Downham, Norfolk in 1988. A lone male returned in 1989 and called forlornly for a mate, without success. The newest (2013) Bird Atlas for the UK shows a few pairs now scattered from Scotland to the West Country and breeding has been attempted elsewhere recently.

and Dalmatian Pelican, Pygmy Cormorant, European Roller, Semi-collared Flycatcher and Aquatic Warbler. Nearly all these were new to me ("lifers" in birder jargon) and each in its own way, has as much enigma as Lammergeier. These were my must-see, target species (note the subconscious hunting terminology used in birding; not an accident, I believe). I hoped, even expected, to see them all.

Chapter 3 – Boats

"Are you bright?"asks Roger Short, as I sit in his office at an interview for the dog sniffing project. Prof. Short isn't the sort of tall, well-dressed "suit" who intimidates by a display of status or wealth, but he has an unnerving, challenging look in his eye. He is wearing an unfashionable, tired looking brown jacket and trousers that make him look almost bucolic. A short bloke in his forties with unkempt, thinning hair and a face with bulbous, cheery features, he has an incisive stare that belies a very sharp mind and total confidence in his abilities and position.

Was I bright? How do you answer that – from a man like him? Was it a trick question? I sit and think about it for a while as he peers at me to see how I will react.

"Bright enough to spot a good opportunity and get myself here," I bluff, aware that we are playing a sort of game; the sort I'm not comfortable with. Where I come from you don't ask obtuse questions like that – and I've never felt "bright". In a subsistence farming and fishing community in the Far North of Scotland, being bright isn't of much use unless you want to get out and grow a bit. So here I sit... growing!

"You need to be able to drive. Got your licence?"

Shit! I only have my provisional licence and L plates on my bike. I bluff it again, exuding confidence that I can pass my test in three weeks, no problem (I am so bright after all!). Roger Short takes me on. There is even a small wage for the few weeks allocated to the project. I have to pass my car driving test in order to get around farms, sampling and transporting cotton wool swabs from the cows' rear ends – all carefully labelled and recorded, and all in the aid of science! I also have to transport some future Fido, once appropriately trained, to identify oestrus from the swabs. Happily, I pass the driving test first time. Riding my wee Suzuki around town for a couple of years must have given me some road sense.

I move on to the next step – learning all about training dogs. I spend a week with the army dog-training unit in Melton Mowbray (love those pork pies) and I have a meeting with an American animal behaviourist who has started a similar project with dogs in the Texas farming belt. A trip to the States is in the offing and it's all getting very exciting for a young lad who came from the sticks near John O'Groats to the grand old seat of learning that is Edinburgh University. It feels as if I am well on my way to scientific super-stardom; the man who solved the riddle of spotting oestrus in cows... and to riding a big bike down a legendary road in the south of France.

Or so I thought...

✱

The day I booked the ferry to Santander was very significant. By then I had decided which bike to take, the route was planned, I'd bought some camping gear and other bits and pieces, but I hadn't committed to anything. Now it was definite. At the very least, I had spent a couple of hundred quid on the first key part: the ferry for me and the bike from Portsmouth to Santander on the north-east coast of Spain. Remarkably, it changed my whole approach. I started truly eating and sleeping bike trip. There is perhaps a lesson here for others: if your plans are getting bogged down, if it looks as though you'll never get down to it, then commit to something (perhaps your first night's accommodation, a train ticket or a deposit). Until I'd done that, even buying gear on eBay and seeing it delivered to the house, didn't make it real.

My friend John had to back out of the trip. His return date from New Zealand became uncertain and he didn't want to hold me up (he knew I was in a "now or never" place). Bizarrely, I went through a sort of reverse anxiety, suddenly becoming nervous about going alone, but it didn't take long for the whole thing to become my baby again. This gave me even more incentive to get on with things; it was all up to me now. I phoned round some Honda and BMW dealers to arrange test drives of bikes on the short-list and the following two or three weekends became dedicated to finding a new bike. I would turn up with my Honda 600, dressed in decent bike gear, trying to look serious.

"I'm doing a round-Europe trip," I'd announce, hoping that they'd take me seriously, and in general they did. Bikers (most of the salesmen owned a bike and were enthusiasts) are very tribal and will usually embrace a fellow nut-case with interest and advice, so I found the whole test-riding experience very encouraging; another shot in the arm for my sense of momentum.

At the Honda dealer in Ruislip, I tried two bikes: a hybrid off-road/on-road tourer called a Transalp, and a Deauville, a budget ready-made touring bike. When I got back on my trusty 600, it felt so much better than the bikes I'd been testing, and a little voice began whispering, "Why not go on this bike?"

At the BMW dealers, things were a whole lot more intense. I felt a little out of my depth looking at these big brutes – and that was just the salesmen! At Park Lane BMW in Central London, I went in feeling flush: in theory, I had £7000 to spend which I knew would get me a decent used bike – even a BMW – but I soon realised that, here in Park Lane, ten grand was a more likely starting point. Many new bikes typically cost a lot more than that. I fully intended to try out the Boorman/McGregor 1200 GS monster, but I was just too short in the arse department and was relieved to score them off the list. Instead, I gave their baby brother a try: Robert Tymistra's 650. I liked it, but it was so different to my 600, I couldn't warm to it. Finally, the BMW 800 ST was a "sports tourer" that might be a great compromise and an exciting bike to ride on the trip. I loved it. Unlike my Honda, it had a low down riding position and it flicked round corners much more nimbly. Unfortunately, it was a new model in the BMW range, so there would be very few used ones on the market. Any brand new BMW was simply too expensive, both to buy and to kit out for touring. The 800ST might also not be the best choice in terms of riding position for covering thousands of miles.

In the end, leaving central London behind, I rode off comfortably on my Honda 600, knowing that I wouldn't be replacing it. This would save me close on £5000, and the bike I bought as a starter machine was going to be the one to take me round Europe... fancy that! Thank you Guy and Spaceport Honda.

By this time, I had given up work and we had moved to Suffolk. Having also given up work to become Anne's full-time carer, I no longer needed to worry about taking time off. I was due to leave in early April and by January I had bought all the gear I needed, including an expensive satnav system specially designed for bikes. I had made all the arrangements for bird guides and stops, and the route was planned carefully day by day so that I knew where I should try to get to for when. I even had a couple of days arranged with friends near the Italian lakes as a break. The bike needed a service and I still had to fit luggage carriers and a windscreen... otherwise, I was ready.

Except for Serbia. Ah, good old Serbia! I read somewhere that you still needed a "green card" to back up insurance in Serbia, presumably since it wasn't part of the EU and was still to be formally recognised in terms of financial and commercial regulations. The Home Office confirmed this, blithely stating that you should make sure your insurance company issues green cards for Serbia[10]. They didn't! I tried re-insuring the bike with anyone who would issue one, to no avail. I even tried a German outfit who publicised online that they provided this service but, to cut a very long story short, they didn't. I had no option, but to set off without insurance for Serbia and hope for the best at the border or at worst, take a 300 mile detour around it, through Hungary and Romania.

I had I thought I should get in some advanced rider training before leaving, but as it turned out, all I could fit in was an

[10]Latest Home Office advice (Dec 2018); "If you're bringing a vehicle into Serbia, you must have vehicle registration and ownership documents and a locally valid insurance policy. European green card vehicle insurance is now valid in Serbia, but the requirement to hold a green card is no longer in effect. You should confirm with your insurance company that your policy covers Serbia "

initial assessment from the Institute of Advanced Motorists. A mere three weeks before my departure date, I met John, the instructor at the Tesco car park in Haverhill and we rode round the (unfamiliar) Suffolk roads for a couple of hours. I got lost. We managed to keep together somehow, but I found the whole thing unsettling, so close to my day of departure. When we had a de-brief at the end, John went through my performance;

"Have you ever heard of counter-steering?" he asked.

I bluffed a guess as a reply, which he ignored.

"You're all over the place on the bends. You should be taking them far faster, and sticking to your line – and you're in too high a gear most of the time."

"I thought I needed to move over to see further round the bends," I protested. He got that but, logically enough, asked why I had to move over in the first place; I should be in position before the bend. I was soaking it all in like a hungry nestling, but at the same time, it was making my confidence ebb away.

"Counter-steering," he explained, "is pushing down on the handlebar the opposite way to the turn as you lean into it. Doesn't sound right, but once you feel it you'll see how it works."

My expression must have said it all. He sighed in mild exasperation and continued;

"Look, you're probably doing it without realising. You took some of the bends just fine, but it's inconsistent. Give it a try. Just push down on the opposite handlebar and you'll feel it pull you round tighter."

"So do you think I would cope with a trip round Europe?" I asked, hesitantly.

It felt like an absurd question after he had more or less told me how crap I was.

"Sure!" he said, "you'll have a great time. Enjoy it."

And, you know, he meant it. I'll never know if he was really thinking "I hope that bloke comes back in one piece.", but his airy response lifted me and I was left with a determination to put his advice into practice as soon as I got back on the bike – and all through the journey round Europe. Counter-steering for me from now on!

The day before I was due to leave, I tried packing up the bike with all the gear. I had a top box pannier behind me, two side panniers either side of the rear wheel, a large waterproof roll bag that went across the back seat straddling the side panniers, a tent behind that, and a tank bag that clipped with strong magnets to the fuel tank in front of me. I had never had it all on the bike at the same time and I knew something was wrong as soon as I pushed the bike off its centre-stand. It felt unbelievably heavy. The suspension sank alarmingly and I could hardly hold it upright. I was sure I had overloaded it, but jumped into the seat to give it a try. I say jumped because, with all the bags and panniers, it was not possible to swing a leg over the seat as I normally would. It took a ballet hop to get into a riding position. Once there, it was so heavy, I had to push hard sideways with my knees just to get the bike to an upright balance ready for my first trial run. I set off down our narrow road to the end where I tried a turn. Impossible. The bike was definitely too heavy. If nothing else, I'd never lift it if it went over and I was worried that the suspension was overloaded. I felt bad at expecting so much of my steed – the first, but not the last time that I would have an emotional attachment to the bike.

The technical advice about luggage weights in my Honda owner's manual was confusing and unhelpful[11] so I set about ditching all the heaviest stuff. The blow-up air mattress and its pump had to go, as did several of the camping ready meals that I had packed ("… they'd have been disgusting anyway, " I told myself later on a dictaphone message). I got rid of some bird books as well until I felt happier with the feel of the bike. God knows how I decided what felt right, but I went from being worried that I wouldn't be strong enough to hold the weight, to feeling confident about setting off on a six thousand mile

[11]The manual states 14 kg as a luggage limit, but that isn't much and anyway, a pillion passenger could weigh 80 kg (average bloke). From many sources of advice on bike touring, what I was carrying seemed fairly normal. I've never found out if the 14Kg was a misprint.

adventure on a big heavy motorcycle. I unclipped the panniers and took the weight off. Again, I felt for the bike as if it were a horse or a mule being relieved of an unbearable burden. The next day we would be setting off to Portsmouth and we both needed a rest (humour me; one day you'll understand!).

I left on April 12th on a bright spring day. Opposite the house, a field of young spring shoots stretched away to my right, giving an air of fresh optimism and new beginnings; a fine day to be setting out, but there was no fanfare when I finally rode off.

We had recently moved to our new home in Suffolk so neighbours were still relative strangers, and most were out at work anyway. Friends lived miles away and my daughter, Claire was finishing her final year at Vet School. It was left to my wife and son to do the send-off, and a low-key thing it was too. Anne was in her wheelchair and really didn't want me to be going anyway: she was facing weeks of an untried and inconsistent pattern of carers in my place. Iain was to be the first of those carers (helped by professionals, morning and evening) and the burden of "the send-off" fell to just him, at a time when he must have been nervous about being left on his own to look after his mum. This all felt wrong, but as I rode away, I tried hard to be "in the moment": low key or not, this was truly the start of something. I had first dreamt of this moment way back, over 30 years before, and it had taken me three years to get ready. It all came flooding back: the training, the test, finding a bike, riding it to and from work through all weathers just to get used to it, kitting it out for a long trip, finding bird guides, organising the route and all the documents needed to ride through fifteen countries and – not least – putting together a package of care for Anne, more or less against her wishes. Yet here I was, tentatively riding away from home on the first step of the way.

I later wrote in my blog;

"Why does everything seem to be a first? This is the first blog I've ever done, it's the first entry while on my travels... and this is my first bike journey of any description – ever!"

That was how I felt now, gliding along the narrow track from home on my Honda 600, packed up for the first time with all the gear as it would be for the next two months. Every aspect felt new and unfamiliar, but I also had a sense of comforting containment; despite my reservations about the weight, the bike felt so good, it seemed that all we had to do was trundle along and I'd make it. "Trundle" was going to prove hardly the right word, but in essence, that's how it felt as I turned left off our little track and out onto the main road heading south.

"You should have done some trial riding," I thought loudly to myself, feeling a little anxious that here I was, setting off on this epic journey with no practice at all. But I wasn't listening. I didn't care if I'd failed to do the sensible thing. It seemed right to be just getting on with it. I gradually picked up speed, testing the feel of the bike in a straight line, round the bends and under braking. All seemed smooth and not so different to normal. Apart from being unsure how far I could lean as I cornered without catching the side panniers, my confidence grew and I started making swift progress. I had a hotel booked in Portsmouth for the ferry next day to Santander so there was no rush. In fact, a mere half hour after setting off, I was pulling in just east of Cambridge for my first stop – pathetic! I was meeting a friend and his daughter at a transport caf' for a photo-shoot and a "documented" send-off.

Mike and Lizzie were already there, sitting in the weak spring sunshine, at a table outside the café. Lizzie was working her way into photography as a career so she was taking it seriously. With tripods, light meters and a heavy-duty camera, this photo session became the true beginning. It seemed to mark this stage so much better than the under-whelming departure from home. It set the right tone for me and it was fun to feel a tiny (very tiny!) bit of celebrity, there in the public car park. It seemed appropriate and I allowed myself a bit of self-indulgence, posing in the car park with the bike looking good. Mike treated me to a bacon sarny in the World Famous Comfort Café then, with a wave, now immortalised in Lizzie's photo, I took off again, this time for real.

From here, until Alan and Collette in Northern Italy, I would meet no one I knew and, once on the ferry, I'd be covering ground I'd never seen before and might never see again.

The ride to Portsmouth was punctuated by more firsts: first pull over on my own at a motorway service station and first time leaving the bike all packed up – a surprisingly memorable experience. It felt very odd walking away from the bike with all its gear so exposed. I was convinced someone was going to cut the webbing and run off with my roll bag and I was totally paranoid about the TomTom Rider satnav, which clipped to a bracket on the handlebar. It had to come with me everywhere, as did the tank bag which, with its strong magnets, I had to yank off in order to lug it into the services. This tedious yet comforting little routine was to become second nature, but here at the leafy Fleet services on the M3, every move I made felt gauche and seemed to be scrutinised by all in the car park. Looking back now, I can clearly recall that no-one gave me a second glance! Still, as waves of disbelief swept over me, I was enjoying it all. Here I was, on my way... on my own... on The Trip.

I pulled in to the Travelodge perched high above Portsmouth, feeling tired by the adrenalin-fuelled ride of "day 0". Being on my own and not looking after Anne was sheer luxury: no one to call me or say how and when I should do things, the luxury of having a bath just when I wanted to and for as long as I wanted, a cup of tea from the hospitality tray – without feeling guilty about how indulgent it was. I slumped into this simple luxury and, stretching out on the big double bed, watched a feel-good film on the telly – "The Holiday" with Kate Winslet, Jude Law, Jack Black and Cameron Diaz – perfect!

Next day I rode onto the ferry – another first. Joining about twenty other bikers in the queue dedicated to motorcycles, I waited. I felt acutely like the new boy, the only one not on a customised BMW 1200 GS, with all the matching, colour-coded gear (panniers, suits, luggage). With my "naked" Honda 600, kitted out using second hand eBay bits that didn't match, jeans (with protectors in a pair of leggings underneath, instead of kosher bike trousers) and non-matching bike jacket, I felt like the poor relation. I certainly didn't look like them: serious bikers. The bike suddenly looked small and a bit of a cobbled-together affair compared to these huge, upright monster machines. I was the amateur among professionals, a boy amongst men, but part of me was secretly proud that I was doing this my own way, not as an expensive, colour-coordinated clone of Long Way Round. I was happy to be doing it on a relative shoestring. Helmets started coming off as people settled in for a bit of a wait and a few conversations started about where we were all off to and for how long. I merely succeeded in insulting a bloke about his Triumph motorcycle, showing my ignorance by accusing him of riding a Yamaha. He was distinctly un-chuffed! Eventually, the loading crew waved us aboard and I self-consciously manoeuvred the bike across the unforgiving, rail-bisected metal deck. Struggling once more with low-speed bike handling, I eventually got the thing into position for the deck crew to strap down for the passage. Stupidly, I hadn't thought about taking only what I needed for the night in a cabin, leaving the rest behind, so I seemed to be unpacking the whole damn lot! I also needed my telescope for some sea watching out on the Bay of Biscay (there were pelagic birds to be seen[12]). I felt rubbish at all this in the bare metal box of a cargo deck, all cold, echoing and smelling of diesel oil, with these hard-core bikers confidently and naturally unbuckling this and refastening that, lifting bags and stowing helmets. Eventually, by copying what they were doing, I joined them on the trek up to the main decks to find my cabin. I hated leaving the bike.

I find being "trapped" on a ferry oddly settling. There isn't much you can do (unless you're a workaholic) so you can allow yourself the indulgence of... indulgence. I wandered about a bit, drank coffee, ate food, drank more coffee, tried some sea watching (unsuccessfully) then struck up conversations with fellow passengers.

Steve and Thomas made a real odd couple. Steve was a short, greying, jolly cockney type, good looking with a twinkle in his eye. He was a worldly, self-made man who was driving a

---

[12]Pelagic bird watching is a specialised form of the art. Basically, it involves getting on a boat and leaving coastal waters for many, many hours in the hope of seeing wandering seabirds that don't come near the coast other than at night or in other parts of the world. Petrels, shearwaters, phalaropes and maybe, just maybe, an albatross. Pelagic trips are often unutterably boring.

Transit van full of 70s British furniture and semi-antiques to sell on in Spain, while Thomas was his Spanish contact and a skilled furniture restorer. Steve had truly been around. He described anecdote after anecdote of how he had "taken the main chance" in life.

"You've got to see an opportunity and go for it"

"I'll give you an example, " he said, "One time, in Fulham... ooh, way back in the 80s, I was passing this cleared building site and all that was left was a long old wall. Well, I saw more than an old wall, see? I saw bricks – thousands of them. All I needed to do was get them to a mate in Kent who sold reclaimed building stuff. Transport has always been my key. If you can move things to where they're needed, you can sell em, right? Right!"

Steve's wisdom was unshakeable, grounded and proven. He went on to explain how he had then asked permission to take down the wall;

"The site boss said I could do what I liked as long as it was done by Monday. Over the weekend, I got a JCB and a crew of mates, and we had that wall down and ready to deliver to Kent by Sunday night. Made a few quid out of that, I did."

"You must have run out of walls though Steve. What are you up to now?" I asked, intrigued by this self-reliant, interesting man.

"Been doing the same sort of thing all my life," he replied, "and I've got a place in Hong Kong where you can make a good living off the main chance – or at least you could until the bloody Chinese got hold of it. Now I'm selling old British furniture to the Spanish – they love it. Thomas here makes the reproduction distressed stuff look new again – cos the Spanish don't get that new-made-to-look-old thing."

This bloke demolished then sold a wall he happened to see on a building site. He now sells renovated reproduction "antique" furniture from Britain (of which he had a van load on the ferry as we spoke) to the Spanish, and he's had another life doing similar deals in Hong Kong. He told me about some of his antics in Hong Kong and it became clear that here was a survivor – and a very different character to me. I had taken the safe route: education, qualifications, a bit of scientific research, then into college lecturing, where I stayed (bar a few promotions) for most of my working life. Safe. Dependable. Secure. It seemed so unambitious, so unadventurous a life compared to Steve's. I had more admiration for this man than for any high-flying career success that I'd met or heard of. Steve would be able to look after himself, come what may. I on the other hand, really wondered how I'd cope if I had to live by seeing an old wall as an opportunity. Steve's story also re-affirmed why I was there; out of the "comfort zone" (sorry, hate those clichés, but that particular one works for me), testing myself and doing it alone. It was heartening that both Steve and Thomas were just as interested in my adventure as I was in theirs.

Thomas was the furniture restoration arm of this business. He showed me with great pride some photos of his workshop in London, his specialist chisels and other tools all hanging up on a wall. He related an incident where he did a restoration job for a "tiny, pretty woman" whom he didn't recognise, but who turned out to be Kylie Minogue! Thomas got increasingly drunk (why do people do that on boats?) and less coherent as he spouted forth his philosophies of life. He also became a pain in the arse and I took Steve's lead when he turned to make conversation with Andrew, a mild-mannered Brit who was on a trip like mine – but by pedal power. He was cycling to the south of Spain, into France then picking up a coach which would transport him and other cyclists home via some other hot cycling routes. We talked about luggage: I was curious about how he dealt with the sheer weight of his gear after my panic with the motorbike.

"I'm carrying 40 kilos," he said, "Most of it is food (so it'll get lighter!) spares and a few bits of clothing."

I was flabbergasted.

"40 kilograms!" I said, "I've only got 60 or so on the bike – and it feels over-loaded. I had to remove some because I was worried about the weight. Maybe I was over cautious."

To this day I haven't resolved the weight issue. I'll probably never know if it really had been necessary take off some gear or if I would have been fine, but Andrew lugging two-thirds of my luggage weight on a push-bike was very impressive and a little confusing. How did he ever get along?

" You only feel the weight going up hills," he said, in his typically understated way.

Considering that this lot had to be pushed by leg power whereas a powerful combustion engine was propelling my luggage, I felt inadequate for having worried so much about the weight.

"How do you navigate? Can you have satnav on a bike?" I asked him, now very interested in the comparison between our modes of transport. He got out a pile of papers from his little cyclist's rucksack.

"I checked it all on Google maps first. I've got print-outs of all the major junctions and towns so I don't get lost." He showed me a few pages of printed road maps.

"I just pull over and check when I need to. I'm not going so fast that I need instant feedback like satnav."

"I guess that's the key difference between us, " I said, "you're going slowly enough to take everything in and at a pace where you can keep track. I'm travelling so much further and faster, satnav really works."

I told him I hadn't owned a satnav gadget until then because I really value my sense of direction and I like to know where I'm going. When you think about it, satellite navigation for the masses is one of the most astounding developments in the whole internet/communication revolution. No wonder it is so seductive. Now everyone has one, but until this trip, I'd had no intention of following the trend. However, it was to prove invaluable going across Europe – far more so than driving around home and parts of the UK. I had decent maps with me of every country and even some detailed regional maps (for birding mainly), but in foreign lands, with unfamiliar road signs, place names and general geography, my TomTom Rider was to become a very useful friend (strange things happen to you when you're on your own on a trip like this!).

I ate, had coffee, ate some more and tried sea-watching with the new (pink!) Nikon telescope I had bought at the Bird Fair, but it was pretty hopeless on the vibrating, wind-swept decks. It did give me the first trip bird though: Gannet, that stunning torpedo of the sea, all daggers and black and white, flying over the swell and spray, occasionally plunging into the water like a giant dart. Everything about a Gannet is pointed: that dangerous bill, the wings, even their tails are sharp. There were also a few Fulmars and gulls (Greater Black-backed mainly) and I thought I saw a shearwater, but it was too distant to be sure (at a glance or at a distance, Fulmars and shearwaters look alike). Shearwater didn't go on The List then – pity, because that was to be the only one of the whole trip... that's birding for you!

Coming back inside, happy to be out of the relentless, buffeting wind, I ran into two Polish blokes wearing orange KTM t-shirts. KTM is a brand of rugged off-road bike – serious stuff. At first glance, these two seemed to be the real deal: tough experienced bikers, but in fact they were a pair of obnoxious drunks wandering about the boat, polluting the friendly atmosphere with their loutish, foul-mouthed behaviour. Was I being a reactionary prude or did the women, whom they thrust their beer guts and unwelcome pelvises at, have justified looks of disgust on their faces? Getting pissed seems to be an obligatory pastime on ferries.

I wandered around the boat some more, happy to be trapped at sea, anticipating things to come, writing my diary, leaving dictaphone messages and chatting to people on board. I sat down for my nth cup of coffee and mused on whether I really would make it all the way to Lithuania and Wilma's grave – that seemed so, so far away. Lost in this reverie of possibilities yet to be decided, I looked up and saw a familiar face, just a few tables across from me. I was only half looking, as I remained absorbed in thoughts of my trip to come until I realised who the craggy features and distinctive blond curly hair belonged to: this was Robert Plant of Led Zeppelin fame! I was unexpectedly celebrity-spotting… and I hate that. It's stupid pride with me; I don't like playing up to the whole celebrity thing – even if a big part of me would have loved to walk up, acknowledge him and say how much his music had meant to people like me over the decades. I could have had a conversation that I would remember for the rest of my life. But I didn't do that. I also have a thing about being "unwelcome"; if I feel my presence is annoying someone or I'm not welcome in some way, I just want out, no questions asked (harbouring all sorts of resentments of course!). Celebrities like Plant must get sick of being recognised and maybe sicker of having the same conversation with endless fans. I'd have felt unwelcome before I even got within a few yards, so I didn't go near. This was a shame because I got talking to his assistant later and even used her laptop to write my blog entry. She disappeared, asking me to look after all her stuff – which included all sorts of open documents and bits about Plant's arrangements and contacts for recording and touring. I could have done some mischief with that lot! She could have been the perfect chance to talk to Mr Plant, but I didn't push for an introduction. I should have, but settled for suggesting to her that he read my blog and donate some money to the fundraising. I wondered why he was on a ferry, as opposed to first class on a plane? Did he not fly for some reason? Or was it that he was less likely to get hounded by the press and adoring public on a bog-standard ferry? Was he on tour with a pile of equipment in a lorry – or even a bike – was he on a bike trip too!? I never got these questions answered and Robert Plant never did donate any money – bastard!

Eventually, after a good night's sleep in my comfortable cabin (or "stateroom" as they grandiosely call them), it was time for breakfast and departure. Back on the vehicle deck, there was more re-packing (as time went on, I was to get heartily fed up with all that), unstrapping the bike, more low speed cajoling out of its slot and then, in convoy... off in a roar of bikes. We all headed out like a group of Hell's Angels, into the daylight and down the ramp onto tarmac terra firma. Great! The beginning begins. Santander may be a lovely place, but I just wanted to get out and get going. Some bikers had to stop at petrol pumps just outside the ferry terminal while the rest of us went on out of the town, waving goodbye. It was surprising how quickly all those bikes dispersed, until I was a lone biker again, riding out of Santander, on the brand spanking new A67, south towards my first destination: Salamanca, the Cambridge of Spain.

Chapter 4 – Espana

The week I spend with the army dog-training unit in Melton Mowbray is very isolating (despite the pork pies). None of the army personnel know what to do with me. Although Prof. Short had used his position and maybe contacts to get me booked into the barracks for a week, no-one knew where I should go or what I should be looking at.

I get up every day far earlier than normal student rising time and wander over to the mess in the hope that someone I recognise will be there for me to latch onto. As it turns out, a corporal has been reluctantly attached to me, as much to make sure I don't get in the way as anything else, but during the week, I get to see experienced dog handlers train and practice new dogs for the role of attack, restraint, and detection. The sniffer dogs are just amazing. Mainly to seek out explosives, they go about their tasks with such enthusiasm and vigour, I am enthralled. Although I feel I am learning a lot of basic techniques for the oestrus detection role my dog is to carry out, the army handlers are very sceptical. Who was I to think I could just walk in and do their job with so little experience – and how is a dog going to sniff a cow's behind anyway?

*

From the north coast of Spain, the land rises quickly to form the spectacular Picos de Europa Mountains. I had read about them during my planning for the journey, and the heart of this region sounded wonderfully wild. In fact, I came across warnings of how isolated, dangerous and inhospitable the area can be. With peaks at over 2400 metres and gorges 1.5 kilometres deep, this was a serious mountain range. Ben Nevis, our highest point in the UK looks gentle by comparison at a softly rounded, and slightly puny, 1300 metres. I was nervous about taking the bike across such a wilderness so early in my journey, but I needn't have worried; the Picos were well west of the A67, the new motorway, which somewhat disappointingly, took me over the eastern end of the Cantabrian Mountains, missing the Picos in a single sweep.

Nevertheless, the first thing I had to do on leaving Santander was climb and climb until the air became cold, clouds rolled in and rain threatened. The peaks in the middle distance were covered in snow, and after only forty minutes, I found myself pulling in to don wet weather gear. This was totally unexpected and a little confusing; I had mainly worried about getting too hot in Spain, not about shivering my nuts off on a cloud soaked mountain within minutes of setting off. Still, there were compensations: I used the stop as an excuse to warm up indoors and have the first of many, many coffee-stops. As I sat clutching my silver Aria helmet, another biker rolled in and perched on a bar stool next to me. He had parked up his Harley and wandered in for a coffee too. We got chatting and swapped life stories while preparing for the rain. Sean was a professional photographer who had recently got divorced and come out to his half of the settlement: a villa somewhere near Portugal. He gave me his card for future contact. I told him I was a travel writer (what a lie!) and gave him my blog details.[13]

Sean suggested we ride together for a bit so, dressed for the damp, cold air, we set off down the smooth new tarmac of the A67. It twisted and turned, bike-friendly, and it was glorious to have a companion. Imagine *me* riding along with a Harley dude! We rode side by side for half an hour or so, taking up two lanes and having fun, then in single file until Sean signalled his imminent exit. A few minutes later we were both waving goodbye as he carved his way off west. I was alone again.

The road slowly dropped me down from the cool air of the high mountains and onto flatter plains until warmth from the sun slowly filtered through my bike clothing. The landscape became more agricultural, more gentle, and I picked up speed to make

---

[13]I had printed off 50 slips of paper with my name and blog address to give to people as I travelled, mainly to boost my fundraising attempt and to get a bit of momentum and comment on the blog.

better progress. After an hour, the sun was out in earnest and I began to feel over-dressed with waterproofs on top of the already bulky bike gear. In a deserted truck lay-by somewhere between Palencia and Valladolid the jacket came off and as soon as I removed my helmet, I heard birdsong: a Corn Bunting was singing nearby and Crested Larks hopped around the rough sandy ground.

Taking the Red Spots out of the tank bag for the first time, I stretched my legs to have a look at the larks. A sea of deserted, brand new tarmac, the lay-by was an inauspicious venue – but I was birding! The plaintive, whistling song of a Crested Lark sounded just a few feet away. Cresteds are dull brown, but strongly streaked and mottled larks with a sharply pointed crest. They are common throughout Europe, but still look exotic to us Brits. This is why I love birding abroad: the commonplace feels exciting, every time.

I became increasingly happy as I warmed up in the lay-by watching the larks and, to celebrate, I broke open a cereal bar from the cavernous tank bag. The joy of that simple act will never leave me. Looking back, it is for those unexpected (and at any other time, mundane) moments that travel is so worthwhile.

I heard again the tinkling of a Corn Bunting and wandered off to find it. Corn Bunting must be the classic LBJ (Little Brown Job!), totally nondescript, small, dull brown and boring but for one thing: their song, which is lovely and very distinctive. It is said to sound like someone rattling a set of car keys, and that works for me. I found this particular fat little LBJ singing his heart out beyond a culvert that led out into the arid Spanish countryside. The pallid browns of the landscape matched the colour of the bunting (and the lark); classic camouflage, I supposed.

I was somewhere near Palencia, and had covered my first hundred miles since leaving Santander. I set off again, now determined to reach my first stop, Salamanca. With around the same distance to go and most of the day still to come, I was doing well, despite the earlier rain and cold of the Picos. Back on the bike, I rolled along, happy to be in the moment, but this existential nirvana didn't last long; minutes after I had picked up speed, a male Montague's Harrier flew up alongside the bike. It flew on, in an adjacent field, then crossed the road ahead of me. Within yards, a Marsh Harrier drifted across the new, snaking dual carriageway – and I couldn't contain myself, whooping and shouting in the helmet. Both of these harriers are large, stunning birds to see up close, but Montague's is particularly exciting, being yet another rare bird in the UK. I hadn't seen one for ages and this was unexpected, so close to the bike and flying along with me (*Bikes 1; Cars 0*). It was a male, with his splendid grey and black livery and fluttering, buoyant flight. He was notably "skinnier" and more rakish than the similar Hen Harriers I had seen from time to time in Caithness and I was even able to see the tell-tale black bars on his black-tipped wings. The Marsh Harrier which rose up quite suddenly in front of me, mere yards after the Montague's, took me even more by surprise (or perhaps I had surprised it?). A much bulkier, more buzzard-like bird, the Marsh flapped heavily over my head and disappeared. As I rode along, I added Black Kite, Buzzard, White Stork and an eagle that I couldn't identify.

With birding now unexpectedly under way, I twisted the throttle grip to increase the pace and give biking some attention. After those Harriers, a little adrenalin was pumping and I flew along, faster than I intended to. I made good progress, but when I saw the speedo hit and go beyond 90mph, I reined myself in a bit; I didn't want to get stopped for speeding this early on. The road surface was new and very smooth; it was easy to let the speed creep up without realising. On these roads, the bike proved more than willing to eat up the miles.

My delight at how well the trip was going proved to be short-lived. The warming brightness of the sun gave way again to dull, threatening clouds and within minutes, I was surrounded by thunder, lightning, rain and hail. Glad to have donned the waterproof trousers at the stop with Sean, I rode on into the rain, but it became too intense. I pulled over just in time to avoid a complete deluge. This wasn't fun. I turned the stop into a late lunch, eating a tapas-style thing called Lomo (some sort of lamb stew) with a baguette. As it brightened overhead, I headed off again, only to be driven under cover thirty minutes later by another intense downpour. Where had sunny Spain gone? The roads became rivers of rainwater and people seemed mildly shell-shocked, unsure quite what to do or say. Resorting to camaraderie born of mutual adversity, they smiled or shrugged at each other (and me). This time I sheltered in a petrol station. I filled up while waiting for the rain to stop, paid for the petrol, waited another 15 minutes then tried again, riding off into the drizzle and spray. Within a couple of hours, including a stop for some of the ubiquitous and fabulous coffee, I was approaching Salamanca, my TomTom satnav showing the way.

I had already played with the satnav a little and chosen options for the display, sounds and connections. Among many others, the voices available included a Welshman, an English Rose, another female English voice, a kiwi, a couple of yanks, a South African... and Tim: classic BBC English. I chose the latter and the TomTom became known as Tim, my travelling companion. I was later to find that I'd left the charger for the Bluetooth headset behind (on the ferry, I thought) so after the charge ran out, Tim became mute! The headset, which otherwise would have delivered Tim's voice into my ear within the helmet, was from then on redundant and I lost one of the major features of satellite navigation systems: the annoying verbal directions, whistles, sirens, squeaks and pops that accompany the satnav user on every journey. I didn't miss them one bit and there was something quite endearing about a mute Tim.

I had no plans for birding near Salamanca, being content to just get there – the first stop after my first day. I did, however, have intrepid plans to camp in the grounds of the Hotel Regio but, having arrived damp and fairly exhausted, I couldn't face a hard cold night in a tent, let alone having to erect the bloody thing in the first place. I booked a room and relaxed after unpacking *(Hotels 1; Camping 0)*.

After a fairly late night making my first proper entry to the blog (use of the hotel computer and internet was free!), I got up just in time to have breakfast. As I was finishing off by making a roll for lunch, the two Polish guys from the ferry turned up. We spoke briefly as they sat down to breakfast, clearly hungover – again! They were quiet and pleasant compared to the drunken idiots they'd been on the ferry. One of them was absolutely huge – a real gentle giant. They'd been out in Salamanca until three in the morning, looking for women and no doubt getting as plastered as they'd been on the ferry. They were now contemplating a ride on their big KTMs all the way to Gibraltar; 700Km in one day! They were probably 30 years younger than me and maybe could live and travel like this, but I left them to it, happy not to be invited to join them, their whole ethos being so different to mine.

Salamanca is billed as the Cambridge of Spain, having the oldest university in the country and of considerable historic and cultural interest, but to me, it became just another big bustling town to get lost in – with cobbles designed to tip me off my bike for good measure. Tim came to the rescue and I slavishly followed his directions out of town. Unfortunately, Tim had no knowledge of the roadblock on the main road south – in fact, Tim had no knowledge of the main road south. Spain had been famously undergoing a decade-long infrastructure program with new roads springing up all across the country. Consequently, Tim's comforting map and picture of a little person on a motorcycle, showed the bike storming across fields, open water, ditches and woods. With a little faith and some hand-drawn directions from a Spaniard at a local filling station (which I passed at least three times as Tim took me back again and again to the roadblock), I finally escaped the clutches of Salamanca. It was a beautiful small city though – if you like that sort of thing.

The Gredos Mountains seemed to hang in the distance to the east as I wheeled along the A66 towards Plasencia, the gateway to Monfrague, my much anticipated first true birding destination. The Sierra de Gredos is a long spine of mountains that rise spectacularly out of flat plains, splitting central Spain in two almost from Madrid to Portugal. White capped with snow, they kept catching my eye as I continued south until finally, they had slipped behind and Spain flattened before me. I could still catch a glimpse of the Gredos in the side mirrors and I felt sad to leave them behind.

Skipping round Plasencia with a developing phobia of anything resembling even a large village, I rolled on until I passed a sign that said "Monfrague National Park".

There had been more rain on and off and the road was still wet after a recent shower, but the sun was out and things were rapidly drying. I stopped by a river meadow for my first picnic. A couple of horses grazed the meadow and Red-rumped Swallows zoomed around me. Bee-eaters called as they flew through on migration, their bubbling whistles all around. I leant comfortably against my Honda, eating a roll constructed earlier from the breakfast buffet. A fellow biker rode by and gave me the usual salute: a casual, sideways raise of his left hand. This was another moment like the lay-by near Valladolid; a true spring day after all the rain and cold, it lifted my spirits. Once again, the bike felt like a companion, more than a machine (*Bikes 2; Cars 0*). It looked so self-contained. Everything I needed was right here under and around me: fuel, power, spares and emergency bits, food and drink, optics, maps and books, tent, clothes and, of course, Tim. I patted the large silver fuel tank as if it were a horse. It all looked so dependable and here I was in Monfrague, having a picnic in the sun beside a little stream within a shimmering green meadow. The bike had taken me here and now it served as my seat. The two horses grazed. I ate my roll. All was well in my world.

The Monfragüe National Park lies between Plasencia in the north and Trujillo in the south with Navalmoral to the east. It is a lush area with craggy hills, lakes and gorges, free of towns and development. To the south lie the more open, arid steppes, but here the land is wooded and deeply undulating. The park includes a long mountainous ridge, cut by the River Tagus, creating on the western side an impressive rock face, the Penafalcon. On the eastern side is the ruined Castle of Monfragüe. Another river, the Tietar, joins the Tagus just to the east of the Penafalcon and its course forms another rich birding area. There is only one village in the park, the tiny, reconstructed museum that is Villareal de San Carlos (population 28!) – and a lovely little place it is too (but don't expect to find the campsite – that had disappeared eight years prior to my visit, despite still being in the guidebooks).

Surrounding the park and throughout Extremadura are the unique "dehesas". These are large areas of common land found in this region of Spain (and in neighbouring Portugal where they are called "montados"). Dehesas are the result of people growing cork oaks to harvest the cork layer from beneath the bark, grazing cattle underneath the trees and growing cereal. The outer bark of a cork oak can be stripped one year in ten without harming the tree, but it leaves them looking strange, with narrow black trunks for the first metre or so above ground, then the more usual grey bark up into the dense, twisted branches. I'm sure the trees would rather not be de-corked every 10 years, but it seems to do them no lasting harm. The result is a diverse, ancient woodland based on native plants with lots of uncultivated scrub, which is fabulous for wildlife, including the endangered Iberian Lynx, Spanish Imperial Eagle (with a population of only 130 breeding pairs – more of which later) and Bonelli's Eagle.

Spain and Portugal have more than half of the cork oak woodlands on the planet and produce around three-quarters of the world's cork. Natural wine corks make up most of the value of the cork market, but we like screw tops or plastic stoppers in our wine bottles these days, so the bottom has dropped out of the cork market; the dehesas are under threat. There have been conservation campaigns to preserve this traditional industry and the dehesas themselves, but such a habitat, which is so reliant on human activity, may have to change. Still, it is such a wonderful place, it may get the protection it deserves – even if only for people like me to go and see it.

The roads through Monfrague twist and turn as if they were designed for biking. Around every corner a new vista opens out: a wooded valley of interlocking hillsides, a lake bending out of sight or a ridged escarpment promising a soaring raptor. Monfrague has the largest colony of Eurasian Black Vultures in the world (more than 200 pairs) and the highest concentration of the rare Spanish Imperial Eagle (more than 10 pairs). In all, three species of vulture breed here along with five species of eagle, three kite species and two species of harrier. As if this is not enough, the arresting and beautiful Azure-winged Magpie is relatively common in this area of Spain, being found nowhere else in the world outside South-east Asia. It has the weirdest distribution of any bird I know; maps of where they occur show a tiny blob only in this part of central Spain and another blob in China/Japan/Korea – and nowhere else![14]

So here I was, in this fleshpot of continental birding. It was only 4pm when I passed the entrance to my campsite, the road still wet from earlier rain. Further on – I knew from a previous visit – was Salto del Gitano (Gypsy's Leap), an awe-inspiring set of crags and pinnacles, which form a gateway for the main lake at the heart of Monfrague. This place is the site for an impressive display of soaring vultures, kites and eagles all around the crags, many at close quarters. There is nowhere better in Western Europe to see vultures so I rode on rather than face "the camping thing".

Monfrague proved to be great for riding as well as birding; sweeping curves on a good tarmac surface with lots of lay-bys to take in a view or to catch a soaring bird of prey, Red Spots at the ready in the tank bag right in front of me. I crossed a viaduct over a narrow part of the reservoir which lies at the heart of the park, leaning the bike round fabulous chicanes before reaching the well-constructed viewpoint at Salto del Gitano. Here, a huge, jagged tooth of rock – a mountain really – rises out of the water across the reservoir: the Penafalcon. All around the pinnacle, there were vultures, some high up, some wheeling low, and others perched. These large, free-soaring birds echoed what I loved about riding a bike; they seemed to bank into the

---

[14]DNA testing has proven that the two groups of Azure-winged Magpie were isolated 20,000 to 100,000 years ago, the land covered in ice over central Europe, leaving only the extremes of south-west Europe and south-east Asia as habitable zones. This kept the two populations apart and they are now regarded as being separate species. It begs the question; why not the same with other birds or mammals of these regions?

thermals the way you lean a bike into a bend. Here at last, the Biking Birder was well under way!

The evening was drawing in and I was getting tired. Even the scores of Griffon Vultures and the promise of others couldn't keep me there. I planned to return early next day in any case so I rode the 20 km back to the campsite and set up my tent on the damp ground.

I am very unfamiliar and uncomfortable in campsites, an animal out of its natural habitat. I don't know where to go or what to do. I don't even know where I can and can't pitch the tent; you'd think that would be obvious – it's a campsite for God's sake! – but no, I end up making a meal of it and taking ages just to pick my spot. As one of my dictaphone messages says in bewilderment;

"What is it with this camping thing?"

My tent, a Banshee 200 two-man tent, was cramped with just one man – and a little one at that! I had to wear a head torch to see into my various bags, which I kept in the tent with me for security, and I could hardly move to find anything. In what universe could two people sleep in this thing?

"You have to take a torch to go and wash your face for God's sake!" I quipped into the dictaphone, the reasons for camping becoming more and more fallacious as the journey progressed. I was also the only person using a tent, all the other pitches being occupied by mobile homes. The pitches were covered by a roof – sort of – but it meant there was no grass, just bare, compacted mud. The ground was hard as a rock.

"Bloody Spaniards won't go to bed, kids still running round at midnight," was my next dictaphone comment, the indignation in my voice becoming palpable. Then I almost blew a gasket as someone with a van started moving stuff about in the pitch dark. I began to think I'd prefer to be in a farmer's field somewhere.

It rained all night and I could hear a river of water running around the tent – right next to my ear. Would the bike stay up on its stand or would it slowly sink into the wet soil until it fell over? Biking Birder might become Walking Birder! I slept fitfully, the plop of raindrops becoming loud bangs in the quiet of the night and the partial delirium of broken sleep. (*Hotels 2; Camping 0*)

Damp and cold the next morning, I peered out from under the flysheet. The bike was still standing. And the rain had stopped. Hallelujah! I got up and had breakfast with a couple of strong coffees. It was Saturday 17th of April and in the welcome warmth of the campsite restaurant, there was the inevitable flat screen TV on the wall, magnetically drawing everyone's eyes like something out of a zombie movie. I was less vulnerable to its spell because I couldn't hone in on the language, but some images of an explosion caught my eye. From the captions, it seemed that there had been a major terrorist incident – a bomb – in Iceland of all places. Having no idea what "bomb" was in any language other than English, I tapped a fellow camper on the arm and made an explosion gesture accompanied by a questioning shrug (the internationally recognised sign for "bomb", of course).

"Si, Si," he said, directing my gaze to the TV with his open hand (the internationally recognised gesture for "of course, you idiot – look, it's on the telly").

Then there came an image of Gordon Brown mumbling in English, talking about the bomb no doubt, which I couldn't hear because of the hysterical babble of the Spanish commentary. I had forgotten that back home they were caught in the hysterical babble of a British general election. All that seemed so far away, even after just a few days on the bike. The TV images changed to show airports closed because of the bomb, and Gordon Brown – again – this time next to some naval ships. My God, it must be a big deal, I thought.

Leaving my large bag and locked panniers in the tent, I rode light, back to Gypsy's Leap, the small, lightweight Nikon ED50 telescope with a super-light carbon fibre tripod in the rear box and my beloved Leicas round my neck, ready for vulture watching. On the way, I picked up a little group of Azure-winged Magpies dashing across the road and into the scrub, their blue, beige and black colours flashing as they flew – stunning birds. Within minutes of arriving at Salto Del Gitano, a storm brewed: a vicious, gusting wind lashing horizontal rain in nasty squalls. I threw a cover over the bike and sheltered behind it. As soon as I had crouched down, however, I felt a gust catch the heavy machine and tip it onto me. I stood up quick, putting my back against the bike to prevent it falling all the way. No more sheltering for me... and couldn't those Italians in their huge mobile home not have offered to let me in out of the storm?!

Even with the rain, there were still a few people there (mostly Spanish, with a few Dutch birders) and sure enough, as the storm passed, Griffon Vultures by the tens soared in around the pinnacle and across the lake, sometimes flying below us, but still at tree-canopy height. The sun came out to show the subtle browns and blacks in the upper wing of both adults and juveniles. With the 'scope, I could get close views of perched birds on any of a hundred craggy ledges. Behind, as I craned up with binoculars, yet more Griffon, Egyptian and some Black Vultures wheeled and perched on sheer rock faces that rose straight up from the road. As a break from vulture watching, Gypsy's leap also provided close views of Blue Rock Thrush, Rock Bunting and Crag Martin (it has only just struck me how appropriate all those bird names are to an area made of rocks and crags!)

I got soaked, but with wet feet and dripping gloves, rode on via the northern park road to Rio Tietar. Stopping at a well-known viewpoint, I found a Lesser-spotted Eagle perched on a pylon and passed it on to a group of Spanish birders. All the way through the park we leap-frogged our stops, passing on the "bird gen" at each one. The group befriended me, sharing their typically Spanish picnic lunch and a welcome, warming coffee in a stone-built shelter overlooking a small lake. The park rangers who led them were intrigued by my "Biking Birder" adventure. We struck a chord and they showed me "their" nesting Black Vultures, Black Storks and Egyptian Vultures, the latter two with nests, just across a small lake from the hide.

Black Vulture

All around Europe, I found the same helpful interest in what I was doing; this lonely, wet figure on a bike, looking for birds.

"Have some food," one insisted.

"Are you from England?" another asked.

"I live in England, but I come from Scotland." (I always use that; it's a good opener)

"Ah –Scotland! But you have eagles there, no?" (see!)

"Golden Eagles, but hard to find and no others," I said

"And why you come by bike?"

That was the first time I'd been asked and I didn't have an instant answer. I'd have to think about this a bit.

"Oh, it's been a dream since I was young."

"But I love birds too," was my lame response.

I passed them my little slips of paper with the blog address on and explained what it was for. All smiles, they took them, intrigued. Every time I gave out one of those I hoped the person concerned would take the time to have a look and leave a comment.

Here I must confess to a birding faux pas: I failed to recognise the importance of Monfrague for Spanish Imperial Eagle, one of the rarest birds in the world and – being a dirty great eagle – one of the most exciting to see. But I left the park without it and, of course, wouldn't see any on the rest of my trip (Imperial Eagle, maybe;, but not *Spanish* Imperial – different, you see!). If I'd done my homework better, I'd have known to ask these friendly park rangers for local gen on where to look. There were to be other misses of that sort, but they would be conscious decisions and less crucial in birding terms. Even now, I kick myself for that one – what an idiot![15]

Blissfully unaware of my folly on the eagle front, the damp, the cold and increasing weariness eventually drove me back to the campsite. Monfrague, even in the rain, had been wonderful (again), but it was getting late and petrol was low in the bike. The search for birds had taken me down roads that I wasn't sure of, but good old Tim pointed the way. Unfortunately, he wasn't playing ball with petrol stations; according to him, there were none nearby. It started raining again. The fuel warning light came on; I had even less than I had thought. Bugger! In the middle of nowhere, half way up a mountain and with no one around to ask, all I could do was get out a map. I navigated to an area with small villages, going further away from the campsite on diminishing fuel. I had to find a local to ask, before running out of fuel even further from where I needed to be. When I eventually ran across someone, through the usual sign language (we Brits really are crap at foreign languages), I discovered I had travelled 8Km in the wrong direction. I know this is a classic and many people have been in this position, but somehow, in that place, in the rain, on my own with a bike (no car to shelter in – *Bikes 2; Cars 1*), I felt a minor disaster unfolding. All I could do was ride slowly back the 15 Km in the rain to the village where I was told there *might* be petrol. I did, there was and (apart from getting soaked – again!) all was well, but that incident stuck in my mind as a reminder of how vulnerable I could be on this journey. I would fill up every

---

[15]I have since returned to that exact spot with three birding pals. We were rewarded with Spanish Imperial Eagle practically dive bombing us before relieving his mate at the nest. I am exonerated!

hundred miles from now on, even though the bike range was well over 160 miles (not good as a touring bike, by the way).

The campsite was a welcome place after all that. Through its friendly arched gates, there was a warm, heated reception hut where I'd left some of my stuff for safekeeping. I had a coffee in the cosy restaurant before taking down the still damp tent and packing up the bike for what seemed like the hundredth time (*Bikes 2; Cars 2*). Spain was remaining stubbornly cool and damp (no, let's be honest; bloody cold and wet!), but at least there was no rain falling as I left.

Five in the evening was late to be moving on, but I was only a couple of hours from my next stop: a warm dry bed, food and, hopefully, a birding welcome at El Recuerdo, the home of Martin Kelsey. Martin is a very knowledgeable academic ornithologist[16] who now runs a birding tour company and acts as a guide to the local area, particularly the steppes around Trujilo, the nearest town. I rode across and around the steppe country: open, flat plains of gently undulating farmland, the home of unique flora and fauna, some of which I hoped to connect with the next day.

The bike bumped along the tracks leading to El Recuerdo and I finally pulled up at a pair of large, black, ominously closed metal gates with a strange hole in one at about waist height. Since the tiled sign said "El Recuerdo", I guessed I was in the right place and stuck my hand into the hole to investigate. Just as I felt a bolt on the other side, I heard it: a furious barking and rattling as some enormous beast came tearing up a gravel drive on the other side. Pure reflex pulled my hand back – just as a great big wet nose and black muzzle came shooting through the hole, followed by a pair of demented eyes.

This was Martin's dog, a big black chap called Holenose or something (part Labrador, part Rottweiler!).

---

[16]"Ornithologist" – another sect in the hierarchy, except that it isn't really in the hierarchy at all, unless used incorrectly. Ornithologists are people who study birds as a true science and as an academic career. I almost became one myself, having started out as a zoologist early on, but I didn't have the stamina! Bill Oddie is not an ornithologist, Peter Scott was. Most ornithologists are not famous.

This hole was clearly his window on the world. I said hello and he disappeared. After a little while, I peered in through the hole and opened the gate. The little burst of adrenalin, fuelled by the appearance of Holenose, subsided and left me feeling suddenly very weary. Getting the bike in through the gates and up the gravel drive was draining, all the while watching out for the reappearance of Holenose. Despite all the barking and clashing of gates, the engine noise, and my cursing, no-one appeared. I unclipped the top box, unfastened the big roll bag containing clothes and nearly everything for an overnight stay, and dragged myself to the door. Going inside, I realised why no one had come; they were having their evening meal and I was late – of course. But Martin leapt up, full of smiles, helped me with the bags and introduced me to his other guests: Barry and Dawn, a couple from Britain, Ray Tipper, a wildlife photographer who lived in Portugal and another couple whose names I didn't catch. I noticed the slightly wide-eyed look I got from everybody. Did I look that outlandish or was there something wrong with me that I couldn't see? (It was to take me some time on the trip to realise quite how rough and travel bitten I came to appear).

Martin's wife, who runs the business with him, appeared with some soup as I sat down in the small, but cosy dining room. I had washed and changed clothes, and the wide-eyed, don't-kill-me-you-biker-maniac looks were now a little less obvious, having morphed into suspicious stares. The soup was delicious and the chat began. Barry and Dawn, in particular, were very taken with the whole concept of my biking and birding journey.

"Where did you set out from?"

"Suffolk."

"Oh, we come from Suffolk – which part?"

It transpired that Barry and Dawn lived just up the road from me, in Ipswich. Small world 'n all that.

"So what about this bomb in Iceland?" I enquired

"What bomb?" replied the un-named couple.

"The thing that's been closing all the airports," I said, "I'm surprised you haven't been caught up in it – it's all over the TV news. I keep seeing it in cafés, but can't get the details in Spanish."

"It's not a bomb," said Barry, "it's a volcano. Where have you been? There's a big ash cloud covering most of Europe and no flights are running. We've been stuck for days. So have thousands of others – especially Brits."

So my bomb turned out to be something much more interesting and, sad to say, unusual.

"Yes, we might have to stay on here for another week," said Barry

"Isn't that awful!" added Dawn with a twinkle. They both clearly didn't mind being stuck at El Recuerdo for a little longer. I liked Barry and Dawn instantly. They were both in their mid-fifties I'd guess and they had a gentle, refreshing outlook on life. Maybe I liked them because they seemed to genuinely get the point of my trip and were (or seemed to be) really interested in where I was going, but Barry was just a calm, easy to talk to chap and Dawn had that twinkle in her eye that made me relax in conversation with them over the smooth wine that Martin had poured. A long discussion followed about the state of air transport around Europe and it transpired that they were all staying several days longer than planned at El Recuerdo. Barry and Dawn seemed sanguine about it, having fallen in love with El Recuerdo and the birding. Ray asked if I'd seen any good birds.

"Well, Monfrague was really my first stop and I haven't been anywhere else, but I got everything I wanted. Black Vulture and

Black Stork on the nest, lots of other raptors, Azure-wings, Rock Bunting. No Black-shouldered Kite though"

"Have you seen any of the Bustards?" he asked.

"No, only just arrived from Monfrague, but I'm hoping Martin will put me on to the steppe birds tomorrow."

"Oh he will, you're in for a treat," said Dawn, "the birding round here has been fantastic"

"Will you be going out again if you're stuck here?" I asked

"Can't," said Barry, "Martin's booked up elsewhere and we might not have the time or money to keep going out in case a flight comes up. Gordon Brown keeps saying they'll send navy ships and the Spanish have said they'll fly Brits home, but now they think the cloud will even affect here."

This was clearly the hot topic du jour and these people were caught up in it, even though they had this nice place to stay and were, at that moment, sitting comfortably conversing over some pleasant, post-dinner wine. I sensed their unease and tried not to make light of it, although I kept wondering if secretly it was a bit of an adventure and, in their shoes, would I be quite happy to be stuck there for a few days? The un-named couple had jobs to get back to and made a good case for how difficult the situation was for them, but I found myself thinking it would be a wonderful excuse for absence... "Sorry I couldn't come in last week, I was in Spain, stuck in the volcanic ash, you know". But then, I've always been a bit juvenile like that!

Sleeping the sleep of the blessed and after a fine breakfast, I set off on the bike next day to explore the Spanish steppes around Trujillo, armed with local birding advice from Martin. Before that, I parked next to the beautiful bullring in Trujillo to look for Lesser Kestrel and, within seconds, they were there. I didn't even have to get off the bike. Red Spots out of the tank bag again, I watched a pair displaying and courting around the orange tiles of the bullring roof, mere feet from the ground. A little boy stood near a puddle, transfixed at this man straddling a big motorbike, binoculars in hand. He stared, as kids often do, but the locals generally paid no attention; maybe Martin put all his guests onto this little gem of a site.

The bullring was a rather lovely building and well worth a visit with its low profile, white and orange arches and that endless curve, topped with bright terracotta tiles[17]. The Lesser Kestrels fluttered like butterflies around each other, more delicate and agile than Kestrels, the male bold with his rust and grey wings and pale, gently spotted underside. It was spring and here was a wonderful sign of it: Lesser Kestrels displaying in courtship flight around the bullring roof. Superb.

From Trujillo, I rode along quiet back roads to the west. Here was the true Spanish Steppes. A bit like going back in time, the landscape looked almost uncultivated: broad sweeping plains and fields with washes of colour from blankets of spring flowers in yellow and purple. Big open skies (that reminded me of home in both Suffolk and Scotland) met distant horizons where the Gredos Mountains rose like the scaly ridge of a dinosaur's back, ancient and a little menacing.

Following the route that Martin had sketched out for me, I rode helmet-less with scope and tripod slung over my shoulder along quiet minor roads towards Santa Marta de Magasca. Some of the fields became smaller and walled in, another sign of bygone agriculture. A farmer tilling his small field on an ancient red Massey Ferguson tractor was being followed, gull-like, by a flock of 30 white storks. It was an unexpected pleasure to see so many of these big birds together instead of the more usual pair, bill-clapping in a huge nest atop some town chimney.

Farther along a quiet rural road, I pulled over to scan across a sweeping vista of typical steppe habitat. A black and white post, far away in a field of wild flowers, became a Little Bustard once I got the scope on it, and a flock of Pin-tailed Sandgrouse wheeled around the nearby hillocks chuttering noisily. The bustard was distant, but splendid with his jet-black neck and contrasting white stripes as if wearing a cravat. Otherwise, a standing Little Bustard is really a chicken – until it lifts its wing or takes flight when more black and white contrasts boldly

---

[17]Trujillo is a beautiful and ancient, orange-roofed, compact town. Worth a look in itself.

against a tan-coloured back. Unfortunately, I only got to see the chicken display.

I continued my search of the steppes for the main prize: Great Bustard. Ahead of me, a muddy track meandered into the distance with two large gateposts rising out of the low ground about half a mile along. Martin had told me to look out for these as a marker for where to walk. My bike is not an off-roader, but I had to give it a try; time was running out for long walks. Because of all the recent rain, the mud got deeper and more slippery as I went. What looked like a large muddy puddle from the road had turned into a quagmire of gloop stretching out for another hundred yards. I got scared; if this heavy machine fell over here, in the middle of nowhere, I'd never be able to lift it. Slowly, I inched it round (a 21 point turn!) and rode it back to dry land. With aching limbs and some relief I parked the bike, hid my bag in the grass nearby and set off on foot. I waited. I searched. No sign of Great Bustard. Black-bellied Sandgrouse flew, landed, flew and landed in a little covey of six to ten birds. Bee-eaters rocketed by in small groups, clearly passing through on migration, and a Calandra Lark turned my head several times as it imitated their calls.

Eventually, I saw a large, turkey-like head and neck rise cautiously on the horizon. In the scope, it was clearly a female Great Bustard (Big Tick!), but I didn't come all this way for a turkey's head. I was standing in a dip and needed more height. Behind me was Martin's landmark, the pair of large stone gateposts – height! Up I climbed, tripod scraping against the stonework. I scanned around from my new vantage point and there, in the middle distance, appeared a large, fluffy, black, tan and white mass, quivering in the long grass: a displaying male Great Bustard. The prize! And a major target bird for my trip. Both bustard and both sandgrouse species, Bee-eaters, several lark species, Montague's Harrier, Booted Eagle and Lesser Kestrel; the Spanish Steppes were magnificent. The empty roads across open, undulating grassland were also a joy to ride on a bike.

I rarely leave a bird site happy that I've seen all I can see, but this time I rode back towards Trujillo completely content with my lot. I stopped at the Little Bustard field to have another look, but it was gone or hiding. The sandgrouse were a little closer, but took off when I stopped so I took my leave of the steppes and headed for El Recuerdo to pick up my bags and move on. I really wished I could stay another night instead of having to now pack up and ride for a few hours. Finding birds is tiring and there was a little adrenalin surge involved in getting a lifer like Great Bustard. Now the adrenalin had gone, leaving me feeling flat and tired. Back at El Recuerdo however, Holenose gave me a replacement adrenalin shot by bolting his head through the hole in the gate once more, just as I approached to open it. Bloody dog! I said my thank you and goodbye to Martin and all at the guest-house and set off towards Madrid.

Martin had tempted me to plan a stop near Saucedilla back towards Monfrague for Black-shouldered Kite, but as I approached the area and took stock of the time, I realised there was no chance of finding more birds that day. Now was the time to put some miles behind me. I decided rashly to get around Madrid before stopping for the night – a four-hour ride, starting at 4. pm with nowhere to stay.

It was hard work on the motorways around a big city like Madrid. Tim was a lifesaver, but I was still in trouble: it started raining – again! (this is Spain for God's sake!), I was getting cold and, to cap it all, warning signs of an accident appeared in the spray; the motorway ground to a halt. I filtered past the stationary traffic (*Bikes 3; Cars 2*), but still only managed 20mph for over an hour.

Storming on past the big city, I became determined to find a hotel well beyond the suburbs, but drizzle and darkness fell quickly and there were no brightly lit hotel signs. In fact, nothing was brightly lit as I passed monolith after monolith of warehouse and industrial estate. I carried on and on until, at around 9. pm, I got a little unnerved and pulled in at a late night services to ask. Luckily, a young waiter vaguely knew of a place with a hotel not too far up the motorway and I set off again, weariness now sapping any optimism I had for finding a bed that night. As the street lights petered out, all became black again on that inhospitable strip of dark, warehouse-lined tarmac and there was no sign of habitation, let alone hotel. Worry started to take hold and I cursed myself. "Never do this again, you idiot," I scolded into the helmet.

A few lights marked a junction and with relief, I pulled over. For a few heart-stopping minutes, I couldn't find anything like a hotel, despite the brightly lit streets, but after a couple of dead ends and dreaded U-turns under the eerie glow of yellow street lamps, I pulled up at the Hotel Azucueca de Henares. Never have I been so glad to see a crappy business hotel in all my life! The concierge shook his head when I asked for just one night, but I stood there, a desperate looking, immoveable object and he relented. Relief!

Despite my weariness, I still had to unpack the bike and, in this dodgy-looking, anonymous Madrid satellite village (what Watford was to London, perhaps?), I felt the need to lock the bike to the biggest post I could find (*Bikes 3; Cars 3*). It was a struggle with the heavy chain and gone 10.30 pm before I finally shut the door, collapsing exhausted into the safety and comfort of my room. Bliss.

Next day, after some internal debate about what day of the week it was (immortalised on the dictaphone as, *"Oh, yesterday was Sunday; that explains a lot!"*), I made a slow and fairly late start after a lack-lustre breakfast in this adequate saviour of a hotel. I sat in the adjacent café with a coffee and croissant, looking out over the scene of last night's desperate arrival. It all looked so mundanely normal, if a bit tawdry and out of the way. The bike stood chained like an abandoned dog, almost accusingly, with it's back to me on the far side of the parking area, right up against a chain-link fence that marked the edge of a piece of wasteland... which, I suddenly thought, might be a good place for an unexpected bird: maybe a Hoopoe or better, a lark or a warbler. I wandered outside with the Red Spots, but that's all it was – a piece of wasteland. I had been unkind to Watford, and that was my cue to get going.

The road heading on from Azucueca towards Huesca and the Pyrenees also looked remarkably normal in the daylight, compared to the threatening tunnel of darkness from the evening before. In fact, it opened out to became a fast and pleasant ride. After putting sixty miles under my belt, a petrol top up and another delicious café con leche, I phoned Josele Dias, my next contact, host and bird guide, (and the one I hoped would put me on to Lammergeier). It would be several weeks until my next guide, a lifetime away in Bulgaria, so I wanted this one to count; I had two nights (*two whole nights!*) with Josele at the Boletas Birdwatching Centre in Loporzano, a small village near Huesca.

"You must go for the Dupont's," came Josele's strong Spanish accent

"Will I have time? I'm still three hours from you," I told him

"Yes, yes, no problem. It will be difficult to go back to the Dupont's site from here and you should go to Aguilon for Bonelli's Eagle."

I looked quickly at the map in front of me and guessed how long it would all take.

"I won't be with you until 8.00 or 8.30, Josele."

"Probably later. Dupont's sing in the evening – you want to be there at 7.00, then come on to here. You *must* go to the Dupont's site!"

I recognised the tone. It said, "No self-respecting birder would be where you are and pass by a chance to see Dupont's Lark." I *had* done my homework on this one; it is an extremely rare bird – globally – and only occurs in Spain and North Africa. It is also classified as threatened or endangered by conservation organisations, since it's population has been in decline for the last thirty years. But to be honest, I had thought it looked like just a boring lark and given it fairly low priority. I wasn't really hunting rarities on this trip and had yet to appreciate the significance of my nonchalance over Spanish Imperial Eagle. I was fairly lukewarm about old Dupont and his lark. However, I had already jotted down the site near Belchite very roughly on a map, but had no idea exactly where to go. Scribbling furiously, I copied down some additional directions from Josele, along with more for Aguilon and Bonelli's Eagle. His insistent enthusiasm made my mind up: I'd go for it.

"Thanks, Josele. See you later."

He asked if I wanted to eat with them... as if he needed to! Proper, home cooked Spanish food? Absolutely. I'd be there a little late, but then I had found the Spanish didn't contemplate eating until around 9pm anyway. I gave Tim the details for Codo, a village just outside Belchite, checked the journey time (which Tim usually over-estimated) and rode off up the A2 towards Zaragoza, fired up for some bird hunting.

My mood was buoyant and the road was dry (for a change!). I had a goal, a time to be there, and I wasn't facing the prospect of finding accommodation in the middle of the night. A town called Siguenza had caught my attention as a possible non-birding stop. It looked architecturally and historically fine but, as I approached the junction to leave the motorway, it just didn't feel right. Although the riding was going really well, I might need all my time to locate Josele's birds and, yet again, I just did not feel like battling with town traffic. I wimped out, letting the bike carry me swiftly on past the turning for Siguenza. I believe it is a lovely small town and will go back some day. Time for a coffee stop!

I must pause here to do justice to – or admit to – the number of road services I stopped at and how important they became to me as a solo traveller. After the running-on-empty incident back in Monfrague I would stop for fuel at the drop of a hat and turn it into a coffee stop at the drop of a bike stand. These stops, especially on roads smaller than motorways, also gave me a slice of contemporary culture in whichever country I was in. For example, I noticed a puzzling bit of behaviour in these Spanish service areas: people stood at the bar with cigarettes, espresso coffee, tapas or other sorts of food, dropping the resulting debris where they stood. Very often, the scene was one of ankle-deep litter, approaching knee-deep as the day wore on. If I were lucky, I'd hit a place just as one of the staff got out a broom to perform the two-hourly sweep of fag butts, serviettes, chocolate wrappers and assorted debris. Surely better for everyone to put the stuff in a bin in the first place, I thought, completely puzzled by the charming inefficiency of it. But there were no bins – which left this Brit a little confused: where do I put my own rubbish? I couldn't bring myself to get all Spanish and jettison it where I sat. Another little observation of contemporary road culture: while I would sit down to rest or to eat and have coffee, the Spanish almost all stood, either at a bar or at small high tables dotted around the room. Those who sat, like me, were almost exclusively elderly women. That made me feel uncomfortable (not very macho to be sitting with all the Spanish old dears!).

Leaving the filthy services near Siguenza, site of my non-visit, the bike hummed along nicely, Honda's famous reliability holding true as the miles slipped by, lubricated by far more coffees than I needed. The local road I had to take to Cannena appeared quickly and I swept out into an opening plain. From the A2 motorway at La Almunia de Dona Godina it is 15 miles of dead straight road to Cannena. The sense of speed was exhilarating as I rode deeper into the plains, although they were mostly flat fields cultivated with what looked like vines. The roads gradually became narrower and less well maintained as I followed Tim towards Tosos. When the sign for Tosos appeared, I turned right down an even narrower road which began to twist and turn. I stopped to check the map; Tim sometimes did daft things to take the "shortest route". He was, after all, just a piece of software in a computer – not a lot of common sense going on in there – and more than once he had me bumping over mountain tracks rather than take a few miles more on fast, smooth tarmac. Tim was not to be trusted out in the sticks. But this time, he was spot on: the only route to Aguilon and Bonelli's Eagle was via Tosos and this slow, twisting road.

After a couple of miles, road works signs began to appear and I knew I was in for delays or, God forbid, the closed rural road that means a two hundred mile detour to reach the other side. There had indeed been big road works going on, but all the machinery and signs were packed up along the side. The road was not only open – it was spectacularly open, widening out into a smooth snake of new, twisting tarmac. The riding became sheer joy. Despite the luggage, I threw the bike into the bends, the newly banked road allowing me to take the curves like a racer, flicking it from side to side. A bird flew across in front of me, up into conifers. I knew it was something new and worth seeing (black and white, size of a sparrow – maybe Lesser Spotted Woodpecker?), but I really was in biker mode and couldn't have stopped anyway. The bike and I swung and dipped our way through the trees and hills, meeting not one other vehicle or person. I couldn't say how many miles of this wonderful road had been re-built like this (or even why – perhaps it had completely collapsed?), but the smooth bends and hairpins lasted until I reached Tosos. Here the road abruptly turned back into the poorly surfaced track that I had been expecting, so I stopped to draw breath after my track race through the hills. Bikers travel miles for roads like that, but it was so out of the way and so new, I doubt if anyone other than a local on a scooter had given it a try[18].

Stopping in Tosos, I got out the dictaphone to record the events of the last few hours;

"I've been dodging rain on and off, having followed Josele's directions, and insistence that I come here to more southern birding sites, 'on the way'. They're not 'on the way', Josele, it's a big fucking detour – but without it, I'd never come to these places, I'd never be in a place like this. This place is called Tosos."

My voice on the recorder sounded excited and pleased to have left the beaten track and ended up somewhere so unusual; the "big fucking detour" was clearly very welcome!

"Not a thing here," I continued, *"everyday buildings, bit of a mess actually, above a muddy river, but... behind me there are these incredible rock formations, well, they've been eroded*

[18]For bikers; it was part of the CV102 from Santa Barbara to Tosos (and on from there to Aguilon). Fabulous landscapes on an empty narrow road. Worth a look.

away and are going to fall over soon. They look like something out of a Roger Dean painting. I'm sure he must have seen something like this as an inspiration"

Roger Dean was a well-known painter of rock album covers for bands like Yes and Greenslade in the 1970s, and these sandy rock mushrooms that rose up behind the dwellings in this naff little village looked identical to the rocky creations he placed in his invented, other-world landscapes.

These lumpy 30ft columns stood like fat sentries right on the edge of a small cliff, which rose behind the low buildings. I stared at them for ages, taking a few photos as a reminder, but the voice recording does more to capture my sense of wonder at stumbling across these precarious pillars right in the middle of a nowhere village.

There was nothing else in Tosos, not even a coffee shop so, with dark clouds threatening rain, I moved on (my parting dictaphone message being;

"Been dodging rain all the time... better go, it's gonna start pissing on me in a minute!"

I was now on the look-out for Bonelli's Eagle. Josele had told me to look anywhere round the Aguilon area, so I rode on with more than half an eye on the outlines of the surrounding hills, anticipating the silhouette of a large bird of prey round every bend. As I turned one corner, a narrow cultivated field of grass spread below the road to my left. Something caught my eye in the middle of the field and I turned to look: five or six large mammals were sauntering warily across the field, grazing as they went. As I stopped, they looked up. They were big goats with enormous pointed horns, some with black chests and legs, but otherwise, all were a dark fawn colour. As they noticed me, they made a more definite move to cross the field. By the time I got the camera out of the tank bag, the leader had started scrambling up the hillside – definitely some kind of mountain goat. I got a few hopelessly unfocused, distant photos before the whole group had jumped up and disappeared with perfect camouflage onto the surrounding ledges and scrubby rocks. I made myself rehearse the characteristics of these creatures so I could find out later exactly what they were[19].

Just as I was about to move off, a shape soared up over the ridge above the goats – definitely an eagle, and a big one. My first thought was Golden Eagle, it was so big and dark against the sky, but as it changed its position and the light caught it at different angles, I felt a quickening of the pulse: Bonelli's! I looked hard for the ID features that I'd memorised, hoping it was a nice adult to make my task easier. Indeed it was: a beautifully marked bird with characteristic dark wing patches beneath, contrasting with a pale body and hind wing. As it wheeled closer overhead, it was clearly smaller and more agile than a Golden Eagle. I watched it soar around for a while, eventually seeing a patch of white on its back – the final tell-tale

[19]Spanish Ibex

mark of Bonelli's Eagle. They are a prize among eagles because there are only around a thousand pairs in the whole of Europe – and because they are bloody lovely birds. Spain has three-quarters of them, the rest being restricted to a few coastal Mediterranean countries. To come to this place and actually find such a bird was hugely satisfying. I could just as easily have travelled right through here and not come across a soaring Bonelli's Eagle. I felt lucky and privileged as I carried on into Aguilon just to have a look at the town.

And a lovely little place it was too, marred only by lack of an open bar or coffee shop. The whole village seemed to be closed, so I took the bike up a rough track out of town to get into the heart of eagle country, in the hope of another Bonelli's and to have a picnic up in the hills. The forest track became far too rough, but I persevered, coaxing the heavy Honda like a reluctant pack mule, up onto a sandy rise where I stopped to eat a roll and an orange. The panorama across those Bonelli's hills was beautiful in the clear air and, in the far distance, I saw something that made me catch my breath, the Pyrenees, covered with snow. Sweet Jesus, I'd have to cross those in just a couple of day's time, I thought. By what route I had no idea and the sight made me realise how far I had to go. I had better give up on finding more eagles, get those Dupont's Larks and shift my backside on to Boletas.

It was well after 4pm before I left Aguilon heading north on another twisting, challenging mountain road (high fun factor though!) and my mind turned once again to the Transfagarasan in Romania: could that be any better than this and would I ever get there? I turned right onto the larger, faster A220 and sped along towards Belchite; a fabulous ride on a fast sweeping road with open plains stretching all around. Tim took me round Belchite with its arresting architecture, which I thought looked of Moorish influence, but later found to be ruins of Belchite old town, left after destruction during the Spanish civil war in the 1930s. Franco had decreed that the ruins be kept as a monument to the war and the superiority of his forces and ideology. He ordered New Belchite be built next door, leaving the ruins undisturbed; more a warning than a memorial, I thought.

I rode straight through all this history and on to nearby Codo, another tiny little Spanish village. I was getting caffeine withdrawal and it had become aridly hot, so the bar-come-coffee shop was a must-stop. The recent excitement of road, goat and eagle had taken its toll and I was tired. I sat inside out of the sun, being stared at by every local who entered (they clocked the bike before even coming in) and I got the very strong impression that tourists just didn't come this way much.

I needed to get a map out for the next bit because El Planeron, the exact location of those Dupont's Larks, meant nothing to Tim. He became not only mute, but dim (Dim Tim!). My map though, was well up to the task, being of a large (or is that small?) enough scale to show every little footpath and track. After the caffeine shot, bike and rider took off again. The landscape was now back to massively spreading plains; this was more steppe country, a few hundred miles from those around Trujillo, this time framed by the foothills of the Pyrenees, rather than the Gredos mountains. The nearby low hills were curiously flat-topped. It looked as though a giant had come along and sliced the top off some mountains, leaving just the base. This whole landscape was like another world.

A little pink sign pointed left off a bend to El Planeron and the road became a dirt track, dry and dusty brown after a day in the hot sun. I rolled along slowly until I saw a vehicle pulled up ahead. Two people were out with telescopes pointing into the low bushes. This is what a tired birder wants to see: someone else who can tell you where the bird is – or save you the bother if they've spent the entire day looking with no luck. The couple turned out to be from France, so I had a go at asking them in French if they had seen the birds. Unusually, they replied in French – I didn't really understand, but got the gist: the Dupont's Larks were there, right in front of me... somewhere. I couldn't believe my luck. This never happens; first Bonelli's Eagle, exactly where they should be and now one of the rarest lark species in the world, right on cue. In a foreign country and on my own, I truly did not expect to find these birds with any ease, but this was becoming magical. The light was falling into a lovely, still evening with reds and pale blues merging above the gently rising land all around and across the plains, when I heard this plaintive, almost pathetic little song coming from a bush, no more than twenty yards away. It was one of the most fragile sounds I think I have ever heard. The French couple looked at me and pointed.

"C'est le Dupont's," he said

"Oui, oui, oui," was all I could get out as I concentrated on finding the bird in the scope. Another song started up nearby, but I just couldn't find the owner. The light was failing rapidly, and you can't count a bird on just song – well, technically you *can*, but there was no way I was going to be there, with the birds singing right next to me, and leave without seeing them. The French couple drove on, leaving me to get on the birds. It's always more satisfying to find a bird yourself but, at that moment, I disliked the couple for nonchalantly wandering off before I found the birds (bit of a birding faux pas, that), but it turned out that they weren't keen birders and the larks were just a bonus activity while they enjoyed the sunset. For me, the sunset was the bonus because, unlike the French couple, I wouldn't be able to come back another night.

That plaintive song had a ventriloquial quality and it seemed impossible to locate the singer, but eventually, I found the right bush and there it was – Dupont's Lark! It was sitting right on the edge of a low shrub, only two feet off the ground, looking just like a lump of the bush itself. Unlike other larks, this bird sat much more upright, and it had a long down-curved bill. To be honest, it looked a little boring -a classic LBJ – but its song and the setting, here on a fine evening on a remote Spanish plain, made it one of the top birding experiences of my life. I couldn't tear myself away. Selfishly unconcerned about arriving very late at Josele's (it was his fault I was here anyway!), I moved further along to get a better look at these birds. Another struck up a song, clearly defending a small scrubby territory in this vast landscape, although such a thin, delicate little call seemed more of a plea than a threat. As before, I couldn't find the songster very easily, getting only fleeting glimpses. I found out later that they have a penchant for running between bushes rather than flying – pesky birds! I stayed, listening to the song until around 8pm-when they stopped.

It had been a hypnotic experience, one that I was reluctant to let go until the disappearance of both light and birds. After all, I would most likely never return here to re-live this magical moment. But fade the light did and, unlike me, the larks went to bed. I now had a fairly long ride to Loporzano in the deepening gloom, arriving yet again in the dark.

As I entered the small village, my little mental picture of how to find Josele's "Boletas Birdwatching Centre" made no sense. I had to phone him and ask for directions several times before I finally rolled down a slope just opposite his house, food and a welcome bed.

"Welcome! Welcome!" shouted Josele as I stiffly swung my leg off the bike.

" Sorry I'm late Josele. Nice to meet you." We shook hands

"Did you get the Dupont's?"

"Absolutely!"

His eyebrows raised and the delight on his face was clear; he had another happy customer. I know how rewarding it is to send someone off for a bird, hoping they see it, then hearing their satisfied happiness at finding it. Of course, it can work the other way – then you feel apologetically responsible for their failure.

"And Bonelli's?"

"Yes, that too."

"Oh-ho-ho!" he exclaimed, opening his arms wide, dead chuffed with himself – and I felt like the star pupil.

"Would you like to eat?" offered Josele.

"As long as you're sure it's not too late, yes, thanks."

Josele's wife, Esther duly appeared with some fresh bread, soup and a salad, followed by some sort of fried lamb chop with a thin, delicious sauce poured over it. Red wine washed it down and made me sleepy. Chat as I might with Josele about the state of Spanish conservation, I couldn't stay awake. I struggled up the stairs with bike panniers to the homely, stone-walled bedroom and hit the sack with the minimum of unpacking. Next thing I knew, I was waking up in a comfortable bed to the loud, insistent tune of my phone alarm. I was in Boletas, and it felt good as breakfast beckoned.

Josele had guests to meet at the airport, so he wasn't free to guide me. Instead, he gave me advice and directions for a walk from the village into a local valley. As I walked out in the sun, I thought how good it was to have the whole day and a second night here without having to move on. I realised that this had been a weakness in my planning: too many single nights in different places, one after the other. It was becoming obvious that I had crammed in too much for comfort, but at least today I could concentrate on birding.

Loporzano was sleepiness itself, with a church tower at the centre, on top of which perched a storks nest containing two of the huge black and white, bill-clapping birds. Classic. I stopped at a little panaderia for some bread. Places like this just don't exist in Britain any more. It was a tiny shop, selling only fresh baked Spanish bread – and it could make a living for someone. This would be unheard of in Tescoland, UK.

Carrying the warm baguette (no doubt called something else here in northern Spain), I crossed the main road and started my walk along a bush-lined path. I left a couple of messages on the dictaphone, one moaning about the skulking, uncooperative *Sylvia* warblers[20] that were eluding me in every bush, and another about the amount of gear I was carrying:

"I've got binoculars, telescope and tripod, sunglasses, baseball cap (borrowed from Josele), sun-tan lotion, a hip bag with bird book, map and notes, water, a small picnic, including the bread, the dictaphone and an iPod. It's a nightmare!"

---

[20]*Sylvia* (Genus, meaning "wood") are a group of warblers such as Blackcap and Whitethroat. Confusingly, Wood Warbler is in a group known as "leaf" warblers (Genus *Acrocephalus*), along with Chiffchaff and Willow Warbler.

All this gear certainly weighed me down and I sort of wished I was just going for a walk, not intrepidly hunting Lammergeier, my goal for the day.

Lammergeiers are a type of vulture but, unlike many of the others, they are just beautiful. Like many birds of prey, they soar effortlessly on thermals near mountain slopes and valleys. They have comparatively narrow, pointed wings, but are still enormous birds. The really distinctive feature of a soaring Lammergeier is its tail: an elongated diamond following behind. No other bird of prey has a tail quite like that (if you're keeping notes though, beware of Egyptian Vulture). With a good view, you can see the pale orange body, legs, neck and head, contrasting with long dark wings, which carry them on endless mountain patrols. I have wanted to see one for as long as I've been birding.

Shamefully and very sadly, Lammergeiers are endangered. Throughout the 19th and 20th centuries, they have been steadily approaching extinction across their already restricted mountain ranges, having disappeared from places like the Alps and the mountains of Bulgaria and Romania between the 1930s and 1950s. In Europe, the only place to see them now is in the Pyrenees and even here, you really need to check out where they are likely to be seen – especially if, like me, you only have a couple of days to look. Finding one of these beauties was my main reason for being here, near the Pyrenees (and the next day, in the mountains themselves).

The path abruptly opened out onto a flat scrubby plateau with a few buildings and a large walled cemetery. Birds flitted around and wild flowers grew in profusions of yellow bushes and pink mats. The edge of the plateau looked across a huge rocky canyon, not pretty, but quite grand in scale and flanked by barren pointed hills far on the opposite side. A ruined castle sat on top of the highest of these at eye level with me; a stunning vista over this imposing valley. A few larks were flitting around the cemetery wall catching insects that were sunning on its warm surface. Josele had told me to check here for the rather scarce Thekla Lark which, in the books, looked almost identical to the more common Crested Larks I'd been seeing since day one. I followed one bird as it ran, train-like along the flat ground between grassy tufts, bushes and little piles of rock. Looking for signs of Thekla Lark (a stubbier bill, a "spectacled" look and maybe a less pointed crest), it took me a while to realise this bird had no crest at all; it wasn't even a lark – what an idiot! I was looking so hard, I forgot to check the obvious. So what was I looking at? I settled in for a prolonged ID session. Picking up the scope several times and following this pale little bird from a distance, sometimes hiding behind a corner of the cemetery wall, I eventually got clear views up close with the telescope. My first instinct proved right when I checked the book (and later with Josele). It was a Tawny Pipit; washed out, with a stripy looking head and five or six black spots showing very clearly on the side of its folded wing.

Wandering around that desolate cemetery, I did find a Thekla Lark along with Woodlark and Woodchat Shrike. I spent ages taking half decent photos of a very obliging little Woodlark who sat perched while I fiddled around, holding my crappy digital camera up against the eyepiece of the 'scope. I wasn't trying to take impressive bird photos on this trip, but I wanted some decent records and I needed something visual for the blog.

Time was getting on and a long walk down into the dry valley lay ahead of me. I tramped off in the increasing heat, encumbered by all the paraphernalia, spending fruitless, frustrating minutes trying to "get on" pesky little warblers who didn't want to be got on. A Black Wheatear completely captivated me for a while (I didn't even know such a thing was around in these parts of Spain), followed by it's congener, Black-eared Wheatear; both lovely little birds with bouncy flight and a habit of perching up on the curve of a rock, showing boldly against the distant far side of the valley.

I descended further, sometimes scrambling over huge fallen boulders and picking up more birds typical of this sort of habitat. Nightingales sang in the background, cheering me on my way. Something made me check all my gear and I found the map I needed was missing – I had dropped it somewhere.

Cursing, I made my way back along the difficult track, leaving the scope and tripod perched on the path. I found the map (not dropped, but carelessly left behind) and, uttering more profane self-abuse, I grumpily trudged back again. Without the scope, I was able to move a little better, so when a dark shape appeared above me, I got on it very quickly with the trusty Red Spots. It was close, it was a big raptor – and I knew that silhouette as if I'd been watching it all my life. Lammergeier! My birding friends know if a bird is a goodie for me by my usual profane reaction;

"Fuck, fuck, fuck!" I shouted to the world, "Lammergeier!" (my eloquence knows no bounds!)

"Oh... you beauty, you beauty," was all I could say after that, other than, "Ah!" and "Oh!". I tried to spin out the sighting by craning my neck, binoculars fixed to my eyes, shuffling my feet along the precarious path and generally not letting the huge bird out of my sight. I drank it all in, consciously trying to see all the features of this gorgeous creature. A true lifer for me, but more than that, one I had lusted after for years, I took in the unmistakable outline: that diamond-shaped tail, the long, relatively narrow wings and luckily, I could see the pale orange body and head, like a bullet in the middle of dark wings. Try as I might, I couldn't stop the bird eventually sailing out of view round a nearby hillside. I contemplated calling it a day. How could I top that? Maybe I should go and relax somewhere rather than slog on down to the river, as recommended by Josele. Then the thought of seeing another Lammergeier popped greedily into my mind and, of course, there were many other possible goodies around a place like this – especially birds of prey. I carried on downwards.

At the river, right in the bottom of the now hot valley, I soaked my self in water to cool off, had a picnic lunch (the panaderia bread, two pieces of toast glued together with jam, and a yoghurt, all taken with me from the breakfast table) and I sat for a while. Nothing much appeared at the river and I couldn't hear any song because of the rush of water. I decided to head back. A magnificent young Golden Eagle swooped up over a ridge as I got back on the track and I picked up a couple of Red Kites on the way. The eagle gave a display flight, folding its wings and stooping into a dive then rolling out of the stoop, and away. A fleeting glimpse of another (or the same?) Lammergeier was the last bird-induced panic until I strolled back with heavy legs to Loporzano, Boletas and Josele and Esther. *SO* nice to be staying put this time; no riding on, no mad dash for accommodation, no concern about cost and finding a campsite. Excellent. Take a tip from me: on a trip like this, plan two-night stops as often as time will allow.

"How did you get on?" asked Josele at dinner

"Lammergeier!"

His eyebrows raised and my heart sank a little; surely he wasn't going to tell me it was very unlikely – because there was no way I'd have accepted that – even from a local expert. He asked where.

"As I walked down into the valley. It soared over the edge then disappeared to the north."

"Ah, yes. They've been seen there before. I think at this time of year they're just patrolling. They do that."

"I saw another later from the valley floor. And a Golden Eagle."

Josele nodded sagely. Thank God! No awkward session where the local expert casts disabusing doubt on my finest hour!

"You were asking for some guiding," said Josele, "tomorrow I am free after all, but only in the morning. Would you like to go out for Wallcreeper?"

Would I?!

"Sure. But I need to get across into France by tomorrow evening. What would be the best route and would I have time after birding in the morning?"

I had decided that it wasn't so essential to get right up into the high Pyrenees to see Lammergeier any more and I wanted to capitalise on my luck with those fabulous vultures by crossing the mountains in one go without more birding stops on the Spanish side.

"You will have time. If you go by the Bielsa tunnel, it will be quick. We will look for Wallcreeper in the morning."

Part of me felt disappointment that I would be effectively going under this stunning mountain chain that separates Spain from France, rather than over, but the thought of finding Wallcreeper and other Pyrenean specialities with this very knowledgeable local expert was too tempting. I also had in the back of my mind that the great Transfagarasan in Romania would fill in that gap – if I ever made it that far.

Next morning we were out early. I had no idea where I was being taken and Josele drove like a lunatic. If you've ever wondered what those crazy Spanish drivers are like in the flesh – meet Josele! We drove to Riglos, the site of a towering group of red sandstone pinnacles right at the edge of the Pyrenean foothills (or pre-Pyrenees). They look like 300 metre high chimney stacks, all fused together, huge and rising straight out of the surrounding slopes. Popular with climbers, they are also a site for Wallcreepers in winter before they return to the inaccessible high peaks and gorges for the summer. Josele knew which face to look on, according to where the sun fell on the pinnacles but, despite some tenacity on his part, his own prediction that the birds had already left for the peaks proved correct. No Wallcreeper – but there were some good new birds for the Trip List, including Peregrine Falcon hunting around the pinnacles along with tumbling groups of Chough high up and Rock Sparrow on the ragged rocks below. I had a couple of other possible sites for Wallcreeper, but these were a long way ahead in Bulgaria and Romania. By the time I got there, they too might have pissed off for the summer.

By mid-day, we were back at Boletas and I was packing up the bike. With all the avian excitement and a whole day off from the Honda, it felt ok to be once more attaching, tying, strapping and locking all the various bits onto the bike. I oiled the chain, checked the water and tyres then set off with a wave to Josele and Esther, heading for the Bielsa tunnel on Josele's advice.

"You should go today," he told me, "the weather is bad for tomorrow and you might not get through. You are lucky at the moment – sometimes the roads are closed even in May."

Tim was primed with the destination, south-east on the A22 then North at Barbastro towards Ainsa and the tunnel. This was a change of plan. I had had every intention of riding over the mountains in the hope of catching Lammergeier, but this seemed unnecessary now and I was a little perturbed by the amount of snow visible on the peaks; the idea of a tunnel with a good fast road really appealed.

The road to Ainsa was spectacular to ride, following lakeside shores and valleys with a good wide surface. Some miles before the town, road works signs began to appear with worrying frequency, among them a big illuminated red cross above the lane in which I was riding. I took no notice and rode on into the small town. It was mayhem. There was some sort of carnival going on, along with major road disruption all around the town. When some temporary road signs appeared, I began to realise the significance of the red crosses: the Bielsa tunnel was closed! I had ridden 70 miles and taken two hours – for nothing. Using some very difficult English/Spanish communication with a couple of helpful cops, I gleaned that the tunnel would be closed for two months. I couldn't believe this. Surely Josele would have known? Can a major route through the Pyrenees be closed for that long in late Spring? The police radioed some colleagues elsewhere and helped me to plot another route; apparently, I would have to avoid the obvious one via main roads back to Sabinanigo because it too had bad road-works. My journey would now go via Fiscal and Broto. This meant trekking north-west for 50 miles along twisting mountain roads to El Portalet, a pass over the mountains. I would be going over the top after all – literally. The cops had given me dire warnings about how bad the road out of Broto would be on a bike – at least the sign language looked dire when one of them drew his thumb across his throat as he gestured down at the bike.

With no other option and not the faintest idea how long it would take me to cross the Pyrenees, I set off for Fiscal at 2pm, really far too late to be heading up into the high peaks; although it was the 21st of April, there was still a lot of snow on the mountains that occasionally loomed into view in the distance. The road to Fiscal was good though: a snaking ribbon of smooth tarmac, and a wonderful ride along a wooded river valley, slowly climbing through the foothills of the Pyrenees. Bend after bend, I made good progress and my mood of apprehension lifted. This wasn't the difficult challenge I had expected after all. Part of me was disappointed, but I still had the cut-throat road after Broto to deal with, so maybe the adventure was yet to come. Broto was to be my first stop, but after another hour on the road, covering only 25 miles, I was ready for a coffee (of course).

Broto is like a mini alpine village with high pitched roofs and wide overhanging eaves for dealing with winter snow. It also had the tacky appeal of a tourist spot in a mountain area where towns and shops are sparse. After a coffee (for which I was charged twice, but was too tired to argue over or even be sure of) I decided to throw caution to the wind and, for the first time, buy a tacky souvenir. There was a sort of supermarket selling postcards, car stickers, inflatable toys, shiny varnished wooden carvings of animals, key rings with mountains scenes, fridge magnets and much more of the same. But I couldn't do it; it was all such rubbish. Instead, I bought a sticker for the bike saying "Broto" on a flowery heraldic sign, and a couple of postcards. I liked Broto for its small scale and simplicity but, unless shopping for shopping's sake turns you on, and once you've had a coffee with something to eat, there isn't much to stay for – except the dogs. Big chunky brutes they were and I immediately thought they must have something to do with the Pyrenean Mountain breed, but without the pure white shaggy coat. I took a photo of one of these for the blog (for some reason, I decided to take pictures of all the dogs I came across and they all went on the blog as "Trip Blog Dogs"!).

The road out of Broto was fine at first, but it very soon started climbing and switching back in tight hairpins. After a few miles, it narrowed and tightened even further and the surface became rutted in places. It kept climbing. This was the real ascent – the one the police had warned me of back in Ainsa. I had pictures of snow appearing and blocking the road. It became hard to do any speed and I struggled with the counter-steering that I'd learned with John of the Advanced Motorist session (now *that* felt like an age away!). Still, I was having a lot of fun with this wonderful machine on these hidden and challenging roads. Just keeping to my own side of the road became impossible, either because it was too narrow or because the bends were so tight. My CBF600 isn't exactly a racer – bit like me – but we went well together and this was the most exciting riding since the road into Tosos. Again, I thought ahead to the Transfagarasan in Romania. Would I make it to that Holy Grail of biking roads?

It took nearly an hour to cover the 18 miles from Broto to Biescas. As the day wore on, it became tiring and my body clock was saying "time to stop" but, as at Madrid a few days before, I became determined to get on; across the Pyrenees and into France before stopping for the night. Thankfully, the road to El Portalet was fabulous; recently engineered into a wide, smooth and winding route high up into the mountains. The bike flew as I leaned and banked round the bends, climbing and climbing until the air began to feel noticeably cooler. On a bend, a dam came into view, beyond which was the green lake it retained, with the village of Lanuza nestling on the far shore. It looked perfect and I stopped for a photo of this tiny little place with its high, steeply sloping roof-lines and jutting eaves, just like back in Broto. An eagle of some sort wheeled over the ridge above this idyllic place, too far away and too purposeful in its flight for me to get binoculars on. The bike seemed to almost start itself, eager to get going, and we pulled back onto the road. Directly ahead, an enormous, double-peaked tooth of a mountain rose into the sky in the near distance, draped in snow and dominating the whole landscape. I stopped again for a photo of this arresting and slightly daunting sight; that was where I was heading.

I came across a few cars, but not many, and no bikes at all. In fact, I had been struck for some time by the lack of bikers, local or otherwise, and especially here, I really felt that I was on my own, possibly one of only a handful of riders to come this way – certainly at this time of year. The fine road steadily climbed, easy and fun to ride at a good speed. The landscape became more and more imposing. More of those jagged, snow-encrusted peaks pointed skyward: the white carnassial teeth of the Pyrenees.

At El Portalet, the road opened alongside an empty car park with stationary ski lifts running alongside. I was passing a ski resort. Warning signs of a border ahead began to appear until I rounded a corner to see the border post open out in front of me. The scene was a little on the desolate side; a sea of tarmac spread out all around and it was totally deserted (as was the border post itself[21]) – not a soul, not a car, no one. Also, the mountain peaks were now all around me, as well as popping up in the distance, covered in more snow than I was prepared for. They were stunningly beautiful, if ominous and threatening in the dull of late afternoon. But what a moment: my first international border, and what a place! I stopped for a while to savour it all, but the sense of isolation became a bit too much and the cold started to bite. I wanted away and down out of these forbidding peaks to wherever I'd next be laying my head. A blue sign proclaimed "FRANCE" in white capital letters and I rode on, leaving wonderful Spain behind.

[21]I learned later that the border post is now deserted and that this road is often closed until late May. I was extremely lucky to get through as early as April 20th

Chapter 5 – Being Continental

Back in Edinburgh, I am driving round in a Morris traveller – the one with the wooden frame like a mini version of an American station wagon. It's great and it takes me round some of the local farms, collecting cotton swabs from the rear end of cows and methodically placing each in a plastic sample bottle. The bottles, which are like the ones you put urine samples in, sit in an ever-increasing array in a large flat box on the passenger seat next to me and I constantly think how very weird this is.

I am awaiting the arrival of my dog when, out of the blue, one Saturday night in my tenement flat off Easter Road, I have an epileptic fit. Exactly a week later, I have another. They are both "grand mal" (major) seizures and with one on top of the other, I end up with a badly bitten tongue which ulcerates into the worst mouth ulcers I've ever had, my jaw has gone out of alignment so I can't open it properly and I have pulled several muscles in my back. The medical community swings into action, assuming that one seizure could have been an aberration, but two is a pattern. I spend the next few weeks attending hospital appointments and undergoing a battery of neurological tests. I am told I have "idiopathic epilepsy". I go on medication, which I have to remain on for the rest of my life and I lose my driving licence. I am no longer allowed to drive or ride anything for at least three years. The rest of life goes on hold. I can continue with my Zoology course as long as the fits are controlled, but it spells the end of the dog-training project. All realistic thoughts of biking evaporate and I sell my Suzuki Bloop.

It is 1977, the bike dream fades... but doesn't quite die; by chance, just a year later, I hitch-hike that Provençal road between Grenoble and Nice with a petite, dark-haired girl called Anne. We fly down the dusty mountain bends in an old Mercedes, driven by a barefoot German taxi driver who is touring the South of France. I promise myself again: one day, I will ride a bike down this road.

*

If a call came into my mobile, Tim would flash up a number on his display. The phone was in the top pocket of my bike jacket, but was linked to the satnav by Bluetooth. Another mind-boggling bit of technology, it allowed Tim to let me know if my phone was ringing as I rode along, deafened by wind and road noise (*Bikes 3: Cars 4*). Like most people, I suspect, I hate taking work-related calls while on holiday. They seem to gatecrash the party and jolt you back to your other life when you least want it. This unwelcome intrusion was even more jarring when some unknown (or known) phone number appeared in front of me as I rode along, immersed in the landscape, the bike and the road, on the look-out for birds. It happened once, early on when Tim was still vocal; a loud beep sounded in my ear and I glanced automatically at Tim's screen, thinking it was one of his warning sounds for a speed trap or change of direction (if Tim had remained vocal, these would have driven me mental!). Accompanying Tim's sound alert, an incoming call was flashing on the screen with a mobile number. I touched the screen to connect the call, amazed by the power of the technology at my fingertips.

"Hello!" I bellowed into the microphone in my helmet, aware now of the rushing air all around my head. I had forgotten too that I was wearing earplugs because of the noise.

" Is that Rob?" came a crackly voice inside the helmet.

It was Kathy, an ex-student from one of my adult college groups. She had kept in touch after going on to start a Pharmacy degree and had become a good friend. Kathy had also been very supportive of the trip and was one of the first "followers" of my blog.

"Where the fuck are you?" she added.

"I'm on the bike right now. Can't hear you very well. I'm riding and there's lots of noise. Can you hear me? How you getting on?"

She told me briefly the latest saga in her university course and life, which she was finding difficult. She was effectively on her own, but with older dependent offspring. Their actions and demands sometimes made her life hard, especially in trying to complete a science degree, working for a living and looking after them. She was in many ways typical of the Access students I had dealt with during the last 15 years of my college teaching: people who had aspirations above some dead-end job, and who were willing to do something about it, despite failures in the education system in the past. I had a lot of time for people like that and I didn't mind so much that it was Kathy on the phone.

"I'll have to pull over to hear you."

I stopped the bike in an opening. Kathy was just phoning to see how I was getting on and to wish me luck. We had a bit of a chat, but I still didn't want to be so connected with everyday life – this was meant to be an adventure! I was just at the beginning and still in a Western country where such contact is taken for granted. This wasn't to be the case further on.

Crossing into France meant rolling headlong down the other side of the Pyrenees. It really was downhill all the way, slaloming and twisting on another great biking road, this time a main road where I could keep up speed despite the bends. At intervals, I passed under concrete balconies constructed to hold off winter snow, avalanches, meltwater – or all three. Currently it was the latter; water gushed in torrents over these artificial overhangs as I roared through, engine noise echoing loudly. I was impressed by how well these tunnels worked to keep the pouring water off the road and I guessed that this was meltwater in full flow.

The towering, foreboding mountains seemed to be falling in on me and I ceased to enjoy the scenery, feeling instead an urgency to get down; down to some open land where I could see far ahead to where I was going. I had been brought up in Caithness in the Far North of Scotland where sweeping moorland, big skies and ten-mile vistas were the norm. I often found it claustrophobic being surrounded by mountains for too long. I opened up the throttle and tore round the bends, longing for some open skies.

The bike, Tim and I sped on until we passed through a tiny place called Les Eaux Chaudes, still in the high hills, but marking a noticeable change in gradient. We were now in the bottom of a valley and the road became flatter as it hugged a river. If anything, we romped on even faster. It was getting late and I had nowhere to stay – again. But thankfully, along with the softening terrain, houses and farms began to appear. The first campsite, I thought, stop at the very first campsite. A road sign with the familiar tent symbol popped into view on a sharp left-hand bend, just as we entered a small village. I followed it, aware that there wasn't a soul around – dinnertime, I guessed. The desertion eventually became a bit unnerving, but I found the entrance to the campsite. There were water hoses lying on the grass along with abandoned gardening tools, as if there had been recent activity, but nothing was happening and no one was about. I turned the bike around a few times, trying different approaches to this ghost village, but had to give up in disgust and head on to the nearest town.

It turned out that I was already in the outskirts of the nearest town: Laruns, centre of a large tourist area for walking and spa bathing (hence Les Eaux Chaudes, the Hot Waters, a few miles back). By the time I rode into the pretty French town centre, it was getting too late (again!) to consider camping. Besides, all the indications were that the main tourist season wasn't under way and wouldn't be for some time. I parked the bike between some black painted bollards in a cobbled section of the square and wandered over to a fountain in the centre. From there I spotted a cute little hotel and thought it looked good for a night. Inside, it was small and cosy. I set my heart on the comfort of this place after my mountain adventures, but they wanted 75 Euros for the room. This was near as damn it sixty quid, double what I hoped to pay and six times the cost of a campsite. I returned to the bike, dejected, but thinking I'd have to just pay, when three teenage boys came over asking if this was my bike.

"Oui c'est la mienne," I said, knowing I couldn't keep up much of a conversation in French, and not really wanting to. The lads had an air of mischief about them as if they were sussing me out to see if I'd be a push-over for a bit of scamming. Their accent was a very thick French that I could barely follow, but I got the gist when they asked if I "smoked". I ignored this with a wave and a shake of the head.

"Vous recherchez un hotel?" one of them asked, pointing at the hotel I'd just come from.

"Oui, mais cette hotel est trop cher pour moi," I said in bad French and I was getting tired of talking to them; they seemed to be just messing about with me. They were also showing an unhealthy interest in Tim and my luggage, but they became very animated at my mention of the hotel being too dear. I didn't catch all that they were saying, but I heard "Eaux Chaudes", "La Caverne" and "bon marche", which I took to mean an inn that was cheaper and good. They pointed at themselves, and I guessed it was where they were staying, which put me right off, but beggars can't be choosers, so I decided to ride back to Les Eaux Chaudes and check it out, leaving the boys jumping around trying to cadge a ride on the bike. I felt a little unnerved by their brashness and swagger, and I didn't trust them not to send me off on a wild goose chase. I was glad to be shot of them.

Les Eaux Chaudes was only a few miles back into the mountains, but it was getting dark, there were no street lights and the looming peaks pressed in like malevolent giants. I really was not feeling great about all this when, right on the main road, a restaurant came into view, all lit up inside and with signs outside. Called La Caverne, just as the boys had said, it was a welcoming, sturdy building of pale stone with green painted windows and blue shutters. Jolly signs outside advertised what was on offer: "La Caverne, auberge, bar, gite". One of the signs was, for some reason, a life size cut-out of a leaning bear wearing a flat cap, carrying a rucksack and raising a frothing glass of beer. He stood in a flowerbed and symbolised the quirky, but welcoming ambience of this place. I eased myself off the bike and strolled in under a little wooden arch with plants growing all around it. It was like a café inside with stairs going up in a far corner and a narrow archway leading through to the rest of the premises. A small bar/reception desk was pressed against the far wall with a couple of tables filling the rest of the interior. A typical elderly Frenchman wearing a tweed jacket and flat cap sat at one of the tables. He looked up as I entered.

"Bonsoir monsieur," I said. He returned the greeting with a grunt.

"C'est votre hotel, monsieur? Vous avez des chambres?" I asked in stilted French, unhappy at having to do this when I was feeling so tired. He grumbled something and shuffled off shouting,

"Annie! Annie!"

Annie duly appeared: a smiling, middle-aged, but youthful woman who seemed open and at ease with life. She was an ex (or-not-so-ex) hippy, I could tell, and this made me relax. I asked if she spoke English.

"Un peu," she said, as they all do (un peu more than my French, I bet).

"Do you have rooms here?" I asked and told her about the boys back in Laruns. She knew them, they were staying there and yes, she had a room in a dormitory to myself. They were finishing with meals, but I could eat straight away if I was ready.

I was ready all right!

As usual, now that I had found somewhere to stay, the weight of weariness fell upon me. I just couldn't be bothered to take the luggage off the bike, drag it all upstairs and then change before eating. I let Annie show me to the room then I went straight down to eat as she had requested. This was the first time I had eaten an evening meal dressed in bike gear, but I didn't care. Another group was at the coffee stage of their dinner and the atmosphere was typically post-meal French: relaxed, convivial, unhurried. They nodded and raised their wine glasses in my direction with civilised "Bonsoirs". As a waitress served me some soup, I couldn't have been happier.

The meal was country-French: earthy and wholesome in parts, but deliciously delicate in others. For some reason I wasn't particularly hungry and struggled with the main rice dish (a sort of fricassee of chicken). The sweet was a sublime lemon mousse and red wine was served automatically, but the coffee I needed wasn't forthcoming. It was getting late and Annie was helping her waitress to clear up so I didn't ask for coffee. Instead I took the hint and reluctantly headed off to unpack the bike. When I got there I looked at it in the dark and decided not to take the locked panniers with me this time. I removed the roll bag and anything that wasn't locked to the bike and lugged it inside, worrying about leaving the panniers out there all night. I knew that many (or most?) bikers treat these luggage boxes like the boot of a car: it's locked, and locked to the bike so leave it where it is, but I had got into the habit of taking it all off and humping it inside wherever I was staying. I felt that if the boxes got broken into it could be a major setback, even the end of the whole trip, and not worth the risk. Here at La Caverne, with Annie and these lovely French people, I took a chance. But I'd forgotten about those three lads, who had by now returned to their billet.

I sat on the bottom of a bunk bed in a spartan, wood-floored room with three other empty bunk beds, wearily getting ready for sleep after having a wash in a large communal shower down the hall. The closed door to the room was right beside me. A loud knock made me jump and I said a tentative "Hello?" forgetting to use French. No one entered so I got up and opened the door. As I did so, a giggling and shuffling of running feet disappeared round the end of the hallway. It was those boys being juvenile – at 11.30 pm. Oh God, I thought, are they going to be up all night playing pranks – and maybe even messing with the bike in their obvious boredom? Worried as I was about the bike, I settled in my sleeping bag on the welcome bed. So tired, I was out like the proverbial light.

More charging around in the corridors woke me again, but it was morning and I had slept the sleep of the righteous. I leapt up, pulled on some jeans and a t-shirt and went to check the bike. It was still there, parked off the road and locked to La

Caverne railings, packed up like a faithful mule that hadn't moved all night.

At breakfast, I asked Annie about the boys and why they were here. Through a combination of English and French, I established that they were reform school bad lads who were here with a minder to get out into the countryside as a form of rehabilitation and release for some of their energy. This whole Laruns area of the French Pyrenees is a well-known nature/hiking/activity playground for French people, famous for its springs, mineral waters and spas (hence Les Eaux Chaudes).

"You will try the waters?" Annie asked and I seriously considered it – since I was there, right next to the spa building 'n all. But breakfast went on, I downloaded some of my photos and dictaphone messages to a memory stick using Annie's little palmtop, wrote up my notes over a second coffee and just sat, enjoying the atmosphere in this lovely little auberge in the heart of rural French countryside, as Annie busied herself around me.

"I don't think I have time," I replied, knowing full well that I'd just let an hour or more slip by for no reason other than comfort and inertia.

"I have to get to Millau today to see the bridge."

We talked about my journey and her business here in the Pyrenees. She had definitely been a hippy in her younger days and had carried some of that love-and-flower-power stuff into her life here. She ran the place as a sort of social experiment (hence those boys), revelling in the wholesome therapy of being in a wild place like that and looking after those who seek its solace. She was one of a kind.

The three boys came charging round a corner followed by a small, gruff, dark-haired woman with a rucksack on her back. They looked every inch city kids on the lookout for trouble, but I had misjudged them a little: they had sent me here in good faith, they hadn't messed about all night, nor touched my bike and they were about to go off into the mountain wilderness with this lady who they clearly respected. She was probably their probation officer who could hike them back to borstal as soon as let them loose in the hills, but they seemed well mannered if a little boisterous. Annie had nothing, but gentle smiles for them too and I felt a tad guilty for my cynicism so I made a fuss of taking photos with everyone. I gave Annie my blog details and promised to put La Caverne and the boys on it.

"They will be very pleased," she said. She relayed some of this in French to the boys' minder and a conversation ensued with some glances over towards me. Annie spoke to me, a little concerned:

"We must ask permissions from the parents of these boys if you will put the photos on a website. It is the law for them."

"Don't worry, I can just delete the ones with them on," I replied, and then I had an idea.

"Annie, could you ask this lady if she could send me the permission so I can use the pictures on my blog. If they say no, I won't use it. Is that ok?"

Annie dutifully asked the minder and the atmosphere relaxed with nods and waves. Annie returned to me all smiles.

"They are very excited about the photos. They think they will be famous!" she said.

"Would you like some more coffee before you go?"

Annie's warmth was beguiling. I didn't want to leave this place. For a moment I had one of those crazy thoughts: I could just stay here and not go anywhere – ever. For a moment, I was in love with La Caverne, Annie and the whole feel of the place. I think she recognised the look in my eyes. She came over with the coffee and placed her hand on my shoulder as she set the cup on the table.

"That was good for them. They need to meet people like you. They see there is more to life than smoking and drinking and stealing. Merci Robert!"

Her hand stayed on my shoulder. I was choked with emotion. I patted her hand and smiled.

"It was good for me too. I just saw them as bad boys, but they sent me here and they seem fine."

"C'est merveilleux!" she said brightly, breaking the spell and moving off to tend her little bar.

I packed up the bike, reluctant to go, but at the same time wanting to make a start. As I took a final photo, Annie appeared and waved goodbye, shouting:

"Bonne Chance!"

As I pressed the starter button and the bike growled into life, I caught a movement down in the gorge above which La Caverne was built. A bird flitted up into Annie's garden, landing perkily on a fence wire with its tail quivering. A female Black Redstart had come to have a look, flitting around like its relative, the Robin, but showing only a dull rust colour in its tail, which flicked and shivered characteristically. Although the male is much more striking (black with silvery grey), this was a nice send off from La Caverne. It was a new bird for the trip and it reminded me what I was about. I pulled away sedately with no sense of rush for a change, heading back into Laruns to begin my journey through the South of France.

My next target wasn't a bird, but a bridge: the Millau Viaduct over the River Tarn and its wide valley. From the moment I first saw images of this structure in magazines and on TV, I was captivated – like most of the world. This motorway bridge was a stunning piece of modern engineering, which seemed to float above the clouds that formed in the valley, and I had wanted to see it for years. It takes the motorway from Paris to Bezier across the Tarn valley between two plateaux, bypassing the town of Millau, which gives the bridge its name.

I tapped Millau into Tim and checked the route he suggested. It was a long motorway curve to the south, right to Bezier on the coast then North again to Millau. Tim was being ridiculous. By default, he had given me what he called the "fastest route". If I went that way, I could stay on the motorway until I crossed the famous viaduct, but then I'd have to travel to the next junction to turn south again. I also wanted to minimise motorway riding because there were going to be several days' worth of that ahead. I asked Tim for a cross-country alternative. He plotted his "shortest route" and it looked much better: a full 60km less, but only ten minutes longer. You have to be careful with Tim and his mates: they'll take you miles out of the way on a motorway or send you up stupid dirt tracks just to save a few theoretical minutes. But in this case the route looked good, passing through rural, un-touristy France and approaching the Millau Viaduct from minor roads in the valley below – which sounded very cool.

According to Tim, the journey time was nearly six hours. It was past ten o'clock when I left La Caverne, stopping in Laruns for some money at a cash point. Millau was too far: I'd be seeing the bridge in the dark![22] I made a firm plan to stop just short of the bridge, but with plenty of time to find a camp-site. This time I was determined to camp, and at a reasonable time of day. Tim, the bike and I set off towards Tarbes and "La Pyrénéenne", the main route to Toulouse (I love the names the French give their motorways!) with birding taking a back seat for a while. I kept my eyes open of course; we were in the South of France and good birds could pop up anywhere, but now I was enjoying the experience of riding my bike and travelling through France – something I have always loved, but not done enough. I resolved to stop at the first decent looking café and have my first coffee in "La Belle France".

Having left Laruns on "Rue des Pyrénées" (how nice is that!), it was a single road all the way to Tarbes and the motorway. Although still in the foothills of the Pyrenees, the riding was fun, with plenty of dips and bends at a good pace, but without too much challenge. The bike seemed happy too, pulling eagerly and dropping into those traffic-free bends all on its own – almost. The landscape became cultivated, but still very rural, not unlike England, with green, hedged fields and farms dotted around as the land levelled out away from the mountains. I began to pass through village after village, soaking up the "Frenchness" of my surroundings: shuttered windows of parched wood, old road signs, peeling plaster and render, old twisted roof tiles and the general earthiness of streets and buildings. After an hour of fast riding along a good road, leaning round the bends then powering out of them along the straights, I

[22]Apparently, though, the bridge is quite beautiful at night, being lit up as a thin, 2km strip of light, right across the valley. Maybe worth seeing.

was ready for that first French coffee. I pulled into the local square in a town called Pontacq. It was very inviting with Plane trees surrounding a gravel square where I could park my bike in the shade (the sun had come out and I felt hot in the bike clothing for the first time since that lay-by in Northern Spain).

As I swung my leg over the bike seat, with a few young locals looking on, I noticed something not quite right near the rear wheel of the bike. There, resting on the gravel was the chain I used to lock the roll bag to the rear seat behind me. Scuffed and battered, the key was still in it. It had been dragging along the road for over an hour as I tore around all those bends. How it hadn't got mangled in the rear wheel, I'll never know. I breathed a sigh of relief at not losing the key or damaging the lock when I noticed something else not quite right: perched on top of the unlocked roll bag were my credit card wallet and sunglasses. Miraculously, they had also stayed put through all the swinging and bumping around. Losing the cards could have been a serious setback. I cursed myself and lambasted my folly. I must be losing it, I thought, getting worried that I wasn't keeping on top of things properly. How could I have set off with the packing up so unfinished? And shouldn't I have noticed the lock dragging along? (With all the wind noise and having to concentrate on riding, perhaps not).

After that little clutch of near-disasters, my coffee in the Café Central was very welcome. In our family, my lingering over a coffee is called "Dad being continental" and my son, in particular, doesn't get it. To me, one of the great pleasures of life is sitting in a French café, with a delicious continental coffee, watching the world go by – just as the French themselves seem to do. Of course, it is one of the luxuries of being on holiday, so it has relaxing and pleasant associations, but I try to recreate "being continental" whenever I can. Here in Pontacq, I raised my coffee quietly and whispered a toast to Iain, enjoying it all the more.

A chocolate coloured dog of the hound variety came over to my table and leaned against my leg. I spoke to him, gave him a stroke, and took his photo for the blog. After that, he wouldn't leave me alone and "being continental" couldn't be stretched out any longer. I made my way back to the bike. This time, I packed up very carefully and even wrote out a "pre-flight" list of all the main things to check before riding off – including credit cards and sunglasses! That list stayed right in front of me in the transparent map cover of the tank bag for weeks and I referred to it every day until I felt too ashamed of myself for needing it.

I rode on for hours, non-stop apart from toilet breaks at the beautifully named service and rest areas on French motorways: Aire Des Bandouliers, Aire de Bordes and other attractive sounding places where you could pull over, some with a café or a shop for refreshment, some just pleasant wooded sites with picnic tables and water. The town of Albi was my destination, via a detour around Toulouse, following Tim carefully to avoid being sucked in by the black hole of a large city.

Three hours after "being continental" in Pontacq, I found myself riding round Albi and out the other side. It was 4pm and for the first time I started looking for a campsite at a sensible time of day. The area I was going through was very agricultural, not the least touristy and with few towns. It was hard work, mile after mile, looking ahead and hoping for some sort of settlement that might have a campsite when, I caught sight of a sign in the corner of my eye as I sped past, saying "Camper de Ferme". That'll do, I thought, and turned the bike round as soon as I could find a lay-by. The insignificant sign pointed hopefully down a lane into the depths of the French countryside, its tepee sign confirming the presence of tents or tent sites. I hit a bit of loose gravel on a bend and almost came off the bike, but carried on gingerly until I came across Le Poujet farmyard with another sign for camping; only seven Euros... result!

I tentatively rolled the bike into the yard, passing a midden, a farmhouse and some large modern corrugated iron sheds. The place was deserted. Ahead I could see the camping area with lawns, a toilet block and a cabin – all quite small scale and looking a little on the closed side. A farm hand, alerted by the sound of the bike, appeared round the corner of the large shed.

"Bonjour!" I shouted and tried some awful French

"Vous avez le camping ici?"

My accent, grammar and generally outlandish arrival must have freaked him, for he disappeared without a word. A much older man took his place, gruffly asking what I wanted.

" Camper est fermé. Nous commençons en Mai," he said

May! God, why was everything so late starting?

"Est-ce juste vous?" he added and I replied that, yes, it was just me. I told him I didn't need much. He seemed to relent and stuck out a huge hand with fingers like bananas. We shook and he gabbled on in French about it being too cold for camping, mentioning a cabin and a load of other stuff I didn't understand. I followed him around as he opened up the cabin and the toilet block, apologising that the water would be cold (no heating yet – it was only April!).

"C'est parfait," I said, standing inside the cabin. In fact, it was far from perfect, but much better than having to set up a tent and, with a bed, much more comfortable. I made positive noises, expressing my gratitude (lots of "mercis" and "magnifiques" – we are *SO* crap at foreign languages!) while he unlocked doors and bumbled around, blaming his wife for not having the place open yet. Seemingly he was the farmer, she was the campsite commandant and I caught the words "lait de mouton" and "pour le Roquefort". I asked a little about this, but once he got going on the finer points of Roquefort cheese and sheep farming, I got completely lost (except that he clearly thought more of his sheep than his wife). All I could do was nod, smile, point and say "Ah! Oui?" with a ridiculous caricature of the French questioning style. It started to become embarrassing. I did learn, however, that we were close to Roquefort-sur-Soulzon, home of the famous cheese and this farmer produced the ewe's milk for making it.

"Vouspouvezgarervotremotoiciparcequ'ilvapleuvoircesoir", he said in a babble as he ushered me into an open barn full of farm implements. I caught "pleuvoir", the verb for rain and only understood the rest because he pointed at the bike and a bike-sized space in the dry barn, but I got the idea: he wanted me to move the bike inside because it was going to rain. How nice! All

111

this was working out well. We had gone from "camper fermé", to a cabin, a bed and cover for the bike – all before dinnertime.

I stopped this lovely farmer from doing any more as he was about to pick up a broom and apologetically sweep out the cabin. He eventually ambled off to his solid stone farmhouse and left me, broom in hand to sweep up the mouse turds. The cabin had been closed up all winter. I recognised the signs from our cottage in Scotland; years ago, it used to lie closed throughout winter until we arrived in Spring to a musty smell, dampness and signs of various creatures sheltering inside. This place was one room with a double bed, a kitchenette, a curtain to divide sleeping from living areas, a fridge and a free-standing cupboard for crockery and cutlery – and mouse poo all over the lino. If it had been a hotel room, I'd have been disgusted but, under the circumstances, it was a real find and as far as I was concerned, I was camping.

I considered trying the camping stove to heat one of the long-life space meals, which had survived the weight-reducing exercise back home, but I just couldn't get excited about that. I went to bed in my sleeping bag, exhausted by the day's long ride and not bothered about food. Annie and La Caverne seemed an age ago, although I'd only left there that morning. Spain felt like a world away after just a couple of days. This bending and stretching of time is a hallmark of travel: the constant shift in place, people and experience, the newness and unfamiliarity, all combine to warp one's perception of time. It was still only mid-April and I wouldn't be heading home until the very end of May.

Next morning I had to track down the farmer and pay him before setting off for the Millau Bridge. He duly appeared as I was ready to roll, but he didn't want any money! Again, the French language stymied me, but he seemed to be saying he couldn't charge me for a cold, dirty cabin with no hot water or shower. I insisted, shoving a twenty-Euro note at him, but he wouldn't have it. I dug around for something smaller, but could only find a two Euro coin. He clearly didn't have change or couldn't be bothered with it.

"C'est tout J'avez", I said getting my verb ending all wrong and wincing inside.

Again he refused any money. Finally, a little unwilling to leave him the whole twenty Euros, I pushed the coin in his hands and made determined, manly moves to get on the bike and ride off. He would take the two Euros and be damned!

"Merci beaucoup, monsieur, merci", I shouted and rode off. He waved jovially, clutching his coin. What a lovely chap. I was torn between being chuffed at such a bargain and embarrassment at even offering him so little. Still, twenty for a mouse-infested cabin and freezing cold water would have been ridiculous, so I rode off, content with the deal. Onwards to Millau and its Bridge In the Clouds.

In the next village, I did battle with Vodafone because my mobile had refused to connect or even accept any top-up money – despite a jolly little text saying: "Welcome to Vodafone France!" – one of many to come pinging in, impressively prompt, every time I crossed a border, regardless of whether the system would actually let me use the phone. This system was called called "Vodafone Passport" – really? One hour and £10 (spent in a bloody payphone!) later, I got some credit from them to carry on using the phone. This was really important for me, not just to be connected back home, but to arrange and stay in touch with guides in Bulgaria, Romania and Hungary, as well as the friends in Italy. I could write pages about the nonsense I had to put up with while "Roaming" with "Vodafone Passport", but I won't; suffice to say, "Fucking Vodafone" appears many times in my trip diary, on the dictaphone and in my notes for this book.

Stressed, and still a little worried about how to keep in touch with people if the phone system was going to die on me like that, I felt I deserved a coffee and croissant. Of course, I did! Sure enough, right in the centre, was a typical village café next to a Boulangerie. I sat, being continental for a while, calming down about the phone until I was ready to push on. I asked for directions to "Meelaow", as I had always pronounced it, only to be met by a blank look.

"Pour le Viaduc du Tarn?" I asked, trying some new information (I knew the bridge spanned the valley of the river Tarn)

"Ah, Mee-ow!" exclaimed the man I had asked.

"St Afrique," he added and reeled off a pile of unintelligible stuff about the route, which I let wash over me, thinking only of sticking St Afrique into Tim and getting on with it. The pronunciation of Millau, sounding like a cat, amused me as I rode off. I kept repeating it in the helmet, "Mee-ow, Mee-ow, Mee-ow!" Travelling on your own does that to you.

The D902/903 route to St Afrique and Mee-ow was stunning as it dropped down to follow the river Tarn and its valley: more lovely twists and turns, more tiny French villages, a few castles and bridges, and a beautiful sunny day. I realised I had been bird-less for some time when a Red Kite came into view in a field, soaring quite low over a hedge, like a slow motion Sparrow Hawk on the hunt. Big, but agile in its flight, with that long, deeply forked tail twisting russet as it steered the bird. It was truly master of its surroundings. It had disappeared by the time I drew level, the only bird of note that day.

The rest of the ride to Millau (I'll stop saying Mee-ow now!) was unremarkable. I gave up looking around me, concentrating on the riding when, as I rounded a corner, the bridge appeared. It was fairly distant and didn't seem that remarkable, but it came in and out of view as I changed direction or dipped below a rise. Each time it re-appeared it seemed to grow in stature; I hadn't realised how far away I was when I first saw it. To fully appreciate the span of this magnificent structure, I had to stop a mile or two before reaching the base of its gigantic, needle-sharp towers. At this point, the Tarn valley was wide and tame, low hills rising on either side with a gentle, cultivated floor in between. Beyond, where the bridge carried the motorway and all its traffic, the valley rose to a high plateau on each side, now re-connected after eons by this gossamer of concrete and steel. Although thin and elegant, the towers, the supporting cables and the roadway all filled the valley. Unexpectedly, I wasn't that convinced of the architect hype; this bridge was supposed to complement its surroundings, to be of such elegance and delicate proportion that it did not spoil the natural beauty of the Tarn Valley. I recorded a dictaphone message about the bridge;

"It seems out of place... and I suppose you'd expect that. It's like two or three Queen Elizabeth bridges that span the Thames in Essex. It's quite lovely, but it doesn't, and would never, suit the place. They've gone for architectural beauty over blending in with the surroundings. This bridge is even more imposing than the already imposing valley of Le Gorge du Tarn"

As I left that message I sat in the grass over a hedge eating a Kit-Kat, trying to decide what I thought of the viaduct. Firstly, I was a little disappointed to be there on such a dull, yet cloudless day – no sun to reflect off concrete or steel and no shadow to pull out the detail of edges and curves. I knew it would look better on a bright day. But I carried on looking and eyeing up the scale of this thing. Far from being unobtrusive, I decided, it strode across the valley like some static alien... and it was beautiful!

Seven thin towers of increasing length marched out into the centre of the valley where the three tallest, with needle-sharp tops, dropped from sky to valley floor. They planted unseen feet on the ground and stretched out many thin arms to the next tower. These suspension cables formed pyramids between the towers, down to the roadway, holding it floating across the valley in precise contact with the high plateaux on either side. Each tower had a split in its upper section, just like the eye of a needle. The road deck looked as if it passed through them, thin and true as a stiletto blade, slicing its way across the valley.

The Millau Viaduct is the tallest bridge in the world with one of its towers reaching 343 metres above the base. At "only" 270 metres above the River Tarn, its road deck is not the highest – but it is twice the height of any other bridge in Europe and high enough to regularly put the road above clouds that form in the valley; at times this wonderful structure seems to hang in the sky above the clouds like magic. I wish I could have seen it like that. Instead, I rode to the base of one of the enormous supporting towers where there was a large car park with turnstile entrances into a visitor centre. Unsurprisingly, this place was already well and truly on the tourist map with video presentations, guided tours – and entrance fees to match. I opted not to wait half an hour for the 2 o'clock show, but spent my time looking up at these monsters as you do with skyscrapers in New York, neck bent right back to see the top and nearly falling over with vertigo. As I left, I wished again that I could have seen the bridge in the sun or rising above a cloud-filled valley; my photos looked unimpressively dull compared with those images. But, I'd made the detour to come here, I'd seen the bridge from afar and from right underneath, and it was by no means a disappointment. Now I wanted to get on the motorway and cross the bridge as it was meant to be crossed: flying high over the valley on my Honda 600. With Tim's help, we headed to Millau. Before riding all the way into the town and out the other side to the junction that would take me south over the viaduct, I stopped to check that it was possible to get on to the bridge at that point. According to Tim's magnified map of the roads, it seemed not to be; there was no sign of a slip road or entrance onto the southbound side. With some incredulity, I turned south on minor roads and onto the motorway at the next junction, well beyond the bridge. It felt entirely wrong to be here, on the A75 autoroute, "La Meridienne", and *not* go across the famous Millau Viaduct, but I had a long way to go on this motorway with nowhere to stay that night[23].

La Meridienne swept me down towards Montpelier and the south coast... and an exhilarating death-ride it was. The motorway dropped in endless fast curves, down and down at breakneck speed. I wasn't used to this. Like some huge racetrack the road wound itself into long, long downhill bends, first a curve to the left then a sweep to the right. Because of the

[23]On later investigation, I discovered it is perfectly possible to get on the bridge at Millau. In fact, Tim did show a slip road, but it didn't confirm the direction of traffic flow – basically, I wimped out of travelling a few miles to see for myself. A poor decision and my loss.

gradient, the speed of other drivers and a little insanity on my part, I rode those bends at over 80 mph, leaning into them for what seemed like forever, excited and scared in equal measure. Being fairly high up, there was also a buffeting wind to contend with and, for the first time, it felt as if I was fighting the bike. The crash barriers flashed by, so close I could reach out and touch them. They were there mostly to stop you rocketing over the edge of a sheer drop, so the view beyond the barrier was of an uncompromising chasm. This was no speed to be so close to metal barriers with nothing but empty space beyond. The landscape around this section of motorway was spectacular – not that I could really look at any of it.

That real-life theme park ride probably only lasted ten minutes, but it seemed like half an hour and it sapped my energy. By the time the motorway levelled out, the wind died down and all became calm, I was ready to stop again. The services I chose were beautifully tranquil, unlike me after the Ride of Death. I relaxed with a ham baguette and a strong coffee, sitting outside in the sun. I followed this with a fabulous fruit tart (even in motorway services, the French know how to make those babies!).

A big bike glided into a parking spot right next to where I sat and a couple slowly got off, surveying their surroundings and going through the routine of disembarkation from a motorcycle. I watched them, coffee and tart in hand, thinking how different it is for the car driver: he or she just pops out, slams and locks the door and walks off. Not so with a bike. First you make sure the bike is pointing up hill – so you don't have to heave the heavy brute backwards up an incline just to leave a car park. Then you take stock, you breathe, you get the helmet off and re-equilibrate with terra firma (especially after a Ride of Death!), you probably sit astride your steed for a few moments before kicking down the side-stand and leaning the bike carefully onto it. Watching the couple perform their version of arrival and dismount, made me feel part of their clan. They spotted me and nodded. When they returned with a tray of drinks and pastries, they sat at the table next to me and we talked. The man addressed me in English (how did he know? – maybe he saw the bike registration and/or the Scottish Saltire sticker on the screen). They were French and just out for a few days, but still travelling long distances. We talked about my trip and their bike, a big Honda Pan European designed for luxury touring. It looked lovely, leaning in its parking space, gleaming black in the sun, all moulded fairings and panniers, with a huge, swept-back screen. The passenger seat was a separate affair with a backrest as part of the rear top box, which sat high up behind the bike. I showed my ignorance by asking if it was a Gold Wing. I let myself down sometimes, I really do. I should have known better (I *did* know better, it just came out – I am a real biker, honest!). Honda Gold Wings are huge: bikes with a car interior slung around them (not a proper bike at all, in my expert opinion).

"Non, non, it's a Pan," he said

At that point, he would probably have given up on me if I hadn't redressed the Gold Wing faux pas. I squinted at it in mock surprise, as if I hadn't looked properly the first time or as if the sun's glare had spoiled my view.

"Oh yes. Lovely. I nearly bought a Deauville for my trip. That's a bit like a small Pan European."

He nodded in affirmation.

"At our age and with two of us, we like the comfort. The Pan is so smooth and we don't rush. We don't need a sports bike."

We spoke about my trip, my bike and where they were going.

"The Italian Lakes. Maybe Como," the man said

"Hey! That's where I'm going," I replied, "not Como, but near Varese, which isn't too far. I have a couple of friends to stay with. Is it a long drive? Maybe six hours from here?"

He looked at his girlfriend, they both smiled and shook their heads. She spoke:

"It is a lot more than six hours. I think you will take eight."

A little perturbed by this, I was keen to check with Tim to see what he thought. We had all finished eating and it was a natural time for us to get on our way. As we said our farewells, I passed the lady one of my slips of paper with the blog address on and we wished each other good luck. He ended with:

"Ride safe man."

"You too."

With hearty thumbs up, they were gone, gliding out of the car park into the sunlight, and away. I followed, going through my checklist first: tank bag, Tim, maps, phone, money, keys, cards, earplugs, helmet, shades, gloves, then... broom! Start the bike and... go. I too slid out of the car park, slowly swinging my feet up off the ground onto the foot-rests, breaking contact with the ground and becoming part of the balancing act that is riding a motorcycle. We were one again, powering along the slip road with a twist of the throttle, merging onto the motorway once more. I had given Tim the scent of St Gilles, a town on the way to Arles and he was sniffing his way along the route. In just over an hour I'd be looking for a campsite.

I was heading to Arles for a rather spurious reason; Claire had gone there on a school trip and come back with tales and photos of these amazing Roman buildings. Being a complete cultural philistine, I had no idea that some of the best-preserved Roman remains are outside Italy and her photos of them captured my imagination. But there was another reason for stopping in the area – the Camargue.

The Camargue is an enormous flat delta where the Rhone meets the Mediterranean Sea. It is an unrelenting expanse of lakes and reclaimed grassland: 360 square miles of salt pans, fresh and brackish wetlands – and flat as a pancake. Not my favourite habitat, but a magnet for breeding and migrating birds, especially wetland species. The Camargue is Western Europe's largest river delta, famous for its white horses, their cowboy "guardians" and black bulls, bred for bullfighting. Despite all this, I had no time to do such a huge area justice. I was already committed to several days floating around the Danube Delta in Romania: four times the size, a lot further from home and not so easy to re-visit as the Camargue. Nevertheless, with an hour or two to spare next morning, I planned to have a look for Flamingoes. Twenty thousand pairs of Greater Flamingo breed in the Camargue and there are few other places in Europe to find them.

The route I'd asked Tim to plot cut across the northern part of the delta rather than sticking on the main road into Arles; I thought I might get a feel for the place on my way into the town, fluke a Flamingo and maybe find a campsite on the way. I must confess, I hadn't done much homework on distances, public access points, where to go for specific birds or how long it might take to cover the ground. The northern section proved to be several miles from the true wetlands and it was made up of endless flat fields stretching out on either side of the road. I arrived at Arles, Flamingo-less. The main approach road into the town from the west crosses a bridge and becomes a charming, leafy avenue with restaurants and cafés on the left and an open park on the right with a bandstand, a carousel (of all things) and a tourist office – which was shut. Rather than park up on this busy street, I rode the bike illegally across the gravelled park to the tourist office. Although it was closed, it had one of those maps of the area with little bulbs which light up if you press a button on a menu of adverts surrounding it on all four sides. There were ads for three or four campsites. I pressed each, in turn, to see the little light bulb glow hesitantly somewhere on the map, pin-pointing the locations in an endearingly lo-tech way. The last time I'd seen one of these was as a teenager in Wick, in the far North of Scotland where I grew up. It was probably removed in the seventies or eighties, but here in Arles, this one was working well. A little bulb lit up to show me a campsite right out of the town, back towards the Camargue. When I phoned the number, they answered, but were closed until May – amazing! However, the guy said I could still come, even though they wouldn't be fully open. I didn't care; I'd have somewhere to go at least and, hopefully, I wouldn't have to sweep out mouse turds or wash in freezing cold water.

I had arranged to eat in Arles and arrive at the campsite later, so I made my way to some sort of central area, following my nose along narrow old streets and alleys (how you'd get a car down those, God knows – *Cars 4; Bikes 4!*) until it all opened out into this fabulous small square, the Place Du Forum, filled with cafés, bars, restaurants and small hotels. It was buzzing in the warm evening air, the chat of people filling the night like subdued cicadas. The coloured parasols, canopies and awnings of the tightly packed shops made the square look like a covered market. It felt very welcoming and cosy. As per usual, I found it hard to decide where to park. Still suspicious (especially in towns), I wanted to be able to see the bike as I sat. Then I couldn't decide which of the many eating-places to go to, preferably one where the bike was well in view. My indecision is legendary – especially when it comes to where to eat, where (*exactly* where) to sit in a restaurant and what to have from a menu. My Grandmother was the same apparently; maybe this sort of incipient autism is genetic. I am like Sheldon from the excellent US comedy "The Big Bang Theory": can't sit by the door in a restaurant (cold and too many people coming by you), can't sit bang in the middle of the room (too many people around you), uncomfortable facing a wall (too many people behind you), don't want to be where people or staff keep passing by (too many people, full stop). In a far corner, back to the wall, surveying the door and all that is going on: that is my perfect spot. If I'm allowed to think about it too much, it can spoil a meal. Sad.

With no such seating perfection available, I sat in the middle of the square, next to a Canadian family. We had a chat, took mutual photos and then I had a meal of aubergine gratin, washed down with a glass of red wine. Being continental again, I was spoiling myself in this lovely ancient square, unaware of how close I was to the Roman buildings, just a few streets beyond.

It was getting dark and I still needed to locate the campsite in the gloom. Reluctantly, I tore myself away from Place du Forum. I finished my, now cold, coffee, got on the bike and let Tim guide me back to the campsite. What a wonder he is in those situations; in the dark of a strange city, he will find you the best way out to whatever obscure backwater you want to get to – in this case, a campsite out in the sticks of the Camargue. Once signed in, I picked my grassy pitch more easily than before and set about unpacking the things I needed from the bike. Tired, and with the night adding to my weariness, I put the tent up quickly in the beam from the bike headlight. I stowed the valuable/nickable stuff inside the tent and headed off to the shower block. This aspect of camping I do not like: the brightly lit block of toilets, basins, showers and laundry seem cold, impersonal and definitely not inviting at 11pm. The cosy privacy of my minuscule (two-man!) tent positively beckoned.

With all the important or valuable stuff either around me in the tent or just outside in the "porch", I settled down to sleep, checking the phone before I did so. The phone! Where was the phone? I had a specific pocket in my bike jacket for it, but it wasn't there. No panic, it must be somewhere else. But no... panic rose in inverse proportion with places to look until I was simply hunting in the same places over and over and getting increasingly worried. The cramped confines of this tent didn't help and it took some time to convince myself that the phone wasn't in there somewhere with me. This was a disaster. It may sound minor, but I really needed that phone to text or ring key people in up-coming countries for meetings, accommodation, directions and guiding to bird sites. I should have been less reliant on it, more intrepid and more positive, but being on my own, with so far to go and so many contacts to make, the phone was crucial. It had numbers and dates stored and I'd given the number to all manner of people who might assume they could get me on it. I imagined Dimiter Georgiev in Bulgaria texting at that very moment to change dates for our meeting (to find Black Woodpecker at the nest). Alina from Ibistours could be trying to get me about arrangements for the Floating Hotel. Now I was being stupid! I could ride back into Arles right now and find the phone (I had decided I must have left it on the table in Place du Forum – so much for the checklist!). I looked at my watch; by the time I got there, it would be well past midnight and most likely everywhere would be shut. I might also struggle to get in and out of the campsite at those late hours. No, I had to wait until morning.

The whole thing made sleeping difficult. I was tired, but fitfully awake. A nightingale sang loudly in a bush right outside, then the frog chorus started up. The Camargue is a wetland paradise for amphibians, and these little green Mediterranean Tree Frogs were everywhere, making their acoustic presence felt in the marshy night. The cacophony added to my agitation and, at that moment, my love of nature went temporarily AWOL. My love of camping had never been enlisted in the first place so this awful night made me hate it even more.

I woke after about two hours of proper sleep, wrecked, but immediately awake, worrying about the phone. The nightingale was singing beautifully and in full flow, its rich, fluting notes hanging in the damp air. I dressed in a blur, left most of my stuff in the tent and rushed off into town, back to Place du Forum. The square looked so different in the light of early morning, ancient and still, with some of the debris of the previous night still lying on the tables: an empty glass of wine, a cigarette packet, left by a late diner or a tired waitress. Even in my nervous state, I noticed the calm as an old bloke swept the pavement outside his café. I tried to locate the table where I had eaten, in the hope that the phone might still be there, but it was surprisingly difficult to be sure. In the daylight, it all looked so different: now there seemed to be more sections within the central part of the square than I remembered. I scoured two or three likely looking tables until I was sure the phone wasn't still lying around. With no sign of it, I needed a smarter approach. The area where I'd been sitting had green parasols with "La Caverne du Forum" written on them and on the adjacent side of the square, just across the narrow street from the tables, was a café of the same name. It occupied the corner where a narrow alley met the square, mustard coloured plaster peeling in patches and a glazed front door with shutters painted a dull pastel green. Its awning and sign proclaimed "Café Restaurant Pizzeria Creperie". So this was the place that had produced my aubergine gratin. It was shut. At 6.30 in the morning, of course it was. These places may only be open in the evening and God knows when someone might come to set up. I asked at another café, where the owner was serving breakfast.

"S'il vous plait, monsieur – Il est ouvert a quelle heur, cette café ici?"

The café owner looked blank and shrugged, the way only the French can shrug and he carried on wiping tables. Given that I had just said to him:

"Please, Mister – It is open has what time, this coffee here?"

This was not surprising. I tried again.

"Pardon monsieur. J'ai perdu mon mobile la-bas, hier soir. La Caverne Forum est ouvert quand, s'il vous plait?"

This did the trick. He looked up at the café, then at his watch and replied:

" Een serty meenoots."

My turn to look blank.

"Sevun o'cluck," came his very thick accent. He was now speaking English, having realised how bad my French was (what a cheek... "serty meenoots"!?).

"Merci, merci," I said, with genuine relief that the place would be open soon.

As I wandered over to see if anyone was already at La Caverne du Forum, it occurred to me that I had just admitted to spurning this man's establishment for my meal the night before. I felt a little disloyal having now bothered him with my problem and inflicted such tragic injury to his language. The Cave of Forum was dark and deserted – but it was only 6.45 and I was relieved that I didn't have to make a decision about waiting here all day. Within ten meenoots, a middle-aged woman appeared and I accosted her with:

"Je m'excuse madam. Je pense que j'ai perdu mon mobile ici, hier soir, la-bas, peut-etre sur un de votre tables."

Immediately, she whirled round to look where I was pointing then started rummaging in her handbag, obviously for the door key.

"Oui, Oui," she said breathlessly, now very animated over what I'd said. I thought I must be getting good, but she replied in (pretty hopeless) English,

"Somzeeng eez put een zee boite d'argent, zee box, last night. Come, come".

She was brilliant. So concerned to help, she seemed to realise how worried I must have been. With some bustle and typical French flair, she unlocked the cash-box and produced my phone like a magician revealing flowers from a hat.

"Voila!"

It may as well have been magic, given the effect it had: waves of relief, sheer pleasure and considerable tiredness swept over me. Coffee, I had to have coffee. And Breakfast. And Croissants. Sod the tent, sod the Romans, sod the Flamingoes; now was the time for being continental – big style! With a mixture of gestures, her hopeless English, and my rubbish French, I worked out that it was ok to wait inside until she had opened up... but there were no croissants or pastries of any kind, I'd have to go to the Patisserie a few doors down for that. Oh, the hardship! To say I was in my element cannot convey how happy I was to be walking around this square in a southern French town for a breakfast croissant from the Patisserie, and back to La Caverne du Forum for coffee... with my phone!

As the café woke up and filled with its normal clientèle, a young woman (the owner) swept the floor with a traditional flat broom. A little black puppy appeared, pouncing on the broom, making a general nuisance of himself.

"Non Manuc!" she scolded.

Little Manuc flopped over to me and started attacking my feet instead. I sipped the strong coffee, bit into my croissant and distracted Manuc. He was the perfect entertainment and I couldn't imagine "being continental" coming any better. After he got bored, Manuc rested his head on my knee and looked up with sad mischief in his eyes.

I could have stayed there forever. Forever turned out to be a full hour and a half, two coffees and the disappearance of Manuc, before I dragged myself back into adventure mode.

Lazing around in a sleep-deprived haze hadn't exactly injected a sense of momentum but, eventually, I rode back to the campsite to rescue all my stuff and pack up, ready for a very long motorway ride all the way to northern Italy. First I wanted to see those Roman remains and I fully intended a detour to approach the French coast on the road that started this trip way back in the 70s. That would all add up to at least 400 miles and seven hours riding, according to Tim, and it was gone ten o'clock before I swept out of the campsite – oh, and I wanted to look for Flamingoes too! As if I had time for all that now – what an idiot!

I took a southern route back into Arles to get as close as I could to the nature reserve section of the Camargue and if I didn't see a Flamingo from a roadside stop, I'd have to leave without one. For no good reason, I really thought I'd see a few in the distance, maybe in flight, if not standing; after all, there were forty thousand of them around here somewhere. From a lay-by near the main lagoon, the Etang de Vaccares, I scoped the distant waters edge, scanning and seeing blobs that could have been Flamingoes… or swans… or big gulls… I had to concede defeat: I was just too far away (ten miles as it turns out!) and those Flamingoes were just not Flamin'going anywhere near me! In fact, I left the wonderful Camargue with not a single new bird. When there is a list of 400 species for the area as a whole, that is truly pathetic. In my own defence, I had decided with some justification, that time would be better spent getting to other, more far-flung places and hunting for even less accessible birds than Camargue Flamingoes. I could come back here relatively easily another time. Feeling thus justified in my abject failure as a birder, I packed away the under-used optics and headed off to Arles for some Roman remains spotting instead.

I was impressed indeed. The amphitheatre, in particular, seemed to dominate the town, just outside the central part where I had dined earlier. By contrast, there also seemed to be lots of little fragments of Roman stonework, embedded within newer walls: a doorway here, an arch there, rubbing shoulders with houses, shops and cafés. The restoration work being done was intriguing because the sharp edges and pale faces of newly cut stone gave an impression of how the buildings would have looked when first built, yet they stood incongruously clean and neat within the old weathered ruins, part of them yet apart from them at the same time. With gaps filled in like this, particularly in the arches of the amphitheatre's grand circle, it did allow you to see the building as a whole rather than a collection of fragments, but I had heard that this sort of "complete restoration" could be very controversial. Can we be sure how it would have looked? Is it better to leave the ruins as ruins rather than recreate and possibly "lose" the original? I'm no historian (*that* is an understatement!) nor an "arts person", but being there made me think a little. I decided I liked it. The new stood out from the old so you could still see the ancient Roman sections while the new stonework filled in the gaps nicely, helping to stop the thing crumbling any further. That's what a mere ex-biologist thought anyway.

Back on the road, it was a case of reeling in the motorway miles with multiple short services stops to refuel both bike and rider. Sadly, when it came to finding the road of my dreams, my heart was not in it at all. Even though I took the necessary detour away from the coast, off the motorway and up towards Grasse, I couldn't muster the enthusiasm at this late hour. I knew I wasn't giving it the requisite time and I was thinking of the long slog that lay ahead, getting into Italy and up to the North. After 30 years, I would have had to sit down and really check out the route that I had fixed in my memory. I hadn't done that and all I could do was ride about twenty miles up the road that I thought I had taken. None of it rang any bells. It didn't open out into that dusty snake of tarmac that I so clearly remember taking me down from the mountains, as Anne and I hitched a lift in an old Merc. in 1978. This road was almost suburban; tame and populated, it was a great disappointment. Clearly, a lot of development had taken place in the last few decades, but I also knew that my memory might be a bit imprecise, and I'd probably have to ride for miles inland to find my fantasy road. I could even have the wrong route altogether. With the Flamingo débâcle earlier in the day, I felt I was losing the focus and grasp on what I was doing. I gladly abandoned my quest, but with feelings of failure, set Tim to find my way back to the motorway for Italy.

It felt good to be making progress, even on a boring motorway, and I always enjoyed my coffee stops after a hundred miles of riding, some of which took me right up to the high coastal cliffs where France and Italy meet on the Mediterranean.

Just after the border, I stopped at a fairly tacky Agip services with its "Autogrill" café. I went for a walk to stretch the legs and discovered that, tacky though it was, this service area was at a particularly beautiful spot, perched high on one of the many sea cliffs overlooking a typical Riviera scene. Bright sprinkles of sunshine danced off the calm blue sea below the cliffs. Palms and cacti grew among trees and shrubs, which were in bloom around the terracotta topped villas that nestled on the cliff sides just below me. This idyllic scene contrasted with the coast-hugging motorway itself; miles and miles of it went through tunnel after tunnel, some of them a few kilometres long. They were poorly lit, considering that drivers and riders entered them from the blinding light of the Cote D'Azur. Every time I entered a tunnel it was as if someone had turned off the sun. A bike headlight isn't quite as powerful as two bright car lights and it was like being plunged into a cave. Some were long bends cutting through the cliffs so there was – literally – no light at the end of the tunnel. This was hard work. As a way of hiding a fast road along this very attractive, but busy coast, these tunnels did their job. I could see why they were there, but they got to me.

After crossing the border into Italy (a surprisingly formal customs control affair), there were yet more tunnels and, as the night approached, a strong wind got up. Illuminated signs began to appear above the motorway lanes flashing, "Atenzione. Forti Venti". With the buffeting I was now subjected to, it didn't take much to work out what those signs meant and it confirmed the need for care. It made me a nervous rider. The winds got worse as the motorway turned North towards Milan and Alessandria. At times, I had to crouch down below the screen for a break from the cold buffeting air. At other times I had to lean the bike over into the fierce side wind just to keep in a straight line; a weird feeling since leaning would normally make the bike go into a turn. As darkness fell it became very cold and, at one of my increasingly frequent stops, I took time out to put on the cold weather gear. There was a distinct déjà vu about all this and it spelled "Madrid"! Here I was again, riding into the cold night on a foreign motorway, well past the time when sane people would be nursing a nice glass of red wine after a meal and flopping into a warm bed. The difference this time was wind instead of rain and, at the end, a stay with friends in their comfortable home instead of a room in a dodgy hotel.

Relying almost totally on Tim to get us in the dark to Bodio, within striking distance of Alan and Colette's place, I phoned ahead with a rough arrival time.

"Hi, Robert. Where are you?"

It was wonderful to hear a friendly and familiar English voice.

I looked at the ETA on Tim's screen.

"We're probably under an hour from you," I said

"Oh... have you brought a friend? I thought you were on your own."

I had got so used to thinking of Tim as a companion whom, along with the bike, I thought of as "we".

" No, no it's just me, sorry. The bike's become a firm friend!"

Alan laughed, but I didn't have it in me to explain all about Tim (I also thought it might sound a tad crackers).

We got to Bodio just fine, but then Tim lost heart when the little track to their house flummoxed him. He was making insistent gestures on his little screen that I should turn round. If I could have heard his voice, I'm sure he'd have been swearing at me. I phoned Alan again.

"Wait at the petrol station and I'll come and get you."

He arrived about fifteen minutes later and led me in, like a lost ship guided by a pilot. I had left Arles at 2.30pm and now it was 10.30 at night, a total of 8 hours. I was a little embarrassed to be arriving so late.

"Sorry I took so long. The winds were so bad I had to keep stopping."

"Don't worry, its fine. It's the weekend and we were half expecting you tomorrow. You've come such a long way already, we know how things can go wrong. You've done really well to get here – from Arles, was it? How's it been going? Good birds?"

"Yep, from Arles via Grasse. A long slog, especially with those high winds. Are they normal? Great birds, Alan: Monfrague in Spain is just the best. I got most of the steppe birds near Trujillo and the Pyrenees for Lammergeier. Missed Black-shouldered Kite though."... but don't ask me about Spanish Imperial Eagle, I thought, embarrassed at the very idea.

"I've never birded that area. We can have a chat about that at home. Follow me."

After what seemed like a long time on a minor road to his house, Alan directed me into a garage where I parked the bike inside for the first time. I removed the personal bits I'd need for a two-night stay then followed him into the house. Being here marked a major milestone: a sort of psychological halfway point, where I could relax a bit, regroup, think ahead and be looked after for a while before heading off to Eastern Europe. It was therefore with great relief, gratitude and warmth that I shook hands with Alan and gave Colette a hug. I had made it.

Colette had cooked a late meal for me, which I was more than ready to eat, having survived at various services on coffee, pastries and a bit of pizza. I had been to their house once before on another birding trip and I remembered well its lived-in charm. It was a large villa on two levels with open living spaces and quiet rooms tucked away up or down stairs. Typical of places that get hot summers, it had tiled floors, shuttered windows and a huge roof-covered rear balcony supported by large white pillars. The roof extended on these pillars to create a shaded outside patio. It felt comfortable and welcoming.

I met Zoya the rescue dog (the previous canine incumbent having expired some years before) and chatted a little with Alan and Colette then headed off to bed. Alan had planned a birding trip next day to the rice fields, a little drive from their home and a place he hadn't been to for some time. I needed Alan to inject some much-needed oomph into the bird quest after a pathetic total of only 2 new birds on the trip list in the whole of southern France: Black Redstart and Black-headed Gull. For now, though, all I could think of was sleep. The punching winds I had fought to get here were coming back to me, the way the movement of a ship comes back once you stand on dry land. Weariness descended like a theatre curtain and shutting the bedroom door felt like closing a chapter on the journey.

I woke at 4.30 am, having slept a deep and satisfying sleep. Why I woke so early I don't know, but it meant I was up and ready in good time for an early start to the rice fields. Colette had made a packed lunch for us all (this was good) and Alan was getting books, notepads and optics ready for a field trip. I would be a passenger in a car for the day (also good) and Alan was going to be the bird guide (even better).

It made a pleasant and slightly unfamiliar change to be a passenger in a car. Our destination was the rice fields near a town called Livorno Ferraris, about 20 miles north-east of Turin. We seemed to drive a long way with the Alps in the distance, massive, snow-topped and rising high, hovering among the clouds. Somehow, Alan found tiny, obscure turnings into flat fields and onto raised dykes until we came to spots where he had been birding before. We got out and walked a little from the car until we overlooked flooded fields and planted ground. I had no idea there were rice fields like this in Italy but, thinking about it, where did risotto rice come from? Arborio, Carnaroli and Vialone Nano were familiar names, but it hadn't occurred to me that the rice itself would be grown here in Italy. I had assumed (if I assumed anything) that it was grown somewhere in the Far East and processed in Italy – or something vague like that. My ignorance knows no bounds! This was the flat and fertile plain of the Po Valley where the river has deposited rich silt, near towns like Novara and Vigevano. The irrigation system for these paddy fields was originally designed by Leonardo Da Vinci and rice can be grown on these flat lands because of a plentiful supply of water from the Alps, which were omnipresent in the background as we drove around.

The rice fields were like those you see in film and photographs of Thailand or Vietnam: flat rectangles of mirror-smooth, shallow water, held in by low irrigation channels of mud and stone. There were occasional bushes or hedges, perhaps there as windbreaks, but otherwise, it was a fairly featureless scene, as is often the case where birds find food. I saw no rice growing, but it was only April and maybe the rice was yet to be planted. We looked for birds over the whole area, but particularly around the edges of these water pans where very shallow margins would allow feeding. Being in such a unique habitat, I was expecting to add birds to the Trip List as a matter of course, but Alan looked around everywhere in an "anything might turn up" mode: it was Spring migration time, after all.

Alan had been introduced to me many years before (by my old friend and birding partner, John) and we'd met only a very few times since, but I knew him to be a very keen and meticulous birder. Considering that I was supposedly the scientist (by training at least), Alan's approach and skills put me to shame. Like most other birders I know, his knowledge of song and field recognition were so much better than mine and here, of course, he also knew the area and what to expect. Alan used a dictaphone at intervals to list the birds before moving on. I had a similar machine with me, but didn't even consider using it to keep track of the bird list.

After a slow start, we began to pick up large numbers of Wood Sandpiper, clearly on passage through to the North. I hadn't seen many Wood Sands and none for a couple of years so these were a welcome sight for me – especially in such numbers, maybe tens at a time.

At one point, well into the day, Alan wheeled around and pointed out a small group of terns flying and dipping around a pool behind us.

"White-winged Black Tern," he said, binoculars pressed tight to his eyes.

The terns were close enough not to need a scope and as we watched their numbers grew. They had come out of nowhere and it seemed likely that they had just arrived en-route from South Africa, possibly moving further North. More appeared until a dozen or more dipped and dived over the mirror calm water, picking insects from the surface. White-winged Blacks are in my top ten of stunning birds: rare, accidental visitors to Britain, they really are eye-catching with sooty black body and head contrasting so markedly with the crisp white of wings and tail. As they twist in flight, it's as if they are showing off this contrast. Perhaps they are – to each other, at least. Other birds around the rice paddies included several "shanks" (Green, Red and Spotted Red), Ruff, Whimbrel and Black-winged Stilt: all wading birds to be expected here, along with several duck species. We picked up a few herons and egrets too, the best of which were three Purples Herons, several Night Herons, spooked from bushes in a hedge as we walked along, and a few Cattle Egrets.

By a mixture of driving around the field boundaries and walking we covered a big area, stopping at ostensibly similar spots, but gradually picking up more and more new birds. Alan was a little disappointed at how quiet it all was, but I was more than happy to be seeing my first Night Heron for a few years. He was working hard at this and I recognised the signs: you get an odd and unjustified sense of responsibility when you take someone out birding. Somehow, it is your fault if birds don't turn up and you feel responsible if the target bird doesn't show. To an extent, you can cock this up by going out at the wrong season, tide or time of day and (if you're a bit of an arse, like me!), taking people to the wrong place, but it should be much more "C'est la vie" than that. I wasn't bothered. There were plenty of new birds for me, the place was unexpected and interesting, and chatting with Alan and Colette about life – and birding – was such a pleasure.

After a picnic lunch from the back of the car (Stock Dove, Tree Sparrow and Whinchat), we headed home via a couple of other rice field sites (Little Gull, Cormorant, Common Tern and Lapwing). By the time we got back, I realised another difference between Alan (and Colette) and myself – stamina! I was bushed, but he seemed to be taking it all in his stride. Maybe I was still recovering from two weeks on the road and perhaps he was a little more relaxed in his home surroundings. Either way, the rice fields had tired me out and I was glad to be staying another night before heading off.

Over a meal, we chatted about life and birding.

"Dupont's Lark!?" said Alan, "Good one. You'll have to leave me the site directions."

On my previous visit, Alan had taken John and myself up into the Alps to find Wallcreeper (and other mountain species). He was an experienced and skilled birder. It felt so good to be able to pass something on to him, rather than the other way round.

"It's at a place called El Planeron, near Belchite. Quite easy to find," I replied.

I started to copy out a little sketch map with some directions for him.

I asked how life in general was going and his health in particular: Alan had had a serious health scare some time previously and I wasn't sure how it had all gone. Despite his thin appearance, he said all that was fine now and he was fighting fit – except for his work.

"He's thinking of giving it all up," said Colette

"Things have changed at work. I don't feel my contributions are accepted or respected anymore," explained Alan

"He's never been stressed about work before, but now he comes home all dissatisfied and tense, don't you, my darling."

Colette was clearly worried about him. I could see all the signs too. Somehow my trip gave me a different perspective. I wanted to say to Alan, "What are you doing, man? Jack it all in and concentrate on all your other interests before it kills you,", but I didn't know him or Colette well enough. My own epiphanies, which had come late for me anyway, were ill-formed and no more relevant to someone else than what I liked for breakfast. Instead, I put Anne's situation and the reasons for my trip before him and let the question hang. Nevertheless, I found myself making over-familiar comments in an attempt to bring a fresh view to his situation:

"Don't wait too long Alan; you've done the job for a long time, you've had a bit of a scare with your health and now you're not enjoying the job. You can walk away, you know... it's allowed!"

Sometimes you need to hear something like that to make you realise that only habit and fear are holding you back. I wasn't sure they were ready to hear it from me though, so I couched it very much from Anne's point of view and, by association, mine.

"See – you should think of retiring Alan," said Colette and, turning to me, she continued, "he's not enjoying work now and he's not usually stressed like this." She was clearly worried about him.

"All I know Alan," I said, " is I felt I had to do this trip before it was too late – mainly with Anne's health, but potentially mine too. It would be awful, feeling the way you do about work, if you became too ill to do all the things you assumed you'd do some day. You both seem so active outside work, you must have loads to get on with – even just the birding and travelling?"

I left the question hanging again and hoped that if he felt uncomfortable or ganged-up on, the mention of birding might allow him to change the subject. Inside, I wanted to make him write his letter of resignation right then, but I felt any more preaching from me might be pushing too hard. I hope Alan finds his way with all this and I wish them both the very best.

Chapter 6 – Trapped in Tarvisio

I finish my degree in Edinburgh in 1978 and move to Cambridge to start my first ever proper job: research into animal behaviour, specifically courtship behaviour in doves. Surprisingly, I don't take to the world of academia (or more specifically, Cambridge academia!) with its one-upmanship, self-justification and precarious career structure. Three years later I decide to do a one-year teaching qualification as a second string and move into halls of residence in Roehampton, right on the edge of beautiful Richmond Park.

Living with epilepsy proves to be only a matter of recovering from the effects of those two fits, waiting for the return of my driving licence and re-applying for it every three years... and taking three little pills every night. There are awkward issues with insurance and financial institutions and I am nervous about how it might affect job applications (especially if I go into teaching): epilepsy in the seventies is misunderstood and treated with ignorance and prejudice. But I am very lucky; I have no more seizures. After three years, I decide I don't even have epilepsy and come off the pills – without consulting a doctor! A year goes by and I have no fits – see I don't have epilepsy, told you!

Almost exactly one year later, while living in those Roehampton halls with their open, communal stairways, I wake up in the middle of the night and I don't know where I am or why I'm there. I am completely disoriented, but I recognise the sickening feeling: I've had it before – twice. Despite the disorientation, I'm still aware that Simon, a fellow student, is in a room one floor above me. I leave my room, stark naked and in a state of utter confusion. I climb the communal stairway and knock on Simon's door. God knows what he thinks I am up to, standing in the hallway, starkers in the middle of the night, but he quickly sees that I am worried and upset. I know what has happened: a third fit, in my sleep, one year after coming off the medication. The doctor tells me off for stopping the pills without medical supervision, but agrees not to inform the driving licence authority because I brought it on myself. I am on those pills for life.

*

Extract from my online blog (Tues, 4th May);

> *Since the last blogette at Alan's, I rode on through Nth Italy right up to Tarvisio on the border with Slovenia – a long, tiring motorway ride. For some reason, I get determined to reach a particular point and ride into the night – NOT a good idea, because finding your way/accommodation is quite difficult and stressful in the dark. But I'm now at the hotel El Cervo in Tarvisio. I have promised myself to stop and camp or find a hotel by 4pm from now on. Camping has been blown out in the last few days, mainly because hotels or hostels are so cheap east of Slovenia (and who wants to set up a tent at 8. pm in the dark anyway!).*

I pulled up at the El Cervo hotel, well after dinner time, exhausted and fed up. It was raining – again – and, I was weary of it. The dull clouds and a wall of high grey peaks around the town made it seem dark as if the day was giving up for the night. The atmosphere was oppressive and heavy.

I eased the bike up a wet and slippery cobbled incline to pull up right in front of the hotel entrance. It was modern (and open!) with a slight step up onto a concourse of crazy paving and a flat covered roof supported on two large concrete pillars. Tired, I inched the bike forward in front of the concourse... then my whole world turned upside down – literally. I tumbled headlong into a forward roll over the handlebars and onto the tarmac. The bike belly-flopped onto its side and the engine started revving madly. I hadn't a clue what was going on. It felt as if someone had pushed the bike over with me on it, but there wasn't a soul around. I got up and rushed over to twist back the jammed throttle and kill the engine. I couldn't work out what had happened. I was just too tired for all this.

Once I had turned the engine off, I took stock and recalled the feeling as the bike had tipped. I had misjudged the width of the rear pannier and brushed a pillar as I pulled in: the last thing I was expecting, but enough to unbalance the heavy bike. My old bête-noire from bike training days with PMT had raised its predictably ugly head. At way less than walking pace, the bike had tipped and landed on the left handlebar There was little damage, but the clutch lever had snapped in two – no gears. Bugger!

I dragged myself wearily into the hotel to seek help with lifting the heavy bike. The place was deserted. It took some time and a lot of linguistic incomprehension to find someone who knew what I was asking for. Eventually, an Asian porter called Apul came with me and helped me to lift the beached bike back onto its wheels. At that point, Apul was a smiling lifesaver and I made a mental note to give him a decent tip once I was sorted out.

Although it seemed like a lifetime ago, I had risen at 6am that day to say goodbye to Alan before he took off for work and I got on the road again for the long motorway slog to Slovenia... and the rest of Eastern Europe. I had no intention of doing any more birding or sightseeing in Italy; the exotic East beckoned.

Saying a grateful and fond farewell to Colette, I set off on a long motorway ride through northern Italy, past Venice and on to the extreme North-east, towards Tarvisio and the border with Slovenia. I battled my way through the miles, enjoying too many stops at motorway services for a rest and some strong coffee. By then, I found myself making comparisons between the different services within and between countries. I became a services geek and observed keenly how tawdry the Italian ones were compared to those airy French respite stops (but nothing like the Spanish places where they drop litter everywhere until wading through it becomes a chore). This unexpected theme was to go on right through Eastern Europe and it has its own cultural interest on a trip like this: mainly a wistful reflection on modern lifestyles, but I found it interesting how each country managed to hold on to its identity even here, in such mundane places. I doubt if this is true in the UK. We seem to have embraced the ways of America, to the exclusion of our own; would you get an edible Lancashire Hotpot anywhere within 10 miles of a British motorway?[24] In Spanish services, they have decent tapas and here in Italy, passable pasta and pizza dishes. I was spending too much time on motorways!

Heading for Tarvisio and the Julian Alps, which show no respect for the border between Italy and Slovenia, I thought ahead to mountain birds like Nutcracker, Snow Finch or Alpine Accentor, maybe woodpeckers and flycatchers in the high cool forests and more chance of eagles or other birds of prey. The Julian Alps are the south-eastern extension of the alpine range with Mount Triglav and Triglav National Park stretching into Slovenia: too much to cover in a "passing through" trip, but I planned to try the Kranjska Gora ski lift just over the border in Slovenia as a quick way of getting up high then walking around the tops for those elusive alpine species.

I'd never heard of these Julian Alps until researching for this trip, but now, here, approaching them from afar on the A23 motorway, they loomed large in the distance, a wide range of peaks and domes rising from the flat land that I was biking through to reach them.

"Proper Alps 'n all" was my dictaphone description (very evocative!)

It was – yet again – dark and cold. At one services stop, I even had to put on my waterproof gear to keep out the cold wind which had risen in the gloaming to make riding hard work. And it started raining as I headed into the Julian Alps, approaching Tarvisio. I was so tired it was small wonder that I dropped the bike outside the hotel.

---

[24]To be fair, this comment is only true of a few years ago; UK service stops have improved hugely in the last ten years or so. It still costs an arm and a leg, but at least you can get something decent on the road in Britain these days. Go, UK!

Tarvisio looked abandoned, the hotel El Cervo looked abandoned, I felt abandoned. Even Apul had disappeared after lifting the bike with me. It wasn't a Sunday, and as far as I knew, not a holiday or a religious occasion. More likely it was simply quiet, being out of the ski season. The place was dead. The skeleton crew seemed surprised that anyone would want a room. After checking in and lugging all the gear in off the bike (three panniers, two bags and the tent – *Cars 5; Bikes 4*), I strolled round in search of a coffee, now feeling more civilised. After several minutes of fruitless wandering, all I could find was a deserted bar. God, this place was desolate, even compared to the closed campsites and the many sleepy villages I'd gone through over the weeks. Somehow, being a fairly large hotel, it seemed worse to be so dead. I expected Jack Nicholson to appear at any moment, hatchet in hand screaming, "Here's Jackie!". I started to panic for lack of sustenance and strode off to accost the first member of staff I could find: Apul!

"Hey Apul, any chance of some coffee?"

"I will find someone for the coffee," he said, in his weird Italian-Bangladeshi English accent, and he scurried off to locate the bar person.

A bar lady appeared, dressed for the part in crisp black and white, and I ordered coffee, expecting a fresh brew of strong continental caffeine, but when it arrived, it was cool, weak and from a semi-automatic machine, not one piloted by a barista as I'd become used to. Furthermore, I had missed the two-minute dinner window by ten seconds and couldn't have anything to eat. This hotel was clearly running at idle.

I drank the insipid coffee then wandered out to check the bike and maybe see if I could fix the broken lever. As I approached reception, all hell broke loose – in the form of a million pre-pubescent teenagers. They were disgorging into the foyer from a couple of coaches, accompanied by enormous cases and the endless trappings deemed essential by twelve-year-olds. There were training shoes, small pink rucksacks, bum-bags, more pink rucksacks and a plethora of headphones, wires to headphones, mobile phones and iPods. The kids themselves seemed to have more arms and legs than they could possibly own, and the noise was deafening. The dull quiet of my arrival suddenly seemed comforting by comparison and I left the bike to see if I could rustle up some food.

First, I tried a powdered soup; Apul supplied a cup of tepid water for the purpose.

"Does this place not have hot water?" I asked balefully into the dictaphone, once back in my room.

The soup was vile. Next, I thought about the camping stove: maybe I could heat up some water in my room and even "cook" one of the space meals I had brought with me. I had the choice of chicken dopeaza, beans and pork sausages (of all the canned, processed crap, beans with pork sausages is my favourite) or chilli con carne with rice. I elected for the chilli and set up the stove in the rather nice, fully tiled, clean shower room. It wasn't to stay clean for long! The stove I had was a mountaineering "Whisperlite" which would burn anything, including petrol from the bike. I had gone for this option in case I ever ran out of fuel for the bike (two birds 'n all that). With the bottle of petrol on the floor next to the loo, I pumped up the stove and... lit a match. The thing burst into a huge yellow flame and coughed out black smoke and ash (flichters, we used to call them in Scotland), which billowed up to fill the room. Panicking, I managed to stop the stove as petrol oozed out across the floor. In horror, I looked up to see a smoke alarm.

"Christ!" I yelped, "the alarm will go off and they'll catch me trying to burn down their hotel!"

I spent the next hour with cubic yards of toilet roll wiping away all the evidence of my stupidity. Those little black flichters had gone everywhere and, in a toilet where everything was pure white, they settled in a grubby layer; the nice clean room had become a chamber of grime. Luckily, the smoke alarm didn't go off – but I still had no food. I ambled down to the bar area just for some company (maybe old Apul would be around) and to scrounge something to eat. The bloody teenagers were all in the huge dining hall, shouting and gyrating around and – *eating a meal!* The look on my face and the drooling stance I had taken at the door prompted a maître d' to address me with;

"Eet eez not for you," by which she meant: this was put on especially for the late arrival of a large group of kids and the dining room was not open. I, however, took it as the slap in the face that it really was and I determined to get some of the grub. I hung around until Apul appeared again and asked him straight out if I could have one of the many sandwiches or pieces of fruit that were stacked up for the obnoxious little bastards-and he smiled, went off and returned with the goods. Definitely a big tip for Apul! I didn't even have to pay: he just shook his head conspiratorially when I gestured about money. I sat and ate the cheese baguette sandwich with another poor coffee but, under the circumstances, it made a fine and comforting meal. I felt good and the hotel even took on a cosy glow with the feasting teenagers murmuring behind the closed dining room doors.

I slept well in the comfortable bed (the hotel proved fairly luxurious) and got up ready to fix the bike and head off for the mountains. The first bit was easier than expected: I had packed a spare clutch and brake lever (having learned early on that dropping the bike and busting these levers was fairly likely). The small tool set I had with me was good enough to undo and redo the various nuts and bolts. The second bit – heading off to the mountains – was impossible by comparison: Tarvisio (like the hotel) was closed – at least until 2 or 3 o'clock. I needed cash and petrol before attempting a ride across the Julian Alps where there would be no civilisation of any kind (or so I thought in my less-than-intrepid frame of mind). To my credit, I did try a little excursion out from the town, up a track into the hills and had a little picnic of breakfast plunderings while hoping for some tasty mountain birds like Snow Finch or Nutcracker (like a huge spotty Starling, but only found high up in mountains like these). To be honest, my heart wasn't in it at all. I took some photos of unusual forest flowers to ID later and returned birdless into Tarvisio, pulled back by its tractor beam of inertia.

I shouldn't make so light of this little excursion into the mountains because everything was unfamiliar and I was still a biking/touring novice. The rough tracks I followed in my attempt to find Nutcracker were small, twisting and unsigned. It took a lot of effort to ride the bike in terrain like this and although I didn't go more than twenty miles, I found it tiring.

Back in the town, I did battle with the banks, the language, the currency, the petrol station and with Vodafone (again). The garage attendant asked about the bike and where I was going.

"That ees Scotland, no?" he said, pointing to the Saltire sticker on the rear pannier.

"Yes. The Saint Andrew's Cross," I said, surprised that he knew this.

"Scotland ees like Tarvisio, no?" he said, sweeping his hand towards the mountains in a theatrical gesture.

"Not such high mountains in Scotland. They are very old," I replied, not quite sure what I meant by that.

As he stopped filling the bike tank, he asked where I was going. When I told him Croatia and Serbia, his response was immediate and vehement;

" No Croatia, no Serbia… they steal your bike, for sure!"

Getting myself out of Tarvisio seemed to take so long. Embarrassed at myself, I didn't leave until 4 pm, tired out by a day of getting nowhere, but I was out of Tarvisio's grip at last, and glad to be so. It wasn't such a bad town to be trapped in, nestling in a deep valley, surrounded by mountains with a wide, clean street of (closed) shops and skiing distractions for the wandering visitors, but I really needed to get on. Having gone back to the hotel to give Apul a decent tip for all his help, the magnetic grip of the town faded and I felt light as I rode out. It was a little like something out of Star Trek: waking after years of suspended animation in some other world and passing through a space warp into reality, the Starbike Enterprise flew around those mountain bends, carrying me to the next stage of my adventure. I was approaching the first border with a (former) East European country: Slovenia. This felt like a significant point to have reached: more or less halfway and leaving the West behind. Anxieties about Serbia returned; soon I'd find out if I could ride through that country without some sort of fight or scam over insurance at the border. Still... Slovenia and Croatia first!

The border with Slovenia from Italy was no problem and this ex-Yugoslavian province proved beautiful to ride through. It is a lovely little country with beautiful rolling scenery, from green valleys to high mountains and cute villages nestling, alpine style in tranquil meadows. Each village seemed to have its own church, sharp-spired, well kept and painted in white and terracotta livery – very attractive to ride past. I was tempted to stop several times, but I couldn't, having wasted so much time in Tarvisio. The roads were excellent and I smiled when I saw a big sign over the road;

"Please be patient; Slovenia is building motorways for you."

The high, jagged-toothed mountains of the Triglav area gave way to flatter lands and gentle, attractive Slovenian countryside with lime green rivers and open plains, as the mountains slipped behind. Away from those oppressive, cloud-cloaked peaks, I hit a good patch of weather. With the sun shining, and dry, clear air to ride through, I elected to keep going. I gave up on the idea of ski lifts to the mountaintops. My heart just wasn't in something as long and demanding as that so late in the day. Instead, I planned to get a campsite not far from the capital, Ljubljana, near a little place called Podpec where Gerard Gorman assured me it was worth a scan for raptors from a church on a hilltop.

I couldn't find St Ann's church on top of a hill and general birding yielded just a few White Storks feeding in a field. In Podpec, a nothing little place, neither touristy nor steeped in history or culture (just a place where people lived), I asked around for the campsite. This was not easy with so few speaking English, but I gleaned some information from an interesting guy. He was a paraglider and all round adventure sports fanatic who told me there was no campsite near Podpec, but there was a sort of hostel/bunkhouse where bikers were made welcome. I was very tempted, but couldn't quite see me rubbing shoulders with Slovenian Hell's Angels (take my word for it – theAngels are big in Eastern Europe). Maybe I missed a little adventure there, but I took the paraglider's further advice and rode back to Ljubljana where there was allegedly a fine big campsite that was definitely open.

With distinct unease at going anywhere near a city, I approached Ljubljana from the North where the campsite was located, a few miles from the city centre. Tim did a good job and we pulled into the site with little trouble. And a fine place it was too. I may have bombed with the birding, but at last, I was camping, and at a sensible time of day- for a change. It was six o'clock on 27th of April, the weather was warm and gentle, I was relaxed, not too tired from riding or chasing birds, and I felt more like I was on holiday. It felt good. I needed a rest, a re-group before the next challenge; I had to get back into the birding somehow.

But for now, I settled into the campsite, putting up my tent and parking the bike like a pro. My little plot looked cosy and self-contained: a patch of grass surrounded on three sides by mature hedges and trees, just off the site access track. I even had a washing line made of two long strings twisted together with the washed garments held fast in the twists to dry (a neat little trick I got from a bike touring website – no need for clothes pegs!). My orange two-man tent looked good too, all zipped up and hiding my stuff from view. It was great to be dressed in everyday clothes. Soft jeans and training shoes made me feel light and free compared to the biking gear with its unyielding protective pads and tough waterproof layers. Across the track, occupying another plot was a large blue motorhome which looked more like a converted truck or horse box than a standard production camper-van or RV. Next to it stood a big blue Suzuki V-Strom motorcycle. A blonde, Scandinavian-looking guy emerged from the truck to fiddle with the bike. I wandered over and said hello, gesturing at the two bikes as a common bond. He jumped up smiling and thrust a hand out in greeting. We shook hands and established English as our language (like most Scandinavians, his English was better than many indigenous Brits).

"ThorstensenErikssonnFjordSonSon," (or something) he said

"Robert."

"Well, Robert, what are you doing, travelling on your motorcycle?"

I told him proudly all about my trip, the birding and some of my experiences so far.

"I'm heading for Lithuania, where I want to visit the grave of a friend who died before I got another chance to see her in Britain. Where are you headed for?" I asked, sweeping my hand towards his motor-home.

"I am on a one year trip from my job. We get this in Finland, so I converted this truck into a travelling home and I am going around Europe. My interest is in architecture in European cities. I am taking many photographs to compare the churches."

That should have been my first clue, but this guy seemed amazing: he had *built* this camper-truck himself (or so I thought) and when I asked him about the bike, I was bowled over.

"I transport the bike in here, " he said, opening a large luggage hatch in the van, low down behind the rear wheel. Inside, I could see a cage-like contraption where the bike would be stored while he was on the road.

"I had this loading apparatus made in the University where I work."

"Are you travelling alone in this thing?" I asked.

"Oh yes, I am having a sabbatical year, but will meet colleagues in Universities if I can, and maybe do some work on the church architecture." (More clues).

We spoke briefly about our immediate plans: he said I could join him for a coffee (fresh coffee, he elaborated), but I was off to eat somewhere and he didn't want to join me, having all he needed in his camper-juggernaut. I got on the bike, less all the gear for a change, and found a pasta restaurant on the main road into Ljubljana. By the time I got back, it was almost dark. I hung around for a bit, taking down the washing, sorting out bags, tent, sleeping bag and sleeping mat (self-inflating... as if!), all by light from the bike headlamp. There was no sign of Thor, but lights were on in his camper-wagon. I bit my lip indecisively, wondering if I should remind him of his coffee invite (which had become obsessively appealing), but this felt rude so I carried on making I'm-here-you-know noises around the tent and the bike. Eventually, driven by desperate caffeine addiction, I went over to the truck and knocked on the door.

"Still ok for coffee?" I asked breezily.

I knew I wasn't exactly giving the guy much choice, but I had to have coffee! – and he had invited me after all. The door opened and, with the self-justification of any good drug addict, I was in, climbing into this cave of a van, over the driver's seat and into the rear compartment. I was actually being quite rude, and I knew it.

"Come in, come in, take a seat," said Thor, slightly taken aback.

The place was astounding: so beautifully converted, it could have been bought from a forecourt. As he explained the conversion process, I could see the tell-tale signs of DIY, but I doubt if I'd have noticed had he not told me. He had a kitchen area, beds, a workstation and a built-in Hi-Fi. I sat at the work area/table where he had some of his academic papers strewn around. They were all titled with impenetrable philosophy gobbledygook and I began to get an inkling that here was an intellectual of the rarest kind (another clue).

"Would you like some music?" he asked, opening a large case of CDs, all of classical music. I chose some Bach so as not to offend him and he scurried around to put it on, pleased with my choice. No sign of coffee. I made the mistake of politely asking about his work and talking on a semi-philosophical level when he did. This seemed to open some sort of floodgate (seep-gate would be more accurate): for the next thirty or forty minutes (though it seemed like four hours) he went on and on about architecture and various philosophies – and his academic work. Some of it was engaging, even interesting and I occasionally got him off onto a bit of politics, but even here I was given a treatise on economic philosophy – *his* economic philosophy – and still no bloody coffee!

"You see, the Italian Renaissance economy was not much different to ours, but we don't *inhabit* our economy the way they did, and it shows in the architecture, not only of the time, but of our time, of what they have retained, don't you agree?"

"Is the coffee ready?"

I didn't really say that, but it was the only thing going on in my increasingly numbed mind. This man was the Most Boring Bloke In The World and I was slowly dying inside. I have never wanted to get away from someone so much – with or without coffee. I was genuinely nodding off as he droned on, but finally, he remembered the coffee, jumped up and started to put the kettle on. I woke with a start, but had the wit to see my opening and I fired a stream of mundane questions to get him off whatever subject he'd been slaughtering for the last ten hours.

"Tell me about this vehicle... and your bike... would you say you're a biker? I'm not really... where are you headed next?"

Thankfully, this brought him back to earth and he conversed in a manner more appropriate to nearly midnight with a stranger. Over coffee, I heard about his plans for his year of travel around Europe. He told me how he had designed the modifications to the truck, but how the university workshop had done most of the wood and metal work. This made more sense: I couldn't see this chap wielding saw, drill or hammer. The conversation was more bearable now (maybe it was the arrival of some very nice coffee, which I felt I had fully earned), but he was still going on about how, during his travels, he would probably write a paper on the Philosophy of European Architecture (or something like that). I'm not a blokey bloke or a philistine, but there are times when I just want a good chat about basic issues (or birds) of the day, not an intellectual discourse.

After a coffee top up, another foray into the academic life of a Finnish University (which explained a lot!) and more Philosophies of Thor, I extracted myself from the cosy, but now unbearable motorhome and collapsed into my tent. Disbelief at what had just happened sent me into hysterical, uncontrolled, slightly manic laughter – potentially quite disturbing to anyone outside the tent. Like old Thor, maybe I'd been on my own for too long. I fell asleep, exhausted.

Camping advice: take an inflatable pillow. They can't weigh much or take up much space, but the benefit will be huge, trust me. I slept relatively well, but an unforgiving, dirty bike jacket as a pillow had taken its toll: my neck was stiff and my face all crinkled against the hard fabric. After my late night with Thor, I was a little worse for wear and took my time over breakfast and packing. This campsite was part of a bigger hotel complex so the restaurant was well supplied and set out. I lingered over breakfast until I felt more awake then I strolled back to pack up. Thor was out winding a heavy ratchet to lever his big bike into the luggage compartment.

"Do you want a hand?" I shouted over

He mumbled a reply, but he seemed much more reticent than the previous night. In fact, he seemed very shy and nervous, but I was intrigued and impressed at the ingenuity of his motorbike handling so I ploughed on.

"That's a brilliant idea. I'm very impressed at your resourcefulness and spirit."

This seemed to please him and he relaxed a little. Thankfully, it didn't open another seep-gate, so we wished each other well, exchanged details: me the blog website and him a business card (which I lost, hence the nonsense about his name), and parted company. I felt a little bad at my reaction to his personality the previous night, but he seemed more content now to be on his own. Maybe he was, as he seemed, a loner.

Before setting off, I had half an hour bird watching in the extensive grounds of the campsite itself and got two new birds for the Trip List: Short-toed Treecreeper[25] and Wren (normal-toed!). Amazing to think that I hadn't seen a Wren until then. I kept this activity low key because you can get suspicious looks,

---

[25]I went for Short-toed Treecreeper (as opposed to just "Treecreeper"!) because, this far east, it was the more likely and I got a good view of its "dirty" underside (not white). However, for any geeky birders reading this, there is an American-led conspiracy theory that, in fact, there is only one species and we European birders are just winding up the yanks by pretending we can tell the difference.

wandering round public places with binoculars (think peeping Tom). Onward to Croatia!

Slovenia continued to be beautiful for bike riding, building motorways for me as I went, so I was a little sad to reach the border. But that feeling didn't last long: a stern looking female cop called me over and asked for my papers. She was immaculately and officially dressed in what was clearly kosher cop uniform and she informed me that I had to pay 150 Euros for riding in Slovenia without a vignette. 150 Euros – for a *what?!* Vignette?! Vignette?! What the hell is a vignette? I'd never heard of a vignette – not even with all my research into European touring (even the Serbian insurance shenanigans hadn't come up with vignette!). For a while, I was sure this was a piece of Eastern European border corruption, with the police lining their pockets. For all I know, it was, but Slovenia didn't seem that backward, this police check was by no means unconvincing and the lady cop even gave me a glossy government leaflet all about the vignette system, which also seemed very legit'. Nevertheless, I protested (if it is a scam, why give them an easy time?), but before I got to the bit about asking for a receipt, which is supposed to flush out the rogues (so I'd been told), she volunteered a receipt. I had no more rounds in my inadequate gun.

"Eet weel be 300 Euro, but I sink you do not know vignette and we are not seeing you before, so eet weel be 150 Euro."

In a major huff, I sat and read the leaflet thoroughly, making her wait, still unconvinced about the whole thing. Sure enough, the leaflet proclaimed a fine of 300 Euros, so I was "lucky" to be let off with half that. She made this clear during my protests and I knew I wasn't going to get anywhere. Paradoxically, her autocratic and somewhat casual decision to reduce the amount made me more suspicious of foul play than ever. But what could I do? Finally, when she took the money by credit card, even I could see it had to be official policy. Cynical exploitation of the Western foreigner it may be, but a credit card payment couldn't end up in her pocket, surely? Nevertheless, the rosy glow around Slovenia was fading fast and I began to have serious worries about Serbia, the real "Border Bad Boy". If nice Slovenia had such a sting in the tail, what would all those "evil" Serbs have in store? And who knows, Croatia in between might be another dodgy Eastern Block experience... "They Steal Your Bike For Sure" began to haunt me again.

Birding hadn't been going well since the rice fields in Italy with Alan and Colette. I had done lots of motorway miles and, once more, my heart wasn't in it. I had lost my birding mojo. Belief is a large part of success in finding birds, rare or otherwise; if you don't have some optimism, you won't look properly, you'll get distracted, tired and want to do something else (in my case, have a coffee somewhere!) and you will simply miss the birds. Also, birding in foreign lands is hard work if you're only passing through. You don't know the terrain, the distances, the right spots to stand or walk and if you don't have local info, like a breeding site or a migration route, you can spend hours looking in the wrong place at the wrong time. I was losing faith in my own ability and it seemed painfully obvious that a guide was essential.

According to my Trip List, I'd seen a total of 121 species of birds with 16 lifers. The 16 firsts for me was pretty good, but a total of 121 after nearly two weeks in Europe was dismal. To give some context: many people have 400 species on their *British* list (I have only 345), top twitchers are now chasing 600[26]. A half-decent Europe list would have nearly 600 and a world list goes to around ten thousand. 121 was pathetic! Things had to change. I gave myself a telling off and vowed to spend a full day birding at a proper reserve somewhere over the border.

150 Euros lighter, I crossed into Croatia. It looked just like Slovenia – apart from the relative poverty. Roads weren't as clean or well kept, the countryside was wilder, less tamed by human hands, and towns, villages and buildings looked less

[26]At the time of writing, there is some debate as to whether the Top Twitcher is Steve Gantlett on 599, Ron Johns on 586 or Steve Webb on 543. The large discrepancy in those numbers is because much rancour ensues when twitchers and authorities (like the British Ornithologists Union) start arguing over which race or subspecies can or cannot be counted, and which list is being used (Britain, or Britain & Northern Ireland). Top twitchers will have now thrown my book in the bin!

affluent. Perhaps the war in Croatia in the early nineties had held things back; Slovenia got off lightly in the Yugoslav wars compared to Croatia and Bosnia, and it showed in how well developed Slovenia appeared by comparison.

But here I was… in Croatia! I carefully checked that I did not need a bloody vignette in this country and took off for my immediate destination: Lonjisko Polje nature reserve, near the town of Sisak. In my usual city-phobic way, I sped around Zagreb on the E70 until Tim told me to turn off. We found our way into the centre of Sisak, looking for a campsite on the way. This place was not for tourists though and Tim's knowledge of campsites seemed highly suspect. We went round the one-way system a couple of times before settling on a main street with bars and shops. I felt really foreign. Nothing about Sisak said "welcome travellers" and I could see no tourists around. The buildings were nearly all from the 1960s with almost no old architecture to be seen. One small, but grand old stone building on a side street had pillars, balconies and ornate overhangs, but it was peppered with bullet holes: a legacy of the war, I supposed. It was a perfectly good town, but a bit out of the way and not used to Brits riding in on motorcycles with no Kuna, the Croatian currency. Desperate for a drink, I tried using Euros in a bar, only to be directed after much language failure to a bank. Luckily, it was still open at 7.30 pm, so Kuna were obtained, a drink was had and I thought about finding a campsite. My little language-busting drawing of a tent (looking more like a wigwam), brought no signs of comprehension from residents or staff in the bar. The only alternative was to drive round and ask as I went. This strategy led me to the Hotel "*i*", a characterless block right on the biggest crossroads this side of the USA; acres of tarmac spread out in front of the hotel like a runway.

The Hotel "*i*" was a business hotel and the staff seemed a little bemused by this figure in bike gear appearing from the other side of the crossing. I got it in my head that this place had to be a budget hotel. 350 Kuna (about £50) seemed extortionate so, for the first time on the trip, I bargained. I was offered a discount for cash at 304 Kuna, still expensive for this part of the world, but it seemed ok. I settled into the *"i"*.

My *i*-room overlooked the runway junction and, in the disappearing evening light beyond, I could see birds flying to roost. Deciding to have an early evening recce, I rode away in pursuit, the Honda feeling light without luggage. Almost immediately, some familiar shapes flew across the bushes to my left where the river Sava ran: Night Herons flying in to roost. I was birding again! Further along the river, nightingales seemed to be singing from every bush and although I saw no more birds of note, I went back to the "*i*" full of anticipation for the next day.

i-breakfast was a rare affair: cardboard for cereal (where do they get that stuff?), sour milk for yoghurt and precious little to nick by way of a packed lunch, but I managed to steal away a box of runny yoghurt, a roll with some unidentifiable ham-like slice and a couple of pieces of toast stuck together with glue – sorry – jam. Despite the birding boost of the previous night, the dour surroundings and the uninspiring breakfast, I sat writing my notes (these notes, in fact!), procrastinating like crazy; I just didn't want to move. This had been happening more and more as the trip went on. I left a pensive message on the dictaphone;

"Feeling weary. I think it's doing it on my own, in unfamiliar surroundings. I don't mind <u>being</u> on my own, but <u>doing</u> it all alone is hard work. Unusually for me, I find myself seeking places (for short times) where there are people around"

"Come ON!" I scolded myself and made an effort to get going.

It was a fine warm day and, with a little more enthusiasm, I settled into finding the Lonjisko Polje Nature Park via a careful ride along the river Sava, through Posavina (the river basin area south-east of Sisak), towards the village of Cigoc. Cigoc was famous in this part of Croatia as the "Village of Storks", where these birds outnumber people and there is a "Stork Day" every June. It is also a centre for natural and cultural conservation and education. All this gave good vibes for a day out birding, but for one very good reason I wasn't keen on having a wander – Gerard Gorman's "Author's Tip" on the area:

"At all times keep to roads and marked tracks in the wider regions here, as unmapped minefields may still exist."

Nightingales were still bursting into song all along the river and the flat, but richly wooded countryside felt full of promise for birds. The riding was easy on a fairly good, even road and I could keep an eye out for shapes and movements. The Red Spots were out ready and it didn't take long for the first heart-stopper to appear: Pygmy Cormorant, flying parallel to the bike along a line of trees which I assumed marked the course of the river. This was a new Trip and Life bird and a target species from day one (122!). Pygmies are only found in these Eastern countries, mainly along the Danube and its tributaries, of which the Sava is one, but I really didn't expect to see any outside the Bulgarian or Romanian river basins. The flight silhouette was unmistakable, a little cormorant with fast wing-beats and a fat little head. Even though I'd never seen one before, there was no doubt. This was all I needed to get the birding juices going again and next up was the first Red-backed Shrike of the trip (way too late – I should have seen several riding through France or Italy). I mentioned my love of shrikes in chapter 2 and this extends even to the commonest, the Red-backed, with its rust, grey and white plumage and a dashing black mask across the eyes. Being the first one of the trip, this was a special encounter indeed. Riding along on a high now, I was eagerly scanning. With nothing on the road, it felt safe to let the bike steer itself (almost) while I kept an eye open to the sides. Minutes after the shrike a larger shape appeared over the trees ahead: Buzzard perhaps? The flight was a little too laboured and the bird generally too pale: maybe a small eagle? I stopped the bike and got off, losing the big bird in the process, but it appeared again with another and I got some good views of both. What were these birds? I kept seeing black armpits and undersides to their bodies: Rough-legged Buzzards, as far as I knew. I noted some other characteristics and got the ID book out as they disappeared from view. Rough-legs are only this far south in winter and should really have been way up in Scandinavia somewhere. These were probably late individuals, still migrating North in mid-April. Although I tried to turn them into small eagles as I watched them in the binoculars, Rough-legged Buzzard they were; a better find for the time of year and I was unlikely to see any more as we went deeper into Spring.

This flurry of Ticks restored a sense of purpose to my travels and my faith in finding birds. It felt great. I rode on towards Cigoc to find the reserve and maybe a guide to help me really get into the wildlife of this unspoilt wetland. The road took me alongside the river at times, past a ribbon of houses on the opposite side. These houses were unlike any I'd seen. Rows of big wooden shacks, they were clearly a traditional style: the Posavina house. Many were dilapidated, some beyond repair, but still very attractive and eye-catching. Shacks they may have seemed, but in fact, they were substantial two-storey buildings of thick, grey-weathered timber with huge dovetail joints at the corners, overlapping feather-board gable ends and wonky, but strong wood-framed windows set into the timber walls. They had steeply sloping, tiled roofs and projecting tiled overhangs above the windows, making them look almost alpine (maybe they got lots of snow in winter here?). I stopped to marvel at these little architectural gems from a bygone age and took some photos, but as I moved on I could see a different pattern emerging: many of these buildings were falling down, neglected and some were clearly being kept as tatty summer retreats. Others were being flattened and replaced, inevitably, with some brick and concrete "improvement". No doubt these would be modern, centrally heated structures, more comfortable, easy to maintain and with all mod cons, but I preferred to see the few people who were there doing up the old style shack and retaining this little bit of Croatian culture.

I pulled in to the Park Visitor Centre in Cigoc, riding right into a school party which was assembling just outside the centre office. I had to pick my way past all these little bodies and their warden leaders, but I managed to park the bike without squishing any of them. A girl dressed in a crisp khaki warden's uniform spoke to me distractedly as she tried to herd the kids into one place while her assistant pointed out a pair of Cigoc's famous White Storks in a roof-top nest right next to the centre. She was lovely and very interested in what I wanted to do. She seemed pleased that I had come just to see "their nature", as she put it.

"Would you be able to guide me round the reserve this morning?" I asked

"Oh no, I am sorry... ," she broke off to rattle some admonishment in rapid Croatian to the kids about queuing to use the telescope. The storks were just a few metres away and there were nests on every second house roof in Cigoc (a lovely sight, so close), but I suppose the 'scope was too much of a draw for the children.

"I cannot guide you today. Many school children. Also, for the bird trail, you must go to Krapje. Go to house 16 and ask for Mr. Bigovic."

She sold me a ticket and a map and pointed the way. I didn't think Mr. Big would make as pleasant a guide as this young lady, but "bird trail" sounded the business. Krapje was only a few miles along the road, twisting and turning with the deep curves of the river, at times riding beside the water's edge where Little Egrets stood guard every few hundred metres. House 16 sat right on the road and was, in fact, another visitor centre, one of those beautiful old wooden Posavina houses which had been sympathetically renovated and extended to provide a fitting office and meeting place for the nature reserve. Modern Croatia was making some effort to conserve and preserve its natural and cultural heritage and I thoroughly approved.

Mr. Bigovic wasn't in and none of the other rangers could guide me that day, but there was a bird trail and I could leave my stuff in the office, so disappointment gave way to a pioneering spirit. I'd find my own birds then and enjoy it all the more. Deep down, I knew I wouldn't see half of what was around without a guide, but I didn't care. It was becoming enough of an achievement just getting to these places and I was happy to now have a personal hunt for a few new species and simply enjoy the rest of the day.

Recklessly, I left all my gear in the visitor centre, except for the optics and a rucksack with the packed *i*-lunch and I set off on a seven-mile hike around this vast wetland. For the first time it was hot and sunny – anyone who knows me knows I don't do hot and sunny. I was a walking shop-stand for the solarly challenged with sunglasses, baseball cap, suntan cream, water bottle and a long-sleeved T-shirt. This was all in addition to being festooned with binoculars, telescope, tripod and camera. I became grumpy again, but once more told myself off and got on with it. I enjoyed the walk along a sun-dappled lane, hearing more nightingales and other warblers in the mature shrubs and trees which lined the track. I thought about the wisdom of leaving all my stuff in the unlocked reserve office and when I realised that it included all my money, credit cards and passport, worry started to prey on my mind. I had come some way, almost to a point of no return. Throwing caution to the wind I strode on, hoping for the best, but unconvinced.

When the heat and the long walk started to get to me, I diverted off the track into a cleared area of woodland and sat on a stump for some lunch. Birds sang and bees buzzed all around as I ate and drank the surprisingly satisfying *i*-lunch. A very loud staccato rasping call kept coming from the bushes until I could ignore it no longer. I had to identify this bird, but just could not see it, or rather, them. They'd been calling at several places all along one side of the path, but never from whichever bush I was searching in – infuriating! At the same time, I kept seeing and hearing little skulking warblers that I continually failed to get binoculars on. They just would not stay still for a second and when they did, it was to play hide-and-seek behind a leaf or a branch. The bits and pieces I was carrying definitely impaired my reactions, but I felt that a decent birder would know what these flitting little shits were – even more infuriating! I did sort out Lesser Whitethroat, Blackcap and

Willow Warbler, but there were at least two other species that I just could not nail.

After my lunch stop, I determined to find the rasper and, after a lot of hunting, discovered that the sound was coming from well beyond the bushes. I also realised that the call was familiar – and common as muck! I really should know this, I thought. All became clear when I found a break in the bushes and could see that the rasping bursts were coming from reed beds behind the shrubs that lined the path: Great Reed Warblers were "singing" from the giant reed stems. I had seen and heard them abroad several times (and even twitched a rare one on Spurn Point in the UK), but had simply forgotten their insistent racket. I liked these birds though because they weren't skulking around; they were giving their all to proclaim territories from the top of long reed stems. Great Reeds are also big, chunky chaps compared to other warblers and, despite being a fairly boring brown colour, they deliver their racket with mouth wide open, displaying a vivid orange gape; all worth a telescope view and a photo or two. Getting my bird, common or not, was very satisfying and it spurred me on.

I walked and walked in the heat, passing dilapidated look-out towers (shooting?), rusting agricultural implements and even a couple of old buses which had been ingeniously converted into multi-storey beehives. They no doubt served the dual purpose of producing honey and pollinating crops, like the yellow rape that was growing in the surrounding fields. After three hours of walking and birding (Red-backed Shrike, Short-toed Eagle, Yellow Wagtail, Wheatear) I saw not another soul until the track opened out to reveal the full extent of this wetland area: a drying marshland stretching out into the distance. About a mile away, around the other side of a complex of fields, pools, reed beds and scrub, I could see a large observation tower with one person, a dot, moving towards it. I decided to go as far as the tower then continue on if a circular route presented itself or head back if not. I hadn't walked so far in years.

The observation tower was a hefty wooden structure with a large roof-covered room at the top. It was fairly new and positioned there for a reason, to overlook a breeding colony of Spoonbills. From this splendid vantage point, I looked down on several of these glorious birds, like big white herons perching incongruously amongst the low treetops. These were mostly breeding birds, showing a smart collar of dull orange at the base of a long, swan-like neck, a crest of plumes on the nape and, of course, that eponymous long bill with a yellow spatula on the end. To see so many of them flapping a little ungainly among the small branches was new to me; we are used to the odd one or two vagrant birds in Britain, but not a colony like this[27].

I rested in the hide for a while, picking up several other birds including a few more wetland species (Night Heron, Purple Heron and Little Bittern) and a huge colony of Tree Sparrows (sadly, rare in Britain these days). I am sure a Bluethroat[28] popped up singing briefly, but it was so fleeting, I couldn't tick it; such an unfamiliar bird in the UK would need a decent view. This was to be one of several frustrating occasions where I only just failed with this colourful relative of Robin and Nightingale. Other birds were kicking about too, making my time spent in the hide well worth the long walk, which I now had to either re-trace or continue with, in the hope of finding a circuit back to House 16.

I chose to re-trace in case the circuit was even longer or in case I got lost (and blown up by a mine!). Tired and drained by the long, hot walk, I trudged up to the door of the centre only to find it shut! The gate into the compound was unlocked, but there was not a soul in sight. Panicking a little, I went to the office door to see if anyone was still in and, to my horror, I found all my gear piled up outside the door, admittedly hidden behind a banister, but just sitting there for anyone to come and nick. With more hope than trust, I checked all of it and found nothing amiss. Torn between relief and anger, I sat down for a while. I

---

[27]Since around 1995, there have been a few Spoonbills attempting to re-colonise the UK at secret nesting sites where chicks have been raised. By 2011 a colony of 8 breeding pairs nested successfully, fledging 14 young at Holkham, Norfolk, and in 2017, a pair bred as far north as RSPB, Fairburn Ings reserve in Yorkshire.

[28]Bluethroat is also a northerly, more Scandinavian/Baltic/Siberian species; a sighting in Croatia would have been good!

soon came to see the good in this little mishap: they had looked after it all, left it out so I could get on my way and no-one had touched it, despite there being a lot of cash and other valuable bits and pieces. I felt a little ashamed of my distrustful attitude and left a thank you note with a donation in their post box, a little sad not to have met Mr. Bigovic.

The road hugged the Sava River, that wonderful tributary of the Danube, providing some great biking and a perfect antidote to the long hot walk. The by-road which took us back to the main E70 was in a shocking state; at one point it was as if a fault line had opened up along its length. I had to be very careful not to let the bike plunge into one of the deep ruts which, surprisingly, were lined with tarmac – some repair job!

Through gentle green countryside we passed a strange communist sculpture right in the middle of an expansive grassy field. It was an enormous concrete tulip with a little bird perched on the top of one of the petals. I stopped to look at the bird only to find it wasn't a small bird, but a White Stork made to look small by the massive bulk of this weird concrete floral effigy built in the middle of nowhere.

As I pulled onto the fast E70 motorway once more, thoughts turned to "That Border". Tim informed me that we were 150 miles away, but it was now 5pm and getting late in the day, I was too tired to face some border horror and I didn't want to spoil my good day. Tim seemed up for it, but we decided to go only a short distance and kip on the Croatian side, facing the Serb frontier fresh in the morning. Most likely, there would either be some hassle and extortion of cash or I'd be bombing through Serbia with no insurance, hoping to get across into Bulgaria unscathed. The alternative was to turn round and loop hundreds of miles north to enter Bulgaria via Hungary. Tim was apathetic so I put all such thoughts out of my mind for the day and pulled in at a Croatian services. They were cute. All of the staff, including the pump attendants (still common in Eastern Europe) wore smart grey uniforms with yellow collars and cuffs. A group of them on a break sat around a table drinking bottled lager (I'm sure that wouldn't be allowed on the job at home, break or no break) while I had my obligatory afternoon coffee and pastry – one of several.

All that walking, birding and riding came over me in a wave of exhaustion as soon as I relaxed into the coffee. The stop confirmed it: no way was I going on, especially not to a fight with Serbian border guards. It was 7pm, I'd been riding for two hours and didn't want to go any further. It was fortuitous, therefore, that just across the parking area stood a chalet style hotel/motel affair. Unless the place was a total dump, I had my bed for the night.

Looking like a mock alpine chalet, the little hotel was as cute as the services attendants. I had an attic room with a bath, a bed and a chair under deeply sloping eaves. But it was self-contained and cheap, providing breakfast in the morning as well (more nice coffee). We were at Luzani, a small town near Slavonski Brod, only 70 miles from the border. Next morning, 30th April, I fed the bike with unleaded, Tim with coordinates and myself with breakfast then headed off towards Serbia.

The motorway ride down the E70 was unremarkable, the open cultivated countryside having flattened out in a wide river valley with small modern towns and business estates lining the road. Croatia was also building motorways for me and this one whisked us ever closer to the border with little to distract. Finally, the smooth new tarmac opened out ahead of me into a concourse like a toll entrance; this was the Croatian side of the border. No problem here, just a glance at the bike, through into no man's land and the approach to the Serbian side. Paranoia fed paranoia until I found myself hiding the bulk of my cash as I queued so I could protest that I only had 20 Euros and a few Kuna; blood and stones were springing to mind. Because I was on a bike, I got waved through to a separate, shorter queue. This is it, I thought, I'm being singled out because I'm on a bike. As expected, I was asked for my passport and the burly guard questioned me about why I was going into Serbia.

"Holiday?"

"Yes." Don't mention birdwatching, he won't get that at all, I counselled myself

"I'm looking for your wonderful nature," I added, sweeping a gesture at the uninspiring landscape around us. He just nodded silently.

"Where you go after Serbia?" he asked.

I told him Bulgaria then Romania. With slow and weary resignation, he shook his head.

"Een Bolgareea, they weel steal your bike for sure... and in Romayneea."

He wagged his finger and tutted.

"Enzoy your time een Serbia-and be carful," he said, handing back my passport and pointing at the bike, "Somtime Serbia roads no good."

Was that it? No extortion? No intimidation? No grilling about insurance? No long waits while papers are checked? Just, "have a nice time in Serbia"?! I almost felt cheated, but it didn't matter to me that I had no insurance, Serbian or otherwise, I was simply delighted that all the tales of doom and corruption proved wrong. And no vignette either (I asked).

My elation lasted for several miles down the continuation of the E70 into Serbia, but the uncomfortable reality returned: I was driving in this "untouchable" country with no insurance whatsoever. If I had an accident here, as a foreigner with no papers, I'd be taken to the cleaners. I doubled my determination to ride through and out of Serbia as quickly as I could. Consequently, there isn't much to say about poor old Serbia, the apparent black sheep of the opening East[29]

The road surface deteriorated (Serbia not building motorways for anybody, it would seem!) until, racing through Belgrade on an urban section, the bike was bucking like a bronco over rutted, un-repaired tarmac. There was dust everywhere and central Belgrade looked like a dump. To be fair, I was hardly giving it a chance and probably not seeing its best

[29]In researching this episode, I used Google's Streetview to remind me of the border set up and, interestingly, Streetview switches off at the Croatian side, to be replaced by still images of road signs and fields. Serbia has not joined the fold yet – even Google is not allowed in! Then again, the same applies to Bosnia and even Germany, where strict privacy laws and culture have excluded Google from everywhere except the large cities.

from a flyover, but nothing made me want to pull over for a look. Beyond Belgrade, the countryside of Serbia had a very definite bygone feel; people worked with hand tools, tending small fields, horse and cart was the norm and what machinery there was looked ancient. I saw little evidence of Western development or intensive agriculture. This is usually a very good sign for the health of the natural environment and meant it was a real shame not to be doing any birding here. In my defence, even Gerard Gorman, the guru of Eastern European birding, had left out Serbia from his excellent guide-book, and I hadn't found an alternative. I wouldn't have had a clue where to go and most likely would have ended up blown to bits by a mine, mugged by some ex-communist Mafia or kidnapped and trafficked as a rent boy.[30]

My time in Serbia was spent on the 400 miles of road or in services for fuel or food... or coffee. These service areas were basic and fairly run-down, but everything was cheap, they would sometimes take Euros (but no small change) and their coffee was just fine.

As I approached Bulgaria, on the E80, I got glimpses of some wonderful looking gorges and unspoilt (unvisited?) river valleys with that strange pale green water that I'd been seeing since Croatia: mineral deposits from some local geological phenomenon, perhaps. Tempting though they were, I had neither time nor inclination. I have since had confirmation that these parts of Serbia are indeed worth visiting and the birding is good... another time maybe.

The journey through Serbia became a blur of unremarkable services stops, prostitutes languishing against crash barriers, the occasional bird appearing above the horizon or in a nearby field and, finally, the approach to the border with Bulgaria, which started in full daylight in a long queue. So, was *this* where they nabbed me: on the way out rather than the way in, just like Slovenia and the vignette? Because of the long delay I began to

[30]Home Office advice on travelling to Serbia (Dec 2018); "There is still some danger from residual mines and other unexploded ordnance left over from the 1999 conflict in Kosovo and in Serbia"

develop Border Anxiety again, imagining all sorts of difficulties as I sat astride my bike with the daylight fading fast. In part, this Eastern Europe border paranoia was fuelled by the Charley Boorman and Ewan McGregor experience at frontiers in Long Way Round. Would I get stung for a vignette despite earlier assurances? Is this where the insurance card is played? If so, I had lost the option of detouring round Serbia and would have to pay up or spend the rest of my life in a Serbian jail. The rapidly falling darkness didn't help and I could see the lights of the Bulgarian side just a few yards away. Out of boredom I got out the Red Spots to look wistfully over the border post; "Republic of Bulgaria" proclaimed a big banner, but I was getting suspicious looks from the Serb guards and hastily put the binoculars away.

With a terrific sense of relief, I eventually got through without any financial or other molestation. I was told (wrongly) that I needed a vignette in Bulgaria so I stopped at the first petrol station to buy one. Seven Euros friendlier, the attendant came out and explained where it should go on the bike and I set off into the darkness of a Bulgarian evening to find a hotel, pointless vignette proudly stuck to the windscreen.

Chapter 7 – Melnik & The Devil's Throat

Four years after meeting Anne on that road in France, we get married. It is 1983, we are both 26 years old, starting out on careers and taking life by the scruff, but within a few months, Anne begins to have horrible sensory loss, tingling and numbness in her arms and legs. She goes through all the "usual" tests, including a horrible lumbar puncture, the after-effects of which are far worse than the relatively mild symptoms being investigated: it takes her weeks to recover from the headaches and dizziness. Meantime the diagnosis she fears comes through: she has Multiple Sclerosis (MS). After my "close call" with epilepsy, it seems like some unpleasant God is taunting us. Somehow, Anne brings her usual and admirable strength of character to bear on her situation – life goes on. Luckily, her MS relapses are infrequent and she makes almost one hundred percent recoveries. The fear subsides and although it seriously affects our plans for the future, from the mundane, such as insurance and mortgages, to the deeper decisions about having a family, we buy a wreck of a house together-and just carry on. Many years later, Anne is often to say to me, "You should never have married me".

*

Bulgaria is far better developed as a birding destination than the countries I had just come through. It has UK based tour companies, well-researched sites, nature reserves and recognised areas to visit for particular groups of birds and particular times of year. Because of this, I had done much more homework on "BG" than on Slovenia or Croatia: Trigrad for Wallcreepers (my second chance at these beauties, since failing in the Pyrenees); the Sakar Mountains for eagles, other raptors and Masked Shrike; the Black Sea coast with the banks of the Danube for... too much to list!

I had planned a partial route and made contact with some potential guides for the eastern part of the country. Now that I was actually here, it was time to get in touch with these contacts and make arrangements. I sent a few texts, hoping that Fucking Vodafone would behave itself:

1st May, 09.40
Hi Dimiter. I am in Sofia now – need to confirm arrangements for guiding in BG. Hope all is well with you. Thanks, Robert

Amazingly, a reply came straight back;

1st May, 09.43
Hi Robert. Glad to hear you are here in BG! Your guide in Burgas will be Dimo, the warden on 4 and 5 May if you will make it. Here is his number. I will give you name of guide in Sakar tomorrow. I have booked for you Sakar Hotel, Topolovgrad on 3 May. I meet you in Varna outside the cathedral on 5 May at 10.00. Good Luck, Dimiter.

Dimiter was some sort of head of the BSPB (Bulgarian Society for the Protection of Birds), at least in eastern Bulgaria, and he had kindly offered to set up guides in various parts of the country. I replied with thanks and sent another to the guide he had named;

1st May, 09.49
Hi Dimo. I am in Sofia now, Melnik & Trigrad today & tomorrow, then Topolovgrad on 3rd. I should b with u in the morning on 4th at Poda for guided birding. I am meeting Dimiter on 5th in Varna. Hope this still ok. Thanks, Robert Duncan.

I sent these texts sitting outside the Motel Yubim in the outskirts of Sofia, Bulgaria's capital city, and it made the trip feel like a real unfolding adventure! I had found this place with great difficulty in the dark the previous night, assisted by a local cop who had already flagged me down for some reason. I have no idea why he pulled me over and I suspect he forgot too in the onslaught of my foreigner's request for directions. I even dragged the poor guy over to a road sign, declaring "Motel Yubim 500m", to show him where I was heading. I think he got caught up in the Mystery Of The Motel Yubim and he ended up encouraging me to "Go – stranger from a strange land – go and find the Motel Yubim." (he didn't say that).

The owner of the Motel Yubim had practically forced me to take the bike round behind the building to a locked yard full of coaches and trucks under repair, guarded by an Alsatian. So the bike would be safe then, I had concluded, but I found it worrying that a local like him felt the bike would not be safe parked outside the Motel Yubim. This sense of vulnerability and incipient, all-pervasive crime, set the tone for my expedition into Sofia the next morning, in search of Internet access.

The highway into Sofia centre was just that, a highway, six lanes wide, but with no road markings or verges – one huge tarmacked dirt track! Workers, mostly women dressed in red tunics, seemed to be continually sweeping the verge of this road by hand with witches-broom brushes. Maybe the road wasn't constructed to successfully shed dust and dirt into culverts? Most of the vehicles managed to go into town on one side of the road and out on the other, but apart from that, it was mayhem! No one kept to a lane – because there were no lanes; it was a total free-for-all, but the bike was good for weaving past the snaking lines of cars and trucks (*Cars 5; Bikes 5)*. The traffic lights had a count-down in seconds to warn of an impending change, either to red so you could prepare to stop or green to get ready to go. I thought this a brilliant idea: it made impatience and stress less likely, it stopped people jumping the lights, and it removed the uncertainty of whether to brake at or accelerate through, a changing signal. I'd never come across this anywhere before. Maybe it was a necessity here, on this chaotic artery into Sofia, but I'd like to see it everywhere – well done Bulgaria!

Less welcome was the Cyrillic script, an unfamiliar and ancient alphabet, which seemed more prevalent here than in other countries I'd visited[31]. It was everywhere and in common use on road signs, shop fronts and notices. Given that early Cyrillic was developed here in the 10th century during the first Bulgarian Empire, it wouldn't be surprising if there was considerable national pride in it, but to a total non-cyrillicist, it was gobbledygook and made getting around all the harder.

Once in this capital city, Sofia proved to be a hellish network of cobbled streets and deep tram-lines designed to throw the unwary off his fully laden Honda CBF 600. It was such hard work to get the bike parked – illegally – right next to a sign depicting dire tow-away consequences for anyone staying for more than a few seconds. I'd like to describe Sofia here to set the scene, but in all honesty, I can't; most of the time, my gaze was fixed firmly on the road in front of the bike in order to negotiate all those cracks and grooves. At that time, I thought the city was a busy, unremarkable place.

I decided to pull over and see if I could request some directions to a legal parking spot from the first person that showed willing. This turned out to be a genial, English-speaking (sort of), young bloke. He was quite dark-skinned and didn't look particularly Bulgarian: maybe Greek or Turkish? Perhaps in his mid-twenties, he was dressed informally in smart T-shirt and pale green three-quarter length shorts (the kind that, for the last ten years, I've been swearing will come to look ridiculous). He was affable, smiling and very willing to help.

"I show you, I show you parking. Yes, yes, come with me... up here."

I jumped on the bike then took ages turning it round on the undulating cobbles, but my guide waited patiently then walked alongside the bike, directing me.

"I walk, you follow. Good parking is there." He pointed ahead, across some tram lines and up a cobbled incline. Across

---

[31]Cyrillic is the official alphabet in many Russian and north-Asian languages, but of the Eastern European nations I visited, only includes Serbia and Bulgaria, (along with neighbouring countries like Bosnia, Macedonia and Montenegro)

another intersection, rutted with tram-tracks and more cobbles, I saw him waving and pointing at a space. Stoically, I ventured into the maelstrom of trams, cars, cobbles and people (I hate cities!) over to the parking area that he had found for me.

"Thanks," I said, shaking his hand. "Do I have to pay somewhere? Is there a ticket machine?"

"No machine, you pay later." He gestured enthusiastically at his chest like a male gorilla.

"I am the, the... ," he struggled to find his words, then he pulled himself up proudly, "I am boss of parking!"

I was nonplussed for a moment. What?... What? How could this young bloke whom I just happened to stop as he walked along the street, and who looked like a Greek tourist, be in charge of parking?

"Are you a parking attendant?" I asked him.

The way he was dressed, even that seemed unlikely, but I made a mime of checking a number plate, writing a ticket and slapping it on a car.

"No, no. I am **boss** of parking. My name is Marco."

He countered my mime with a circling gesture to indicate the area, or maybe the entire city. None of this computed. My warning hackles started to rise; who was this guy? He did know exactly the right parking spot (or so it seemed to me, the foreigner) and he had made some effort to get me here. I remained friendly and grateful, but wary.

"Why you come to Sofia?" he asked

"I'm looking for an Internet café. Is there one near here?"

"You want Internet?"

"Yes, do you know one near here? Not too far from the bike. In one of these streets?" I gestured at the buildings, which, I was only just beginning to notice, were old and rather fine.

"Yes, I know good cheap Internet for you. Not here, you follow me," he said, beckoning. I hesitantly started to remove the tank bag and lock up the bike. Everything on the bike was secured in some way, either hidden away in the locked top-box or panniers or strapped to the seat and locked with a visible chain. I still felt it was vulnerable though; a bold thief could take the bits on the seat fairly easily. I wanted to put another heavy padlocked chain around the rear wheel and frame, as I normally would, but that seemed ridiculous here in a main street among parked cars so, doubtfully, I relied on just the steering lock and joined Marco.

As we walked away from the bike, I felt more and more uncomfortable, having this internal debate about what Marco was really up to. Was he leading me somewhere dodgy to rob me, or lure me away from the bike so a partner in crime could fiddle with or even steal the bike?

"You are the parking boss?" I asked, "do you have other workers who check the tickets?"

"No, it is just me. The others are there and there." He gestured vaguely around.

A little further on, he bumped into a couple of people and stopped for a chat with the usual handshake and informal street swagger of continental youth. Was this just one of many acquaintances he would surely have as a local "boss" of street parking, or was it an accomplice being directed back to my bike in order to steal it? The scam version of these unfolding events was taking a paranoid hold in my imagination. I asked loudly how far the Internet café was as we turned yet another corner, further and further from the parking spot.

"Not far, you will see, it is good, cheap Internet."

Across a big square, along a street with scaffolding and a pedestrian detour, right turn at the lights, left at the next street corner. I was beginning to make mental notes of landmarks so I could find my way back – in a hurry!

"This is too far Marco, " I said in a serious tone, "too far from the bike, I don't have time to walk so far."

"No, no it is fine – just over here, not far," he said reassuringly, "good Internet, you will see."

We carried on down more streets with shops and cafés until finally, we took a turn into a grey residential road with blocks of flats. This was so wrong. I stopped, ready to turn back.

"There, you see: Internet!"

He pointed at a sign outside a doorway into the flats saying; "Toxo Internet". Bugger me! He was right: an Internet café all this way and in a dodgy looking block of flats. But my warning hackles were unconvinced. Why all this way? And if he were some sort of parking official, surely he would have known somewhere more public on the main street? I wanted an Internet café amongst the shops where I could get a decent coffee – not here, worrying about exactly when I was going to be mugged by the local gang of estate dwellers in this anonymous block of flats.

We went through the doorway and he pointed up a scruffy stairway.

"Internet upstairs. I come back soon, then you pay me for parking."

Ah, right, now we were getting to it! He was still smiling and affable, but it was clear this was at least part of the sting – he wanted a back-hander for parking and I had no way of knowing if the bike was being dealt a ticket by a real parking attendant or even if it was being pilfered.

"Oh, don't I pay at the bike? How much will it be for the parking?" I asked in as innocent a tone as I could muster.

He told me some small sum in Euros (two I think).

"I need to go to the bank Marco, for money," I lied, "Is there one near here?"

"Yes, yes, bank just outside. You go up to Internet now, I go somewhere. When I come back, I take you to bank."

No way, mate! He waited for me to mount the stairs and I started climbing. He left. I turned round, back down the stairs and headed out of the door. He had gone. Thank Christ! Now I had to find my way back to the bike. My heart was pounding. Would he (and the gang?) be waiting around one of the corners? I started to run, fearful that this had all been a ruse to get me a long way from the bike so it could be ransacked or stolen. I had visions of Marco's accomplice turning up with a van or lifting truck and simply removing the whole bike. This is not as paranoid as it sounds – it happens in the UK and is a major method of bike theft, especially of valuable BMWs and the like.

It had taken us a good fifteen minutes to get here, I was lugging the heavy tank bag, it was warm, I was sweating, and I had no confidence in my ability to re-trace all those twists and turns. I broke into a run until lack of fitness brought me puffing to a trotting walk; back across the square (beautiful buildings, but never mind that!), along the scaffolding, then... where? I had lost my bearings and became even more convinced that this had been Marco's plan all along: get the tourist lost a long way from his vehicle. I took a left, but didn't recognise any of the shops or signs in this street. I retraced back to the intersection and saw a statue that I remembered passing on my left. I went on, so that it was on my right, and got back on track. After another ten minutes of trotting, sweating and panting, I turned a corner, back to where all this had started. The bike was still there, sitting quite happily where I'd locked it.

A wave of relief swept over me, but I was certain Marco would be around somewhere to demand his parking fee, if nothing else. I just wanted out of this horrible city – but needed a drink first. I unpacked a bottle of water, leaned back on the bike and took a deep draft. If Marco turned up now, he could just fuck off, I thought. No more, "Ok Marco, I'll just follow you blindly". What an idiot I had been.

To this day, I wonder if he was genuine and I too paranoid, but there had been too many danger points that made it a very unwise thing to have done. If nothing else, why did he ask for parking money after that long walk to such a dodgy, out of the way place? Maybe he was just a young bloke trying to drum up business for a local Internet enterprise and I had shown spectacular paranoia and lack of faith. Maybe, but at least I was still alive, unharmed and everything was intact.

I programmed Tim to get me out of there, but as we rode off, I felt that Sofia deserved a better look. I had walked (and run!) across its fine National Assembly Square where people were milling around in the sunshine, enclosed by impressive white stone architecture. I had seen the Parliament building with flag flying, but I hadn't noticed anything else. Despite my bad experience with Marco and a desire to get the hell out, I rode the bike around a little until I found the square again. I grabbed a sandwich and sat on the bike eating it (no more parking for me!). A statue of some First World War General on horseback dominated the centre of the square and I noticed behind the town hall a spectacular looking wedding cake of a building with two fabulous, gold-plated domes. This was the spectacular, multi-storey St Alexander-Nevski Cathedral. Sofia was looking more and more like a place worth visiting, so I rode round to have a closer look at the cathedral. Its golden dome and bell tower shimmered in the bright sunlight and it looked even more like a giant wedding cake, with its many layers supported on short white pillars, topped with coppered green roofs.

Despite all this architectural and cultural splendour, I was still in a distracted state of mind and not feeling good about Sofia. The cobbles were still getting on my nerves and I wanted to be out in the wilds again, birding.

"Take me out of here," I said to Tim as I gave him his next destination: Melnik, a hundred miles away in the far south-east corner of Bulgaria. We sped off over the cobbles, hoping to soon find the main road south.

Tim did a fine job and the roads gradually widened – but the cobbles remained. We were clearly on a major arterial route out of the city (the A1 in fact) but, for nearly three miles, it was a horrendous, bucking, rippling surface of ancient cobbles. Was I being a philistine, a product of modern living, unhappy unless on a tarmac ribbon, speeding past everything? At that time, after my experience in Sofia, probably yes. I just wanted out of the city so badly; I couldn't see any charm in this busy, major road still being in such a bad state, cobbles or no cobbles. It would probably have been fine in a car, more so back in the centre with the tram tracks 'n all *(Cars 6; Bikes 5)*. Even so, it gave a real pounding to the suspension on every vehicle I could see – including my bike.

Melnik was a gem and the ride there, a perfect antidote to Sofia. Yet again on this trip, a ridge of high, snow-capped mountains accompanied me in the distance as I passed through small villages on the way to Sandanski, where Tim instructed me to turn off towards Melnik. The road to Melnik was a bikers dream: a good surface of undulating, twisting tarmac through a mix of wooded and cultivated hillsides. A distinctive baldness to some of the hills made the landscape seem open and fresh, while the high Pirin and Rila mountains formed a crisp, snow-cool background in the distance.

This Melnik road also provided two good birds as spectacular fly-pasts. My first Golden Oriole of the trip flew across the road in front of me. He took his time flying through the field on one side, and across the road into an almond orchard on the other side, giving fine close views of his patched black and yellow livery. I stopped the bike as he disappeared, then in the silence, I heard him give that wonderful rich fluting call for which Golden Orioles are rightly famous (when I first heard it, it used to remind me of notes in the Blondie song "Denis", but I can't quite hear that any more).

On the same stretch of road, coming into Melnik, a similarly cracking view of Red-backed Shrike sealed the biking-with-birds experience for the day. Again, the road as it approached the town was restfully beautiful with rounded, sculptured hills dotted with olive groves and scrubby bushes. In the near distance, I could see some odd, sandy-coloured hill formations, like peaked sand dunes rising from the shallow valleys, and beyond that, the omnipresent, snow-crested Pirin/Rila Mountains. This part of Bulgaria really was beautiful and distinctive.

Melnik is a very strange town. Billed as the "smallest town in Bulgaria" with only 385 citizens, it is no more than a strip of dwellings lining a partially dried up riverbed. It is right in the middle of nowhere, yet it has something like ten restaurants, several gift shops, two hotels and numerous guest-houses. There are also lots of wine shops, more of which later.

I had decided to head in this direction because it was on the way to Trigrad Gorge, home (I hoped) of some Wallcreepers, as well as some other wildlife and spectacular mountain scenery. Melnik was a good stopping point and its description in the guidebooks was tantalising. It had previously infected my daughter Claire: she too had been here recently, coming back with confirmation of how crazy a place it was. Melnik also had a section to itself in good old Gerard Gorman, which was back on track now, having left Serbia, the no man's land of Eastern European birding.

Another unique thing about Melnik was its high-peaked, sandy hills all around (the Melnishki Pyramidi).

I couldn't stop looking up at them as they towered behind the small town. They must be the most photographed objects in the whole of Bulgaria. At first sight, these peaks seem to be made entirely of sand. They jut high above the town and surrounding land like Matterhorns, jagged and impressive, often several in a row like teeth in a dinosaur jaw – and about as ancient. Yet, I couldn't help wonder why they were still there; surely erosion by rain, wind and ice would have broken the sand down long ago? Apparently not – in fact, they have been tunnelled out and used as wine cellars for centuries.

Wine! As if the landscape, the town and the birding aren't enough, Melnik is also famous for its own unique and – trust me – *gorgeous* wine. Claire had brought back a bottle of Melnik 13, which I had therefore tasted – gorgeous, gorgeous, gorgeous! Full-bodied, rich, fruity and definitely not plonk – but as cheap as chips and not available in the UK[32].

I eschewed the big El Greco hotel in Melnik in favour of a cheap guest-house, further through the town. The owner played a game of cat and mouse at first.

"Yes, we have room. How many?"

When I told him it was just me and just for one night, he changed his mind and shook his head. But he was clearly a Bulgarian Basil Fawlty: not quite all there and not quite in charge. After speaking to his wife, Sybil, he came back shaking his head, but handing out a key, clearly unhappy (mind you, nodding in Bulgaria means "no", so the head-shake could have meant "yes, fine – if you must"). The room turned out to be a little self-contained suite including a separate wet room, lobby and bedroom – very nice.

I went for several walks through the little town and its ancient alleys, which peter out quickly into a scrubby, wooded valley immediately behind the houses. Here, the general birding was superb: Golden Orioles fluting from several bushes and back gardens, three species of woodpecker (Syrian, Lesser Spotted and Green), Nightingale, Hawfinch, a small falcon flying around those sand pyramids (Hobby or Red-footed Falcon), Alpine Swift and a weird looking Sardinian Warbler. I watched the latter for ages wondering what was wrong with it. Eventually, I thought I'd better make some notes;

"Black cap/cheek, heavy-ish bill, makes head look a bit "honking", pale eye/eye ring, grey back, pale/white underneath. Song? No song, just alarm like Blackcap with scratchy trills. Black & white tail when flying off, white outers?"

---

[32]If you search really hard or are some sort of wine expert, you can probably find Melnik wine in the UK, but I've never seen it in any shop, online or advertised for UK sale, let alone Melnik 13 itself.

All that said Sardinian Warbler to me, but this thing looked strange: maybe eastern Sardinians were a different race compared to those I'd seen in Spain and elsewhere? I needed a book.

Back in the guesthouse, I consulted my Collins Guide to Birds of Britain and Europe and took some time working out that I'd seen an Orphean Warbler (Eastern race). This was a mythical bird to me, not because I knew much about it nor because it was a first (there are *lots* of birds I haven't seen!), but because it has such a fabulous name: "Orphean Warbler" – it sounds like something out of Greek Mythology. It wasn't on the Target List because I had always thought of it as a Mediterranean/North African bird – but that's wrong, as I found out. In fact, I could have seen them in Spain and they are often found in Greece by holidaying birders. Nevertheless, a Bulgarian one was very good indeed. My notes checked out well, the pale eye being a clincher (Sardinian Warblers have a staring red-brown ring around a dark eye). Being in the far south of Bulgaria, very close to the Greek border, it seemed perfectly possible that Orpheans bred here. Gerard Gorman also confirmed it as occurring here in Melnik, which I hadn't picked up. He also had a mouth-watering list of other species but, with just one day in Melnik – and Wallcreeper still to find, I missed most of these. I went back out to double check my bird, found the Orphean Warbler again and confirmed my ID. Result! An unexpected Life, European and Trip Tick – and a lovely little bird too.

Food! That evening, I celebrated by eating well in one of the many little restaurants in Melnik. I tried another version of the famous wine and even tracked down Melnik 13. Heavy or not, three bottles were coming home with me: one for Claire. Now here I must make a note of dissent: Melnik is lovely and all that, but there is an element of self-fulfilment going on. There are only this many restaurants, guest-houses and the big El Greco hotel – because of tourism. I was here early in the season, but I could picture the coaches rolling up, disgorging their passengers and filling the tiny town with hordes of wandering shoppers. If nothing else, you could tell by the presence of several tacky little outlets selling trinkets and Melnik memorabilia. No different to many a quaint seaside village in Britain or anywhere else, but being in such a far-flung location, in a relatively undiscovered part of a relatively undiscovered country, it seemed wrong. But this is an old, not particularly original hobby horse of mine and I was there partly for the same reasons. I stopped having wistfully negative thoughts about the cancerous effect of rank consumerism and quaffed my delicious wine to wash down the meal. A warm glow replaced those uncomfortable thoughts and I headed off to bed, content with Orphean Warbler, Melnik 13 and a fine evening's walk back to my room.

Next day, I left Melnik on a road out of the town, which was not the one I'd come in on. The guest house owner advised me to leave the town on a different route for Trigrad – and it seemed to make sense. Three bottles of wine heavier, Tim, the bike and I set off on this unknown mountain road, in search of Adventure, Birds and Trigrad.

Melnik turned out to be the furthest south I would be on the entire journey and now we were heading North for the first time since arriving in Tarvisio five days earlier. Tim seemed happy with the route (you can tell if he's unhappy because he keeps telling you to turn round, never with any annoyance, just insistently), but increasingly, the bike and I were not happy at all. The "road" degenerated into a slowly climbing dirt track, full of potholes. It was wide enough for cars to pass,or even trucks (not that any came by), but the poor surface, and having to steer around endless holes, made my progress painfully slow. It was also hard work. Compensations were the clear, sky-filled views out over open, barren hills, vineyards where the beautiful wine was made and several lark species flitting around, but the track just went on and on, flattening onto a plateau before heading down again. I came into a one-horse town called Hastovro (not on any map I have seen), took a photo of the horse and rode on through. There was nothing there, not even a much-needed coffee stop. I have no idea how long that mountain track was, but it took over an hour just to get back on a tarmac road that felt like it was going somewhere. I consulted Tim and a map to find that we had only come a few miles from Melnik, and Trigrad was still 90 miles away on relatively slow mountain roads. It was now 1 o'clock, which meant I'd have to stop well before Trigrad, just to make sure I had some accommodation.

The proper mountain road E198, proved to be wonderful for both biking and birding. There were raptors round nearly every bend, mostly small eagles, floating along and over the richly wooded hillsides as if they owned the place. The road itself was superb, with tight bends, long straight inclines and the odd hairpin thrown in.

It took us through deep valleys so that I could look across and down at vast green hillsides, a new and more spectacular view appearing each time I pulled the bike up after leaning round a bend. Some way on, a perfect picnic spot opened out in a natural lay-by. We pulled over, parking on a hard piece of ground and I sat in the shade on some fortuitously tumbled boulders, eating some lunch. Birds were flitting around the dense scrubby bushes, but the little buggers were playing hide-and-seek.

I tried recording a dictaphone message about this idyllic place, but it was full of interruptions;

"Uh-oh – bird!" followed by*;*

"Fucking things won't stay still for a second! I can't get on them. Uh-oh – bird!"

It started to irk me until I spotted something flicking around the top of a pylon, way across the deep valley next to where we had stopped. Binoculars told me it was something different, colourful and active, but its size was difficult to judge – I needed the 'scope. Luckily, this bird seemed to like perching and fly-catching from his high pylon perch, so he was still there by the time I got the 'scope set up: Rock Thrush! – another bird that had eluded me on trips abroad, from Majorca to Spain and even Israel. There was some heat haze spoiling the otherwise superb view, but this bird's striking colours were clear – and a dead give-away. It was a male, showing in the bright sun his beautiful muted blue head, orange underparts, flickering black wings and white on his back. He flew back and forth from his favourite perch on the pylon, catching insects and flashing these colours until another joined him, this time a dowdy brown female. Then they both disappeared. Another fine Life and Trip Tick.

After such a magical pit-stop, I was ready to go on. Tim was all fired up for a mountain detour ("shortest route" according to him), but I'd had enough of rough mountain tracks and walking pace progress so I ignored him. An old-fashioned map showed us a more sensible route: the road we were already on! (Tim didn't argue – he's good like that). Full of confidence and joie de vivre, we resumed the leaning and banking, the braking and counter-steering (John, of the Institute of Advanced Motorists, would've been proud of me!) and hared along that lovely mountain road... until an enormous pothole appeared without warning. We were on it before I had time to react. The front wheel crashed in, bucking and twisting, pulling the whole bike off line. To keep it upright, I almost went into the path of an oncoming car, which sailed by oblivious on its pothole-free side of the road, leaving me stopped astride the bike, a quivering wreck, stuck in this chasm where the road should be. I kid you not, the hole was almost the width of the road, about four metres long and around 30cm deep. It was ridiculous: a normal tarred surface had suddenly degenerated into this dangerous mess. There were no warning signs before the bend and, from the state of the rubbish in the bottom of this crater, it had been there for some time. The crash barrier to the right was all bent, with boulders wedged under it. On the opposite verge, next to the hillside, there was a similar pile of loose boulders. Clearly, a landslide of big rocks had damaged the tarmac and it had been cleared to open the road, but nothing else had been done. At home we moan about "Health and Safety gone mad" or "The Nanny State", but this is what happens in a poor economy with poor bureaucratic infrastructure. This near-death experience in a Bulgarian pot-hole made me realise the value of all the systems and laws which keep our roads, homes, hospitals, schools and workplaces safe and comfortable – even if sometimes they are a bit OTT.

The bike seemed undamaged, but it took a long time for me to believe the suspension hadn't been broken somehow. Also, from this point on, there were many more potentially lethal craters, materialising like Black Holes, waiting to suck me into oblivion. The abandoned joy of this lovely road had gone. I could no longer lean and bank and counter-steer (sorry John of IAM). I rode like a learner, expecting to fall off at any time – and for good reason. This was, after all, an isolated mountain road. It must see winter damage like this from ice, floods and landslips all the time and it would take huge resources to keep on top of it. Perhaps a road like this in the UK, even by early May, would be in a similar state. Somehow though, I think the

British Highways Agency would have swung into action – with some warning signs, at the very least.

Borino was the first town after all that. With slow, pot-hole impeded progress, it was also the place to stop, and it had a spa hotel that looked comfortable, if modern and characterless. I locked the bike to a post in the car park and settled in, a bit tired, but relaxed after a long day, with several experiences to relive and make notes on. After a shower and a change of clothes, I went in desperate search of a coffee. The foyer bar was small, but open. A few well dressed young locals were sitting round a table, chatting excitedly, but they were restrained and polite, giving me waves and beer bottle salutes as I sat down; a nice atmosphere in which to write my notes and leave another dictaphone message. They were taking group photos and I offered to take one of them all together, which perked them up even more; one of the men even offered me a beer. The camera belonged to a birthday girl who was out celebrating. I accepted my bottled beer, returned her camera and gave her a birthday kiss – which caused more excitement. I was pleased to have catalysed a little event there in the hotel foyer of a southern Bulgarian mountain town, but I left them to it and went to bed with a warm glow. A very good day (except for the Black Hole!).

At breakfast the next morning, a text arrived:

3rd May, 08.08
Hi Robert. The name of the guide [in Sakar] is Dimitar, like me :o)! Here is his number. I hope you are enjoying BG and our birds! See you in Varna on 5 May. Dimiter

I sent a thank you text in reply, then one to my new contact;

3rd May, 08.21
Hello Dimitar. I am going 2 Trigrad now & will b at hotel Sakar this evening. See you tomorrow at 7.30. Thanks, Robert Duncan.

183

Trigrad was 12 miles east of Borino: close enough to head out from the hotel and back without all the luggage. Having failed in the Pyrenees with Josele, I was now, for the second time, in earnest search of Wallcreeper. The big brown sign for Trigrad's gorge, the "Devil's Throat", came into view fairly quickly after leaving Borino. I turned right and barrelled down the narrow twisting road.

The hillsides rising from the road gradually got closer and closer as I rode further in until they formed sheer rock walls rising vertically for hundreds of feet on either side, with only room for a small stream in the bottom beside the road. This was the Devil's Throat, a deep rocky gorge of sheer cliffs cutting its way into the mountains – and home of the legendary Wallcreeper.

Uncharacteristically for me, I found myself in a well signposted car park with an information board, depicting the wildlife of this extraordinary place. The car park was at the end of a short tunnel hewn into the rocky cliff – literally the end of the road. There were even some people around: car park stallholders selling local jam and herbal tea infusions. But I was on a mission. I took off, walking up one of the marked tracks, now with some knowledge of the terrain required for Wallcreepers. I scoured every massive rock face and crag for the little birds, looking for a tell-tale flash of red and grey, black and white. These little gems are indeed stunning but, being only the size of a Blackbird, they look very small against enormous slabs of mountain, especially when flitting around high up, as is their wont. It was hard work – and I failed again. There were Crag

Martins and Alpine Swifts wheeling high and low through the gorge, a Peregrine Falcon around the cliffs, a Dipper and a Grey Wagtail on the stream, but sadly, no Wallcreeper.

Back at the car park, I bought some fig jam and a box of herbal teas from a friendly and genuine local lady who explained all about the infusions and how they were good for one's health. This seemed to be a feature of the Bulgarian approach to life; natural remedies and knowledge of them seemed much more mainstream than in the cynical West (which included me, I was ashamed to realise).

Just as I was about to leave, a car arrived and I heard the arrestingly familiar tones of a Northern English accent; two middle-aged holidaying couples got out of the car, draped in binoculars and telescopes. I chatted to them about my Wallcreeper failure. They said a little about having seen them here before;

"Last year, we saw them just above the mouth of this tunnel, at the other end. They had a nest there."

"I've looked all up the gorge for as far as I could go with suitable habitat. No sign," I told them

"We'll start looking at the old nest site then, " one of them said.

I tried to engage them in further conversation, but they seemed keener to get on, the ladies in particular, who wanted to stretch their legs. I watched the two men, bristling with telescopes, tripods and cameras, disappear into the tunnel while I packed up my own optics ready for the ride back to Borino. As I emerged from the tunnel, I slowed to see where the two guys had gone; they'd positioned themselves on the other side of a crash barrier next to the stream and were looking back at the rocky arch which formed the tunnel. I don't know what made me get off the bike and join them – but I'm so glad I did: they were watching a pair – a pair! – of Wallcreepers, just a few metres away. The luck of some people! I didn't even bother setting up my scope: the birds were too close. We got the impression that they were once again near their nesting crevice, flitting around together, flashing their wings like butterflies.

Wallcreepers are a little like giant grey Wrens in overall appearance, but with a long curved bill, black chin and, when they flick their wings, a very handsome flashing pattern of red and black with big white spots. What makes Wallcreeper so sought after by birders is not just this unique beauty, but also the extreme and highly specific habitat in which they are found. They are almost exclusively mountainous and nearly always clambering and flitting around ledges and crevices on huge cliffs of rock in out of the way places – just like Trigrad Gorge, in fact. Although they move from the high tops down to foothills and even onto town buildings in winter then back up in spring, they are non-migratory so there have only been four lost individuals found in the UK in the last 60 years: a rare, difficult and beautiful bird indeed.

One of the blokes[33] had a camera on his 'scope and I asked him for some copies of the photos as a record of a momentous event and a beautiful, beautiful bird – a Trip Tick with spots on! To have tried and failed in Spain and so nearly failed here in Bulgaria, it felt exceptionally good to have this particular target bird on my list. It had been many years since I'd seen my first and only Wallcreeper (with Alan, whom I stayed with in Italy a few days before), and they were quite distant views across a huge valley of rock in the Swiss Alps. This was much better, and a truly fabulous "re-tick".[34]

[33]His name was Ian Mislebrook and I made the classic faux pas of putting his photo, which he did very kindly send on to me, onto my trip blog without acknowledging him as the source. Apologies Ian, I hope I rectified it with suitable speed, and thanks again for the pic – it makes a wonderful memory.

[34]Re-tick; seeing a good bird for the first time in a very long time.

Chapter 8 – Dimiter, Dimo, Dimitar

For most of its victims, MS is a stretched out affair. Its progress can be imperceptibly slow, but punctuated with sudden collapses, as if all the nasties have been stored up over time then released in one hit. It reminds me of an earthquake: tension building unseen between tectonic plates deep below the ocean; huge amounts of energy, stored as if in a giant coiled spring. Then with devastating consequence, out of the blue, all that energy is released – MS is like that. One minute Anne is walking around, bright as a bee, then the next it's as if an earthquake has gone off somewhere in her nervous system... tingling, numbness and spasm turn her into a disabled, frightened and angry person. For a few weeks she battles with the symptoms until, slowly, thankfully, normal function returns – almost. With one of these relapses, Anne loses the ability to write. As a practising scientist, this is very serious: writing is bread and butter for her. It is frightening and difficult in everyday life too... but she recovers.

We go on for years, through the eighties and nineties, more or less ignoring Anne's illness, though she has constant reminders: visits to physiotherapists, hospitals and research units. Anne also continues to work at her job in cancer research – a little ironic, working to help find a treatment for a serious illness while dealing with a worse one herself. This is a difficult value judgement to make, but in terms of treatment, cure and prognosis, MS is one of the worst. Cancer may be frightening, the treatment worrying and severe, but MS has no cure and in those days, no real treatment. Its effects eventually tear away at the very things that make life worth living.

Anne's MS comes to affect normal freedoms for both of us; she works for many years in cancer research and we bring up two children, but eventually, Anne has to give in and resort to walking with a stick. She struggles on, coping with the slow, debilitating progress of MS, in its relentless, imperceptible march. Imperceptible, except for the occasional relapses which shock us into action with walking aids, raised steps, ramps and weekly physiotherapy. I start to see all the restrictions, normally associated with old age, racing prematurely towards us. I get nervous – and a little selfish. Maybe I'll never get the chance to travel to some of the bird watching places that I had always cherished, places that I assumed I'd see "before I die". For the first time in my life, I see how Anne's MS might directly affect me. To Anne's eternal credit, she hadn't allowed it to impact much on anyone else. These thoughts make me reflect and worry. I remember the bike dream and the Provençal road and I become increasingly aware and covetous of all the fabulous birds that I haven't yet seen. I can feel these two things slipping away from me. A sense of urgency takes firm root and I realise I need to act before Anne's condition worsens to the point where I can no longer leave her for any length of time. Selfishly, I don't think of her own freedoms and that she might, with far more reason, be feeling the same way.

*

The ride across Bulgaria was a slog. Dimiter had booked me a room in Topolovgrad, nearly 200 miles and four hours away and I was making a late start from Borino after the Wallcreepers. There is only one (incomplete) motorway in Bulgaria, the A1 running east-west from Sofia to Burgas on the Black Sea, where I'd be heading later to meet Dimo at the Poda Nature Reserve. Tim elected not to use the A1 and this time I trusted his instincts on the basis that his route was 30 miles shorter (but supposedly 20 minutes longer!).

All I remember of this road to the Sakar Mountains were endless bends, quite busy traffic and more of the lethal cracks, dents and fissures in the surface. In retrospect, had I felt fresher, it would have been another wonderful biking route with open stretches through lush woods mixed with tight bends and sweeping curves. The Trigrad end, in particular, brought me down, down and down from the Rhodopes mountains into the valley basin of the River Maritza, reminding me of a gentler version of the Pyrenean decent into France. I was just a bit too Wallcreepered-out to appreciate it at the time.

At one particularly welcome coffee in an idyllic forest services/restaurant somewhere near Asenovgrad, I started thinking about the Transfagarasan, that awesome dribble of tarmac across the mountains in central Romania, and the Mecca for all bikers (and drivers) who want the ultimate ride. From where I was, near Asenovgrad, Romania wasn't that far. Maybe it was the relentless road I was on now, after days of mountain biking here in Bulgaria, but I started having doubts that I'd ever make it to the Transfagarasan – or if I even wanted to.

The coffee was cheap, but good, so I had another one while I checked maps for my progress. I would arrive in the dark (again!), but at least this time, a room would already be booked. I didn't pick up many birds on the way to Topolovgrad (still Wallcreepered-out, maybe?), but while bombing across one featureless, cultivated plain, I pulled over to check out a fat little bird sitting on top of a bush and got my first Spanish Sparrow. At a busy town called Harmanli, not too far from my destination, I also discovered a spot that seemed alive with avian activity: where a rattling old bridge crossed the Maritza river, there were lots of herons, woodpeckers and, sitting on a wire with other feathered blobs, a Roller. I'd seen different species of this chunky, colourful group of birds in Africa, but never a *European* Roller, here in its eponymous continent. This was, therefore, a Life, European and Trip Tick: definitely one from the Target List and a damn fine bird! Although I had turned the bike round in all the traffic and dust to see my first true European Roller, it was actually a poor view, more a silhouette in the fading light of early evening, as it perched enigmatically on a wire over the bridge. Thankfully, the silhouette was very distinctive: Jackdaw-sized with a thick neck and a heavy bill – difficult to miss.

As I rode off, into the dying light on the last leg to Topolovgrad, a text came in;

3rd May, 19.26. Hi Robert, my name is Dimitar, I'm your guide. I'll meet you at the Sakar hotel at 07.30 tomorrow morning. See you.

Arriving in the dark, with the hotel outside the main town, and with dense fog settling in, I didn't see much of Topolovgrad. The Hotel Sakar, however, was a real surprise: it was a collection of chalets deep in the woods, built very close to large trees all around. It felt more like camping. In the fog and the dark, it also felt a little eerie. All the buildings were timber, cabin-style structures, completely clad in wood inside and out, including the large reception, dining and function rooms ("modern rustic" I called it in my notes). Perhaps because well-known local Bulgarians had arranged things, I found it easier to communicate with the hotel staff, including the owner, Nina, who chatted for a while before going off with my food order. We talked about the hotel business here and the connection with birders. I told her about the Birdfair[35] and was very surprised that she didn't know about it, so many tourist businesses use it to advertise. She was very interested and I offered to spread the word about the hotel at the next Birdfair in August. They all seemed to know Mitko (an affectionate derivation from Dimitar, I assumed) whom I was meeting early the next morning for a day's guided birding.

Yet again, the local hotel seemed to be a meeting place: a small group of (friendly) men was gathered round a table chatting over a few bottled beers. They seemed to inhabit the reception area and were on very friendly terms with the staff and the owner. They could even have been family. It reminded me of the hotel in Borino where the foyer bar had been taken over by a group of locals. I was the only one eating and I sat at the end of a very long dining table, like a king. The food was sublime after the crap I'd been eating – or not eating – on the road. There was no menu that I could understand so Nina suggested a few things: to start, a beautiful fresh salad with sliced soft-boiled eggs

[35]Possibly the biggest bash in the birding world – see chapter 2

followed by a sort of stew or goulash with very tender pork in a tomato/onion based sauce (which I likened to Heinz Tomato Soup, but more fresh and clean tasting). Nina had also given me a whole carafe of a local Merlot, which was as nice as Melnik 13 (very, very nice!). I drank the lot and got very tipsy. Dimitar was coming at 7.30, breakfast had been arranged with Nina for 7.00, it was getting late and I was getting pissed… bed!

I was staying here for two whole nights – luxury! The bike, therefore, could be left behind while I went out with Mitko, I could have breakfast without making/stealing a packed lunch from it, and I was looking forward to being driven around with an expert to find the birds for a change.

Mitko arrived with the expected casual and friendly greeting to the staff at the hotel, but with an unexpected wife who was apparently coming with us (unusual). They were a couple in their late twenties. Mitko was a stocky, dark haired young bloke with a neatly groomed beard. He was dressed in light trousers and a T-shirt with an Imperial Eagle and the BSPB logo on it. His wife, Krassy, was an attractive, fair-haired young woman, also dressed casually in jeans and T-shirt. They were both really friendly and easy going. Mitko drove the BSPB 4-wheel drive Toyota Hilux, with me in front to see as much as possible. Krassy went in the back. It was joyous to sit and pay no attention to the road, either directions or surfaces. I could take in the surroundings, instead of concentrating on riding the bike. Sakar was an area of relatively low, wooded hills, but it was extensive and deeply undulating with occasional boulder outcrops, crags and small gorges, interspersed with bits of farmland and olive groves. We had chosen a good day: not hot, but bright and clear, the fog having lifted early in the morning.

"You like Bulgaria?" Krassy asked in good English, as we headed out from Topolovgrad.

"Very much. Melnik was lovely and I saw Wallcreepers at Trigrad. The mountains are beautiful, but the roads are a bit difficult on the bike."

I explained a little more about the potholes.

191

"Yes. The roads are not good," she said, "but we are used to it. There is no money for them, but it is also government corruption."

"Doesn't it ruin the suspension on people's cars?" I asked, "that can be expensive."

"Yes," said Mitko "That's why we all drive old cars!"

"Eagle!" shouted Krassy.

Through the car window, we looked where she was pointing. Flying low among a plantation of what looked like well-spaced olive trees was a big brown bird of prey. It was behaving more like a giant Sparrowhawk, dipping above and below the trees, but we got superb close views as it flew past the car. You don't often see the upper-wing of birds of prey since they tend to be flying, soaring or gliding high above, but this time we could see at close quarters the diagnostic white spot on top of each of those big brown wings: Lesser Spotted Eagle. Tick! As a result of this and several repeat performances, Krassy became known as "the wife with the good eyes".

As per usual, the guide saw most of the birds first and Mitko was no exception, especially where raptors were concerned (having a "wife with the good eyes" helped!). Every soaring eagle was spotted and pursued; he let nothing escape. This is the mark of a good bird guide. He knew why I was there and his default was to get the bird at all costs. A really good guide will exhaust you in their determination to find everything. Several times I've had guides keep at it until a bird is nailed (pardon the gruesome aphorism!) long after I had stopped caring. Mitko was the same – gold-dust! He showed me Imperial Eagle, Lesser Spotted Eagle and, my favourite, Long-legged Buzzard – all with accurate and educational commentary. I wasn't really sure what his targets were for the day, but he was clearly a local expert in addition to his research work with the Imperial Eagles.

One of the first places we drove to was a nest site for these impressive birds and, although distant, I got a good look at them on the nest through the telescope, their distinctive pale heads glistening in the sun. As we drove around the Sakar Hills, we picked up other Imperials in flight, showing the characteristic pale "epaulettes" on the leading edge of their wings. Mitko told me a little about his work on these birds:

"We are putting radio-tags on the eagles to work out their home range and maybe see where the young disperse to. I am doing my PhD at the moment, so it is hard work!"

"Should you be working on it right now? You have time to take me round? I hope Dimiter didn't twist your arm," I asked, feeling a little guilty that maybe he was too busy for all this and had been press-ganged into it.

"What is 'twist your arm'?" said Mitko

He looked at Krassy as much as at me. I let her explain in rapid-fire Bulgarian. He laughed and slapped my back.

"No, no – Dimiter does not twist my arms! Don't worry – I love this. I am so happy that people like you want to see Bulgarian wildlife. It is good publicity for us and it makes some money too for BSPB. And I am here with my wife with good eyes. What could be better?"

He flashed a smile at Krassy and all seemed well.

I have no exact locations for some of the sites we visited (they may well be secret), but somewhere near a town called Shtit (no, the first "t" is correct!), very close to the Turkish border, Mitko took us out into the middle of some farmland to the base of a low hill. It was covered in scrubby vegetation and small trees, possibly a mixture of olive and almonds for cultivation, but it looked completely undisturbed.

"The Mask-ed Shrike comes here in the beginning May," said Mitko, "We are too early, but it could be here now. The first I see is 8 or 10 May"

Masked Shrike! This was the only place on my entire trip that I would have any hope of seeing this Lifer. As I mentioned in Chapter 2, I love shrikes and Masked went on the Target List as soon as I discovered that it was a speciality here. They are fairly common around the eastern Mediterranean, on Greek Islands and the like, but here in Bulgaria, this is a rare speciality. We were less than half a mile from the Turkish border and not much more than ten miles from the border with Greece, so these shrikes were on the extreme northern edge of their range.

"This is a very small population here," said Mitko as we hiked up the hillside

"Only ten or twelve birds here. The only site we know in Bulgaria."

I asked him about a place I had tried near Melnik (on Gerard Gorman's advice)

"No. No birds near Kresna for years," he said, " this is the only place; maybe ten or twenty Mask-ed shrikes in all of Bulgaria. That is why we study them here."

At the top of the gentle rise, the ground opened out. There was the occasional old stone wall, but otherwise fairly open, rough grassland with small trees and shrubs beginning to close it all in. It looked a bit like an overgrown orchard. Covering the ground on foot was fairly easy and we slowly quartered the lush plateau. Birds flitted obligingly across the grassy swathes between the trees and bushes, perching on the many branches to keep an eye on us. They were everywhere: Hawfinch, Sardinian Warbler (not Orphean!), Syrian Woodpecker, Golden Oriole, Red-backed and Woodchat Shrike. Mitko wouldn't give up and we spent hours walking round. We picked up Black-headed and Ortolan Buntings along with more Woodchat Shrikes, each one setting the pulse racing in the hope of Masked – but we "dipped" (birding term for "failing to get the bird"): there were no Masked Shrikes to be seen.

"If they are here, he would find them," said Krassy with a conciliatory shrug, and I believed her.

Mitko was an expert on these birds[36], this was his study area, and if he couldn't find them, it meant they weren't here. I was just that bit too early. This was the name of the birding game: too late for Wallcreeper in Spain (they'd gone back to the high tops), but too early for the return of Masked Shrike in Bulgaria. On a long trip like this, place and date, was always a trade-off.

Once we decided to throw in the towel, the hours of shrike-hunting hit home in a wave of tiredness. Despite this, I was very

---

[36]Some time after I returned home, Mitko sent me a copy of a scientific paper he had written on a study of Masked Shrikes, carried out in that very piece of scrubby woodland.

reluctant to leave: as you walk away from the only place you could possibly see a species, you still feel that it could be there somewhere – just another try, maybe?

"If you could come back next week, they will be here," said Mitko.

For a millisecond, I contemplated staying around for a few days, or detouring back here before going north to Romania but, to make it worthwhile, I might have to wait at least a week in case the birds were delayed in their return. I put those thoughts behind me and tiredness took over once more. Krassy sealed the deal by mentioning the "C" word – coffee!

As we walked down to the car, Mitko told me about the border and a little about the "communist times", which several people had mentioned as if it was a recent, but very separate era, an era that was well behind them.

"That looks like the border, there – see?" he said, pointed to a line of concrete posts with a few rusty old wires draping between them and disappearing in the tangle of overgrown grasses. In the near distance, there was also an old look-out platform rising out of the bushes like a tree house.

"But the real border is a hundred metres further," he continued, "peoples are trying to escape the Communists and get into Greece or Turkey. They get there... "

He pointed again at the line of concrete posts.

"... they think they reach the border, but the alarms go off and the border guards shoot them when they run for freedom. They think they are safe in another country, but they are still in Bulgaria: this fence is a trick."

This tale filled me with sadness. I had, and still have, vivid pictures of desperate people (for some reason dressed in heavy army overcoats) reaching that fence of wire and concrete, climbing over in dreadful fear but, miraculously, getting through to the other side and to freedom, only to be mown down, shot in the back by rifles from the look-out post. What a cruel trick to play – and on your own citizens. What pointless oppression. With the benefit of hindsight and the distance of a few decades, it is easy to see the fallacy of a political system that made people want to leave that badly, but in those days, the grip of ruthless and corrupt communist regimes was iron tight. To be standing there, where I could see the very fence, the very field where this had happened, and to hear it from someone who knew, made it real in a way that no amount of book reading or news reports can. This is the value of travel in the broadest sense.

Mitko and Krassy took me away from this sad place into the village of Shtit to a square where there was a simple restaurant with tables outside and a large hall inside. The square itself was just a dusty flat expanse with no grass or planting of any kind. The elderly couple who owned the restaurant came out, full of greetings. Mitko clearly knew these people well and a meal was arranged in friendly style. Drinks appeared with lots of smiles and chat. The sadness of the border story melted away and I sat comfortably in the weariness of our unsuccessful shrike hunt, letting the impenetrable foreign babble wash over me. Krassy told me that the owners of the restaurant had known Mitko since he was a little boy and this was obvious in the way they addressed him. Krassy too seemed touched by how well her husband was received here. There were lots of smiles all round.

"They have been here for over 30 years," explained Krassy, as Mitko got involved in some friendly banter with his friends.

"Their son lives near here too. He breeds dogs in his kennels."

One of the men in the group spoke to Krassy to ask me about my trip and where I was heading. I gave her a brief summary, ending with my plan to go cn to Romania. Krassy listened to his reply, then translated for me.

"He says, don't go to Romania: they will steal your bike for sure."

Krassy gave up the translating and explaining when plates of food arrived. It was some sort of succulent, grilled chop with salad – beautiful and just right. I was too tired to carry on being polite with uncomprehending smiles and nods (which would have meant "no" in Bulgaria anyway!) so I used the act of eating as a social screen behind which I could relax. I did catch

Mitko's eye at one point and raised my beer bottle by way of appreciation for the whole event. He smiled back, saluting with his bottle in return.

The old man of the couple who ran the restaurant took us inside to the hall where he proudly, but with some mischief, pointed out a big photo of himself on an old tractor. It was a wonderful picture that told many stories: the tractor had Colorado number plates, he sat on it, looking like a rock star with hat, sunglasses and moustache, and next to him was a drug sniffer-dog from his son's breeding kennel. There was clearly a story to be told here, but I wasn't going to understand it.

Mitko refused any money for the meal, saying I was their guest – a heart-warming and very welcoming gesture. Revived, we got in the car and made our way back to Topolovgrad via another couple of well-chosen birding sites. One of these, a more open grassy plain, had an information board showing the species to be seen in this conservation area – which included Isabelline Wheatear, a locally rare breeding bird and another that I wasn't going to see anywhere else. These birds apparently live in the burrows of Susliks (Ground Squirrels) where they use the fur from the squirrels as nesting material. Although hard to believe, I was told that the wheatears cheekily plucked the fur from the squirrels (as opposed to finding bits of it moulted or shed in the burrows?).

At Harmanli, we stopped to investigate a plantation of poplars lining the riverbank, not far from the bridge where I had seen the Roller the previous evening. Mitko was hoping for Levant Sparrowhawk, yet another species restricted to the extreme east and south of Europe, it was a rare and difficult bird to find, but my guide knew this was a nesting site. Suddenly, Mitko whirled round pointing and hissing:

"There, there!"

A shape darted from halfway up one of the poplars, over our heads and out of sight. In the few seconds that I saw it, thankfully, I got a decent view. But it was quick! It was basically a Sparrowhawk with pointed black wing tips: Levant Sparrowhawk (Tick!). Such birds are well adapted for life among dense trees and they can fly very quickly through woods like these. There would be no hope of catching up with it. Knowing this, Mitko suggested we continue back to Topolovgrad via a site for Long-legged Buzzard. Now, this is not a species I had picked up on for the Target List and at that point, philistine that I was, I thought it would be just another buzzard-shaped raptor to tick off. My enthusiasm for it was not strong. I had reached the point where the guide (or the guide's sense of responsibility) was keener than me, and a good thing too.

Mitko took us along a narrow rocky valley with large rounded boulders erupting from the ground to form mini-cliffs, and we waited. Krassy, "the wife with the good eyes", spotted it first: a Long-legged Buzzard, and one of the most distinctive birds of prey I have ever seen, not because it stood out in colour or shape, but in the way it flew. It carried itself on raised wings, forming a very deep V shape and it had a butterfly quality about its flight. When it landed on one of the huge boulder outcrops, I got it in the little Nikon telescope. Its long rufous "trouser-legs" and chest were obvious, as was its pale, dignified head; a very fine, distinctive bird. I was unexpectedly captivated by Long-legged Buzzard and more than happy to end the day on that note as we drove back into Topolovgrad and the Hotel Sakar.

Mitko and Krassy stayed around for a bit, forming part of the ever-present foyer clan, I settled up with Mitko for the guiding and I joined the BSPB through him. The farewells were heartfelt; a day like that didn't feel like an excursion on some package tour – far from it. A lot of personal energy, hope and enthusiasm went into it, on all sides. They wanted me to see the best of their country, specifically the birds, which in Mitko's case, was clearly his life, and I wanted to see it in equal measure. I'm sure he gained as much satisfaction from seeing my joy as I got from his (and Krassy's) efforts. When we finally said goodbye, there was genuine camaraderie. I invited them to stay with me in Britain if ever they came to the UK. I absolutely meant it – how nice it would be to see them again and maybe show them some British birds.

Before Mitko left, I asked him about Internet access in the town. He took me to a makeshift youth centre in Topolovgrad: basically, a room above a shop where someone had set up half a dozen old PCs for gaming and Internet use. I returned on the bike so that Mitko could get off home. The last blog entry had been in Italy at Alan and Colette's. It was now nine days on and there was a lot of updating to do (Slovenia, Croatia, Serbia and now most of Bulgaria). Had I not failed in Sofia with the Marco fiasco, it wouldn't have been so bad. Still, here I was in Topolovgrad with my little digital camera and as much time as I needed to catch up. I started writing:

"Finally, today, I am in a beautiful pre-booked forest hotel in Topolovgrad (East Bulgaria) and have had a day's guided birding around the area (Sakar Mountains). Lovely countryside and-for the birders, get this: Imperial Eagle, Long Legged Buzzard, Lesser Spotted Eagle, Levant Sparrowhawk, Hobby, Sparrowhawk and Isabelline Wheatear amongst Shrikes, Hoopoes, Golden Orioles and more (what a place!). Thanks to Mitko (Dimitar) and his wife, Krassy – with the good eyes! You took me right to the good birds with superb views of most – a great day, thank you. I will have to come back for Masked Shrike!

Right now, I'm sitting with the youth of Topolovgrad in an internet gaming club/café. (Finding internet access without your own lap/palmtop is quite difficult). It's very relaxed as they play their games, although they keep looking over to check out this strange old Scottish bloke in their midst!"

I posted a selection of photos from the previous week or so, including several of the Julian Alps, Thor in Ljubljana, and a few birds. By the magic of email, the Internet, and Smartphones, the chap who had taken photos of the Wallcreepers at Trigrad had already sent me copies which I could post on the blog. Such a thing would have been impossible just a few years before, let alone while on the road like this: truly amazing. I finished the blog, rode back to the hotel for a late meal and went straight to bed.

For the first time on the trip, my journey to the next stop was so short, I could easily do it in one go without stopping: only 60 miles from Topolovgrad to Burgas, a port right on the Black sea, and home of the Poda Nature Centre. I phoned Dimo, the reserve centre warden and my next guide. He gave me directions, but I got hopelessly lost on a dual carriageway, just a few hundred metres from the centre. Dimo came to get me in his beat up old VW Polo and I followed him to the centre.

He was a fairly short man in his thirties, I guessed, with a goatee beard and wearing a "Black Roses MC 10th Anniversary 2007" T-shirt with standard issue green khaki wardens trouser. He was a smiley chap, full of mirth and interest, and the first biker I had spent any time with. He told me that the Black Roses was a motorcycle club with an active Bulgarian "chapter". As I had found with some other bikers, he was surprisingly impressed by my bike, given that it was a fairly bog-standard, "naked" street machine (no cowls, fairings or sports add-ons). Perhaps it did look a bit mean with its black engine and wheels set off against metallic silver on the tank, mudguards and footrests.

I had arrived relatively early at around 10am. We still had the rest of the morning and afternoon to have a tour around the Burgas wetlands of which the Poda Nature Reserve is part. I parked the bike outside the centre: a modern single-storey block which I recognised from photos I'd seen. I recalled how exotic the place had seemed with its big sign in Cyrillic script and the large plaque with an Egyptian Vulture, the emblem of the BSPB. It had railings all round the roof, and part of the block was raised into a second storey with further railings. It was the done thing to go out on the roof with telescope and tripod and view the reserve from there, just as I'd seen in the online pictures. Now that I was here, on the Black Sea coast, I couldn't wait to get up there and fulfil that particular little ambition. But Dimo had other ideas.

"We must do the tour now. I have to go at 3," he said in a rush.

"Time for a cup of tea Dimo?" I asked him.

"Sure, ask Stefan, he will make one... Stefan!"

A fuzzy-haired hippy appeared in the doorway.

"This is Stefan. He is a student here for some experience. Can you make Robert some tea or coffee Stefan? Show him where he will sleep in the education room. I will be back soon."

Stefan and I shook hands and I followed him into the centre. It was a simple place, nothing flash like we have now in Britain with our RSPB flagship visitor centres like Minsmere in Suffolk, Titchwell in Norfolk or Rainham near London. This glorified hut was the Bulgarian equivalent and I loved it. It wasn't old like the converted Posavina house at Poljanski Polje in Croatia, but it was full of purpose, with maps and wildlife conservation posters everywhere. It was functional, modern and clean, but it already had an established feel to it. The odd visitor drifted in and there was an air of peaceful calm, especially with Stefan floating around in his floppy, home-weave jumper, baggy trousers and sandals with socks on (I thought only stuffy middle class Brits did that). Stefan was German and he was there for two months as part of his university course in some weird combination of Art and Conservation. His English was good and for the first time in ages, I could have a flowing conversation with someone. After just twenty minutes, however, Dimo returned full of urgency. He was a busy man, being head of the centre, and I could tell his time was at a premium. We sped off bumping along the rough track out of the centre in his old car.

"We all drive old cars here," he said, with a laugh, confirming Mitko's assertion. I still thought he punished the thing unnecessarily on the rutted tracks.

What followed was a whirlwind tour around the main birding spots in the Burgas wetlands. Dimo was no birder: he just took me to the spots (which he knew well) and politely let me search with binoculars and telescope. He had no optics of his own and he wasn't sure of all the bird species. In this area, however, that didn't matter so much because the birding mostly involved scanning across open areas and everything was relatively easy to see.

A pale beige blob some way away caught my eye.

"Is that a Ruddy Shelduck?" I enquired of Dimo.

"It could be, I think they are here sometimes". He was looking in the opposite direction.

Despite this lack of interest, he took me to some great places including Burgas Bay and Lake, some other-worldly salt pans near Lake Atanasovsko and up to a high point which looked out over Lake Mandrensko. On the bay there were distant pelicans as well as some close fly-overs of both Dalmatian and Great White Pelican. The salt pans had many wading birds, terns, herons and egrets (Caspian Tern and Glossy Ibis, being new Trip Birds) and on the hill above Burgas, I caught a glimpse of a Wildcat, its bushy black-ended tail disappearing into low heather-like scrub. The whole area was fabulous for birding, but my trip around with Dimo was a whistle-stop, so I know I didn't do it justice. Nevertheless, it gave me 17 new birds including 4 Lifers. The Trip List was now a slightly more respectable 160.

In a way, I was glad the birding was short and sweet because the ride to Topolovgrad, followed by a long day with Mitko and Krassy, had left me in need of a rest. The Poda Centre was a haven of peace. On our return, Dimo clocked off for the day at around 4pm and the place was left to Stefan, me and Tex the guard dog. Tex was a scary looking German Shepherd, tied up to a long chain, but he was as soft as warm Playdoh. I took a photo of him and put it on the blog with a load of photos of other dogs I'd come across on my travels; for some reason, I kept noticing dogs – or they approached me. Perhaps it was because I was on my own and, liking dogs, I tended to speak to them. Tex was a friendly chap and I felt sorry for him, being chained up so much of the time.

"Is he really necessary here?" I asked Stefan over a cup of coffee.

"Well, there are problems with vandals and drug addicts coming here from Burgas. It is a port with lots of people coming and going"

"But he's useless!" I said.

"He puts people off, I think," replied Stefan, " – especially kids, and maybe at night, with strangers, he might get aggressive or bark or something. We have a night guard anyway."

"A guard as well?"

"Yes, Thomas comes at about eight and stays overnight. He shares the nights with three others."

I was amazed at the need for all this, but Stefan assured me that bored, drunk or high people come here on the nearby dual carriageway because it's a quick and easy way out of town for a secluded, drug-addled party.

"It hasn't happened with me here, thank God," he said, "but I have heard noises and cars on the track. Maybe they see the lights and stay away, but if Thomas or I were not here, they would climb the fence and then poor Tex would have to defend it on his own."

We chatted for a while longer then I decided to try birding from the roof before it got dark. It was very quiet. Apart from the famous Cormorant colony, I saw few birds from the roof; a major disappointment because I had seen many images of this roof packed with birders and telescopes as if this was *the* spot. I'm sure I was just unlucky because it is supposedly a great place to see thousands of migrating storks and birds of prey moving along the "Via Pontica", the second largest bird migration flyway in Europe (after the one over Gibraltar). The Cormorant colony was famous for a rather dubious reason: they are the only pylon-nesting cormorants in the world! And there they were, sinister looking black shapes sitting on the arms of a line of electricity pylons which were planted in the shallow water of the lagoon that ran north from the visitor centre. In the near distance, across the choppy waters of the bay, the cranes of Burgas port dominated the skyline. It was a small, but busy commercial and industrial centre on the Bulgarian Black Sea Coast.

Food was a bit of an issue at the centre. Stefan had his own thing planned and was clearly not up to sharing in any way and he didn't want to go out anywhere to eat (I think his budget and his menu stretched to beans on toast, pasta or cuppa-soup). I walked up the road from the centre to a sort of transport café and was pleasantly surprised at the food. The owner looked like a member of the local Mafia or a film star (I couldn't decide which), but he was intensely keen that I should try Bulgarian food and wine. The food was simpler than at the Hotel Sakar, but it was a freshly cooked potato and meat hash with chilli and yoghurt, accompanied by another huge salad. The red wine (only a glass this time!) was not quite as impressive as the other Bulgarian wine I'd had, but considering I was in a glorified transport caf, it was very good. They didn't seem to understand the concept of dessert, so I bought a few bars of chocolate in their attached shop and ate some of it with a coffee. At peace with the world and reflecting on my whirlwind birding day, so different to the day with Mitko and Krassy, I sent a text to Dimiter:

5th May, 20.09:
Hi Dimiter. I am in Burgas. Had a good day with Dimo. Will meet you at 10 tomorrow in front of the Cathedral. Thanks and see you then."

He was to be my last guide in Bulgaria and the one who had organised all the others. He was head of the BSPB in this part of Bulgaria, and a popular guide with tour companies and individuals alike. So much so that he wasn't free to do any more than a morning to find Black Woodpecker for me. I have wanted to see one of these since the day I woke up to birding abroad. They are big, black, bad boys of the forest, especially the males who come with a full bright red cap and a dagger for a bill. As large as a crow and just as black, they are not easy to see by any means.

Stefan made another coffee and I gave him a bar of chocolate. We chatted for a while before I settled down on the hard tiled floor of the education room with my "self-inflating" mattress and sleeping bag. I wondered if I should ask for a mattress from one of the unused bunks in Stefan's room (or even to use the bunk instead of the floor), but since it hadn't been offered, I guessed there may be some etiquette to do with who can and who can't stay overnight in the centre. Maybe Stefan had paid for single occupancy of the room, but I would have happily offered to pay a hostel rate, had I known there were free beds.

In the morning, I met Thomas, the night guard, and we had breakfast together, Stefan pulling out a surprising repertoire of cereals (perhaps prompted by the chocolate). I gave Thomas a bar too and he responded by cleaning all the squished bugs off the headlamp of the bike. Chocolate seems to work wonders in this part of Bulgaria! Saying goodbye to Stefan, Thomas and Tex (Dimo hadn't reappeared), I took off towards Varna to meet Dimiter.

Not far out of Burgas, I couldn't connect what Tim wanted me to do with what the road signs were saying. I ended up going back and forth along a two-mile stretch of dual carriageway, which I only got off by "using the force" and gut instinct. Finally, I saw a slip road which had a sign saying "Varna". We were in business. The road between Burgas and Varna was great for biking, fairly flat, but a good surface with lots of sweeping bends. It took me past Nesebar and Sunny Beach, both now well-known beach resorts.

I remember little else of the route to meet Dimiter except that there were public holiday celebrations closing the roads in Varna and it seemed like a much nicer city than Sofia. I had few of the qualms of Sofia while I negotiated the closed roads to find the cathedral, but I still couldn't get my bike to the right spot. I phoned Dimiter and he was there, waiting. In the end, he walked to where I had stopped. He led me on foot back to his office while I followed him on the bike. It was slightly weird, riding at walking pace in the gutter of a strange city, weaving in and out of cars, trying not to get ahead of him. It was a test of my slow riding ability. He was keen for me not to leave the bike parked in the street, or even in the alley outside the BSPB offices. This wasn't the first time that I felt unnerved by a local person's assumption that the bike needed to be locked out of sight (I'd had the same at the Motel Yubim and in Melnik), but at least it would be safe. Perhaps they were aware of how disastrous it would be if the bike got nicked, but somehow, it unsettled me.

The bike took up the whole space of his office and looked more out of place than a beached whale, but there it stayed while we were out. Dimiter was a charming man about my own height and weight, perhaps in his mid-thirties. He had good English and a gentle manner which I took to immediately. As he led me to a BSPB minibus parked outside, we chatted about my trip and my time with Mitko and Dimo. We loaded our optics into the bus and headed out into the busy streets.

"Is it a public holiday today?" I asked

"Tomorrow. Sorry, I forgot to tell you. It is St George Day, May 6th. It is a big celebration here. There will be a parade in the town so they are getting ready. Lucky you did not come tomorrow!"

Varna is a small city so we were out into the wooded hillsides very quickly. Following main roads at first, Dimiter turned abruptly down a rough track, straight into a small wooded valley with tall mature trees. I thought we would have to drive for miles along this track, way into the forest for the elusive Black Woodpecker, but within minutes Dimiter pulled up into a clearing and got out.

"We will look here. There is a nest," he said.

He unpacked his camera and telescope and set it up right next to the bus. I did the same – and waited. Looking around, I could see a bungalow through the trees with a man in the back garden... doing some gardening... what else, right next to a Black Woodpecker nest?! Dimiter pointed through the fresh spring leaves of the trees to a trunk about twenty metres away

"Can you see the hole in the tree?"

I looked with binoculars and the naked eye until I could see the nest hole he was pointing out. I nodded (which meant "no" in Bulgarian)

"That is an active Black Woodpecker nest"

"Here? So close to people?" I queried, pointing to the garden nearby

"Yes, it is unusual, but a good one for us to monitor and show people. The birds may have chicks already. That man keeps an eye on them. He telephones us some informations sometimes."

A nest like this is often selected by conservationists as the one to use for education or guiding. The birds may be used to the presence of locals and less prone to disturbance; this was the one for showing to the likes of me. I was a little disappointed that it didn't take a hike through the deepest, darkest woods, but it was great to get here so quickly and good to know that our presence was unlikely to disturb the birds any more than the gardening Bulgarian just a few yards away. We waited. We watched the black hole in the tree trunk.

"There!" whispered Dimiter, "hear it?"

I heard nothing, then a loud "kree-kree-kree" sounded close by and a bird, like a big black crow, flew straight onto the tree trunk, right by the nest hole.

How I had missed the first call, I don't know: it was shrill and so close. A Black Woodpecker clung to the tree, watching warily, swivelling its head to listen and look. It jerked around the trunk in the vicinity of the nest hole for some time, showing off the red on the back of its cap: a female. The dagger of a bill almost glowed in the dappled light and her pale eye ring stood out like round spectacles. With the naked eye I could see the two long, rigid tail feathers that she pushed against the bark, allowing her to lean back like an abseiler; a stance that looked very cool half way up that tall tree. I got the telescope on her so I could see all these details closer than I could have hoped for. Dimiter took several photos, one of which he later sent to me and which now forms a front piece to the blog and is reproduced here:

While watching this charismatic bird, a Song Thrush appeared and a Green Woodpecker did its mocking "yaffle" laugh at us before flying through. The thrush was, surprisingly, a first for the trip. The Black Woodpecker hung around for ages, up and down the tree trunk and branches, around the other side, flying away and back again – such a great display and so different to the fleeting views of birds like the Levant Sparrowhawk at Harmanli. Dimiter let me relish this for some time and even he had a smile on his face.

"Do you see this often?" I asked him

"No. This is the first time this year. It is good for me too."

He was smiling, genuinely happy at being here. I got the impression that, like most of us, work ordinarily kept him chained to a desk and a computer. He was in no hurry to leave.

"Are your photos ok. Dimiter? Can you send me a copy?"

He showed me the images on the screen of his digital camera; at twenty metres, they were superb, frame-filling shots and a wonderful record of a wonderful bird. Tick!

I liked Dimiter and spent some time back at his office chatting about conservation in Bulgaria. You could tell that he lived in a country where an organisation like his was definitely not considered mainstream. There seemed to be a lot of enthusiasm, especially from the post-communist, younger generation, but unfortunately, they weren't in charge. A lot of development and so-called progress took no account of the effect on places like the one we had just visited. The BSPB had no clout here, unlike its counterparts in the UK. I willingly paid my fees for all the guiding that Dimiter had organised, joined the BSPB and bought a couple of T-shirts from his stock, as presents for home (one of them had a Wallcreeper emblazoned on it and was destined to become a nightie for Anne). Sadly, Dimiter wasn't free to have a coffee or lunch. I would have liked to do something to thank him for the woodpecker and spend some more time discussing Bulgarian conservation and his work with the BSPB.

"Sorry," he said, "I have to go to the airport very soon to pick up three birders who I am guiding next week. This why I could not guide you more."

"Where are they from?" I asked

"From UK – flying from Birmingham, I think. They are with me for a week, so we will be able to see most of eastern Bulgaria. I am taking them to the same hotel I have booked for you in Krapets, near Darankulak"

"Oh, will I see you there then?"

"Yes, I give you some informations, but I must be careful because they are paying for my guiding. These men have sent me their strict requirements: they want to see all the birds – Eine... Zwei... Drei!"

Dimiter made a repeated karate-chop gesture of one hand on the palm of the other to emphasise these last syllables. I got the very strong impression that in his gentle way, he didn't approve, but somehow it had been made clear that these guys were paying and wanted no nonsense. He seemed a little uncomfortable with the prospect.

"I will try to see you there and tell you what to look for," he said, "but now I must give you instructions for some good birds on the way to Darankulak. You will have time to stop – some good places."

I packed up, extracted the bike from his office and said a fond farewell to this lovely man with whom I had spent all too short a time. I sincerely hoped to meet him again in the next few days.

Though it had been just a morning, I seemed to have been off the bike for a long time. I got re-acquainted with Tim by way of setting a new destination; we were heading for Albena Resort right on the Black Sea. This area is a well established coastal strip of beach resorts, some of which have become popular and well known in the UK. I was a little wary of turning up at such a place on my bike, looking for birds, but it was literally on my way and no distance from Varna. Tim took me straight there – and right into a huge car park surrounded by manicured grounds. Dimiter had drawn me a map of the perimeter roads into the forest of mature conifers that lined the beach. I was looking for Semi-collared Flycatcher, an uncommon and difficult bird that Dimiter suggested would be hard to find elsewhere. As with most of the guiding I had experienced, he knew they would be here because this was a nesting site. I parked the bike at the bottom of a huge wooden observation tower that took you right up into the canopy – ostensibly a great place to see any bird life, and hopefully some Semi-collared Flies.

I still have the Post-it note that Dimiter gave me with a detailed map, down to the bush, of where to see these birds, but I saw almost nothing from the tower other than Blackbirds and Starlings, with which the place was crawling. From up there, I could see that the woodland had not only conifers, but a pleasant mix of deciduous trees. At this time of year, their leaves were the fresh pale green of Spring and they filtered the light to bathe the forest in a calm, verdant glow. The bike was parked restfully at the base of the sturdy tower and I could have stayed there for hours waiting for the flycatchers.

Abandoning the tower though, I returned to the bike and rode slowly on among the trees, stopping every now and then to check. Eventually, I got off and sauntered back along the track. A woodpecker that might have been a Middle-spotted flew in alarm then a sweet little call sounded from halfway up a tangled bush. I realised I had been hearing this for a while and dismissing it as the familiar "teacher, teacher" call of Great Tits. This time though, I heard the whole thing in isolation and coming from somewhere close. It was quieter and less "in your face" than Great Tit. Using the song as a homing device, I got the Red Spots on the singer... and sure enough, there sat a black and white bird the size of a fat sparrow, singing away. I could have watched it for a while, ticked it and left, but I knew better: why wasn't this a Pied or even a Collared Flycatcher? Why was it a *semi*-collared? "Who cares?" you may ask, but it would be a Lifer for me; I had to know for sure – this the nature of birding.

I got out the Collins Guide and checked thoroughly. The flycatcher page was a sea of black and white birds that all looked the same[37]. With the 'scope on this little male singing from within a bush of tangled branches, I looked keenly for the subtle markers: a white vicar's collar interrupted by a small bit of black behind his neck, and a little extra hook of white on his wing. Semi-collared Flycatcher it was – Tick! I even got some rubbish photos through the 'scope, but they do show those ID-clinching features and they went straight on the blog (not that anyone commented – bastards!). While I had the book open, I checked the European distribution of this little chap and was astonished to see that Bulgaria and possibly Greece are the only places – in the whole of Europe – where they breed. Double Tick! And thank you, Dimiter.

My Bulgarian work colleague, Mariana had told me about Cape Kaliakra, long before I set off on my trip. It was near where she was brought up and her wistful descriptions filled me with the allure of an exotic place. "Cape Kaliakra on the Black

[37]Try it; page 315 (in the first edition). There aren't many plates where all the illustrations look quite so similar. Any decent field guide will show the same with flycatchers.

Sea coast" sounded far-flung and adventurous. Gerard Gorman had a section on it, describing it as "quite remarkable" because of the variety of habitats leading to the cape and the consequent wide range of bird species. I was heading there, pressing ever North towards Romania.

The roads to Kaliakra were lined with bushes and smaller plants which were in a profusion of flowers. Purple and lilac of different shades brushed the verges and rose in banks on tall, thick bushes. Lower down, plants sprouted yellow and red at the roadside and one or two small trees were aflame with dark maroon. At Kaliakra itself, the cliff-top grassland was a sea of two foot high, saffron-yellow flower spikes from one cliff edge to the other[38]. I wished I had known my flowers, but it made little difference I suppose; the sight and perfume were beguiling. Some of the land around Kaliakra formed steppe habitat with open, sweeping grassland plains of an area known as the Dobrogea. I only really found out about this distinct geographic region after my return. That was poor homework, because I should have looked a bit harder in the wider area for birds like Red-footed Falcon, Saker Falcon, Rose Coloured Starling and Lesser Grey Shrike. As it was, I headed straight for the cape to look for one particular bird that was currently top of the Target List: Pied Wheatear. These little black and white gems aren't really European at all: more Iranian or Asian, they are right on the extreme western edge of their range. I couldn't see them anywhere else in the whole of Europe, east or west. They were true specialities of this tiny strip of Black Sea coast.

I rolled the bike up into the car park where the road stopped almost at the cliff edge of the cape itself. It reminded me of John O'Groats at home in Caithness: the end of nowhere, with nowhere to go and yet it attracted people for that very reason. The cape was a finger of land jutting out into the Black Sea, so narrow you would fall off if you overbalanced. I exaggerate slightly, but the cliffs were over 70 metres high with jagged rocks at the bottom and choppy waves nagging away at them. It

[38]Kaliakra in early May was a botanists dream. The carpet of yellow flower spikes was Yellow Ashphodel.

212

would be easy to get a bit too close and step over the edge. Most of the ground was covered in the tall yellow flower spikes that I had seen on the way in. It was like walking through a miniature yellow forest, and an arresting sight. There were a few stalls in the car park selling Bulgarian souvenirs and people milled about through and over the remains of a medieval fortress, the main attraction here. It was the St Georges Day holiday that Dimiter had reminded me of, so there were more visitors here than normal; families and couples enjoying a break on a sunny, but windy day at the cape. I was the only biker and the only person with binoculars. I made myself even more conspicuous when I got the telescope out.

I started by looking down on the rocks and out to sea, hoping for Yelkouan Shearwater, but I have to be honest, I wouldn't have known how to tell it from a Manx Shearwater, except you wouldn't get one of those here – it all gets a bit esoteric![39] Anyway, there was no sign of shearwaters of any description and I wasn't about to spend time on them. The only birds I could see down by the lapping water were Yellow-legged Gull and Shag (a special Mediterranean race though!).

As I focused on the rocks through the telescope, a little shape flitted across the field of view, all black and white with just the right jaunty motion of... a Wheatear! I tried to re-find it using binoculars, but it had flicked itself well out of view. I was on a path, so picked up the scope and walked on to try another vantage point. As I looked up to see where I was going, there on the path, mere yards in front of me was another familiar shape: this time a female Wheatear. I knew what she was from the moment I clapped eyes on her – Pied Wheatear. She sat right on the path, looking fluffed up and a little unwell. I got her in the scope where, in the sun, she looked more sleepy than ill. Perhaps she had just arrived, a tired migrant from East Africa. She was a lovely little thing, fairly plain earth-brown above, white underneath with the subtlest smudge of orange just below

[39]I'd only just heard that Yelkouan Shearwater had been upgraded from subspecies to species, having only recently been "split" from Mediterranean Shearwater, which itself was formerly a sub-species of Manx Shearwater. So that clears that up then!

the wing, and the distinctive black and white tail of a wheatear. Lovely though she was (and a fabulous Tick for The List), it was her boyfriend I really wanted to see.

I could have stood watching the little female for hours and I took a few decent photos through the 'scope, but eventually, I had to move on to find the tantalising male bird that I had glimpsed earlier. From the same path, just a little further on, he appeared, flicking and hopping around some lichen-covered rocks just over the edge of the cliff.

He was fantastic! A festival of black and white, he jumped around on his rock as if he owned it, flicking his tail to show chequered blocks of snowy white with a distinctive black "T" shape at the end. The white even showed through as a little spot when his wings were folded. I thought this was probably a characteristic of Pied Wheatear. His head was the real clincher though: a white crown and nape with a dirty grey smudge on his cap. He had a black throat and a white underside with smudges of orange on the breast. I spent ages watching him on his rock and managed to get passable photos using the digital camera up against the eyepiece of the telescope. I was so happy. I could have left Kaliakra satisfied with all that, but I had a further look around and picked up a nice Black-headed Bunting; a riot of yellow, black and rust compared to the wheatear. I also found Alpine Swift, Common Swift and a Corn Bunting on my return to the car park.

When I got back to the bike, I left myself a dictaphone message:

"I'm at Kaliakra. It's just beautiful really... a lovely, lovely place. Maybe I think that because I've just seen both male and female Pied Wheatear and taken – for me – amazing photos of both of them. They're around all the time, chattering away; maybe just one pair, but I suspect more. I'm going to take it very easy on the bike now on my way to Dimiter's hotel. I don't want to spoil such a successful day by having a stupid prang on the bike. And I'm gonna have a really nice meal when I get there because I've had nothing to eat all day: no breakfast, no lunch and I think I deserve it.

For now, I'm just savouring the moment here in the car park on Cape Kaliakra. What a day for target birds, and birds I've wanted to see all my life! Mustn't forget Black Woodpecker with Dimiter this morning and the Semi-collared Flies as well. I mustn't forget this; almost can't believe it. I will never do it again. Ah! There's the wheatear – he's just flown in front of me down a little ravine. What a send-off – Pied Wheatear – says it all. I'm gonna give him another 5 or ten minutes to get a nice crisp view. Great, great day. One of the best days bird watching of my life."

There was only one way to go from there: back the way I had come, retracing the route through those glorious wild flowers. As I sped along, now intent on getting to a place of rest, a Middle-spotted Woodpecker flew beside me dipping between the trees which lined the road; my last Kaliakra bird. What a place!

The Yanitsa Hotel, booked for me by Dimiter, was that place of rest. Even with Tim's expert help, it took me a while to find the turning for Krapets, a tiny little village, beyond which was the hotel, right on the beach. After the usual faffing around to park the bike, I went straight for the meal: an excellent concoction of kebabed pork in a tomato sauce, served for some reason in a ceramic Viking longboat (!), accompanied by a simple salad, and washed down with yet another satisfying, sleep-inducing, Bulgarian red. Too tired to stand almost, I staggered back to my room in the dark. What a wonderful day.

I went for a big breakfast ahead of my next bird quest, and Dimiter was there with his group of three British birders. They fitted the stereotype, convincingly dressed in scruffy green clothing and festooned with badges, binoculars and beards. I went straight up to Dimiter, full of smiling recognition, but immediately, I sensed a tension in the air. He was being very guarded. With total innocence, I asked if they had all been out already.

"Yes, yes," said Dimiter, politely with a smile and a hand-shake

"How did you get on?" I asked the Brits

"Oh, not bad, just good general bird watching," one of them said.

(I'm going to have him repeat that one – *"Good general bird watching"*. Hold on to that). After this, there was silence at their table.

Now here I need to explain a fault of mine: in a conversational vacuum, I am hopeless. Instead of reading the signs and shutting my mouth, awkward silences make me gabble (even more than I usually do!) to fill the space, so to speak. They say "nature abhors a vacuum" – well, so does Robert. I do, in fact, read the signs ok; it's my reaction that is somewhat out of control. To fill this particular conversational black hole, I pressed on with:

"I got Pied Wheatear yesterday at Kaliakra. Great place. And, Dimiter, I found the Semi-collareds at Albena, thanks. Any advice for this area? Did you get Paddyfields this morning?" Gabble, gabble... Dimiter made coughing, spluttering noises and the Brits said nothing. I felt foolish and the vacuum seeped back in. What the hell was going on here?

"I will come and see you after breakfast Robert" Dimiter almost whispered.

I need to explain something else: it is a rule – nay, a Law – of Birding that you pass on The Gen to fellow birders. It usually starts with a nonchalant, "Anything about?" or "Seen much?" The expectation is that a string of sightings, directions and advice will follow, possibly taking every opportunity to "grip off" the newcomer with desirable birds that he has just missed and won't see. I was, therefore, completely nonplussed at the sullen response from these guys. And they were Brits too... ? I turned on my heels to find a table.

The murmur of talk around their table told me they were from somewhere "up North", like Yorkshire or Lancashire (I know I have now insulted the populations of both counties). This was perhaps a piece of the puzzle: I had always found the Northern Birder to be a race apart, a subspecies just ripe for splitting into a separate group all of their own, a status which I think many believe they already have. Don't get me wrong, most of those that I've met have been far better birders than me. They have stamina, tenacity, and honour, and they rely on experience rather than guidebooks or hearsay. Hooray for them... but more than just a few seem to be a pain in the arse as well. I can call a spade a spade too. Northern? They don't know the meaning of the word!

Dimiter found me after they had finished their breakfast and he sat briefly at my table.

"Sorry, Robert. I have to be careful with them. They are listing – and paying me to guide them. They expect every bird, no mistakes. You remember?" he said, making the karate chop gesture that he had used before.

"It's ok Dimiter, I understand. You can't spend their time with me."

"I will give you some informations on paper." he said, " You must go to Darankulak and Shabla though. If you need more advice, you can SMS me and I will try to reply, but don't phone, I will be with them all day."

Dimiter repeated the karate chops with a wan smile and got up to leave. I wished him good luck and was left with an uncomfortable feeling of vindication tainted with disappointment at my fellow Brits. I was also very sad for Dimiter and spoke a note into the dictaphone:

"He seems pressurised, almost cowed by them, as if they had made it clear that he isn't to talk to anyone else while he's with them."

With some directions scribbled on a page from Dimiter, I left the panniers behind and travelled light on the bike north from Krapets, along the beach to a coastal wetland called Eagle Marsh, near the village of Darankulak. Immediately outside Krapets, the road degenerated into a sandy track and I was genuinely off-road with the bike for the first time since Aguilon in Spain (although the "road" from Melnik had been pretty rough!). Luckily, the surface was dry and fairly hard, but the track wiggled and bumped its way along the sand dunes, with the waters of the Black Sea just yards away. There were a few hairy moments with twists and turns and ups and downs. At some points, I had to stand on the footrests to ease the bike down into a hole then up the other side. After a mile or two, the track came to an end, very close to the sea on my right and a wood-fringed marsh to my left. I parked and locked the bike then set off on foot around the marsh.

I was, of course, looking for any new and exotic birds but, in particular, Paddyfield Warbler: another eastern waif from Asia. It was clinging on, stubbornly extending its range around the top of the Black Sea into Romania and south to here – but no further. As with Pied Wheatear, I wasn't going to see Paddyfield Warbler anywhere else[40].

I tried to cover all the bases while heading towards Eagle Marsh and found several tern species, Squacco Herons, Reed and Great Reed Warblers and even some Red-necked Terrapins, sunning themselves in the middle of a sodden pool. Ferruginous Duck on the more open water was an unexpected Trip Tick, along with a few waders and several warblers in the extensive reed beds where I hunted for Paddyfields near the end of my

[40]I discovered afterwards that Istria, only 70 miles north into Romania, has Paddyfields in their hundreds; many, many more than the few tens in Bulgaria. Nevertheless, they are still only found in a narrow strip along the Black Sea; rarity is a highly elastic concept! (and anyway, I didn't stop at Istria)

walk. I found one or two skulking and flitting low down in reed stems close to the path, but they weren't singing. I really struggled: why weren't they just Reed or Marsh Warblers? To be honest, I went back to the hotel unconvinced and unimpressed – bloody warblers! I'd check with Dimiter – if I could get past the wall of silence and disapproval from his paymasters.

Just as I decided to give up chasing these pesky little birds, I looked around for my sunglasses – they'd gone (this is not unusual for me, as all who know me will attest). They were bikers' shades that wrapped close around your head for wearing inside a helmet; a present form my daughter for the trip (sorry Claire). I re-traced a fair bit of my walk, but soon realised that, as oft in the past, it could take hours to find the exact spot where they fell, a spot no doubt where I had been totally absorbed with some bird or other. I gave up and headed back to the hotel.

Although the previous evening's meal had been cheap, I was down to a few Bulgarian Leffa and my last 50 Euros. The hotel didn't take credit cards – from me at least – and the banks were closed, even though it was a Friday (something to do with St George the day before?). I headed south into Shabla, the nearest town of any size, in the hope of finding a hole-in-the-wall for cash and maybe a replacement pair of shades. Shabla turned out to be a buzzing little place with wide streets, a sort of central concourse and a few open shops. It had the feel of a Wild West town. I parked the bike close to a pavement and dismounted as if I was in a Western, tethering my horse to the rail of a boardwalk. I got cash at an ATM and, since it had been a few hours since breakfast, I decided on a whisky in the saloon before moving on to the lakes near the town. After cash, coffee and a brioche filled with prune jam, I walked like a bandy-legged cowboy back to my steed, put on my Stetson and threw a leg over the saddle. The bike neighed eagerly, I lifted my feet onto the stirrups and we galloped off.

The road out of Shabla was dead straight and very reminiscent of the approach to Kaliakra. I decided not to rush this one, but check out all the surrounding fields and trees that lined the road. I stopped to take off gloves and helmet, get the

Red Spots out and slowly inch the bike along. I hooked the helmet over a wing mirror and threw the gloves in front of me so they were crooked between the instruments and the screen. I started birding and was doing quite well with Middle-spotted and Syrian Woodpecker and a few lark species, but then a little "life event" took over: as I got ready to move on, I reached forward for the gloves, but could only find one. It must have been shaken out of its "safe" little crook as I had bumped along. I walked up and down the lane, peering along the verge and into the grass wherever I thought I'd been. First the sunglasses, now the glove; I was doing well! It took ages to resign myself to not finding it. This was a minor disaster: you can't ride at any appreciable speed without decent gloves (unsafe if you crash, too cold in anything, but the hottest weather, and bugs, stones or rain will sting or damage your hands) and where was I going to get another biking glove around here? *(Cars 7; Bikes 5)*.

I had walked some way from the bike, almost back into Shabla, when a little white van approached from the distance, towing a trailer. It slowed as it reached me and I bent down to see the driver through the open side window. A big calloused hand holding a glove reached out across the passenger seat. The man reminded me of my grandfather: weather-beaten, no-nonsense, salt of the earth. He gabbled on in Bulgarian, gesturing back towards the town and thrusting the glove at me, smiling. I shook his hand and he grinned, nodding his head with an exasperated expression (which means "I don't know... you youngsters!" in Bulgarian). I was 53, but must have seemed like a foolish youth to him.

This was a "life event", not because I got a little scare then got my glove back, but because of the gesture he made in driving out to find me. It contrasted so much with the dire warnings I'd had in nearly every country about how people would steal my stuff, diddle me in shops or even nick my bike. He, to quote a cliché, "restored my faith in human nature". Not that it had been un-restored, just undermined a little. Having said that, I'm sure there were elements out there in everyday life, that would rip me off or worse if I presented them with the opportunity. But this was just the opposite. I got the impression somehow that they had found the glove back in town, had a big confab about it and decided to come and find me:

"There was a foreigner here on a bike, just a few minutes ago. He was asking for whisky – thought he was a cowboy or something. He dropped his glove just there. Dimitar, you'd better drive out and give it back to him."

"Why me? I don't like foreigners."

"Shame on you Dimitar, you're the only one with a car, and don't you realise he won't be able to ride very far without a glove: the bugs and stones and rain will damage his hand."

"Oh all right then, but if I can't find him, I'm coming straight back with it. He'll just have to come and get it himself."

Something like that.

Before moving on to the lakes, I left a self-flagellating dictaphone message to myself:

"Don't ever let anybody tell me that I'm an intelligent, sensible person. Even after losing my sunglasses, I became careless with my gloves and I lost one. I got into the habit of propping gloves and binoculars behind the bike screen, birding from the bike seat. What an idiot." I followed that with:

"I now officially hate warblers... they are the most boring little farts!"

After the faith-restoring glove incident, I carried on to the lakes area and spent much of the time trying to see and ID warblers; the place was crawling with them. Shabla lakes were similar to the area around Darankulak with reed beds and marsh, but there were more Willow and other low bushes where lots of boring little brown birds (LBJs!) were flitting and skulking around. One, in particular, was very active – but so boring in appearance, I almost fell asleep trying to identify it (it was a Marsh Warbler). Another had a nice white throat, but was otherwise... boring grey (Olivaceous Warbler). Then a fine Savi's Warbler saved the day by getting up high in a reed bed for all to see, clinging on for dear life and reeling its continuous metallic trill for an absolute age. I was hypnotised and even got a misty photo of it; another brown warbler, but this one had style! Shabla was actually fantastic, giving me another Semi-collared Flycatcher (I was now an expert) and a lot of "generally good bird watching".

Back at the hotel fairly early, I lounged around a bit, enjoying the peace and doing nothing. I borrowed the manager's laptop to transfer the huge number of now precious photos, both to free up some space on the camera and to preserve them in case of accident. Dimiter and his Northern Birders returned not long before dinner. They had the air of conquering invaders, heroes who had been out battling the locals – and come back victorious. Dimiter smiled and waved to me. The Northern Birders grunted.

Over dinner, we sat apart, but I had become a little angry and bolshie about my "right" to speak to Dimiter. Before my food arrived, I walked straight over to their table and engaged him in conversation about my day and his; I ignored the Northern Birders. They didn't like this at all.

"So Dimiter, come and have a word after dinner... I'm sitting just over there," and I pointed to my table.

I knew this could be uncomfortable for him, but I hoped he would get what I was doing and stand up to them a bit. Bless the man, he did. He held my gaze as if to say, "You're right, I won't be pushed around by these arseholes any more."

We were communicating telepathically! I patted his shoulder as I walked off; such a nice moment.

I decided that these "sullen birders" weren't that at all: they were just rude people. I watched how they dealt with Dimiter and the waiters and saw the generally oafish way they behaved. I left a dictaphone message over dinner as I looked over at them:

"For whatever reason, I don't like them. Maybe it's just a vibe and I'm getting it wrong but, despite our common ground, I feel more at one with Dimiter and I'd rather sit with the local people here. I wonder what Dimiter thinks of them? Compared to

people I meet on my travels, these Brits are uncommunicative,
stand-offish, insular... and rude. I am disappointed by them, and
a bit ashamed to be British.
When I raved about Pied Wheatear at Kaliakra, the more
amenable one of them said dismissively that he'd had 'lots of
Pieds' on the beach outside the hotel. I had a look and saw
none. I resent these "sullen birders" for taking the mystique out
of my Pied Wheatear. As birders, they of all people should
celebrate a place like this – that is surely why they've come here
after all."

I was really getting into my stride! It was quite a revealing
message to listen back to: sort of says a lot about my pre-
occupations and how I let things get under my skin.

After dinner, Dimiter came over and we had a sort of
farewell chat. I decided against slagging off the Northern
Birders with him. He said he had enjoyed his time with me.

"We have never had someone like you before: biker, birder,
adventurer!" he said.

He seemed genuinely taken with what I was doing.

"The others are good birders, but very demanding and it is
hard work. They want every bird and now I am tired." He
sounded very weary.

I didn't hold him back, but issued a very genuine invite to
come and stay with us in the UK. It was a mutually warm
farewell as we shook hands. I returned to my table, and
immediately left the final salvo of dictaphonic outrage at the
Brits:

"Turns out – from Dimiter – this is their first time in
Bulgaria!! So, even for them, the 'unflappable Northern
Birders', this must be cracking, lifetime stuff. 'Good general
birdwatching', my arse!"

I'd come across this repressive, distrusting attitude before
and decided to think of it no more.

Back in the quiet of the hotel room, I lay on the bed contentedly watching a Sandra Bullock film, thankfully subtitled in Bulgarian, so the soundtrack was in English. I often had the telly on in these hotel rooms – just for company/distraction, but in the end, the dubbed language and sometimes the unbelievable banality of the adverts, drove me nuts, so I could rarely watch anything properly. But Sandra was giving it her best and I zoned out for a while.

Just as I was musing about how suitable this room might be for Anne if I ever came back here with her (I liked the hotel and it was very cheap), the phone rang. It was Anne, as if she had sensed my thoughts. She wasn't happy. She was staying in a local respite centre to cover a ten-day spell when no one could be at home. The centre was run by the local authority and had two residential rooms within a self-contained flat. There was a kitchen, lounge, bedroom and accessible shower room with care and nursing staff to look after it all. It seemed like a Godsend that it even existed. For most of my time away (nearly two months), Anne stayed at home with one or both of our children looking after her, supported by carers, morning and evening. Staying in the home was a new and very unwelcome experience for her. She said she was in a lot of pain.

"I can't get any Paracetamol," she said

"Why not?" I asked

"There's no one here to give it to me. And I can't open the door to get out."

"Can't you call someone?"

"I can't keep doing that."

So the conversation went on and I had visions of those horror stories about "care" homes and uncaring or abusive staff. I felt powerless, but offered to call the home and see what was going on.

"No, don't do that." she said, "I'll get somebody, don't bother yourself. You've dumped me in here. I'll just have to get on with it."

"But Claire will be back tomorrow," I said. "to take you home for the whole day if you want, then at the end of the week you'll be back home with both of them and Hannah. It's not for long"

Hannah was one of the carers who had been coming in to get Anne up in the morning and to bed at night while I was away.

"Are you getting on ok?" Anne asked, with a tremble in her voice. It was a classic diversion: an attempt to stop herself letting out all the anger.

"I'm fine," I said, "I'm about to go into Romania and onto the floating hotel. Bulgaria and the birds have been fantastic. I've met some great guides."

The diversion failed.

"Well, I'm glad *you're* having a nice time then," she shouted, "I'll just fester away in this place!"

There followed a sadly predictable tirade of tears and foul-mouthed recrimination, which succeeded in making me feel guilty, impotent and angry all at the same time.

This was a pattern in my relationship with Anne and her MS, one which I had learned to live with, but could never ignore or shut out. I tried reasoning with her:

"Can't you call someone for Paracetamol? They must have painkillers there."

"I can't reach the button and they don't come anyway. Don't pretend you're concerned. I'm here and you're there. Have a nice time"

The phone went dead.

The sad thing was, by the very nature of my absence, I was the person least familiar with her situation. I had seen inside the home and met some of the staff, but not spent any time there. For all I knew, it could be the sort of place which looks fine on the surface, but is cold and neglectful in reality. I had no reason to believe that and yet, I felt I should listen to what she was saying; it would be awful if she was right about the atmosphere and lack of care. But I could do nothing from where I was, other than contact the kids. I did this by text, asking them to check how things were and to let me know.

Sandra was still at the wheel of a speeding bus when I got off the phone. I was stressed and exhausted with the emotion of it all so I let the film absorb me. There was no point sitting there all alone getting miserable. Sandra to the rescue – of a bus-load of terrified passengers... and me. By the explosive end of the film, I was sleepy enough to just flop into bed and pass out.

The bike needed a wash and some attention: the chain had to be adjusted and lubricated again after all those miles, the tyres had to be checked, and the windscreen was covered in bugs that had to be washed off. There were a host of minor things to look at, like oil and water levels, cables, brakes and various pipes. I am no bike mechanic – far from it – but there was very little out of place and this Honda seemed hugely reliable: it didn't hiccup once. With the bike dry, clean and well lubed, I packed up a little more attentively and it looked really good. I took a photo of the bike, settled up with the hotel and rode off, feeling as if I was making a new start.

With the bike running beautifully, it was a moment to glide away rather than power off through the tiny village. In any case, Dimiter had convinced me that I had not been watching Paddyfield Warblers at Darankulak; my disappointed description had him nodding his head (which means "no" in Bulgarian) and he put me right with more directions and his usual:

"You will see them. They are there."

I didn't like punishing my clean and shiny bike along the sand dune track once more, but I really wanted those pesky warblers. Retracing the last part of my walk, along the seaward side of Eagle Marsh, I concentrated on just the reedbed, looking for yet more Little Brown Jobs. I got more great views of White-winged Black Terns and some beautiful Squacco Herons flying in a small group, like white butterflies, reminiscent of miniature Barn Owls. Right next to the path, with the waves of the Black Sea splashing behind me, a little bundle of feathers jerked its way up a reed stem, uttered a couple of declaratory tweets and started singing for all it was worth; this I had not seen or heard before. With a raised punk-like crown, throat fluffed up from the effort of singing, a pale eyebrow and a black line through the eye, all the tell-tale signs were there: the dainty Paddyfield Warbler – and unmistakeable it was too. I definitely hadn't been watching this bird before. Several of them did the same trick: clamber up a reed stem, sputter out a couple of "peechews" then deliver a rich, staccato song full of turns and twists, scratches and trills, all mixed up in one exuberant shout at the world.

I sent Dimiter a text. I had missed him at breakfast (presumably he'd been dragged out of bed at 04.00 hours by the Sullen Birders and frog-marched around some reed bed, in search of more "good general bird watching"):

7th May, 11.10. Hi Dimiter. I am leaving now 4 Romania. Paddyfield excellent! Got photos. Thank u for everything. Gd luck to you, Neophron and BPSP. Come and see me in the UK. RD

Back on the main road, Tim was showing only ten miles to the Romanian border. Three things seemed to stand out as I rode this significant stretch of tarmac: flowers, football and Red-backed Shrikes. I stopped before the border to leave a final dictaphone message from Bulgaria:

"I've stopped just to record a couple of things that strike me: everything is in flower and it is glorious to ride through just now. The smell is heavy in the air. It's wonderful.

*I've also been struck lately by how often football has been
an international ice-breaker. So many people have recognised
the Scottish flag on the bike screen or just the 'GB' sticker, and
shouted or waved to me. Some have just come up shouting
'Manchester United' or 'Chelsea' then a conversation would
start about the bike or my travels – or theirs. Don't know why
this occurred to me, but I just wanted to make a note of it.
Lastly, there are Red-backed Shrikes everywhere. There seems
to be one in every third bush, including the one right next to me.
Maybe there is a little passage going on here at the moment,
they can't all be local breeding birds, surely"*

I can remember now the exact spot where I left that message,
a male Red-backed Shrike "chacking" his alarm call at me as I
spoke into the little recorder. Every plant seemed to be in flower
and the nascent perfume even drifted into the helmet. I have a
terrible sense of smell, but the air seemed laden with scent as I
rode along, and even more when I stopped.

Much though I hate football and the effect it has on the
average European male, it often provided an opening which was
a great help in striking up a conversation with everyday people.
I could no more discuss football than fly, but for some reason,
British football teams and players are known the world over (the
obsessive TV coverage, I suppose) and it seemed a universal
way to make a connection. I had to grudgingly admit that David
Beckham and his global fame did a lot for international
relations.

As for those shrikes... well, I'd seen a few by then, but this
was how it was supposed to be when I had imagined the trip
way back at the beginning: exotic, with exciting birds leaping
out of every bush. I was still on the Via Pontica migration
flyway and these shrikes were no doubt a late influx en-route to
breeding sites further north and west.

There didn't seem to be any more Bulgaria could possibly
provide and, having inched my way north since Trigrad and the
Wallcreepers, the border with Romania was now so close, it
drew me like a magnet. All clean and lubricated, the bike flew

smoothly on; I really was going to make it to the Floating Hotel on the Danube Delta.

Chapter 9 – The Delta

In the Ashfield café behind Southgate College in North London, I call in for my usual early morning cup of tea and toast before going in to work. I am now a college lecturer and it is the Spring of 1997.

The smiley East European waitress with short blonde hair held in place by a scarf bandanna bounces up with her pad.

"Tea with toast and marmalade!" she says.

"Yes, thanks. You know what I have now."

She scribbles and turns away, nodding and smiling still.

Large works of art have appeared all around the café; distinctive, arresting canvases in a quirky, foreign style. As I look at them, I realise that they appeared not long after this new waitress.

"Did you do these?" I ask her

She gasps and puts her hand to her mouth.

"You think I did these?"

"Well, they look Eastern European or something, they appeared not long after you, and you look more like an artist than a waitress"

She definitely struck me as having more going on in her life than waiting tables in this cosy, but naff little back street caf.

The waitress looks round furtively then sits down opposite me.

"I am so happy that you believe I have done these. It is nice that you see more than just a waitress."

"Oh, it didn't take much working out."

"But you are the only person. Maybe others see the work, but they don't think it is me or they don't say anything. I am so happy that my work connects to me for you"

"I've only just noticed them. How long have they been up?"

We chat for a bit about her painting and where she is from, but in no time she is being called to get back to work.

"*Wilma!*" *shouts her boss with a* "*move yourself*" *jerk of his thumb and a sweeping gesture to show how many customers are in.*

"*My name is Wilma,*" *she says unnecessarily.*

"*Robert,*" *I say, shaking hands with her.*

"*See you tomorrow – tea and toast with marmalade!*"

Over the next few weeks of morning chats in the café, for which she always gets in trouble, I get to know Wilma. She seems very taken with making a new friend in this large foreign city where she hopes to make her name and fortune. Wilma paints her wistful characters in oil and acrylic on large canvasses. She invites me to a private showing of her first London exhibition: a small space in Highgate. I recognise some of the paintings from the Ashfield caf, but others are new: fishermen with blue waterproofs and big yellow boots, drunken Turks around a table with wine glasses, and Sufi dancers from Istanbul done in four separate canvasses which come together to make a large whole. This is a world I know nothing about: artists, art lovers, art collectors, art critics and... arty types.

I offer to help Wilma clear up after her exhibition and it turns out she has nowhere safe to store her paintings. We take them home and they go under beds, in cupboards and one or two hang on the wall. This marks the beginning of a blossoming relationship with Wilma as a family friend; more exhibitions, one of which my daughter Claire fronts for Wilma, greeting the public with glasses of white wine in a Quaker hall in Central London. Wilma represents a stretching of my norms and boundaries beyond the confines of science and education. We get to know her two girls, her friends in London and Lithuania, and we help her to get established, to travel back home and sometimes just to live. In return, she brightens our lives; a happy woman with a child's mind, naïve and wise at the same time. I couldn't know then that my friendship with Wilma would come to determine an important part of my journey, many years later.

*

Having left behind the lakes and sand dunes of Darankulak, a small blue sign appeared in the distance as I somewhat absent-mindedly hummed along: "Romania 3km". I sped past the sign, but realised how significant this moment was. It sort of marked the beginning of a new phase, in a faraway place. Eastern Europe both behind and ahead, the only sensible way home now was to keep going. There was no shortcut and turning back was not an option.

Pulling on the brakes and changing down with my left foot, I came to a halt. The road was deserted, but I knew vehicles would soon appear since this was the main route to the border. Yet again, with familiar trepidation, I inched the bike round in a nervous U-turn, annoyingly having to put my foot down to steady the bike (I hate that – I never did get confident with it). I zipped back to the sign, another U-turn and I pulled up just short to take a photo. It was only a small blue sign on an unremarkable road…, but it said "Romania 3Km". Despite all the wonderful landscapes, birds and people, despite all those miles and experiences, this little sign somehow made it all real.

"Romania 3Km" – sweet! I sped on to the border, now fresh with the anticipation of new adventures.

The Danube Delta was a major goal for me; a bit of a bogey destination. There was always some doubt in my mind: would I make it this far, and on schedule? I had arranged to meet with Alina, representative of Ibis Tours in Tulcea, the main port on one branch of the Danube, just as it opens out into an enormous and fascinating delta. As before, I had used some contacts, guidebooks and Internet research to find the most appropriate local guides for "The Delta": Ibis Tours seemed to be it, in particular, a guy called Daniel Petrescu, whose photographs, I knew, appeared in all sorts of important birdy publications. Daniel turned out to be far more than just the most appropriate guide.

I sent a text to Alina and rode on:

7ᵗʰ May, 12.27
Dear Alina, I am in Sabla area of BG & will be riding my moto 2 Tulcea 2day. I should arrive about 4pm (mayb 5 or 6pm). Can you check there is somewhere 2 store my bike – it is quite big! C u soon, R

After a little while, Tim beeped silently on the screen to tell me a text had arrived. I pulled over.

7ᵗʰ May, 12.47
Dear Robert, call me when you will be close to Tulcea. We will make room for your bike, even if is big. I personally can not wait to see it, I adore bikes. Have a nice trip and see you soon. Alina"

Alina and I had been in touch by e-mail from the UK and a booking fee had been sent by international transfer. I was to arrive on the 8th May and join an existing tour group for four days on the Floating Hotel. The Floating Hotel! From the moment Alina mentioned it in her emails, I was hooked and as I read her descriptions, I could see this was the only way to experience The Delta and its birds.

From Mangalia, the first town after the Romanian border, I phoned her for directions. I pulled over into a dusty lay-by just before entering the town to make the call from astride the bike.

"Hello Robert!" came a female voice with the now familiar East European accent.

"You are here!" She sounded genuinely excited.

"I can't wait to see your bike. I love bikes".

Hearing her voice for the first time was strange – she was now a real person. It all seemed fairly straightforward; go to the Hotel Delta on the river itself and, just along the front, I would see the Ibis Tours boat (sorry, Floating Hotel).

"Is there somewhere to leave my bike?" I enquired, nervous that her text sounded a bit gung-ho.

"Is it very big?" she asked.

"It's quite big, Alina"

"It's ok, I have plenty of room for you." The sexual innuendo wasn't lost on me but, good though her English was, I assumed it passed her by.

In biker terms, my Honda 600 was a mid-size "big" bike. There are many larger, more powerful machines on the road and many much bigger for touring. Still, I knew my bike with all its gear took up a fair bit of room and weighed a ton. I was getting worried that they wouldn't have anywhere to keep it safe after all.

"You can leave it at our guest house in Tulcea while you are on the floating hotel. No problem". Relief!

After that exchange, riding the bike to meet Alina became a goal in itself. It was hard to feel immersed in the passing countryside. The miles slipped by; tough going across wind-swept plains and lakeside flats. I learned later that this plains area, to the south and west of Tulcea, is known as the Dobrogea, and it has its own unique topography, wildlife and environmental importance. In fact, the Dobrogea forms a strip about fifty miles wide between the Danube and the western coast of Black Sea stretching from north-west Bulgaria, into

Romania and up to Tulcea. Geographically and ecologically it ranges from the rugged Black Sea coast like that at Kaliakra to hilly areas in the north-west and from the open plains of the south to the Danube Delta in the north. The part I was in near Mangalia, was low and flat. There were endless fields of bright red poppies with low, sand coloured hills rising in the background. I found out later that I was a bit too early to see the poppies in full flower, but the blush they made in the fields as I rode along this sweeping expanse was eye-catching enough.

I saw few birds, but I wasn't really looking as I flew on towards Tulcea and that Floating Hotel. It still sounded mystical and romantic, but now much more real. My spirits flew. The bike swished along on a good road and I took the chance to open it up a bit: 80 mph on a straight stretch tested the road surface and suspension as well as my ability to hold the bike true in the buffeting wind. The Dobrogea was known for its winds. I slowed, thinking guiltily of the poor bike, but also of Romanian cops on the lookout for a daft foreigner to slap a fine on.

There was a noticeable improvement in the roads and roadsides on passing from Bulgaria to Romania (being on a bike and that much closer to verges and pavements, I noticed these things!). The tarmac was smoother and better kept and the pavements were... well... pavements: proper kerb-stones, even painted red and white to mark them out on the approach to towns.

Mangalia is a major port on the Black Sea where a number of intimidating naval ships were docked, presumably to patrol Romanian waters. The town looked more prosperous and well kept than most Bulgarian towns I'd passed through. Palm trees were planted in the middle of landscaped roundabouts and everything had a fresh, almost Mediterranean feel... except for the dockside, right on the Black Sea, where a few ominous-looking warships were berthed. Surprisingly, Romania has a reasonable navy, despite having one of the shortest coastlines of any of the Black Sea countries. Strategically, however, it is very important, the Danube Delta lying to the north and the Bosporus to the south. During times of war and political upheaval (mainly of the 20th century), Romania has and retains a strong naval tradition. To have a closer look, I rode the bike slowly past these hulking warships (relatively small Corvette class patrol boats, the frigates being moored in Constanta farther up the coast).

As per usual, however, I was just passing through; big towns still repelled me and all I wanted was for Tim to take me around or through the busy streets in short order. Nice though Mangalia seemed with its Mediterranean waterfront, Tulcea was still 150 miles north. The Delta beckoned. I leaned the bike smartly round a palm tree roundabout and, following Tim's video-game view of the way ahead, I twisted the throttle grip to speed out of Mangalia and its grey, dockside warships.

As the port receded behind me, the countryside opened out unexpectedly. I hadn't done my homework on this bit of Romania: these Dobrogea Steppes took me by surprise. It was a unique-looking, slightly barren landscape of sweeping brown grasslands, framed by gently rolling hills in the distance. I knew from years of birding that such unpromising places often have the most rewarding natural history (like the steppes of Aragon in Spain and its Dupont's Larks). Sadly, I had to – wanted to – do nothing more than roll through this area, concentrating more on riding safely in the gusting wind than on birding. The miles slipped by.

For some reason, dusk seemed to descend sooner than expected. I wondered if, at this time of year, darkness would still come a little earlier here than in Southern Europe; maybe I hadn't noticed the effect of riding ever further north. Whatever the reason, it made me feel a little behind schedule; I pressed on across the plains hoping soon to swing towards the sea again so that I would arrive in Tulcea in daylight.

The sweeping, sand coloured plains of the Dobrogea rolled by, pale and empty. I was in a biking meditation, birding far from my mind, when a dark zipping shadow flew towards and over the bike, disappearing behind me. If it had been a soaring raptor, I might have pulled up to get binoculars on it but, keen to keep up speed in this failing light, I let it go. I had a good idea what this bird was, but I didn't know if it would be expected here. Nothing else could have the rakish silhouette of a giant swallow whisking over my head: it had to be a Collared Pratincole, a stunning bird, which I had only ever seen once before, many years before on Majorca. It's deeply forked tail was as clear as day, but I saw no colour or any other marking and I had no idea if these birds were resident here or even just passing through: another one to look up later. It spiced things up a bit though and spurred me on to Tulcea.

As I approached the town, I needed to stop for further directions from Alina. They didn't help. I had to stop again just across a huge set of traffic lights on a major route into the town. I had no idea if I was approaching from the right place to pick up Alina's landmarks. A local biker pulled up and gave me the thumbs up by way of query. You can tell a local by the state of their bikes, how they dress and how they ride. This guy had added all sorts to his orange painted Yamaha in a fairly random fashion: the original yellow turn signal lights had been replaced with trendy clear ones and a new exhaust had been fitted to give the bike a better sound. It looked "custom" in only the most amateur of senses, but it sounded great and obviously worked better than just ok. He knew where I wanted to get to and, instead of issuing further directions, he motioned for me to follow him. He took me right there, through all the city traffic, eventually signalling right and pointing me straight on where I could see the river-front and the Hotel Delta. The biker (whose face I never saw), turned off with a wave.

I hesitantly rode into the car park of the hotel and stopped next to some tour buses. The hotel porters gave me suspicious looks as I wearily pulled off my helmet, but I didn't care... I'd made it!

Walking along the river-front to seek out the Ibis Tours vessel, I was glad to stretch my legs, though I still took the precaution of lugging the all-important tank bag with me. Here was another example of reality not matching one's mental picture; instead of a quaint riverside scene with a few pleasure boats, Tulcea's Danube was a bustling tourist spot, full of life and commerce. In the rapidly closing dusk, the town was lit up, lights from the buildings reflecting orange in the Danube waters. On a high spot like a tumulus above the town, just a few hundred yards from the river, a needle-shaped monument pointed into the sky and below that, a sign had been erected saying, obviously enough, "TULCEA" in huge illuminated letters set out in the style of the famous Hollywood sign. Fairly high above the town, it sort of worked as a confident proclamation. I stopped for a moment to look the other way across the river and there, the Danube itself held sway, steady, timeless and as wide as the Thames. It was dark and still, but flowing strongly, as a hotchpotch of boats moved up and down its length. There were many moored vessels: pleasure boats, rugged-looking cargo barges, the ubiquitous grey naval gunships like those I saw at Mangalia and all kinds of other craft for all kinds of other purposes. Where the Floating Hotel was among this lot, God only knew! I was a bit stumped and resorted quickly to the phone again.

"Hi Alina, I'm here, but I can't find you."

She told me how to get to the boat and I chose to leave the bike in the Hotel Delta car park and walk. Mistake! With my tired legs and carrying the tank bag, it felt like miles. Even when I was very close to where the vessel should be, I couldn't tell if it was the right place. I sat down and waited for Alina to arrive. In a few minutes, a car pulled up some way away and a young woman stepped out. Alina was just as I had imagined her: slim with very dark hair tied back, jeans, a blue satin blouse and a bag slung over her shoulder. She reminded me of my lovely friend Natalie from the college where I used to teach. I sauntered over, aware that I probably looked how I felt – bedraggled and in need of a wash – but she was full of genuine, welcoming charm. I think we both felt we'd already got to know each other, so the hug between us came naturally. That was a nice moment. After the weeks of riding alone, this little bit of female contact made me want to stop biking and sit down with her for a while. I really did not want to trudge back to the bike and ride it round the side streets of Tulcea to find the boats. Sodding bike!

After riding to the right spot, and after Alina had had a good look at the bike, she got a few blokes to carry some of my stuff onto the boat. I let them – such luxury to have a hand! Alina and I chatted for a while.

"You have come all this way alone?" she asked, "It must be a great adventure. I wish I could do something like this. Which country do you like best?"

I'd been asked this before and it's a tricky one. Each time I felt I was being invited to choose their country over the neighbours'. I also lost count of how often I was warned of the dangers I would meet if I ventured cross this or that border into another country. With Alina, I was diplomatic, but honest:

"Well, the roads in Romania are much better than in Bulgaria, but I haven't seen much of Romania yet. I liked Spain" (Spain was far enough from Romania not to offend!).

We talked about travel a little and I was struck by the irony of someone like Alina, working for a tour company and greeting visitors from all over the world, yet unable to find time, money or opportunity to travel herself. Most people I met in Eastern Europe seemed to be in the same position. If they went abroad at all, it was for work, not a holiday. I felt a little uncomfortable, but Alina seemed relaxed about it and not the least resentful or envious. I wished I could take her with me on the rest of my journey; I had a vivid mental picture of her riding pillion behind me, dark hair blowing in the wind from under her helmet.

Costica, Alina's boss and co-owner of Ibis tours, turned up in his car and led me the short distance back to the guest house where I coaxed the bike onto some hard standing. It was to remain there for the next four days while I messed about on the river, sadly without Alina or Costica, who were mostly shore-based organisers. I spent a few minutes unpacking and re-packing the bike panniers and bags, sorting what I would need on the boat from what I could leave behind. My helmet went in the rear top box (couldn't see that being much use out on a boat!), bike boots in one side pannier while comfy old trainers took their place on my feet. A remaining assortment of bits and pieces came with me in the tank bag, now doubling as a rucksack. I had to be absolutely sure not to forget anything for birding: binoculars, telescope, camera and dictaphone, for recording what I knew would be an epic few days in my birdwatching career. I became almost neurotic about leaving something crucial behind, but finally, I had to make sure all was locked up and ready to go. It was odd to be deserting Old Faithful for the first time and, stupid though it sounds, I felt I was abandoning the bike after it had taken me so far. I gave the fuel tank a secret stroke and whispered, "Thanks for getting me here, see you soon." Alina and Costica were waiting – and watching me with slightly puzzled looks.

Another short drive back to the Floating Hotel and I was finally on board. It was a surreal episode; just as I walked gingerly across the decks of adjacent barges, I was met by this upbeat group of senior citizens and a tall Romanian who was exchanging weird in-jokes with the group leader. It was like landing in the middle of some old school reunion. The banter between them was full of forced jollity and I really didn't know what to make of it. It was also a bit relentless, though done in good spirits. Then champagne appeared, toasts to renewed friendships were made, and it all began to make sense – sort of.

The group leader was Paul Hollinrake who, with his wife Louise, ran a natural history tour company based in Orkney – of all places. The tall Romanian turned out to be Daniel Petrescu himself. He was a surprise. Not the typical birding sort (perhaps diffident or shy, bearded and unfashionable), Daniel was a hip dude: good-looking, confident, and speaking several languages well enough to run his eco-tourism business – and dryly funny with it. Among the group, there was a certain amount (a lot) of sycophantic adulation where Daniel was concerned, but he was clearly a very talented, knowledgeable man. This was to be confirmed as the days passed and I liked him as soon as I got a chance to talk to him in person. Daniel's love of the Danube Delta is as touching as his understanding is deep.

Daniel was brought up in and on the Delta. He was raised in Letea, a tiny village way to the east of Tulcea, far up a water channel off the middle branch of the Danube and only accessible by boat. Later, we were to visit this, his home, and experience first hand what it was like to live here; all of Daniel's life seemed permeated by water, boating and navigation. It reminded me of the fen people in Graham Swift's Waterland – very damp! The group I was with, particularly Paul and Louise, were perennially impressed by Daniel's river skills. He certainly knew where to point the small boat in among the baffling myriad of channels, large and small. Our trips into the Delta lasted several hours at a time and not once did he falter or seem lost. Perhaps this is only to be expected but, for sure, he needed that confidence and ability to take groups like us out into that watery heaven for days on end. There was no doubt, Daniel was the best guide I could have stumbled on.

His father, Eugen had been a teacher locally and also a foremost authority on the birds and conservation of The Delta. Leading small groups to the area after the 1989 revolution, Eugen became the Danube Delta Conservation Officer for the Romanian Ornithological Society. According to the Ibis Tours website, Eugen Petrescu "... is probably the best bird-watcher in eastern Romania". It was clear where Daniel got his love, passion and knowledge of the Delta from and, when I learned this bit of personal history, I felt even more that I had struck gold with my guide.

Daniel's mother was also a teacher in the small school in Letea so he had a fairly academic background compared to most people in the village who largely lived off the land or, more accurately, off the reeds. Reed beds, as in the fens here in the UK, were and still are a major source of income. Reeds can be harvested in continuous, yearly rotations as a sustainable resource for fencing, roofing and other building uses. When you live in the largest reed bed in the world, it makes sense!

Now, Daniel co-owns Ibis Tours with Costica whom I had met on the riverside in Tulcea. They have two floating hotels, one or two smaller boats for navigating the smaller channels and a guest-house in the town. It seemed like a flourishing eco-tourism business.

After the champagne, more hearty banter and some small talk, I made my way inside the boat where we were to assemble and later, have a meal. The long central room of the Floating Hotel was occupied by an equally long, lavish dining table, the decks were carpeted or wood lined and I got to my cabin via a wood panelled spiral staircase. The whole thing was very well put together; it may not have been spacious or grand, but "Floating Hotel" was by no means a misnomer and it was easily the most luxurious accommodation I'd had on the trip so far, floating or not. I was to find out later from Daniel, the remarkable and poignant story of how these vessels got to this wonderful stage in their lives.

My cabin was private, comfortable, warm and cosy. When I first shut the door, finally on my own, a big childish grin came across my face. I fell onto the bed and, Bridget Jones-style, kicked my legs silently in the air. If there hadn't been others to hear, I'd have screamed and giggled my delight like a little kid. Jesus! – I'd made it: the Floating Hotel, Alina, Tulcea... the Danube Delta!

Once I'd recovered from my (largely restrained) fit of the giggles, I left a dictaphone message, urging myself to "savour the moment":

"It's so easy to drift, adventurously or otherwise, through experiences like these, but you must stop sometimes and remind yourself where you are, where you've come from and what you've done to get here. Savour this moment Robert – and make sure you remember these feelings; it's why you're doing this."

The group of people I was joining were almost the opposite of Daniel: nearly all were well-to-do, retired professional or business people: a surgeon, an actuary, an official for the National Audit Office. They were all from a certain section of English society, let's say upper middle class, and most were in their seventies or eighties. I too could almost have been their social or cultural opposite (every one of them carefully tipped soup bowls away from themselves in an impressive display of class unity – I sat on the class fence and refused to tip either way), but my birding adventure seemed to catch their imagination and they were full of polite, but genuine interest. They were, after all, very committed to this sort of eco-tourism and I can think of a lot less worthy ways of spending your retirement riches. To their credit, they were the sort of successful, self-made people who understood, even admired, what I was doing. I was very grateful for the way they accepted me into their group; I was a rough diamond, gate-crashing their genteel social set and they could easily have been stand-offish. They weren't though and, as in Spain, I thought I'd end up with some good friends or contacts once we all got back home. When I left this group, I gave them all my blog address, but not one of them got in touch or left a donation. Bastards!

Looking through Daniel's postcards for sale near the charming little bar on board the boat, there were stunning images of pelicans, herons, egrets and superb aerial shots of The Delta. I turned over a card and there, in frame-filling glory, was a Collared Pratincole – on the Danube Delta! I asked Daniel if we were likely to see any.

"Not here on The Delta," he said, ", but they breed on the Dobrogea. We might see them when we go there with the group".

"I'll be leaving you before then Daniel, but I think I had a Pratincole as I was riding along the E87, north of Constanta. Think that's likely?"

"Oh yes, if you're sure of what you saw?" he said, with a little suspicion.

"Pretty sure – like a great big fat swallow and I've seen them before in Majorca."

He shrugged his shoulders and swung his head from side to side as if weighing it up. His gesture just said, "could be". Birding types are like that, but it was all the confirmation I needed: Collared Pratincole! My ID from the brief fly-past on the bike as I rode up here had been correct. It wasn't even on my must-see list. I felt pleased with myself – the usual little rush you get from seeing a new bird, especially an unexpected one... and one which is so cool!

Meals on the boat were superb and started with dinner on arrival and breakfast on the first morning, impressively prepared by a cook in a tiny galley kitchen and served by a lovely waif of a waitress who looked after us, above and beyond the call. I wondered if secretly she thought of us as the pampered rich, tolerating rather than accepting us as temporary friends, but she, the cook, Daniel and the boatmen all made our lives on the Floating Hotel comfortable, easy and safe in the most reassuring way. Such luxury. I was loving it after my solo, self-reliant progress this far.

On that first evening, apart from welcomes, drinks from the bar and introductions (especially of me and my trip, since I was an interloper), Daniel gave a short talk on The Delta, followed by an outline of how we would explore it using the Floating Hotel as a base and smaller boats to venture into the various creeks and channels.

"We will take the small boat up this channel here, off the middle branch of the Danube and explore these channels and two lakes."

He pointed out the route on a detailed habitat map of The Delta then reeled off a list of the birds we were likely to see, along with a little background on the ecology and structure of the waterways and reed beds.

"The largest reed bed in the world," he concluded at one point and the truly global importance of the place sunk in properly for the first time. Daniel exuded the confidence I'd seen many times in teachers and lecturers during my life in education, a quality I hoped I had managed to attain in my own teaching. Watching him, I thought back and remembered that I used to come across with that same authority and conviction, at least some of the time. After my trip, I sometimes thought of Daniel and that time as a sad reminder that I'd given it all up and may never again feel that vitality. Perhaps this was one of the many reasons for my journey – to do something vital again before my role as full-time carer became a permanent, daily reality.

Once we'd had the next day sketched out in such mouth-watering detail, it was time to retire. I made my way down the spiral staircase, a little weariness descending and, with some relief, sank into the cosy calm of my cabin. What a day – and what contrasts: earlier that morning I had been in Bulgaria, watching Paddyfield Warblers in sandy Darankulak, and Pied Wheatears at Cape Kaliakra, with its sea waves pounding rocky shores at the base of high cliffs. I had crossed the border and the Dobrogea plains into Tulcea, meeting Alina, Daniel and this group... and now, here I was in the luxury of my cabin on the Floating Hotel. I took a long-awaited shower and collapsed in that hazy, satisfying exhaustion of travel, left a dictaphone message, got the Pratincole into my notes and lay down to drift off, thinking about all that I'd done that day.

For eons, at least since the Black Sea retreated after the last ice age, the Danube river has been endlessly carrying billions of tons of silt, eroded from hills and valleys throughout Europe, and dumping them here as it empties into the Black Sea. The silt and mud have been continually settling to form what we now see as The Delta: a huge, rich aquatic wetland, extensive reedbeds and areas of unique forest and steppe. It is almost a definition of "biodiversity": species richness like nowhere else in Europe and almost unrivalled in the world. Unfortunately, The Delta is also ripe and irresistible for development as a transport network, for agriculture and even as a sewer for Industry.

The Danube itself is Europe's second longest river (after the Volga), rising in Germany's Black Forest and travelling nearly 3000 Km, through ten countries to the Black Sea. Many stretches of the river are national or international nature reserves, but none more than The Delta itself. Quite apart from the almost exhausting display of birds, which attract people like me, The Delta is an astoundingly important place in conservation terms. The statistics are a list of superlatives; firstly it is huge, occupying an area the size of Kent (3500 square Km), it is the 8th largest wetland in the world (out of only 300 defined by the Ramsar Convention[41]), it has the largest reed bed area in the world and over 300 important bird species, many of which are endangered or threatened internationally. It has around 90 fish species, including populations of sturgeon and it is one of the last refuges for wild European Mink, Wildcat, freshwater Otter and the globally threatened monk seal. It has a glowing list of "awards" in the form of international conservation designations: it is a UNESCO Biosphere Reserve, as well as a World Heritage and Ramsar site. It took me some time to get my head round all this, but those are the sort of reasons why it was so high on my list of destinations for a round-Europe-eco-tourism-bash.

To form The Delta as it is now, the Danube splits into three main channels. One, the Chilia Branch, flows north from just before Tulcea, forming a meandering, twisting border with Ukraine and the northern edge of The Delta Reserve within

---

[41]Ramsar in Iran where, in 1971, an international convention began the listing and protection of the most globally important wetlands.

Romania (around a fifth of The Delta lies in Ukraine, but the most important and more accessible areas are in Romania). The other main channel, the St Gheorge Branch, more or less forms the southern edge of The Delta and the third branch is a smaller, straightened channel, the Sulina Branch, flowing due east from Tulcea for 50km, right through the middle to the town of Sulina on the Black Sea. This middle channel and a tributary from it were to be our main sailing areas. The Floating Hotel was to take us up the larger channels, meeting us further along after our various excursions in smaller boats.

My attire for birding in The Delta had to be a compromise, but it made me feel very separate from the rest of the group. They had "all the gear" whereas I had to use my bike jacket as a waterproof and bike boots if I needed sturdy footwear. It didn't look or feel right, especially when set against the Rohan, North Face, Gore-tex garments that came out in preparation for our first trip on the small boat. I must have looked like a cross between biker yob, birder and total plonker with my bike stuff, dirty old trainers, small pink telescope and crappy digital camera. Many of this well-heeled lot had expensive SLR cameras and they incessantly talked photography with Daniel, who I knew was a wildlife photographer of some renown. Yep, I felt like the poor relation all right... but I knew my birds (at least compared to most of them).

With some very shaky transfers to the small boat (many were on the elderly/infirm side) and, with us all sitting on green plastic garden chairs on the matted deck, the small vessel steered away from the Mother Ship. It was to meet us some miles further up the Danube while we explored the smaller channels. Daniel stood right up front, delivering a dry, witty, sometimes sarcastic commentary about The Delta, its people and how it is being exploited and, of course... its birds. His knowledge and expertise unfolded as each bird appeared, usually seen (or heard) by him first. He could recognise and imitate calls instantly: Black Woodpecker, Thrush Nightingale, Little Bittern and more, were echoed back as they called or he would try to coax a response with his own version if he thought one of these birds might be hiding nearby. I know lots of birders in the UK who can do this, but it was astonishing to see it done for such – to me – exotic and rare species.

Daniel was withering about the local and national attitude towards the exploitation, development and conservation of The Delta. His stories were shot with accusations of stupidity and corruption: river straightening projects that were backed by European Union money, but with little proven benefit (though destined to do untold harm to the fragile ecosystem and its birds), local and not-so-local tourists who use the pristine waterways as a boating and picnicking playground with little regard for the real worth of the place. We saw a few of those. Daniel had christened them "Sausages" in a very amusing, if a little superior piece of jovial banter which, by its constant repetition (every time a Sausage appeared), raised hoots of laughter. We laughed a lot at that. They were called Sausages by the way, because of the habit of local Romanians to descend on the waterways, hop onto a bank, cook loads of sausages on a barbecue, eat, drink and go home... having looked at nothing. Each to his own, I suppose, but I could see Daniel's point: it showed a lamentable lack of regard for what is a precious national and global resource.

In total, I spent three full days and a morning meandering through parts of The Delta, led by Daniel and his assistants piloting the boats. Mostly we slowly plied our way up varying sizes of creeks, sometimes under overhanging tree branches: willow, alder, poplar and oak, which acted as perches or hideaways for a fabulous array of birds. I thought back to the sort of natural history programs I was used to watching on TV: the "standard" David Attenborough fare of arresting, astounding images, tales of nature and the effect we humans have on it. Normally, real life just isn't like those TV programs. After all, dear old Attenborough has an entourage of scientific and televisual experts, all making sure that his backdrops are superb. The whole thing is edited to look as if birds (or whatever) come leaping out of every bush right in front of him. Here on The Delta though, for the first time in my life, birds really were leaping out of every bush – and right in front of me! I stopped bringing the telescope because they were mostly so close (and because I couldn't use the 'scope on a moving boat anyway!).

Typically, we would be chugging up a tree-lined canal and Daniel, from his standing vantage point right on the bow of the boat would shout out every living thing he saw: "Whiskered Tern", "Squacco", "Roller". Everyone would whirl round to see the next bird with choruses of "where, where?" or "what did he say?" and the info would ripple all round the boat until everyone had seen the bird. Birders are nothing if not keen to make sure you see the bird. It's an unwritten rule: everyone has to see the bird. And see them we did – leaping out of every bush, right in front of us! If you're into watching birds and want new ones coming at you faster than you can keep up with, go to the Danube Delta.

There was a rich array of differing habitats, landscapes and vistas to see, hear and photograph: narrow, lilly-strewn creeks, wider channels bordered by willows with branches dipping their fingers into the water like lazy arms, and some large open expanses with trees around the edge, reflecting upside-down copies of themselves in photogenic splendour. At one point, Daniel jumped off the boat onto what I thought was a bank and proceeded to give one of his lectures about the uniqueness of this place; in this case, the very special "floating islands". I listened intently to this fascinating ecological tale. Apparently, large chunks of aquatic vegetation become free-floating, supported by methane and hydrogen sulphide gases produced by natural anaerobic decay within them. This forms a substrate for further plant colonisation by other marsh fen plants: grasses, sedges and even shrubs and small Grey Willow trees. These plant islands float their way around the complex of waterways, getting larger and larger, a process of decay and growth going on underneath which helps add nutrients and form a platform for further growth. As dead plant material adds to the whole each year, it grows until some of these floating islands are large enough to catch the wind and drift, blocking even the widest creeks.

Daniel, standing securely on the floating island, plunged a ten-foot long boat hook into the "ground" to show how thick this particular island had become – the boat hook went all the way in and the end was dripping wet when he withdrew it. Next to him grew a Grey Willow, unique to The Delta, and beside it, an introduced, alien shrub. He explained how this plant, the Indigo Bush, was out-competing the Willows, creating a conservation disaster within the whole area. Daniel made a point of over-enunciating the scientific name of this alien plant.

"A–morrr–pha fruteeee-co-sssa,"[42] he lilted at us. He was clearly immersed in the protection of this, his home, his love and his livelihood. So much to protect and seemingly all the cards stacked against it.

These floating islands became so large and permanent that some villagers in the heart of The Delta even made gardens on them, though mostly they were regarded as an inconvenient barrier to navigation – to the extent that sometimes boatmen had to push these lumbering beasts out into open water to prevent them continually blocking the navigable channels.

One morning (which I later called Heron Day), Daniel took us to a channel where he clearly knew that lots of herons and egrets roosted or hid during the day. The way these beautiful big birds appeared all around us became almost surreal. As our boat slid along, often silently slipping through the still water with engine off, we would come upon a Little Egret, then a Great White Egret, then a Purple Heron, then half a dozen smaller Squacco Herons, sitting like garden gnomes among the lower branches. These birds would wait until we drew alongside, then lazily take off to fly around or through the trees, landing behind us to continue whatever they were doing before our arrival. In flight, they all look like big butterflies, with a slow or fluttering, languid wing beat. They weren't little insignificant scraps of beak and feather, like many of the birds I was chasing; herons

[42]*Amorpha fruticosa* (Indigo Bush); an invasive ornamental shrub which competes with native plants, reducing effective and useful habitat for other species (especially nesting birds in the Danube Delta)

and egrets are pretty much in-your-face, tall, elegant, white or grey birds. Little Egrets are snowy white with bright yellow feet, Great White's are just that: very tall (over a metre) and pure white. Purple Herons are similar, though much darker, with black and beige stripes, giving a "purple" effect. So good to see them all at such close quarters (some superb photo opportunities, not obtainable in any other way) and to have a view of them fly and land, often in flocks of half a dozen. Then Glossy Ibis – a flock of ten or more, feeding with their probing, ridiculously curved bill, in the wet marshy banks or reeds. Unfortunately, there was no sun glistening off their backs to show the reason for their name: that iridescent and ever-changing green, bronze and black.

Daniel took us to an area with clouds of terns of different species: many, many Whiskered Terns with their diagnostic white cheek patch and their flitting, dipping flight onto the water surface; Black Terns and White-winged Black terns amongst them (the three being collectively known as "marsh" terns). It became a game to make sure everyone could pick out these different species and you knew that for many on the boat, these were lifers or at least new to them here. The List is very important on such trips and the marsh terns went on mine, no mistake.

The names of birds cause a lot of piss-taking mirth in my family. My son, for example, thinks I (or collectively "we" of the birding clan) simply make up bird names: anything called a Penduline Tit just can't exist. Every new and more ridiculous one he hears convinces him of this fact ("guess what bird my dad says he saw the other day..." guffaw!). I'm not about to defend the ridiculous names – they are funny, and stupid sometimes – but some are interesting, especially when you're watching something for the first time and can suddenly see just why it has its name. Take Whiskered Tern, with that diagnostic white patch on its cheek? It's like a side-burn, a whisker in fact. I had never thought of this before the tern day on the Danube Delta. It meant that, from that moment on, I would never forget or misidentify Whiskered Tern.

Then there was (European) Roller. Oh, what a bird! This trip was to be my chance to see one properly for the first time. Yes, yes, I know:

"What! – you've never seen a Roller? – call yourself a birder?!"

A bird like this is often known as a "tart's tick": an "easy" bird to see – but yet to be ticked. Here in The Delta, I saw not just one or two Rollers, but tens (maybe 50 in total). And I am sure this is exceptional. They were everywhere. At this time of year, like many of the birds I was seeing, Rollers were displaying to mates or to rivals as part of their breeding behaviour. First, they are gorgeous birds: green, blue and brown, not unlike a great big Kingfisher. Second, they perch high up, right on the tip of a dead tree for all to see (a little distant sometimes, but easy through binoculars). And last... they roll! In flight, often in pairs, they perform a twisting, tumbling display, which includes a roll onto their backs so that, for just a second, they are flying upside down. It was a privilege and a surprise to witness this, instead of just reading about it. I think that is what a trip like this is all about; you may well experience the planned or hoped-for, which is great, but it's the unexpected that stops you in your tracks and makes you savour the moment. I won't ever forget Rollers... rolling!

We chugged on over the four days in our little boat around endless, calm, yet exciting channels, Lake Nebunu, Fortuna and Bogdaproste with their marsh terns, Great White Pelican and the rare Dalmatian Pelican (Tick!), Pygmy Cormorants, two pairs of Red-footed Falcons (Tick!) and on one occasion a slow flypast by a bird which even surprised Daniel: Great Black Headed Gull (Mega-Tick!).

We spent an afternoon visiting Letea, Daniel's home village, and a glimpse of the old Delta way of life with horses and carts, and reeds cut all around in leaning bundles to be used for fences, roofs and even walls. The dirt streets with no pavements were a view of a past lifestyle; past, even for isolated Letea, for there were satellite dishes on many of the reed homes.

From Letea, Daniel had arranged a slightly odd tractor ride (the only way to get around) into a very different area of The Delta: the sand dune forest. The tractor pulled us in a trailer which must have had concrete for suspension, jolting and splashing through swamp and forest puddles, some of which were more like lakes. Dragonflies in their hundreds buzzed among the endless, sparsely leaved trees. I'd never seen so many. I expected to see lots of Hobbies: small falcons which specialise in catching dragonflies on the wing, but I didn't see even one. Maybe a forest like this was not good dragonfly-catching territory – and the dragonflies knew it?

Just as I was getting a little tired of bumping and bucking through this dull, dappled forest with its dragonfly-infested swamp, the tractor eventually pulled out into a more open area of grey-white sand, edged with conifer, oak, ash and white poplar. Again, this was an ancient and unique habitat, full of rare and endemic plants – a treasure trove for the botanists in the group.

Daniel talked of rare ash and oak species[43] and the process of succession which had formed this place: a sand dune system miles from the sea and all of 12 metres above sea level, the highest point in The Delta! Succession used to be one of my favourite bits of ecology teaching. It was grand to listen to someone else explain a fine and unusual example; how one plant species, over the years, changes the soil and shelter conditions for another to take over, the vegetation changing over the centuries, until trees, uniquely adapted to this particular environment, invade to form the final, climax vegetation. In this case, the climax was the sandy forest with its unique blend of tree species on the edge of the vast swamp that is the Danube Delta. Wonderful!

On our way back to the Mother Ship, we came across two blokes in a kayak, looking ever so small and vulnerable in this huge expanse, yet at one with the surroundings and blending so

[43]*Fraxinus pallisae* – species of ash almost unique to this place
Quercus pedunculiflora – oak species, similarly unique
Salix rosmariniflora – a type of willow and coloniser plant of the area

well at water level, with no engine to disturb. The one in front had a camera and tripod pointing forward while the other paddled. A great way, I thought to get superb photographs of what this place had to offer. We gave them a silent wave and drifted on, everyone quiet with tiredness from concentrating on new experiences and trying to take it all in. That was my last trip on the small boat before leaving for Tulcea.

It was good to be back at the Floating Hotel, now moored near a raised bank, along which we walked in the setting sun of a fine evening before my final dinner. The leisurely stroll produced Pied Flycatcher and a distant Sea Eagle. A Kingfisher had its nest hole mere feet away from the bow of the barge and a Muskrat[44] torpedoed around on the surface of the water on the other side. The Kingfisher took to perching on the boat's thick mooring rope, almost at touching distance, while egrets and Night Herons flew past at intervals. This was the magical setting for my last meal with the group: Mr & Mrs Horne from the USA, but still with English accents, Allan the dragonfly expert and his wife (who knew well the road in Harrow in which I had lived for 30 years!), Stephen the ex-surgeon with his iPod full of bird calls, which he played at key times to help us all get the sound or even to attract a bird (I liked Stephen the best) and Bob the auditor. They were very warm about my departure, but the thing I remember most from that evening was hearing Daniel tell how he had come about the two floating hotels.

"They were prison barges from the communist times" he said, "you can see many of them still lying along the river".

I had seen them: beached old hulks stuck along the banks of the larger canals. It was hard to believe that these would be salvageable, but I guessed Daniel had chosen two of the better ones.

"We bought a prison barge and had to strip it out completely. All the bars from the cells and windows were still there and when we pulled out the pipes, radiators and windows, we found

---

[44]Muskrat is an introduced species from N America, very like our Water Vole.

things the prisoners had hidden: money, sharpened forks and razor blades. There were four men to a small cabin".

He sucked his teeth, making a hissing noise.

"Terrible conditions – but that was the communist times; too many prisoners for the prisons. Ceaucescu locked so many up, those were bad days for Romania"

The time he was referring to was easily within living memory and I asked Daniel if he could recall any of it.

"I was only young, but my father remembers it all. Bad times for The Delta. All they wanted to do was use it, exploit it and ruin it. And they didn't care about the people".

This was one of many times in former Eastern Block countries where I heard "the communist times" referred to as a dark era of the very recent past. I couldn't really get my head round having all the symbols, buildings, signposts, statues and street names, such obvious remnants of those days, still in evidence (still lived in even) while at the same time, all had changed politically and people were doing what Daniel and Ibis tours were doing – getting on with building a new future. I felt that, were it me, I would have wanted to clear it all away, but of course, that would have been a waste of effort. These people had better things to do and that was fair enough.

"The boat looks really good though Daniel." I said. "How did you manage all this?"

"Oh, I did it with friends," he replied. "I bought an old bus and we cut the top off," he motioned a sweeping line along the length of the roof, " then fixed it onto the barge. That's where you're sitting now. We just made a new roof across the top and fitted it out inside. This one has been re-done much better since then. We have to upgrade the other one soon"

This shed light on how resourceful and self-sufficient Daniel had had to be to get this far with such a business. I doubted if I could have done all that, even with help. My admiration for this man grew as he spoke. All this (and the tour guiding) was spoken in English which was a little inaccurate, but very fluent and more than good enough to discuss these and other issues of the time. I felt my life had been pedestrian and safe by comparison and once again, I was glad to be stretching myself on this trip; at least it was something challenging and worthy of note.

"Daniel!" shouted Paul, the group leader from Orkney (although he spoke with a broad Yorkshire accent),

"Robert is heading towards Hungary next, but he wants to know of a place to stop. I suggested Gigi Popa's. What do you think?"

"Yes, yes, Robert you must go to Zarnesti and Gigi Popa's," Daniel agreed, "great mountain birds in the Eastern Carpathians and Transylvania. And Gigi Popa is the father of the mountains!"

Transylvania! This reminded me of the Transfagarasan, that magnetic and legendary road. I asked Daniel if it was anywhere near.

"Yes, not far," he replied, "you could detour there from Zarnesti if the weather is good. But it might still be closed. You will have to check"

This was sounding good, if a little optimistic in terms of getting on to Hungary and my next organised stop, with Roy Adams in Eger. But maybe I was going to the Transfagarasan after all?

Louise appeared and made an announcement.

"Before we go into dinner, I'd like to share something wonderful with you all, if you would come out onto the rear deck."

We followed and she faced her audience.

"Listen," she said, pointing vaguely behind her into the massive reed bed which stretched out beyond the raised bank where we had walked earlier. It was a lovely still evening, warm, but not hot. The sun was setting (having already given the photo buffs a chance at some stunning sunsets)... and we listened. Being a bit full of myself, I strained to hear a Bittern booming, thinking I knew what she was trying to alert us to, but I heard no such sound.

"Hear it?" she asked. I couldn't get what she was on about, and then the stillness revealed a hum in the background. Louise asked if anyone knew what it was

"The wind humming in electric cables?" I offered, again a little too sure of myself.

"Nope!" she said with the satisfaction of a magician who knows a secret, yet to be unveiled. I gave up and a few others had a go at guessing

"Not birds, surely?" suggested Steven

One, who shall remain nameless, came up with mating buffalo as a possible source for the sound. Louise realised at this point that her guessing game had gone a bit flat, but the intriguing hum was still there, now impossible to ignore.

"Fire-bellied Toads," she said "Thousands of them, all over the reed bed. They call synchronously and it makes that electric hum."

I couldn't believe it. I listened hard to link the all-pervading noise (which now sounded quite loud) to my mental image of a Fire-bellied Toad. We used to keep a few in the biology lab back in college some years before, so I knew what they looked like: small green and black chaps with a bright orange and spotted black underside. No way could that animal produce this unearthly hum that hung in the air above every reed and all of the reeds at the same time. It was truly magical and formed the abiding memory of my last evening on the Danube Delta: the electric hum of a million Fire-bellied Toads.

Chapter 10 – Alina, Elena, Laura

Wilma becomes a firm family friend. We are still involved with her exhibitions, trying in our own way to find outlets for her work, helping to transport her paintings and decorated porcelain to her shows, and storing them in between. We have "Wilma art" all over the house, in cupboards, wardrobes and under beds. She often comes round, bringing a cheerful and kind breath of air into the house.

We take Wilma on little trips to show her the countryside, villages and stately homes of the Home Counties. One memorable trip to Littlecote Manor near Hungerford sees Wilma rolling down the sloping lawns with our children, Iain and Claire, having huge fun, reminiscent of those famous early films of the Royals doing the same at Sandringham or Buckingham Palace.

Wilma takes Anne's arm as she walks very slowly and unsteadily with a stick around the grounds and dilapidated buildings of the walled garden at Littlecote. It is the time of the Victorian Kitchen Garden, a wonderful BBC series about the restoration and functioning of a walled garden: this garden, here at Littlecote. Sadly, after the filming, the garden seems to have been left to decline once more. I take a few photos. These are the days before digital cameras, and I give Wilma the prints of this magical day; photos of poignant memories... which will resurface over a decade later, far away in Lithuania.

Wilma travels back and forth to her home in Kaunas, to see her daughters and her mother, something she finds difficult, both financially and practically. I get used to driving her to airports and giving or loaning her money to make the journeys. On one trip, after returning home to her mother's funeral, she flies back to Glasgow rather than Luton (we find out later that this is a mistaken attempt to avoid immigration checks because she has been too long in the UK), and she is refused entry. We get a tearful phone call for help. Despite our best efforts to prove that we are her sponsors, Wilma is deported.

By the time she is allowed back into the UK Wilma has bad news: she has aggressive ovarian cancer and is hoping for treatment here in Britain while she continues with her art career. Her hopes are dashed; the NHS won't fund her treatment because her cancer is too advanced and the radiation required will be too much for her system to cope with. She is forced to go back to Lithuania for treatment yet again, but on her subsequent return to the UK she is clearly not well. Despite the radiation treatment given to her at home, her legs swell up like tree trunks and she can hardly move. She loses her hair and is in great pain. It turns out that the NHS doctors were right; her cancer had ravaged through her body and left her (or the treatment had left her) horribly bloated with oedema. She can hardly walk. The radiation has destroyed her lymph glands, the swelling is lymphoedema and there is nothing that can be done. Once more she returns home seeking treatment, but now she is extremely unwell and she knows she is facing death.

I drive her to Luton airport once more, carrying her bags because she can hardly walk with her legs so swollen, and she wears a headscarf to cover her scalp. I can only accompany her as far as security and, after a hug that can never be forgotten, I have to watch her go through customs in floods of frightened tears. She is very unlikely to come back to Britain – and we both know we might never meet again.

*

Leaving the Floating Hotel was a sad affair. I had to go back to Tulcea at the end of my fourth day rather than the next morning. I was tired from a full day out on the river and had, I guessed, at least three hours chugging back up the Danube to the town, Ibis Tours' guest house and Alina.

Daniel and the office staff had decided to swap me for a couple of Germans. They were brought out to the Floating Hotel on a small boat, which was about to turn tail with me on it. I said my farewells to the group and to Daniel and walked the gangplank between the vessels, joining a rough looking waterman who sat in a little skipper's cabin at the rear of the boat. The departure wasn't particularly heart-rending; I hadn't really got to know this group very well and that sense of not quite fitting in remained. The final meal with them had been pleasant enough with lots of chat about what I was going to be up to next, and awareness that I'd be leaving them. Paul had given a little speech saying how well I had blended in with the group, despite some reservations before-hand (news to me, but understandable). He had wished me well and they'd all drunk a toast to my adventure. I waved a little nostalgically to them all assembled on the deck of the Floating Hotel as the small boat put-putted away, but I was happy to sit alone on the small deck with my bags and optics, watching the Danube go by.

It was the 11th of May. We left at 2.30 pm from somewhere deep in the north of The Delta, meandering back via Lake Nebunu and many, many little channels. It took bloody hours, but the birding was great! I wondered if the pilot (who had no English) had been told to take it slow and follow a route for particular bird sites. It was odd, for example, that he slowed down right at a dead tree, with a rookery in it. Great, I thought, as I looked up at the birds jittering around their nests; hundreds of dark blobs populating the tree. Rook was, in fact, a Tick for The List, but there was something else going on here. Other, very dark birds were moving in and out rapidly. One flew from the tree, unmistakeable as a bird of prey and so dark, it could only be Red-footed Falcon. It had come from right in the heart of the rookery. Looking more carefully, I could see there were very few Rooks around; most of the birds were falcons. In theory, the Rooks should have gone, having raised their chicks some time before, but a few seemed to be still here, mixing it with the falcons[45].

Male Red-foots are very striking slate grey, almost black falcons with bright red feet. The hooked red bill seems to glow

---

[45]I am very confused about this; Red-footed Falcons use old Rooks' nests. Rooks breed between February and mid-April. The Falcons don't migrate back until late April/May, yet I saw both birds in the same tree, apparently living side by side. Maybe a seasonal changing of the guard?

like a jewel in a black face. Females have much more contrast with rich buff, almost orange, on the head and underparts, and a dark eye-mask. They nest in a large gregarious colony, often in old Rook nests as was the case here on The Delta. Birds of prey have an aura, a sort of presence that captivates. They always steal the show, but not many give a colonial display like this. The aura of ten or twenty Red-footed Falcons buzzed with energy as they flashed and twisted around the tree. I felt exceptionally lucky to experience this because Red-foot colonies are thin on the ground and disappearing at an alarming rate in Europe (where they are mainly confined to Romania, Hungary and a few in Bulgaria).

I had little else to do, but look out for birds, read, write notes and generally watch the river go by. I left a few dictaphone messages:

"Getting birds all over the place."
"Whiskered Terns everywhere"

I left other, interminable and sometimes inaudible messages, the chug of the engine playing havoc with the recording level of the dictaphone. The boatman had no English, but he gave me a beer (he downed quite a few on that long cruise) and we kept saluting each other with the bottles.

The birding was superb and helped to pass the time no end. A lazy and typically enormous White-tailed Eagle sat on a bunch of dead branches that poked out of the water, its hooked cleaver of a bill shining yellow in the sun, a Dalmatian Pelican boated by us, a pair of Little Bitterns (Tick) flashed cream and black into the reeds and a flock of Bee-eaters rocketed through like a group of bouncing, iridescent green-and-orange torpedoes. Those were just the highlights; The Delta was still putting on a show.

But, by 6.15 and no sign of Tulcea, I was getting bored and tired of the journey. We had left the small, entertaining channels and were moving along the big river. It had interest of its own, but few birds. I tried to maintain an observant eye, taking photos and writing notes, but after four hours on this little boat, I was getting a bit numb to my surroundings. Big barges plied their way past us, carrying cargoes of bundled reeds or logs which formed walls of circular cut ends rising high above the water. Other, more industrial vessels had cranes or winches sprouting from their decks and some had gun turrets instead of cranes; the sinister grey of military ships. A few other little boats like ours slipped between the larger hulks, or even arrowed past like little speedboats, leaving a wake behind. The impact of human activity now swamped the natural world I had been immersed in for the last four days; Daniel's words about the effect of exploitation on the river made total sense here. I felt uncomfortable to be back in such a tamed and disfigured habitat. Some of the boats were abandoned, rusting hulks (like those Daniel had salvaged, no doubt). They became more frequent the closer we got to Tulcea. It was a sad sight. I wanted to be back with my bike and gone – or asleep.

The little boat swung into the Ibis Tours berth at 7.30 pm. We had chugged 25 miles at walking pace and I was drained. Costica picked me up in a car, but I sleep-walked back to the guest house. Alina had gone home and the clean, fresh building was quiet. The bike, with Tim locked in the rear top-box, was still there as I'd left it. All I had to do was eat the simple meal they had prepared for me and go to bed.

You'd think I would sleep. But my tiredness was born of inactivity and some boredom. I couldn't nod off. I got out a book and read for a while. Then dogs started barking outside and they kept it up for ages. When they eventually stopped, I finally lay down, drowsy and ready to drift off.

"Eeeeeeeeeeee"

"Eeeee-yeee-yeeee-yeee"

The unmistakeable, thin whine of a mosquito!

I jumped up in a sleep-deprived rage and literally threw the book at it, along with pillows, towels and my bare hands. I even connected with it once or twice – but it would not go down.

"Eeeeeeeeeee... Eeeeeeeeee... Eeeeeeee"

I stalked round the room, having to locate it several times after it did its remarkable disappearing act. A pillow got it square on, but when I pulled the pillow back, it had gone again. The thing was indestructible! I hunted it for a while longer, but gave up and let it hunt and eat me.

"Eeeeeeee"

Oh, fuck off!

I did fall asleep for an hour or so before breakfast and woke up with no sign of bites from Indestructible Mozzie. Had I dreamt it all?

The cool restful dining room of Ibis Tours Guest House was calming. This was a fairly modern, but stylish, four storey building, marble-tiled with arches and shiny steps between the rooms and floors. It was the alternative accommodation for tour groups while not on the Floating Hotel. I sat alone at a table and Cerisella, Daniel's wife, served various small courses. Her English wasn't as good as his, but we chatted ok.

"Do you miss Daniel when he's away so much?" I asked.

"Yes, we married a few months only. But in not so long he will be back."

"Do you go out on the trips with him much?"

"I would like. Maybe in the future, but now I am here in the office and doing this"

She swept a gesture across my table and me with a smile.

"Good!" I said.

"It is good business. I am very lucky with Daniel. I have good job here too."

I could tell she was happy, but at the same time she seemed a little lonely. Maybe it was just the emptiness of the place with just me as a guest and no office staff in yet; Alina hadn't arrived.

Making a typing gesture, I told Cerisella about my blog.

"Is there a computer I could use?"

"I think, in the office. I ask Alina when she comes"

Cerisella wafted out.

"Robert!" a voice shrieked from around one of the arches. It was Alina.

"You are back. How was it?"

She sat at the table opposite me, looking radiant, her black hair shining and her dark, dark eyes wide with wonder. She was reluctant to start work. It all seemed very low key here.

"Alina, it is the best place I have ever been for birding."

"Lots of people say this. What was your favourite?"

This stumped me a little; I hadn't thought of it and I was a little distracted by the sudden appearance of this beautiful girl at my table. She made quite an impact after all that macho stuff out on the river.

"Maybe the Pelicans flying in formation... or all the Rollers... or the Red-footed Falcons. I don't know, there was so much."

"Sounds like you have a good time. And Daniel – he was good?"

"Yes, yes, the best I think."

"He is our best guide. You are lucky it was him. The others are good too, but Daniel was born out there."

Alina gestured dismissively into the distance. I got the impression that "out there" wasn't her cup of tea.

"Do you go out often?"

"No. I like to, but I like to do the work here more. I am a city girl!"

"But you like to travel?"

"Yes, if I can, but there is not much money – or time. I will travel one day. I love to come with you on your bike!"

She was smiling brightly at the idea.

"Have you got a helmet?" I asked more in jest than anything... although taking Alina on a little trip wasn't out of the question (yes it was!).

"Maybe I can get one... but I must stay here and work... it is just a dream."

She reached out and patted the back of my hand to express regret.

"That's a pity. If you come to the UK, you must tell me. You can visit us and stay – then I'll take you out on the bike."

"That would be great. Yes, I will. Thank you. I must go to the office now, Robert and let you finish your breakfast. Do you want anything else?"

Looking at her sitting opposite me, brightening my day with her smile, I wanted to whisk her away on the bike... but that was mere fantasy, brought on by how relaxed and natural all this seemed. In reality, I was in the middle of this crazy adventure and she was at work; a normal day for her… but I had missed such relaxed, female company, so thoughts of her jumping on the bike and riding off with me, didn't seem out of place.

"Are you all right Robert?" she asked, looking at me with some concern.

I had drifted into that daydream and must have looked a little vacant. The spell broke.

"Can I get you anything?"

"Another coffee would be good... and oh, Alina, is there a computer I could use to do my blog?"

"Yes, I think you can use Costica PC. He is not here this morning. I will turn it on for you. I will tell Cerisella for some coffee."

In the office, things were more normal: keyboards clacking, printers whirring and Alina busying herself on the phone. She had a colleague in the office who smiled when I came in and gestured to the desk where I could use the computer. While on the phone, Alina waved a greeting. I sat for an hour or more uploading photos, going right back to Topolovgrad to catch up. It took ages and, by the end, I felt that I might be overstaying my welcome in the busy little office. I also had to get going; the bike hadn't been re-packed and it had been immobile for several days. This was going to be a late start – even more than usual and I had a long one in front of me. I had decided to head for Zarnesti where Gigi Popa owned a guest house: the place recommended by Daniel and the group on the boat. Alina had phoned ahead for me to confirm that I was coming, but it was a good seven hours riding and at mid-day, I was still finishing the blog entry.

Out at the bike, I was a bit hesitant; in just those few days, I had lost the rhythm of packing up, checking and setting off. Everything had become a little dusty around the old bike, but all seemed in order. I checked the chain, pulling it up to check how much play there was. It still glistened with fresh lubricant and needed no adjustment. I had a look at all the fluid levels too: brake fluid reservoir on the right handlebar, water coolant in a small tank, almost invisible, tucked behind the engine under the seat, and oil, checked with a short dipstick in the engine crankcase. I fiddled with the various controls, brake and clutch levers until finally, I started up the engine. Amazingly (I'm always amazed that these things just keep going) it burst into life as if I'd only been gone a few hours. All seemed well. Eventually, wearing the bike gear, I loped back in to say goodbye to Alina but, having heard the bike, she had rushed out of the office to see me off from the front of the building.

"I wish I come with you on the bike. It looks fun. You are lucky."

"I wish you could too. Thanks for everything Alina and come to see me sometime."

She gave me a big hug. What a lovely girl. Some bloke was going to be very lucky with this one. I hugged her back. The whole thing retained an air of easy friendship; so nice – and genuinely innocent.

With Tim poised to lead me out of Tulcea and on across the Dobrogea once more, we took off, leaving The Delta, Ibis tours and Alina behind. We were now heading west for the first time since leaving home a month before; destination Zarnesti and the legendary Gigi Popa.

It took a while to swing away from the basin of the Danube and into the Dobrogea proper. Thanks to Daniel, I now knew a little more about this area than when I had passed through it from Bulgaria. As I rode towards Harsova I recalled those bare, undulating hillsides and flat steppe grasslands. There was more of the same here in the northern Dobrogea; the Tulcea Hills and Macin Mountains rose to the north as I wheeled on across the lower slopes of the Babadag and Niculitel Plateaux.

Tour groups, like those I had been with on the boats, spent time birding in these areas and the list of species is mouth-watering. It reminded me a little of the Sakar Mountains with Mitko and Krassy so I didn't feel too aggrieved at having to speed through; the journey to Zarnesti in the central highlands of Romania was set to take seven hours.

The flat valleys of the Dobrogea have lots of small villages: tiny communities where people get around as much with horse and cart as with the internal combustion engine. In one of these villages, I stopped to check progress and for a rest. This was one of the few times when I could feel the warmth of the air around me and I was getting tired in the heat. Someone was hammering a piece of corrugated tin, making it ring out in the background as an old Romany lady came walking by on the pavement (was there a pavement? – I can't remember!). She eyed me as she approached. I looked up, took my helmet off and leaned against the bike in the dusty street. Our eyes met briefly and she nodded a welcoming gesture as if to say "Good Morning". I nodded back and felt at ease here. She carried on by, dignified and full of poise as the corrugated tin rang out.

Along these and other roads, I noticed several large, imposing, factory-like buildings, usually right in the middle of a field or just on the edge of a village somewhere. I had seen these places elsewhere in Romania and in Bulgaria. With tall, windowless towers attached to lower accommodation buildings, they all looked like Dungeness power station. Some of them could have been storage silos; tall and semi-cylindrical. There was something characteristically ex-communist/Eastern Block about their imposing size and grey, austere presence. Some could even have been detention centres or prisons – or even just housing blocks.

The communist agenda, Nicolae Ceaucescu's in particular, seemed to have required these developments as part of an economic and social policy. I discovered that at least one of these monstrosities had been purpose-built in "the communist times" to provide local employment – making trainers, of all things. Ceaucescu must have seen a gap in the market: his government decided to build a factory, make trainers and employ a load of people – job done! I suppose when you cut yourself off from the rest of the world, your internal markets can be whatever you want them to be. I never did find out what use they were being put to now; making trainers, I suppose!

In contrast, further on, between the towns of Saraiu and Harsova, I rounded a corner and came across an idyllic little lake called Lacul Hazariac, right by the roadside. I was travelling slow enough to take the turn and still glance to my right. The arresting beauty of this lakeside scene made me slam on the brakes (not forgetting to check the mirrors behind, and do my life-saver glance over the shoulder first… as if!).

Close in, by the nearest bank, a pair of ducks floated serenely along the water's edge. I knew immediately what they were, even without binoculars.

"Fucking… Ruddy Shelduck!" I shouted into my helmet (technical terms meaning, "I have just come across a rare and beautiful bird called Ruddy Shelduck").

My appearance made the pair nervous and the large, pale orange ducks gradually steamed away from the edge of the lake. No chance of a photo, but I got good views with the old Red Spots. Looking more like small geese, they were unexpectedly eye-catching, their rich ochre hue almost glowing in the sun against the blue of the lake. This pale orange gave way to a white head and the male bird had a black choker low down his neck. They both had white flashes in the folded wing and black tops to their tails. Illustrations in the guidebooks do not do them justice; they don't seem particularly bright or showy, but in the flesh (or feather), they were one of the most striking birds of the trip.

As with many of the unusual species I encountered, Ruddy Shelduck are mainly North Asian breeding birds with fairly small, extreme western breeding populations in Turkey and around the Black Sea, including the Dobrogea of Bulgaria and Romania. They don't seem particularly endangered, but any small population is precarious in countries where development is rapid and conservation is not a particular priority.

I clicked the bike into gear, slowly released the clutch and swung my feet up as the bike pulled away. I could see the lake and the birds recede in the mirrors; such a shame not to watch them for longer, not to try for a photo. I slowed to a stop once again. This time, I spun a classic U-turn with little thought (I was chuffed!) and crept back hoping to find a vantage point to watch the ducks from, and maybe even get the scope out for a photo. The birds were having none of it. Being a pair, well into spring, they were probably defending territory or a nest or maybe even chicks. Whatever the reason, they were extremely wary and carried on slowly out to the centre of the small lake. I didn't want to disturb them any more so I gave up and headed off once more. It was a beautiful day; a perfect combination of sunshine, empty foreign roads and exciting, exotic birding.

Like those communist factories earlier, I noticed another, more recent phenomenon: the building of enormous, ostentatious looking villas or mansions in small, otherwise poor villages. A town called Tanderei seemed to have a whole row of them along the exit road. These grand statements were being constructed right alongside shacks and wasteland, gypsy homes and run down shops, or on their own in some roadside field near a town. It reeked of new wealth... or dodgy new wealth. I had brought my potted prejudices with me; probably ill informed or out of date notions about East European Mafia and the rush to capitalism. As I looked at the villas, I could sense the sharks (entrepreneurs or crooks?) creaming off the profits of privatisation, and building these incongruous monuments to their new status. Some of them even came with high walls or security fencing; they were building a miniature Beverley Hills, in the middle of Romania!

The rest was a slog to Zarnesti. I lost all appreciation of where I was and the places I passed through: Slobozia, Urziceni and Poloesti. All roads seemed to lead to Bucharest with signs around Uziceni telling me it was only 50 Km to the south. These ubiquitous road signs eventually showed the distance increasing: Bucharest 85Km. At last, I felt a sense of progress as I drew further from the capital and closer to the magnificent Carpathian Mountains of Transylvania, just coming into view in the distance.

Any sense of progress ground to a halt in a massive set of roadworks somewhere near Sinaia, a lovely winter resort town sandwiched between steep hills in a narrow valley. Although this was just the sort of place for an enjoyable coffee stop, I couldn't appreciate this town and its fairy tale Peles Castle. Instead, I joined huge queues in riverside villages where the traffic was hemmed in by road works on one side and the river on the other. The bike helped a lot as I filtered past teams of workmen and endless lines of vehicles queuing to get by the re-surfacing machinery (Romania was repairing roads for us!). I felt sorry for the drivers; at least I could pick my way past them all (*Cars 7; Bikes 6)*, feet out for balance and steadying the bike in case it started to go over. It was dangerous in places where traffic or workmen weren't expecting a big bike to approach from the queue – and it went on for miles.

Before and after these horrendous works, the road was a joy to ride; fast, well surfaced and increasingly exciting as it rocketed into the mountains through narrow valleys. Beyond Sinaia and Busteni, it got even better. Route 1 or E60 from Bucharest to Brasov was fabulous. It became more twisting, the villages and towns prettier, and the distant scenery more awe-inspiring. Tim counselled a turn onto a minor road for Rasnov and Zarnesti. I didn't argue with him, but I was tired now and hairpin mountain roads had lost their appeal. For any bikers reading; this route is wonderful. It's not the Transfagarasan, but terrific for biking, the E60 is fast and sweeping with a good surface, then this little track to Rasnov (the 73A before Predeal) rises through twists and turns before dropping in a mini-Transfagarasan on the approach to Rasnov. I just couldn't appreciate it quite that way at the time; I was too knackered!

It was practically dark as I approached Zarnesti, which, after seven hours riding, now seemed like the most out of the way place I could ever have chosen. On the way in, traffic had to stop at a rail crossing. When it came to my turn to move forward over the rails, I was shocked at the chasm of metal which confronted me. It was designed as a motorcycle obstacle course; several rails cutting deeply across the road at a sharp angle. The streets of Zarnesti were no better: unforgiving, coarse gravel instead of tarmac. Big chunks of stone juddered the front wheel and dislodged the rear in alarming little skids as I rode around, trying to find Pensione Elena and Gigi Popa.

Some youths playing street football tried to direct me, but I don't think they knew what I was asking for. As they watched me floundering and slewing around on the gravel, I could almost hear the overwhelming, unspoken consensus:

"What is that fool doing down here with that great big bike? Bloody foreigners."

I had to phone Gigi a few times to be directed in. Since I couldn't tell him exactly where I was, this proved difficult. Eventually, I rounded a gravel-crunching, bike-toppling corner to see the tall figure of Gigi Popa standing in a faint pool of light by an archway with a sign which said... "Pensione Elena". Thank God.

"That was as 'off-road' as I ever want to be," I concluded later to the dictaphone.

I had never been so glad to reach a destination: Zarnesti was no place to be lost in, on a bike, in the dark.

"Welcome Robert!" boomed Gigi, "you were lost?"

His tone expressed a little surprise that I'd had such trouble. We shook hands.

"It's a bit difficult to see where you are going and ride the bike on the stones."

I gestured to the ground where great chunks of rock lay, waiting to catch me out.

"Ah yes, we have never had a motorcycle come here, maybe that is difficult. Never mind you are here now, come in. Welcome. Welcome! Bring the moto[46] here."

Gigi was a tall, imposing figure of a man, getting on in age, maybe in his mid-sixties. Despite a bit of a paunch, he was sprightly and upright, obviously proud of his business and

---

[46]I should have mentioned before now; across the whole of continental Europe, "moto" is the equivalent of "bike". Sensible in a way – less confusing than in English where "bike" can mean "cycle"

master of his realm, in a gentle, reassuring way. He gestured the way through the arch and onto a smoothly cobbled yard outside the guest house. Thank God to be parking on a relatively smooth surface that didn't want to yank the bike from under me.

Pensione Elena (after Gigi's wife, a common way of naming small hotels and guest houses, it seems) had a Wild West sort of feel. It didn't surprise me to learn that it had been a hunting lodge. A newly built (or renovated) building of substance, its masonry was painted cream with coffee coloured accents, tiles and balconies. It had an Alpine feel to it with steeply sloping roofs, presumably to shed snow, since we were fairly high up and in the shadow of Piatra Craiului Mountain. The high roofline caught my eye, even in the dark and I noticed the odd way it was built: there was no ridge where the two slopes met, instead, one jutted higher than the other in an overlap. Something to do with snow, I guessed, making a mental note to ask Gigi (I never did!)

"How did you enjoy The Delta? And Daniel, he is well?" Gigi asked.

"The best place ever, Gigi. An unforgettable experience and such good birding. Daniel seems on good form. I met his new wife, Cerisella."

"Yes, he is married now. A good man. He brings his groups here sometimes. It's a good business in Romania. Come in, come in. You are late, but Elena has prepared a small meal for you – yes?"

I hadn't given food a thought. All through this trip, I ate very little (except on the Floating Hotel!). I would stock up at breakfast (but still not eating that much), steal some bits for a packed lunch and sometimes have nothing else all day, not even a meal at night. It must have been the distraction and concentration involved in riding; no boredom-eating on a bike! (*Cars 7; Bikes 7*)

"Yes, that would be great, I'm quite hungry," I lied

Gigi hurried off, shouting to his wife,

"Elena, Elena, he has arrived at last!"

This was all in English and made me wonder if it was a little hint that I had kept them waiting a little too long. However, there was no vibe to that effect as Elena served a fresh light meal with smiles and motherly attentiveness. I don't think her English was as good as Gigi's; she didn't say much. Instead, Gigi re-appeared and we chatted. He told me about his eco-tourism business and the guest house.

"We are in the Piatra Craiului National Park. Piatra Craiului Mountain is behind us – you will see in the morning, from your bedroom!"

Gigi made a sweeping gesture along one wall of the dining hall which made the mountain seem like a seriously dominating feature of life here.

"Many guests come for the bears. We take groups into the mountain to a cabin overnight. Some people go walking on their own with advice from us. You will stay for the bears?"

"I don't think I have time Gigi. I have to head for Hungary. I have a hotel booked there and a few days with a birding group."

"Ah yes, you would need more time to take hike to the cabin. Another time maybe!"

Gigi was like so many of the people I had met on this trip (Martin and Josele in Spain, Dimiter and Mitko in Bulgaria, and Daniel in The Delta): capable and deeply, authoritatively knowledgeable. I felt like a skimming stone by comparison: full of purpose, even energy, but ultimately just scratching the surface. I had no real substance, and I would peter out then sink without really getting very far. But for now, the bike was a bouncing stone carrying me across the landscape of Europe's birds. Maybe I'd reach the other side, but I knew I'd never have the depth of some of those I had met on this trip and elsewhere.

It was the morning of the 13th of May and mist clung to the high mountain ridge as I looked out from the little window of my cabin-style bedroom in Pensione Elena, Zarnesti, Transylvania. Piatra Craiului looked menacing. It rose out of the surrounding land like the ridged back of some ancient dinosaur; like a Plesiosaur breaching the waves. It is billed as the finest walking ridge in the Carpathians and was used for background scenes in the Oscar-nominated film, Cold Mountain. Its dense pine and beech forests hold brown bear, wolves, deer, wild boar, and even the very rare lynx. More than a third of all the European populations of large carnivores live in Romanian forests like these. You can visit the biggest bear reserve in Europe, right here in Zarnesti: the Liberty Bear Sanctuary.

I went for breakfast and for some advice from Gigi on what to do in just one day.

"Go up the track from edge of the town – you will find it – and keep walking up the valley. There is a gorge there for Wallcreeper and other forest birds"

"Might I see Nutcracker?" I asked

"Higher up maybe, but you will need to hike up near the top. You may not have time – and you must watch out for the bears if you do that!"

He was serious. Wonderful though it would be to come across a Brown Bear, I didn't think I wanted to do that wandering around on my own up some Transylvanian mountain!

I set off for Gigi's track, leaving the village as the road petered out into a rough track. It meandered along the course of a stream which flowed with pale green water. Even down here, the wildness of the place closed in as the heavily wooded mountain rose above me. The odd vehicle or horse and cart came by, but otherwise, I was on my own, enjoying a bit of walking for a change. Heading for the Wallcreeper gorge took me way up onto the mountainside itself, the track continuing endlessly on into the trees. Just as the walking experience was wearing a bit thin, a cart drew up beside me and what I took to be a Romany couple gestured for me to get in. A lift! In a Romany cart! What an unexpected surprise. I self-consciously set my telescope and tripod in the back of the cart and hopped in, sitting on a bundle of rags. Full of appreciative gestures and expressions of thanks, I shook their hands. They smiled and the man gee'd up the horse. The couple were undoubtedly the poor of the land; wearing old torn tweed jackets, she with a scarf and a gaudy skirt, he with fraying trousers and a flat cap. Their skins were swarthy, weather-beaten and ingrained with the dirt of a hard life. I'm sure they were the original Roma gypsies, no doubt despised by today's more affluent, Westernised Romanians of the post-communist era. But they stopped to give me a lift and I was chuffed to have this little bit of contact with the Romania of a bygone and disappearing age.

By way of mime and gesture, I learned that they were going way up over the mountain to work in some fields: there were hand tools for cultivation beside me in the cart. I think I managed to get across that I was on holiday, biking and now birding. They could see the Red Spots and I wondered if I seemed like some privileged, rich Westerner to them. I also pondered how or if I should give them something for the lift – or if that would be taken as an insult.

After a mile or so, the cart stopped. The man gestured with a toothless grin that they were heading way up a smaller track to the left and that my route lay ahead. I thanked them with a bar of chocolate, having decided that money would be crass and with nothing else to spare. They seemed touched and happy with my little gift. I was touched and happy with their friendliness and generosity of spirit. I got the strong impression that these poor people in Romania (and in other former communist countries) were seen as second-class citizens by the respectable, aspirational new generation.

I found the gorge soon after and started another search for Wallcreepers. Even though I'd seen the little buggers at Trigrad, it would be great to see them wherever they're supposed to be. With a strong feeling of déjà vu, I scanned the sheer, pale brown rock faces, hunting amongst the crevices and slabs. Nothing. I lost all confidence in finding these birds, doubting that I was even in the right place. I gave up and headed back out of the gorge in search of whatever alternative bird life was around. Back along the stream, I found a few flying objects and managed to get Dipper and Grey Wagtail in and along the stream. These are both specialists of fast flowing water, the Dipper in particular, as it dived under then popped out again onto a rock. Like a giant brown and white wren, it bobbed and darted along the stream. I also came across Alpine Swift, Crag

Martin, Fieldfare and Raven. Seeing a Fieldfare in summer, in the middle of a forest, was odd since we only get them in the UK in winter. Boldly patterned grey, brown and black thrushes, they tend to range widely across open fields in large, noisy flocks throughout the cold months, but here, they were breeding in isolated pairs in the cool forests.

A very obliging little Rock Bunting sat for ages – on a rock! – allowing me ample time to get some decent photos through the scope; it looked like a little humbug with its black and white striped head.

A similar session, taking photos of a beautiful Grey Wagtail sitting on a branch above the bubbling waters of the stream, rounded off my time birding around Piatra Craiului. No Wallcreeper, no Nutcracker, but I'd had a great morning and headed back just as the rain started. I wasn't to know it, but this was the start of some of the most intense and prolonged rain seen in Eastern Europe for over fifteen years.

Back at the junction where the gypsies had dropped me off, I did my best to eat my lunch in the rain, hoping that someone might come along and I could cadge a lift. Sure enough, a bloke in a small white van appeared. He parked in the lay-by, right by the bend in the track where I sat having my damp picnic. As he filled up with water from a little fountain, I decided to be bold and just go over and ask for a lift back to town. With walking gestures and pointing to the rain, I requested hopefully that I jump in the back of his pick-up. He shook his head, got in his van and drove off... the bastard! Contrast that with the old gypsy couple in their horse and cart...

Near the now damp picnic spot and memorial fountain, there were rusting yellow footpath signs back to Zarnesti and on to "Cabana Curmatura", which I took to be the cabin up on the mountain for bear watching. There was also a sign for "Dracula", one of many all over the place in this area. I paid no real attention to them, but this one just had an arrow pointing left and the word "Dracula" written underneath. Its simplicity and understatement intrigued me for a millisecond[47]. I took a quick photo of the quirky sign and plodded off in the rain back towards Zarnesti. The bike gear served as waterproofs, but I only had a baseball cap on my head and trainers on my feet. I must have looked an odd sight.

The track followed the stream closely with its pale green water looking somehow artificial, even polluted. I noticed a yellowy scum in all the puddles and in the rivulets of rainwater running down the track ("Weird yellow stuff", I'd said on the dictaphone). Could the colour of the stream water be related to this yellow in the puddles? After a while, I remembered that I'd seen yellow dust covering everything and guessed that pollen was being washed from the many large mature conifer trees which blanketed the slopes all around. This yellow froth accompanied me all the way into Zarnesti, by which time the rain had made me truly soggy. I only wanted to get back to Pensione Elena and get dry.

The walk back helped me to decide on staying another night here: it had been long, I was soaked and was in no way ready to get on the bike to cover any sort of distance. As I'd found

[47]The sign for "Dracula" pointed up a track to Bran Castle 4 miles SE of where I was walking. Bran Castle is touted locally as the castle of Count Dracula. I didn't go to find out, but according to one Tripadvisor review that I read; "Who could possibly think that this concrete monstrosity is legit?! Don't people research any more? Ever heard about Ceaucescu and his ambitions for tourism in Romania?". Presumably then, this is a modern fabrication, designed to cash in on the Dracula myth.

before, the luxury of staying put for a second night felt so good. I could relax now, write up some notes, maybe do a bit on the blog and... get dry!

"How was your day Robert?" Gigi asked.

"Wet!" I said, and we got talking about birds, bears and my future plans. I asked him if he knew about the Transfagarasan.

"I see how dinner is and I find out some informations for you. You relax, I will be back," he said as he left for his office and the kitchen.

"You missed Pine Grosbeak as well then?" said a fellow guest, who was sitting in the lounge with a drink, looking very laid back and at ease with the world.

"Didn't even know they were there," I replied.

He stretched out his hand.

"Kevin Bell," he said, and we shook hands.

Kevin was a fellow inmate at Pensione Elena, an Irish Canadian who had come to Europe for the bears and a look around the continent. He was a tall, slim distinguished looking man with masses of grey hair and beard. He reminded me strongly of Roger Jenkins, an Irish Maths lecturer whom I had known well at college and played with, in our Irish/Scottish band during the late 1980s. I took to Kevin instantly and we got on well, chatting easily about our respective journeys. He had travelled to Europe from Canada with his wife, but their interests diverged and she was apparently doing her own, more cultural, thing in Vienna, while he was out in the wilds of Romania, looking for bears with Gigi Popa!

Gigi returned with hands outstretched expansively.

"Hello, Kevin. I see you have met Robert. Good. But, bad news Robert: the Transfagarasan is closed. I am sorry, this happens most years, and it is still early for the snow to melt. I think you cannot go there at this time."

After days, even weeks, of deliberation and discussion with people like Daniel and Gigi, it turned out that the famous Transfagarasan mountain pass, now within striking distance on my way through Romania, was likely to be closed until the end of May, possibly early June. Perhaps after winter damage, a few weeks were required to repair and make the road safe for the hordes of Top Gear copy-cats who go there to experience "the best driving road in the world"[48].

On my maps, the Transfagarasan was temptingly close. I would be in the heart of Transylvania, only forty miles away as the Lesser-spotted Eagle flies, but the mountain detour just to get there would take hours (four to be exact). I'd also done a lot of mountain roads and I wasn't about to take off, only to find that this one was still closed; sadly and finally, the Transfagarasan became a by-passed dream.

In a way, I really missed another trick here in Romania: the Piatra Craiului National Park is awesome and the walk along the mountain ridge is apparently one of the best mountain walks in Eastern Europe. I couldn't know about or do everything, of course, but I had a sense of missing out on things that were right on the doorstep: this fabulous mountain park, and now the Transfagarasan. Rather than getting the best of both worlds (biking and birding) was I getting the worst? I seemed to be often scratching the surface like here in the National Park; no time to dwell and yet too many miles to cover to be relaxed about the journey itself. Is it not really possible to enjoy touring for its own sake *and* take time out for a special interest? Or rather, should I have planned it differently? Maybe I was being too hard on myself. I had done the "dwelling" at key places like The Delta and had more to come in Hungary and Poland. I'd also had some fabulous experiences just riding the bike. Perhaps I just needed three months instead of two!

I had stayed the extra night at Zarnesti and enjoyed the freedom of changing plans when it felt right, but now Roy Adams and his birding group at Eger in Hungary were beckoning; Roy was the bird guide I had already contacted in

---

[48]Top Gear took three supercars to the Transfagarasan in 2009 and proclaimed it, in typical Clarksonian style, as the best driving road in the world. It is the second-highest paved road in Romania. Built as a strategic military route during Ceaucescu's paranoid reign (with the controversial deaths of many who worked on it), the 90 km of twists and turns run north to south across the tallest sections of the Southern Carpathians. The road runs between the two highest peaks in the country, connecting the historic regions of Transylvania and Wallachia, and the cities of Sibiu and Pitesti.

advance. I was expected there the next day. I couldn't delay any longer. After doing a blog entry while my clothes dried off, I sent a text to Roy then I left Pensione Elena, Gigi Popa and Kevin Bell. Hungary here I come!

The oppressive rain and cloud had lifted as I headed out of Zarnesti on Tim's advice, towards Rasnov. Rasnov was only six miles away, but it felt like another land. We were now on wide roads with tarmac, signs and traffic. It had a castle on a hill above the town which looked exactly like Colditz. Just below Colditz was a sign like the Tulcea one, proclaiming "Rasnov" in big white Hollywood letters. The bike, Tim and I made good progress through beautiful towns and villages, stopping only to take the odd photo. Places like Saschiz with its impressive fortified church tower and terracotta painted buildings, and the wonderful Sighisoara with its huge central clock tower, were begging me to linger, but I needed to press on. I vowed to return to Sighisoara one day – it looked so lovely: a well preserved and unspoilt medieval gem, bristling with spires and towers, and nestling in its very own valley (I later found out that Prince Charles has bought some sort of hide-away there; always a good sign!).

The bike pulled well, as powerful as the day I set off with never a hiccup along this fabulous road: the E60 towards Targu Mures, another exciting biking road, overshadowed in these parts no doubt by the Transfagarasan, just a few miles to the south. The road was new with a beautifully smooth surface and fast, open curves. Riding these bends was becoming second nature. Snaking, leaning and twisting, I could still enjoy all the mountain scenery as well as appreciate the towns I rode through. Local people often seemed drawn by the appearance of a fully kitted out touring bike and I got a lot of attention in some of these places when I did stop. Maybe all the other bikers were on the Transfagarasan!

My goal was the Turda Gorge, and my last chance at finding a second Wallcreeper. Following Tim into Turda itself (I needed cash), I felt claustrophobically hemmed in. I hated the place. It was rush hour, late in the day, I had nowhere yet to stay, no energy or incentive to find a camping site, and the traffic was horrible, with a large number of trucks lining the busy main road. I found a cash machine then headed out under Tim's watchful eye but, as we shook off the grip of city chaos, I caught sight of a sign in the suburbs of Turda which said "Pensione Laura, 14Km" with an arrow pointing left. Ignoring Tim's silent protestations, I took off down the small road into the residential part of Turda, not knowing if this place would be any good or anywhere near the Turda Gorge. The road became the inevitable dirt track I had come to expect, but I persevered. At one point it turned into the service road for major roadworks on a nearby motorway (Autostrada Transylvania A3) which was "under construction", but mysteriously carrying vehicles. In mild panic, I wondered if I shouldn't really be on that, swishing along towards Hungary. The service road was sandwiched between the new motorway and a quarry and it morphed into a wide, pot-holed dirt track used by large construction vehicles.

We persevered, Tim now looking extremely confused with the little video game biker on his screen heading off across a field, until we entered a tiny village called Petrestii de Jos (where video-biker looked more at home). I stopped and asked a young bloke for directions. He pointed me confidently back the way I had come, out of the village and around on a back road to... Pension Laura with (in the very near distance, only a mile or so away) the Turda Gorge! Its craggy bare rock faces were bathed in early evening sunlight and looked resplendent. What a beautiful, out of the way place. I had followed my nose and come up smelling roses; the gorge being so close was pure serendipity.

Pension Laura was a spanking new guest house built on three floors with external walkways to all the rooms, wooden balconies and a private sauna. It was in the middle of nowhere, but clearly, the gorge was a major tourist attraction, so the guest house was well situated to cash in on the new breed of well-heeled Romanian tourists. The owner had a big Honda sports bike sitting outside and, once again, the foyer/bar area was inhabited by friendly locals (nowhere else to go in this out of the way place). I joined them for a drink, but weariness overcame me; I couldn't stay and explain all the vagaries of biking and my trip to these chilling dudes who would have talked all night. I needed to move on the next day after an early start to the gorge for Wallcreeper and whatever else it held (Golden Eagle, Eagle Owl, Rock Thrush... and more, according to Gerard Gorman).

The idea of an early start evaporated in the middle of the night. I woke sometime in the early hours with a banging headache and feeling sick for the first time on the trip. It was a huge effort just to get up, let alone pack the bike for another day's riding, eat breakfast (retch!) and set off on a foray to the Gorge. I felt truly dreadful, but tried breakfast to settle the stomach (I thought). I should have packed it in and gone back to bed until they threw me out – or even stayed another night – but I stuck to the plan and rode the bike off-road along a rutted track to park at the mouth of the gorge. A man in a tiny wooden shed took an entrance fee and gave me a ticket. I staggered and moaned my way along the undulating path, deeper and deeper into the gorge. I looked for Wallcreeper, but I felt so ill, I doubt if I could have picked one out. My heart just wasn't in it. As the gorge narrowed, the path became more precarious, emphasised by the appearance of a steel rope fixed to the rock face with pitons – so you could hang on when trying to negotiate the path with a raging fever. After taking a photo of a rock climber (which made me feel even more sick), I turned back.

How I got on the bike, along the off-road track and back onto the main route to Hungary, I'll never know, but by the time I covered the twenty miles to Cluj Napoca, Romania's second city, I was in a bad way. While stopped at some traffic lights in the city centre, I had to leap off the bike (only just managing to put down the side stand), dive behind a low hedge and throw up (only just managing to rip off my helmet!). A taxi driver who had pulled up at the same lights was staring disapprovingly at me through his open window. Were I at home, I'd be crawling into bed and telling the world to go fuck itself, which is what I wanted to tell the taxi driver... but I didn't have the energy. A big town like Cluj was not where I wanted to be.

Throwing up made me feel marginally better, but I still had the thumping headache and a pain had started in my back – no doubt from the spasm of lurching behind the hedge and vomiting. Tim, God bless him, helped me out of the city, off towards Oradea and the border. But our troubles had only just started.

Chapter 11 – Wet, Wet, Wet

Anne is the brightest person I have ever known. She has a pure intelligence; not pretentiously intellectual nor reliant on a load of useless knowledge, but incisively analytical with bags of common sense. She did a degree in Physiology and Zoology at Newcastle University, after which she tried nursing – before realising she was wasting her mind.

By the mid-nineties, Anne is a respected scientist in cancer research, with a Ph.D. and several research papers to her name. She attends conferences from California to Italy and is involved in designing and running lab experiments, collecting and analysing data and writing more papers – until her MS has her walking with a stick and stumbling. For a couple of years she carries on with her lab work, but she begins to fall at work and has to face a major change. Her employers (the prestigious, but now defunct Gray Laboratory in the grounds of Mount Vernon Hospital in Middlesex, West London) are very accommodating and offer her a job as a librarian but, for someone with her background and career record, this is a dissatisfying demotion.

Walking and standing become difficult for Anne and she has difficulty driving, generally getting around, and even getting on and off a toilet. She begins to feel a lot of pain, weakness and fatigue, all classic symptoms of advanced, "secondary progressive" MS. Even a job as a librarian is too much for her.

In 2002, Anne gives up work altogether. Helped by Harrow Citizen's Advice Bureau (God bless you Gladys!) and a very generous employer, Anne is able to sort out her pension and disability benefits. With my work, we can afford to carry on more or less as we were, except that Anne is at home all day on her own. The kids are old enough to get themselves to and from school and Anne is able to get herself out of the house or up and down the (many) steps to the garden, while I carry on full time in college.

The time comes when Anne needs help just to get out of bed and up in the morning, all before I set off on a one hour drive to work for 8.30. At home and on her own most days, Anne phones me more and more often at work: sometimes as soon as I finish a lecture, sometimes just as I'm about to start, sometimes during. When I get in, she is understandably fed up and often angry at life; there is rarely a welcome.

"You'll never give up Southgate College; I'll believe it when I see it" is Anne's embittered refrain whenever she feels abandoned.

*

For several days, the weather had been anything but sunny. Since the drenching walk at Piatra Craiului, clouds and a dull overcast fug had become the skyward backdrop. After the vomiting purge, Tim led me out of Cluj, optimistically following coordinates for the Hotel Villa Volgy in Eger, Hungary. I was to camp in the grounds there for a few days, birding with Roy Adams and his tour group. Tim reckoned it was nearly five hours riding.

It's not as bad as you might imagine, riding in the rain. At least not until it starts coming in! Maybe I should have spent more on my boots because, after an hour or so, my feet felt very damp. My gloves, similarly, were wet inside. The rush of cold, damp air as the bike swooshed along through sheets of rainwater turned my toes and fingers into lumps of icy pain. I still felt ill, tired and feverish. My energy was slipping away. All in all, riding didn't feel very comfortable or very safe! (*Cars 8; Bikes 7*)

Twenty or thirty miles beyond Cluj, a chalet style café came into view and with the relief of the desperate traveller, I pulled in. Fruit tea in hand, I squelched over to a table and sat. Without the distraction of riding in the rain, the miserable state I was in almost floored me; my fingers were numb with cold inside dripping wet gloves, one finger going a yellowy white with poor circulation. My toes felt the same inside sodden boots and my head was thumping with the ache from the previous day. I felt feverish and very weak. All I wanted to do was lie down and sleep. Shakily, I peeled off the wet gloves and clung to the hot tea cup for comfort and a little warmth. Finishing it, I heaved off the cold, clinging boots and socks, dropped my head onto the table... and slept. Surprisingly, no one bothered me.

After forty unconscious minutes, I woke confused and aching, but warmer. I didn't want to leave; certainly not into "Le Deluge" outside. In bare feet, I went out to the bike and, with great effort in the rain, extracted a pair of dry socks from the big waterproof holdall. My return to the café brought on some stares. I was now being noticed (like Clint Eastwood in "The Unforgiven": a weird, feverish stranger enters the saloon from the rain outside – if you know the movie, you'll know what I mean!). I bought a coffee and pastry and sat in my damp, steaming corner. It was such pleasure, pulling on those socks! With dry feet warming and fingers around another hot cup I felt a little better. I slept again.

The whole stop took over an hour. I was getting nowhere and felt only a little better. It took some effort of will, but wearily I got myself ready to ride again, paid and left the warm steamy oasis of the café. Back at the bike, a cowboy (well, he was wearing a Stetson!) offered to swap his pedal bike for mine. Was he a delusion? Did I dream him in the blur and fog of fever, confusing reality with The Unforgiven? Delusion or not, we had a jovial conversation about him buying the bike, which lifted my spirits for a few minutes until the misery of riding ill in the rain took over again.

After a further twenty or thirty gruelling miles, I just couldn't go on. I pulled in to a sodden lay-by, almost at the point of collapse. I hung my head, feeling the weight of the helmet and my drenched clothing. Through the raindrops on my visor I could see the sodden mud and gravel of this depressing little lay-by. Puddles sparked as raindrops hit and little rivulets flowed here and there as if to emphasise how wet the world had become. Slowly, and with jarring stiffness, I kicked the side-stand down onto the loose surface and gingerly swung my leg over the bike. Pain shot down my left leg. I could hardly stand up straight now. I looked around, hoping that there would be somewhere to get out of the rain or at least sit down. Neither looked likely. I hobbled over to a sodden, rotting wooden stump and eased myself into a sitting position. Taking the weight off my legs made a difference, but my back still hurt and big fat drops of water plopped onto me from overhanging sycamore leaves. The leaves collected rainwater, concentrating it into great blobs that only added insult to injury by running down the back of my neck, cold and hurtful. At that moment, I felt an irrational dislike of sycamore leaves: as far as I was concerned, the world was against me, it was out to get me and I wanted to go home.

Pulling myself together a bit, I shook the dripping rain off my helmet, gave the visor a wipe and hobbled over to the bike: the one I had bought a lifetime ago in Spaceport Honda. My silver CBF600 stood there leaning on its stand, dependable and ready to go (I hoped). It was my friend and this was not the first or last time I would feel an emotional attachment to the bike. I spoke to it for comfort, "Come on baby, let's go. Take me out of here". We powered off up the road in the rain.

I managed another 50 miles before deciding, at a brightly lit motel, that I couldn't go on. We were less than half way; only a few miles from Oradea and the border, but another 120 miles to reach Eger. It crossed my mind that I might look too outlandish to be offered a room in any hotel; too much like a hobo or a bandit in my drenched and haggard state. But this place was a bright oasis. There was a wedding going on, with kids careering around and hotel staff rushing about. In the main hall, the inevitable wedding band played, people danced, and a bride floated around like a fluffy white blancmange. I couldn't walk out of this bright and comfortable normality, back into the drenched, black hell outside. *Please give me a room!*

The manageress of the hotel was consulted about my request.

"We have a wedding and we are very full," she said in good English, looking me up and down.

There was definitely an element of "do we want this vagrant sullying our hotel in the middle of a wedding?" (what would the guests all think!?).

"I am very tired and unwell. I can't ride my bike any more," I told her, deciding to try the traveller in distress angle.

It was no act; my body language said firmly, "I'm not moving; if you don't give me a room you're going to have to throw me out."

The vibes felt negative, but her response surprised me: making a sudden, silent decision, she grabbed a waitress and said something in Romanian then got the receptionist to check me in. No discussion of money. I didn't care anyway.

"Sorry, we are busy with this wedding, but the waitress will bring you some tea. Enjoy your stay. You look like you should go to bed!"

Gesturing towards me, she spoke to the receptionist again and something told me she was saying:

"Keep an eye on him. We don't want him passing out here in the middle of the foyer."

She was nice. They were all nice. Tea appeared and I sat, wet, but cosy, in the surreal surroundings of the wedding and let the tea revive me. In a psychedelic bubble of weariness, pain, damp, tea, noise, children and people rushing around, I suddenly remembered Roy Adams in Hungary: I was supposed to be arriving there that day! I sent a disjointed text:

15th May, 16.27
Hi Roy. Sorry to mess u around, but I won't make it today. Been taken ill & w the rain, had to stop. V near Oradea & border. Hopefully get to you mid-day 2moro.
A reply arrived soon after:

15th May, 16.42
Not to worry. Hope you get better & are ok to ride bike tomorrow. Don't rush. Best wishes, Roy.

The hotel staff, who were now mothering me a bit, took my wet clothes away to dry somewhere, and ushered me off to bed.

After a fitful night's sleep, I woke feeling no better. For some reason, the wedding meant I couldn't have breakfast (maybe I lowered the tone). I ate the previous day's jam sandwich, and the waitresses made me another tea (mint this time). People were so helpful everywhere.

Sipping the mint tea, I reflected and wrote some notes... all questioning my approach to the trip; was I trying to do much? Too many days constantly on the move? I felt I wouldn't make it to Wilma's grave now and even planned vaguely to fly back out another time to see her grave and meet her family. These thoughts saddened me with a sense of failure. In hindsight, it was clearly the terrible weather combined with illness that made me feel this way. In my notes, I also wrote, "The End Seems Nigh". It felt like things were drawing to a close, even though I still had two more weeks in Hungary, Slovakia and Poland.

A text arrived:

16th May, 09.05
Hi Robert. Hope you are feeling better. A bit damp for birding, but all going well. Just go to hotel reception when you arrive if I'm not around. Looking forward to meeting you. See you later. Roy

I sent a swift reply:

16th May, 09.09
Hi Roy. Not much better, but pressing on – have to get home somehow! Might not camp out after all. Can you book a room for me if they have one? Thanks. See u around noon. R.

Riding through the busy city of Oradea in the heavy rain was tough, but Tim got me there and we pushed on to the border. It was a Sunday and the Romanian side was deserted. I stopped to buy a vignette for Hungary, and changed all the Romanian Lie into Euros. After a cursory passport check, I was waved through with no formality; not how things would have been in the dark communist times of Nicolae Ceaucescu.

In my unhappy state, the emotion of reaching Hungary overwhelmed me: I cried into the helmet again, blubbing like a child. I really felt that I was battling against heavy odds. The roads were awash with water. Sheets of it ran like rivers across the tarmac. It was getting worse. Another thirty miles of never-ending rain and cold forced an early stop. But I had made it to Hungary; surely I deserved a coffee!

This time I scribbled "paracetamol?" on a piece of paper and presented it to the very nice young girl who served the coffee. She came back with just half a tablet, but painkillers here must be extra strong because it worked! I slept again, head heavy against my arms on the wooden table top. Right next to my cheek, blue and white checked material hung in front of the windows with rain streaming down the glass outside as I drifted off.

I woke completely disoriented in a sea of white and blue rain with a stiff neck and steaming with damp. Outside, it was still raining heavily. I stayed there for a while, feeling comfortable and safe. The waitress smiled at me as she delivered the next shot of caffeine.

I sent another text:

16th May, 13.18
Hi Roy, Slow Progress I'm afraid – comb. of rain, cold & illness. Never rains, but it pours – literally. Shd be there by 2.30. Hope things ok w u. Robert"

Revived, we pressed on, Tim navigating and the bike running well. I hadn't had the energy to check its various functions, but it felt fine in these horrible conditions. For some reason (surely not that meagre half paracetamol?), I suddenly felt better. After another 50 miles, I felt ravenous and stopped for coffee and a pastry. The bike was ravenous too and needed petrol.

Cold, aching and wet, but feeling better, we took off yet again, powering on through the sheets of water that formed the surface of the M3 motorway. For some reason, the bike seemed faster, more powerful. Perhaps stupidly, I let it go, jetting through the water at a constant 90mph. We really covered the miles and the turning for Eger came up sooner than expected. As

I rode into the town, (noticing the first Tesco I'd seen since somewhere in the UK!), I shouted and bellowed into the helmet with exuberant tears of joy:

"EGER! EGER!"

Tim took me straight to the hotel... except that there was no hotel. He'd got it wrong. I had no idea where I was, but this was not hotel-land. It looked like any suburban area of any town, with weedy old concrete slabs forming roads to private garages, with the odd low block of flats and a small industrial estate near a railway line.

"What are you doing Tim?" I said to the little screen which showed the cartoon motorbike, lost in a sea of tiny tracks, and a big green arrow pointing ironically backwards.

"No need to be sarcastic," I said.

I turned around, back to a more major road and tried re-programming Tim, but I could give him no further information so he kept trying to send us back to the garage estate (he's a bit dim like that!). Eventually an old bloke in a beat-up Volkswagen Golf with an Alsatian in the back shouted something in Hungarian, which I took to be: "Are you lost?"

"Hotel Villa Volgy?" I said hopefully.

He nodded, gestured for me to follow and drove off. In a panic not to lose him, I kicked the side stand away and skidded after him, the rear wheel slewing around alarmingly; not nice on a fully laden bike.

After many twists and turns (God Tim, where had you taken us?) the old guy indicated left as he stopped at a T junction. He pointed vigorously to the right with his whole arm out the window and turned away waving, his big Alsatian dog rocking around in the back. With no opportunity to thank him or check where I was going, I looked doubtfully to my right: no hotel. I could do nothing other than turn the way he had gestured, and carry on. A little way up a slight incline, the road took a sharp right and there, rising gloriously out of the surrounding bushes and trees was the Hotel Villa Volgy! Thank God for Hungarians in old Golfs!

It was still raining.

The hotel was swish. I wasn't. I stood dripping onto the polished black marble floor tiles, an ever-increasing puddle forming around my feet, just in front of the reception desk. Some tall, well dressed young women were checking in so I had to wait my turn. The puddle got bigger. The group of elegant girls could not have made a more stark contrast to the sodden figure I cast in the hotel foyer. I felt very out of place, but the girls were pleasing on the eye. They looked like a group of senior school girls or young air hostesses aspiring to be models: tall, slim and elegant in their crisp skirts, blouses and heels. The contrast with how I felt became too much and I gave up waiting by the desk. Instead, I mooched over to some low comfy sofas and, hoping I didn't ruin them by sitting down, started removing some of the wet outer clothing which now felt welded to my skin. Once free of the worst of it, I sent a final text to Roy:

16th May, 14.48
"Hi again Roy. At hotel reception. Will ask about room etc & generally hang around in a puddle! Hope 2 meet u soon. Robert"

The phone rang soon after.
"Hello, Robert. Glad you made it!"
"Hi, Roy. Yes I'm here, more or less in one piece. I'm going to try for a room."
"Ok. Tell them you're with me," said Roy, "and you'll get the discount. We're on our way back. The grounds of the hotel are fairly good for birding. You should get Wryneck, a few woodpeckers, shrikes, flycatchers. There's an Icterine Warbler around. See you at dinner, around 7.30."
I didn't care how much the room was going to cost for my three days there, but it was good to know I could name-drop Roy – to save any disapproving looks as much as reducing the bill. My paranoia was unwarranted. The reception staff weren't the least officious or snooty: though smartly dressed, much like those elegant girls, they were welcoming and friendly. The room was sorted with little fuss (maybe Roy's name helped).

A room! A warm… dry… room! Curtains closed, telly on, heating turned up full; I was in heaven. I stripped off all the wet or damp clothes until I was running around the warm room, naked and happy. Running is a considerable exaggeration: my back was still very stiff and aching. Painful jabs shot down my left leg if I turned or moved suddenly. Warmed and less hysterically euphoric, I settled into the shower, letting the hot water cascade down my aching back and into my weary soul. I really didn't feel like meeting a new group of people. I just wanted to stay there forever and get over the traumas of the last three days.

Over dinner, Roy introduced me to his group: the people I'd be birding with for the next few days. Roy was an unflappable, middle-aged chap, a little portly and unassuming, but he ran his own guiding business out here in Hungary, and he knew his stuff.

The dining room was fairly plush with soft carpet, white cotton tablecloths and sharply dressed waiters attending the tables. Wine glasses sparkled on the long table where we sat.

"Evening all," said Roy, "this is Rob. He'll be with us for a few days."

He went round the small group introducing everyone: couples Sue and Richard, Tony and Jane, and Nadia, on her own. They all looked like down to earth types who had formed that intangible "group aura" that you feel as an outsider coming in for the first time. They were open and friendly though and I felt welcomed at once, unlike the exclusivity of The Delta group, which took some cracking and which I never really felt part of.

"You're the biker then?" said Richard, offering a hand to shake, "That must be some trip."

He was a good-looking man in his fifties, greying, but with a full head of hair. He had a gentle expression that put me at ease. I liked him straight away: these were more my sort of people.

"So it's turning out to be," I replied, "the rain's been relentless and I've been ill the last few days."

"Roy told us. How are you feeling now?" asked Jane.

"After half an hour in the shower, much better thanks."

That was a bit of a lie. Even though I was warming to this group and they made me the centre of attention with the bike trip and birding, I struggled to match their enthusiasm.

"Did your clothes get wet? They'll dry them here if you want," offered Roy.

"They're soaking, but festooned around my room at the moment. The shower floor is heated so I've got my bike boots upside down over one warm patch, my gloves on another and the rest hanging off all the radiators."

This brought up the subject of the bike again.

"What bike have you got?" Richard wanted to know.

The conversation took a turn into the details of biking, where I'd been and what birds I'd seen. Since this was a birding group, all sorts of sightings were exchanged. I found out what they'd been seeing, and hoped to see, and I regaled them with tales of hunting Wallcreeper, the Danube Delta and riding in the rain.

"Spain was fabulous too," I concluded, stretching my mind back over the endless expanse of six weeks travelling and birding.

"Lammergeier was the best, but I got all the steppe birds and Dupont's Lark."

They were all impressed by Lammergeier, but only Roy pricked up his ears at the Dupont's: those birds really were a bit of an esoteric Tick.

Dinner was served.

"You'll be glad not to be riding your bike in the rain for a few days," said Nadia over coffee.

For the first time, I realised how true this was: there was now a break of a few days and I consciously relaxed that little bit more as she pointed this out.

"Yes, you're right. I'm going to enjoy being taken to the birds with a lot less effort – and in the dry!"

"Don't bet on it," piped up Roy "we've been a bit damp at times. This rain is never ending. If low pressure sits over central Europe we can get days of it."

"A bit damp would suit me fine, Roy!"

The television in the lounge (in fact every television, everywhere) was showing constant bulletins about the floods, which were now becoming major disasters throughout Eastern Europe, including Hungary and Poland.

"Looks like you were lucky to get here at all, Rob," said Sue nodding towards a Sky News bulletin, which showed torrents of water running through streets, under bridges and over fields.

"She's always glass half full mate," said Richard, "you're allowed to complain – sounds like you had a terrible time getting here."

"But he's here now!" exclaimed Nadia, raising her glass in a slightly inebriated toast.

They all smiled and lifted their glasses, shouting "Cheers!" and "Welcome Rob!" or was it "Well done Rob!"?

Either way, they made me feel very much part of the group and they seemed to realise that I'd been through a lot. Maybe it showed on my face…or maybe I was just such a mess…or maybe we were all getting a bit tipsy on the strong and flavourful Hungarian wine!

They were so much more relaxed and less guarded than the Danube Delta group. Nadia was a short, stocky lady with grey-white hair and an artist's flair. In her mid-fifties maybe, she looked quietly flamboyant and seemed very at home in this group, even though they couldn't all have known each other for more than a few days. Nadia liked to joke and laugh, but she was genuinely interested in everybody, maybe at her own expense; she didn't talk about herself much.

Jane told me a little about Tony's illness and he joined in the potted life histories, along with Sue and Richard; the two couples were already long-standing friends. Their concern for Tony's well being and enjoyment of the trip was heart-warming. He looked frail, but bright and he was clearly unsteady in his walking; a shame because I could see that, without his illness, he'd be a lively, engaging chap. They were all in their mid to late fifties, either retired or approaching retirement. Sue, who like me, had a background in education was a wiry, energetic woman, a true lefty lecturer type – also like me! She had a short spiky haircut and dressed in a trendy, colourful way with drainpipe jeans and a cheesecloth style blouse, set off with a stripy scarf; all very youthful, without being mutton-dressed-as-lamb – a good trick to pull off, I thought. Her partner, Richard, had a more laid back, laconic style, but he was quietly self-assured; an interesting and interested man to talk to. Tony's wife Jane was just lovely; she had a permanently warm expression and twinkly-smiley eyes that I could and did lose myself in as we talked... or maybe it was the "strong and flavourful Hungarian wine"!

With Roy as master of ceremonies, they gathered round and went through the day's birding. It is a usual thing on such organised trips for the leader to provide a checklist of some sort, then go through the sites visited each day to get The List correct and to make sure every sighting is noted. I took a back seat for this, of course, but was keen to hear what they'd seen. Turned out to be mostly rain! The relaxed tone here in Eger contrasted again with the experience I'd had on The Delta. I recalled the feeling of being very much an interloper as Daniel had gone through the day's checklist on the evening of my arrival on the Floating Hotel.

The "strong and flavourful Hungarian wine" certainly oiled the wheels with these friendly, laughing people at the Hotel Villa Volgy and it took away all the hardships of the previous few days. I returned to my untidy room, infested with damp clothes, happy and ready to fall into bed.

We were up early for a pre-breakfast birding forray; this is another norm on birding trips. You get out early for the birds before the rest of humanity stirs and sends them diving for cover. Often this involves getting up at dawn to catch some feeding activity or movement from a roost site or just to hear and locate a songster, which may not sing reliably through the day (like Dupont's Lark!). Today it was a short trip to a local river valley for some warblers (notably River Warbler!) and scrub birds, like shrikes or orioles.

Still not feeling one hundred percent, and with my back sore and stiff from lying, I wandered down to reception where we were to meet. The allotted time of 07.00 came and went. I asked the receptionist if he had seen Roy and his group.

"Yes, yes they are going," he said quietly.

"They've gone?" I was incredulous.

"Yes, here... " he pointed to the door.

This man's English wasn't very good, so I quizzed him a little more, but it seemed that they had gone. I must have got the wrong time. Having all my gear on, including some waterproofs and telescope, I reluctantly set off around the hotel grounds as Roy had suggested the previous day. It was drizzling continuously, dull and cold – central Europe in the middle of May! I was picked up immediately by a local canine who followed me around, barking and scaring all the birds. She was a young, golden coloured Alsatian/Collie type cross with a collar on. It was my own fault for speaking to her and encouraging her. She was fun though and became one of the many dogs that I took a photo of and later put on the blog: another Trip Blog Dog.

She accompanied me in the hunt for woodpeckers, Nightingales and Orioles. She also made it almost impossible to see either of the two Wrynecks which were calling loudly around the Hotel. Wrynecks make a loud, short, repeated screeching note, very rhythmic and unmistakeable, but they are superbly camouflaged to look exactly like a broken off tree branch; not easy to see with a mutt running round barking and wanting to play, despite being told firmly to shut the fuck up! The Wrynecks made a fool of us, calling and moving constantly so they were impossible to locate. It was getting unpleasant in the light, but depressing rain, so I headed back, looking forward to breakfast – and the embarrassment of meeting the group after their early birding trip.

As I turned a corner towards the hotel entrance, there they were, by the minibus.

"Here he is!" exclaimed Nadia.

"Thought we'd missed you," said Roy.

"Let's go. It's not far."

For a minute, I thought they had been looking and waiting for me and were now very late setting off.

"God Jane, have you been waiting for me all this time?" I said guiltily.

"All what time? We've only been here a few minutes. Are you feeling better? You must have been up before us. In fact, I thought *we* were going to miss it. Takes a while for Tony to get going and he's never sure if he's up to joining us of a morning."

Roy hopped in the driver's side and, with a lot of we're-getting-on-the-bus body language, the others moved towards the doors. What the hell was going on? Where were they going now? And what about breakfast!?

"We were supposed to meet at seven, right?" I said.

"Yes, Rob. What's the matter with you – I think you're losing it, dear. You feeling ok?"

"Jane... ," I said slowly, "what time is it?"

The penny was just starting to drop...

"Just gone seven. Stop worrying, you didn't make us late – I told you!"

Jane put a comforting hand on my arm, slightly mocking, but her smiling eyes showed a little concern.

"You know what I've done?" I said, "I forgot to put my watch back, coming into Hungary yesterday. Bugger, I got up an hour before I needed to! And I almost missed this trip!"

"You idiot!" – more twinkly eyes, this time in amusement.

I confessed my stupidity to all, giving them a good laugh, and we set off for early morning birding – Take Two!

"See much round the hotel?" Roy asked as he drove the minibus out of the grounds.

I told them the Tale of Two Wrynecks and Roy reeled off a list of birds I should have seen.

"It was pretty miserable with the rain – and that dog didn't help," I said in my defence.

And I wanted breakfast!

In the heavy gloom of an overcast, cloud-filled sky, the Ostiros-Novaj river valley where we stopped looked inauspicious. In fact, it looked uninviting and unlikely as a birding spot. Uncharitably, I cast doubt in my own mind about how good Roy was going to be as a guide – very unfair under the circumstances – but this place was unimpressive and Roy's quiet, almost unenthusiastic style gave me no optimism for finding good birds. This seemed to be confirmed when I asked what he expected to see here.

"Oh, a bit of this and a bit of that," was his answer.

Turned out that, to him, "a bit of this and a bit of that" meant some damn good birds! Roy was more the fire that burns bright within, rather than on the surface, and I changed my mind about him there and then: he was a brilliant guide. We heard, and some saw, Wryneck, River Warbler, Barred Warbler and Marsh Warbler. Not bad since the first three were Trip Ticks! It was just the weather that, literally, put a damper on things.

The Wryneck we saw was lovely and made up for the unseen pair earlier in the morning. Looking just like a lichen-encrusted broken branch, the bird clung, woodpecker style, onto a small limb of a bush right next to its nest hole. Wrynecks are, in fact, woodpeckers, but they look different to all the others. This one showed off well its exquisite mottled grey and brown markings; boldly barred lengthways to look like the bark of a tree. Roy made sure everyone got a good look (another sign of a good guide – everyone has to see the bird). For the first time ever, I saw a Wryneck do what the name suggests: twisting and, at the same time, lengthening its neck in an alien, snake-like ritual. It looked very strange, but captivating – and unique to this species as far as I know[49].

This group of people was just right as birding companions, Roy was just right as leader and part of this particular mix. We all got on so well; no sense of competition, no "gripping off" (birder term for rubbing it in when you've seen some bird that others haven't) or "stringing" (trying to turn a common species or a brief view of something into a mega-rarity). Everyone was

---

[49]The scientific name for Wryneck is *Jynx torquilla* (torque, as in twisting). They are in the woodpecker family, but in a group all of their own. The odd habit of head/neck twisting was thought to be other-wordly and associated with witchcraft; as in "put a jinx" on someone.

relaxed and we moved around each other quite naturally; no cliques formed and everybody chatted to everybody else. Even the couples weren't very "couply". I was coming to like these people more and more.

Roy got us all onto Lesser Whitethroat, Hawfinch and Golden Oriole before a tantalising, but non-locatable snippet of Bluethroat song ended this damp little birding foray.

At the second attempt, breakfast was very welcome. I'd been up for several hours and had done a lot of tramping around in the rain, still not feeling great. It made me very aware of the luxury of stopping here for a few days, knowing that I could relax in warm surroundings with someone else driving, navigating and finding the birds. We tucked into breakfast before Roy rounded us up.

We were off to the nearby Bukk Hills for woodpeckers and the like, then on to some fish ponds.

"Target birds for today," said Roy, "White-backed Woodpecker and maybe the other seven woodpeckers too, Red-breasted Flycatcher, Collared Flycatcher, Wood Warbler and Hawfinch. Might get Ural Owl if we're lucky."

"Does that include Black Woodpecker Roy?" I asked, keen to see another one.

"Yes, but they can be difficult – especially in this rain. Everything's hiding. Then we're off to the fish-ponds for some wetland birds. Doubt if the rain will affect that much, although the water levels have risen and washed out some of the ground nesting birds like Grebes."

There were murmurs of disdain at this news as the seriousness of the rain and floods seemed to come at us from every angle.

Roy stopped the bus in a lay-by on the main road in the middle of the Bukk Forest, not far from Eger. We walked a little along the road and took our stance on the verge, Roy pointed out a tree trunk with a hole in it across the road and a little way into the forest. We watched it. Telescopes sprung up surreptitiously until we looked every bit the group of twitchers, all intent on one spot and one bird: White-backed Woodpecker.

A flicker of black and white with a flash of pink announced the arrival of the woodpecker at the nest hole. As they all seem to do, it clung to the bottom of the hole having a good look around, before disappearing inside.

"It's the female," said Roy, "can you see the black crown?"

We all murmured assent, peering through our binoculars or telescopes. This was another typical example of local knowledge; I bet hundreds of people, birders included, drove past this spot without realising that there is such an open view of the rarest woodpecker in Europe at the nest. Roy took us straight there, pointed out the nest hole and all we had to do was wait. A little too easy maybe, lacking the extra thrill and panache of seeking it out for oneself perhaps (a tad like going to a zoo?), but this was still a wild bird, in wild country. As the name suggests, White-backed Woodpeckers have a lot of white on the back, laddered and speckled amongst black, rather than the big white blobs of Greater Spotted Woodpeckers, more familiar in the UK. Her head had more white, and that flash of pink rather than red underneath was a clincher.

"The rarest Woodpecker in Europe," declared Roy, as the bird re-appeared to do a little clinging dance around the tree trunk before flying off, no doubt to find more food for its young.

The rain drove us on.

"No point trying to find birds in the forest areas in this. We'll go on to the fish ponds."

It was disappointing not to dwell in these impressive hill forests, especially with someone who knew them so well, but I was also glad not to be tramping round a sodden forest in this rain. We drove on.

The Kiskiore Fishponds were unimpressive as a site. Again, dulled by the overcast weather, we were in a flat, open, artificial area with raised dykes and rectangular lakes set out in front of a visitor centre (or was it an angling centre?). Just as we arrived, a Short Eared Owl flew over our heads (Tick!) and we had fabulous views of a Penduline Tit at a nest. There were a few other waterfowl, but nothing out of the ordinary[50]. I returned to the hotel with the group, happy to be with such easy going people and having seen a few new birds – including the rarest woodpecker in Europe!

We were joined that day by another latecomer: Heather, a tall elegant lady in her sixties who slotted into the group just the way I had. It was heartening how easily people could come and go like that and still strike up relaxed and meaningful friendships, even if only for a few days. Maybe it was wisdom brought about by age or the bond of a shared experience or maybe just common ground and personalities that would bring such a group together. Whatever the reason, it felt warm and safe being here with Roy and this gentle yet interesting group of people.

The Hortobagy (pronounced, I think Hortobashh) is legend in my birding career. It is the largest piece of continuous grassland in Europe, grazed for thousands of years by ancient breeds of semi-wild cattle, and home to a dazzling range of species from large birds of prey like White-tailed Eagle and Saker Falcon to smaller jobs like Bluethroat and Aquatic Warbler with a host of wetland birds thrown in. I had read umpteen bird and conservation articles about the wildlife value and scale of this place. Like the Biebrza Marshes in Poland and the Danube Delta in Romania, the Hortobagy was the stuff of legend for a wannabe European birder. When Roy took us out to this grassland (and the nearby Lake Tisza), I was back in dream mode; I had been thinking of coming here for over twenty years.

Perhaps for the first time on the trip though, I found myself less than overwhelmed by the experience. Maybe it was the incessant rain or maybe I really was reaching The End: perhaps I had taken in as many new, wonderful birding experiences as I could. If I hadn't been with this group and with Roy leading, I may well have headed off – to get away from the rain, if nothing

---

[50]We did see loads of Ferruginous Duck and some Pygmy Cormorants, but these had become a little passé – I hate myself for that. I would have died for a Pygmy Cormorant only a couple of weeks before and "Fudgie" Ducks are lovely chaps that would be an extreme rarity in the UK. We are so fickle!

else. But the birds started trickling in: Roller, Spoonbill, Bee-eater, Great White Egret, Purple, Night and Squacco Herons.

The landscape itself was endless, like the rain: a flat expanse of long grass stretching for miles, lines of bushes or small trees and the occasional lake or marsh. Roy took us to the main visitor centre for the National Park. There wasn't a soul around. We disembarked; a gaggle of birders struggling to put on waterproofs, ready for a walk with Roy into the Hortobagy. Tony elected to stay in the coach for a while. He wasn't up to the walking that day. The rest of us followed Roy away from the centre into the rain.

We walked along a railway track, which felt odd with this great expanse of grassland around us, but apparently, this was the main birding walk. It was miserable! But Roy was right: from a birding perspective, a slow walk along this track with lines of willow and other low scrub in the foreground produced lots of birds. Like us though, they seemed miserable and wanted to hide all the time. We spent ages trying to find a singing Bluethroat (was I *ever* going to get a view of these pesky things?), and a River Warbler kept us all twitching too. I got some half decent photos of a Purple Heron by holding my little digital camera up to the scope as usual, but the light was so poor, the image looked faded and grainy.

We had fairly long drives around this eastern part of Hungary, to Lake Tisza and back to the hotel. On the way, Roy stopped for various birds and we notched up, among others, Saker Falcon, White-tailed Eagle, Eastern Imperial Eagle and Lesser Grey Shrike. He took us to a Bee-eater colony, but all he could show us was a pile of mud below a few sad, unoccupied holes where the birds should have been; their nesting bank, normally a dry wall of sand or soil, had collapsed in a mini landslide because of the rain.

The Imperial Eagle, showing its two white shoulder patches, put on an amazing twisting aerial display as it got mobbed by a Hooded Crow. Crows aren't small birds, but the eagle made it look like a Sparrow! The Saker Falcon was disappointingly distant, but in the scope, it gave me a real lift. I hadn't expected to see one of these large falcons at all – and it was a lifer[51]. It sat way across a typically flat expanse of grassland in a dead tree, but its large size and pale head were clear. I could even see the faint moustache running down its cheek like a black tear from its eye. Lesser Grey Shrike was also a first for me, and a pretty bird, sitting on a power line right by the road. Roy spotted it as we drove past and I leapt out to get this rather nice Tick for the trip list: a compact shrike, all grey and white with the subtlest of pink flushes on its flanks and the tell-tale black Zorro mask of the shrike family.

All in all the birding was superb, as I knew it would be in this wonderfully open, wild yet tamed place. I got eight new birds for the Trip List which now stood at 208; still no great shakes considering the distances I was doing and the number of countries I was visiting, but this was the last thing on my mind. My back was objecting very strongly to all the walking and I needed a rest. Back at the Hotel Villa Volgy, meeting Tony, Sue, Richard, Jane, Nadia and Heather for a pre-dinner drink, I was exactly where I wanted to be for my last night here. We ended the evening with a stroll in the hotel grounds to listen to a Scops Owl "popping" away in the trees, eventually finding it half way

---

[51]Saker Falcons are rare birds, breeding only in these areas of Eastern Europe and southern Italy (and further east into Russia, Mongolia and China). They are considered to be an endangered species and much of this is put down to "unsustainable capture for the falconry trade".

up a conifer tree on the base of a branch, pressed tight up against the trunk so we could hardly see it – an absolutely classic Scops Owl to round off the evening (Tick – No 209!).

Overnight, my back seized up and I could hardly get out of bed, let alone pack up the bike, which by now needed checking and maybe adjusting. Eventually, in a lot of pain, I swung my legs out of bed and pushed myself side-ways into a sitting position. I took my time and slowly, slowly with the help of a long shower, I managed to loosen up enough to head down for breakfast. I was walking like a zombie, the slightest jolt or bump sending shooting pains from my lower back down into my left leg. The others were concerned, the women in particular not happy about me setting off on the bike. But I had no option.

I gave the bike a look over. The chain needed tightening, but not badly, so I left it; perhaps another little sign that I was feeling near journey's end. I was worried that the rain would have helped to wash off the lubricant on the chain, but it seemed to be glistening healthily. All I could do really were visual checks of fluid levels, tyre pressures and various mechanical operations: brake and clutch cables, gear lever down by the left foot and back brake lever on the right. Lastly, I checked the front fork suspension; nothing seemed seriously amiss and the bike sounded fine when I fired it up after two full days of sitting out in the rain in the hotel car park. A little more capable of walking and lifting, I managed to pack up and get all the gear back on the bike. It took a lot out of me though. I looked forward to sitting on the bike, riding rather than walking and carrying things.

After breakfast, the Eger group gathered round for photos by the minibus and the bike. I was leaving them to another few days of birding with Roy. My thoughts turned to where I was heading next and I realised I'd been living in a bubble these last few days. I had given no thought to where I was going except in the vaguest of terms. Unlike the previous destinations, I had no structure, no contacts or guides to text in advance. I didn't even know exactly where in Poland I was heading for or how long it would take. After the group had departed for another crack at the Hortobagy, I sneaked back into the hotel with maps, books and notes in hand to plan ahead over a coffee (or two). I took Tim with me to help plot and time a route.

The only places that I had firm plans to visit for birding were both in Poland: Bialowieza Forest in the east on the border with Belarus and the Biebrza Marshes in the north. After that, it was only Wilma's grave in Kaunas, Lithuania, then I would be heading home. Tim's journey times to these places were frightening: four hours across Slovakia from Eger into Poland and another six hours or more just to get half way through Poland to Bialowieza. Tim and I made a plan to ride right through Slovakia without stopping. He plotted a route to Rzeszow, well into Poland, opting to go south from Eger (the wrong direction, Tim – Poland is north!) taking the M3 and M30 motorways for speed and to detour round Miskolc, a fairly large town near Eger. I went with Tim's decision in favour of swift and easy progress along the motorways, rather than struggling round the tight bends of the White-backed Woodpecker forest in the Bukk National Park. If it had been a bright day and if my back hadn't been tight and sore, I would have loved to set off through that big wild forest, stopping for birds on my way to the next avian adventure. As it was, I just wanted to get on: now the trip had taken on a sense of let's get this done and go home. I was too far from Bialowieza and Biebrza for those places to fire me with any sense of anticipation – and it started raining again!

By the time we got to the M30 motorway, heading North towards Miskolc, I was riding through a swimming pool. Within an hour, I was soaked again and a few short miles further on we ground to a halt, stopped on the motorway by flashing lights and an ever-increasing queue of traffic. The motorway had been washed away by the floods! A traffic cop, miserable and bored from standing out in the rain (doing very little now that a queue had formed) talked to me as I slowly approached and passed him by.

"Where you go?"

"Slovakia then Poland."

"Not good on moto in rain!"

"Very bad. I am wet"

"Why you go Poland?"

"To find birds."

I mimicked using binoculars and pointed at a couple of birdy stickers on the bike. He looked unimpressed.

"You do thees on moto? Why?"

Why indeed! I shrugged and patted the tank to show that I just liked biking, which at that moment was a lie.

"Be carful een Poland. Full of creemeenals – they steal your bike... for sure."

This made a change. Such dire warning and aspersion was usually reserved for a the next country I was heading to – in this case, Slovakia. Maybe the cop was a Slovak.

I smiled and waved a goodbye as the queue took me past him. He cut a lonely figure receding in the bike mirror, obscured by rain.

The traffic was being diverted into Miskolc, which Tim had been desperate to avoid by coming along the motorway in the first place. The long queue snaked its way through the town until we emerged on the E79 heading North again.

Between Miskolc and the border with Slovakia, Hungary was under water. Fields were flooded so they looked more like shallow lakes with trees sticking out of them, pavements and side roads in villages were submerged and everywhere there were little sand bag walls lining fences, gates and doorways. In one flooded field, there was an abandoned JCB digger, sunk up to its axles, and a caravan listing dolefully into the water, its reflection only magnifying how wrong it all looked. I had never witnessed flooding like this: it was something you only saw on the telly. Every second road was closed off and it began to dawn on me how lucky I was to have got through this far. I would also be lucky to continue without major detours. I reckoned Tim was in for a lot of "re-calculating route". We pressed on.

Now heading due North, Slovakia was just a blur (a surprisingly dry blur), but while the roads were passable and my back held up, we just rode through[52]. At one point, a big brown bird rose up and flew alongside in a field to the right: a Lesser Spotted Eagle with two white spots in its upper wing, clear as day. Apart from this, Slovakia became just a place to get through. The goodbyes at Eger and slow packing up had made for a late start. All the flooding with obligatory coffee stops turned a three-hour journey into a six-hour marathon. By the time I got near the Polish border, I'd had enough. I went to the first B&B I could find: a "family pension" in Ladomirova just south of the border near Svidnik.

The ground everywhere was sodden and soft. Although there was plenty of space for the bike in the back garden of the B&B, I had to find a stout square of wood to rest the side-stand on so that the weight of the bike didn't bury the stand into the ground until the whole lot fell over.

I had a kitchen to myself and there was a tiny hut along the road which acted as a local shop. The shop reminded me of something similar that we had in the tiny council house village where I was brought up in the Far North of Scotland. It was really just a large wooden shed owned by a local family (the son, Freddie, was my best childhood friend… ahh, the memories!), but it was a much-loved hub in the tiny community during the 60s and 70s. Such enterprises have long since ceased to be viable in a world where everyone has a car and we all shop internationally at huge, out of town supermarkets (yes, there is now even a Tesco in Wick!). On the other hand, I'm sure the same applies here in northern Slovakia, yet this little shop was still a going concern. Maybe they are like the French: they value their way of life enough to support small local shops (fresh baguettes every morning in every village – yum!). We don't seem to have that sense of value in Britain – until we lose it completely, then we frantically try to re-create it in the form of trendy little bijou businesses selling local "artisan" produce at ridiculous prices.

---

[52]My notes and dictaphone messages say Northern Slovakia around Kosice was beautiful with the Tatra Mountains to the west and pretty towns to ride through, but it all became a bit of a slog and difficult to recall.

After buying a few basics, in this little trip down memory lane, I "cooked" one of the space meals I had carried with me (the chilli con carne that I had failed to heat up in the Bathroom Inferno, way back in Tarvisio). It was splendid. With no desire to explore the area, I had an early night before hitting the Polish border next day.

After a heartless breakfast, and with Lucky the Spaniel supervising, I updated the blog on my hosts' PC:

Slovakia & into Poland. Hello to all at Eger.

Hi all. No photos, sorrz. Borrowing internet from b and b owners and thez not keen on attaching camera. I'm just about to set off for Polish border. N. Slovakia looks beautiful. Have had four dazs riding in the rain, getting soaked and getting dried off difficult (there is onlz the letter z on this kezboard ´I cant find the one I need!)

Bit hopeless this so won't write much more. Hope to be home on the 28th. Getting tired now.

(I found the letter Y! look... yyyyyyyyyy!).

Best wishes to all, especially Richard, Jane, Tony, Sue, Nadia, Heather and Roy at Villa Volgy. Hope your birding etc went well after I left. It continued pouring for me, sadly, but saw a Lesser Spotted Eagle fly alongside the bike near Kosice, just as Roy said. By the way, lots of closed roads around Miskolc, including the main M30 motorway, because of flooding.

I took a photo of Lucky as he barked at a fat bloke on a bicycle and then I tried to get on the bike with the usual hop to avoid hitting the luggage. My back was having none of it. I had to ease one leg over the seat in a stiffly balletic arch then shuffle over to sit up straight. With good old Tim programmed to get us across the border and on to Bialowieza by "Quickest Route", I eased the bike out onto the road once more... heading for Poland... and home.

Chapter 12 – Bialowieza, Biebrza, & The Last Bird

It is summer 2009 and, for the last four years, I have been working only part-time in order to be with Anne more, just to keep up with things. Increasingly, I have had to do nearly all the practical, day-to-day tasks as well as lifting Anne when she needs it: in and out of bed, the car and the loo – because now she can't stand, let alone walk.

In June, I arrange to go down in hours further, to half-time and I go back in September to a new academic year at college, trying to fit classes and other work into a three day week. But the work I do is never-ending. Script marking comes home with me, I can never leave for home when I finish and there are many times when I have to miss meetings in order to stick to those three days. It is a constant battle, reminding work colleagues that I'm not available all week. They are very understanding, but I just know it is a major pain in the arse for them. I am continually trying to make up for it and I carry around a huge weight of guilt and self-recrimination.

Just a few weeks into the new academic year, one September day, I have an epiphany of sorts: I can't do this any more. I can't keep coming in to college, doing this increasingly demanding job, developing it as a career – and looking after Anne. Within days, I hand in my notice and arrange to finish work at Christmas.

*

As I sat in my umpteenth café, somewhere North of Kosice in Slovakia, a large TV screen showed news images of flood disasters from every country I had passed through. There were scenes of inundation and rushing water in Poland, the Czech Republic, Slovakia, and Hungary. Apart from Czechoslovakia, I had experienced them all, along with the rain that began in

Romania. On the screen, an image came up with a sign for Miskolc, Hungary. I had been diverted into that town only the day before when the motorway had been washed away. Livelihoods were being lost, homes destroyed and there were even some deaths as a direct result of the floods. Here on the screen were images of people being evacuated. A state of emergency had been declared in Poland, where two months worth of rain came down in just 24 hours, at least 25 people died, and around 23,000 people were evacuated. The cost was estimated at 2.5 billion Euros and it was stated in the Polish parliament that the ongoing flooding was "the worst natural disaster in the nation's history... without precedent in the past 160 years".

In a bizarre way, all this made me feel a little better about myself. It somehow vindicated the sense that I'd been battling against heavy odds. It gave explanation to the many weary stops and my slow progress, even my weakness and ill health: it was all because of the floods! I now felt lucky to be alive as opposed to unlucky to have got caught in it.

According to a dictaphone message that I left myself at one point, it was "drying up a bit". I don't know what happened to that millisecond of non-rain but, just south of Lublin in Poland, it all changed again. The sky turned charcoal and, all of a sudden, it got cold. This heavy, ominous atmosphere and the sight of a covered petrol station just across a roundabout, sent me scurrying for shelter (if you can scurry on a motorbike!). As I filled up the bike with petrol, a wind got up, black clouds rolled in and rumbles of thunder came drumming through. Lightning bolted across the sky, searing and cracking just above the petrol station. As I ran into the small shop, gallons of water fell from the sky as if from a giant upturned bucket and I got soaked in just a few steps. The bike, Tim and all my luggage were abandoned under the flat cover of the station pumps as rain spewed out of the sky, crashing onto the concrete and bouncing several inches back into the air. I had never seen rain like it.

"You Eeengleesh?" came a voice from behind the counter.

"No – Scottish," I replied.

"Ahh Scutland! Kenny Dalgleeetsh!"

God, was Kenny Dalglish still the only Scottish player of any note abroad? Not that I knew any other Scottish footballers (as you now know, I hate football, Scottish or otherwise!), so it was a miracle that I didn't have to totally bluff, as I usually do.

"Yes, Kenny Dalglish! Hello," I replied.

"You like Polish weather?" asked the voice.

"Oh yes!" I said sarcastically.

Now, through the window panes of the little shop, the rain was so heavy, it looked like fog outside. I walked to the door to check the bike. It was leaning forlornly on its stand under cover, but still getting wet, as raindrops leapt off the concrete to join others in an unholy riot of dancing water. The road was now just a narrow strip of tarmac between two streams of water, running so fast down both verges, it splashed up onto the pavements. For a while I felt that I could easily get cut off here, unable to get the bike out through feet of water. I was in the middle of the Great Flood all right!

"Do you have coffee?" I asked.

"No, but I work here," said a young chap who had now come round from his hiding place behind the counter, "I can make you one. I am Tomek. It is my day off, but I come to see my friends"

Tomek held out his hand. We shook. I was still looking outside worryingly at the bike.

"You can stay here until it stops. I make you coffee. We chat," said Tomek.

There was nowhere to sit and I felt and looked like the classic drowned rat. Beside Tomek, drowned mouse might be more appropriate. He was a burly bloke, not tall, but thick set and healthy looking. I was a drenched, wasted individual by comparison. I had taken off my bike jacket to dry out a bit and caught sight of my reflection in the glass front of a vending machine: a drowned mouse stared haggardly back at me. I looked small, wet and unwell; not at all the intrepid biker, riding through Europe and taking it all in his stride.

"Your English is very good Tomek."

"Yes, yes," he said excitedly, "I lived in England two summers. I worked in a restaurant. I am chef!"

"Oh, where about?"

"Near London, but you would not know it – outside the city, a long way. You have come a long way from Scutland on your bike."

I explained the route I had taken and the purpose of my trip. I gave him the last of my little paper slips with the blog address on it. He wasn't the least interested in birding (most people weren't), but the bike caught his attention.

"Nice bike," he said, pointing outside to a hazy shape in the rain.

I don't really know why so many people said that. They love bikes on the continent and I thought they would all know the humble status of mine. It was nothing outstanding; not a huge impressive engine, like a BMW touring bike, not a smartly dressed sports bike that would look more at home on the Isle of Man TT, not even a monster like a Honda Goldwing; my bike was a basic, 600cc Honda street bike, dressed in second-hand bits from eBay, yet it still drew appreciative looks. Maybe it was because of its outlandish kit. With the panniers, top box, tank bag and extra bags (where a passenger would be), it did look huge and a little mean with its black engine and silver-grey paintwork. Perhaps it was only non-bikers and the less discriminating who saw it as "a nice bike".

"It got me here Tomek, but not from Scotland; from Suffolk in the South-east of England. I used to live near London. Where did you work?"

"You would not know it. A place called Bushey."

"I know Bushey!" I said excitedly, "I lived in North Harrow until last year. I know Watford and Bushey well. I did my first bike training there!"

"You know Bushey!" said Tomek with even more excitement, "No-one I ever met knows Bushey!"

"Which restaurant did you work at?" I asked.

"The Alpine. You know it?"

"Yes, I used to pass it all the time – until last year, when we moved. The Alpine – right on the corner of a crossroads. They've just painted it and done it up."

"Yes, yes, I know. I hear it closed. You know the Alpine! This is incredible! I make you coffee. We will chat. Incredible! No one knows the Alpine!"

Tomek was over the moon. While he made the strongest mug of fresh coffee I'd ever had, he continued with considerable animation to enthuse about the chance of meeting someone who knew the Alpine restaurant in Bushey.

"You will go to the Alpine and tell them you met Tomek?"

"Yes, sure. We go down that way sometimes. Will they be happy to be reminded of Tomek?" I asked, tongue-in-cheek.

"Tomek got in trouble sometimes, but they liked me! I was the salad chef. I made all the salads. Wow! You know the Alpine, but here you are in Poland! Can I take a photo to show my wife? Just married, you know."

He found a camera and took a photo of himself with a drowned mouse, to amaze his friends. I asked if he would go back to the UK. He seemed rather negative about it.

"No. My life is here now with my new wife. We cannot go to London. Maybe in the future."

With Poland now firmly in the EU, I wonder if Tomek ever became one of the many Poles who moved to the UK for work? And if he did, is he on his way home again, now that we are half-heartedly *not* in the EU since the disastrous referendum of 2016 (don't get me started!). Since my trip and writing this, we have had the referendum and are grappling with Brexit. I'm sure I would have been a "Remainer" anyway but, in completing a trip like this, there is no way I could ever turn inwards and support leaving Europe or feeling anything other than European. The experience makes me feel even more that we have made a huge mistake. I think if I was to do my trip now, I'd feel self-consciously traitorous, wondering if someone like Tomek would be suspicious of me; more of a foreigner than I was when I rode my bike through all these European countries, some of which have only recently become members of the EU themselves.

Tomek and I never kept in touch. And I never did go to the Alpine. From our new home in Suffolk, it was just too far; sometimes that sort of thing works out and sometimes it doesn't.

Apart from the rain and the floods, the only thing stopping me from racing through Poland, on to Lithuania and onto a ferry home was the thought of two mythical places: Bialowieza Forest and the Biebrza Marshes, the last birding destinations of the whole journey. I sent a text to my daughter:

20ᵗʰ May, 10.30
Hi Claire. I'm in Poland! Can you look up DFDS ferries and let me know the sailings from Klaipeda in Lithuania to Kiel in N Germany (from about the 25ᵗʰ) then Esbjerg in Denmark to Harwich. I know they exist, but didn't book in advance. Much easier for you to do than me. Thanks. Let me know. Dad x

Her reply would determine how the last few days of my journey would play out. There might not be any ferries when I wanted them, or I might even have to ride all the way across Poland, Northern Germany and possibly into France to get a boat home. Despite all these possibilities and so much of the planned trip yet to come, I was now thinking of this as the final stage. Looking back, it was probably a combination of illness, the extreme conditions and a very bad back that determined this mindset. In fact, there was still a long way to go and a lot to see if I stuck to my original plan: my next goal was Bialowieza Forest.

Bialowieza is one of the last remaining parts of an enormous primeval woodland that once stretched across Central Europe, untouched for over 7000 years. Most of it is in Belarus and is difficult to visit (the border with eastern Poland runs through the forest), but the 40 square miles within Poland is well protected[53]

[53]Until quite recently, this was true; on 13 July 2017, the EU took Poland to court, over illegal logging operations that are destroying Białowieża. The Polish government said it had authorised the logging to contain a spruce bark beetle infestation and to reduce the risk of forest fires. But scientists, ecologists and the EU allege that the

and is home to Bison, Beavers and Birds; a magnet for naturalists.

Spurred on by these thoughts and heading ever northward through Poland, the sun came out and I saw some dry land! The bike pulled well in the cool dry air, the slightest twist of the throttle on the left handlebar made it leap forward eagerly. That often caught me by surprise; a sign that, the way I normally rode, the bike was well below its limit. Just occasionally though, I felt the scary power of that highly tuned engine, almost as if the bike added a little bit more than I'd asked for – a mischievous mind of its own?

We were making good progress on the bumpy Polish roads. When truck and van drivers saw the bike approaching from behind, they would move over, almost into the gutter, just to let us pass; another sign of how much Eastern Europeans seemed to appreciate bikes and biking. Coffee stops were few and far between and I had already learned that there were no pastries or cakes with coffee in Poland. For a rest and to consume lunch that had been cannibalised from the breakfast table, we pulled in to a large lay-by with a few trucks lined up in the dirt and potholes. The lay-by was in the middle of a forest, which grew on either side of the road. I leant contentedly against the bike seat, taking a swig from a bottle, hoping for a serendipitous bird, a rarity maybe, like Black Woodpecker or Goshawk speeding through the trees. Sure enough a bird turned up: she was dressed in tight denim hot pants, an even tighter top-and little else, other than a vacant, drug-addled expression.

"Hello. I Mandy. You like sex?"

Who doesn't dear!

"Oh yes, very much," I replied, gesturing to the bike sarcastically with a disturbing picture in my mind of the two of us balancing and cavorting on the seat.

Mandy was a sad looking case; not unattractive, but puffily wan from doing little else, but this all day, and tragically the worse for whatever substance was coursing through her arteries.

logging is for illegal commercial use of protected ancient forests. How sad.

A text arrived and was a welcome distraction from the dominating presence of this Polish hooker:

"Hi Dad. Hope u r havn a gd time. Ferries – Klaipeda-Kiel on 25th at 17.30, then Esbjerg-Harwich on 27th at 18.45. Can u make them? Want me to book? All ok at home, don't rush, enjoy it. x"

I needed time to think, to check distances and dates, and decide how I felt about coming home well before the end of May – before I'd had enough time to really see Bialowieza and Biebrza. As I drifted, lost in these thoughts, an almost naked female body pushed itself into my space, reminding me where I was: Mandy was still prowling.

"You want sex with me? We find room," she insisted, thrusting her barely contained boobs right under my nose.

"No, sorry, I have a long way to go. No rooms."

I also knew my back wouldn't take the strain! Not that I was tempted, you understand...

"Fuck you!" was her drawled response. Nice.

As a complete antidote to that tawdry encounter, not far from Bialowieza, I rode into one of the prettiest villages of the whole trip. Kleszcele was like a little piece of paradise; immaculate roads and pavements, swept clean and new looking, with a row of tidy houses and cared-for front gardens. This place was so charming, I kept stopping – and the sun was out too! Further along, through the long village, a stunning church appeared amongst the trees on the opposite side of the road, immaculately and strikingly painted in white and blue. Wandering around the outside, I attracted the attention of a gardener who was looking after the place. By means of gestures and smiles, I let him know how beautiful I thought the whole place was. He seemed pleased that some foreigner had taken the time to appreciate what they clearly loved and looked after with some pride. With a tinge of disappointment, I realised, of course, that this was down to the power of religion: through the centuries, across continents and cultures, the poorest communities were made to keep impressive (and expensive) places of worship. I am no fan of the Church, or of most organised religion: it has a lot to answer for in my book. Perhaps Kleszcele cathedral was an extreme example in such a small place, shining, almost dripping with gilding and gold objects inside – but it was an arresting building in a lovely little village. The doors were locked, but the gardener opened them for me, and through a further set of locked bars, I could see all this opulence extending inside. I took a few photos, which for some reason were all out of focus; maybe God resented my harsh judgement.

The rest of Kleszcele didn't look at all like "down-at-heel Poland". In fact, not much of what I saw in Poland looked down-at-heel. At one point, I stopped for an early lunch in a newly built restaurant and had the best burger I'd ever eaten; the bun was light and fresh, the burger itself was succulent, dripping with salad, relish and dressing. The place was run or staffed by a group of trendy, bouncy young people; an optimistic new business in an up and coming country. Poland was feeling good.

The approach to Bialowieza was through endless forest on a dead straight road. I kept stopping for birds and saw plenty, but nothing new: a few woodpeckers, lots of familiars like Song Thrush and Blue tit, a Hawfinch and a Sparrowhawk dashing across the road between the belts of trees, no doubt pursuing some poor little songbird. As I approached the village itself, I kept imagining Bison appearing in the gloom of the trees, like shadows from the past. The sense of entering an ancient, hidden place pervaded the very air. It felt right to be here and the feeling that this was the fag-end of my journey started to lift. I was excited about this place and set about finding somewhere to stay.

Like all places with a super-hot attraction in the middle of it, Bialowieza village was strange. There was a big, expensive Best Western hotel in a place the size of a postage stamp. The trappings of tourism were everywhere too: banners, shops selling souvenir trinkets and, of course, more visitors than inhabitants. I'd done a bit of research on this place and I knew that somewhere there was a major visitor/interpretation centre to do with the National Park; maybe I'd get advice there on where to stay.

Winding through the well-kept village, I passed the Best Western and, as I rounded a sharp corner, a large wooden gatehouse came into view. Next to it was an imposing brick building, like a town hall or a large post office. The gateway was an elaborate structure with a peaked roof of wooden tiles supported on wooden pillars, forming an impressive arched entrance to the park with pedestrian entrances to the side and a cubicle for a steward or attendant. It had the words "Bialowieski Park Narodowy" carved into the cross piece at the top and it looked every bit the grand entrance to a grand place[54]. I was a bit dim about the words: Narodowy (National) confused me and another sign for "Park Palacowy" failed to register that this was the way to the Palace Park where the new visitor centre and huge observation tower now stood.

Riding the bike under the arch of the lovely wooden gateway, I was not at all sure that this was the right way. The tracks became footpaths with people strolling along under tall, impressive trees. I kept going on the widest track until it opened out into a tarmac road and finally a large, block paved parking area in front of a big new building: the Palace Park visitor centre. Excellent! It was a modern, but grand building with an observation tower the size of an airport control centre. I vowed to go up there at some point.

It was getting hot as I pulled up and leant the bike onto its side stand for what felt like the millionth time. It had been a long ride through most of south-west Poland and here I was, right on the border with Belarus and in a place of many dreams: Bialowieza Forest.

Cool inside, I went to the desk and spoke to the smartly dressed reception lady. I quickly learned that this place had

---

[54]In the 16th century, King Sigismund I built a new wooden hunting manor in the village of Białowieża, part of which, I assume is the rather grand entrance to the park. King Sigismund also brought in the first recorded piece of legislation on the protection of the forest; the death penalty for poaching a bison! (bit rich when he'd just built a dirty great hunting lodge, but at least the bison are still here today.)

"pokoje goscinne": guest rooms. I decided to stay here, regardless of cost (within reason – surely it wouldn't be more expensive than the Best Western?). I also felt that I should support the Park with my custom and was right in the heart of the place I had come to see, as opposed to some hotel or pension in the village. To my delight, at 100 Zloty (about £20), the rooms were very cheap and brand new; a cross between a large swish youth hostel and a hotel, on several floors with lifts, carpeted corridors and a separate, modern restaurant. It turned out to be one of the best places I had stayed in so far.

With my back aching from a day on the road, I couldn't face hauling all the panniers and other luggage up to my room as I had been doing; this time I left behind everything that was locked onto the bike and took only a couple of bags up to the room. As it was, it took a double trip. Just as I shut the door behind me, the phone rang. It was Anne. She sounded fairly upbeat, asking where I was and when I'd be home, but the subject of money came up fairly quickly and had obviously been on her mind.

"You didn't leave me any money," she said

"How d'you mean?" I asked, "you've got loads of money in your account."

"I've got no cash here for spending. You didn't leave me any cash."

My mind was completely at sea over this. It came out of the blue, totally out of context with everything I was doing, like something from another, or someone else's life. I racked my brains: had I really left no cash for Anne before I left? For quite a few seconds, I had no idea. I just couldn't remember.

"I'm sure I did," I said, but I wasn't sure, and that must have conveyed in my voice.

"Well, you didn't – off on your little trip. You don't care about me."

As she spoke, I gradually connected back to life at home. The time-line of the preparation for my trip slowly came back to me. Meantime, Anne was getting into her stride:

"I have no money to pay for anything. It's all right for you!"

Eventually, I remembered that I had gone to a cash point and got some money to leave for Anne while I was away, to save the kids, carers or neighbours having to pay for things. But where had I left it? I had no idea.

"I left you £250 in cash," I said, frantically trying to recall where I'd put it.

"No you didn't, you liar!"

She was shouting now.

Then I remembered where I'd put the money, it was found and I felt exonerated, but the damage had been done. Anne's feelings of abandonment had been given rein and she was in full flow. The conversation ended in recrimination and outrage, then the phone went dead.

With no way of making things at home any different or better, I went for a walk – no, a hobble – around the park gardens, Red Spots in hand in this tranquil place, with its grand trees and landscaped lawns. Within minutes, I was craning up with the binoculars at a Pied Flycatcher (or was it a Collared?) and trying to ID a woodpecker that was drumming nearby.

Evening was drawing in as I extended my stroll around the back of the centre and on via board-walks over a reed-fringed lake to another entrance where there were more obvious signs of tourism: a kiosk selling ice-cream and a small shop which acted as a ticket office. In the shop, I booked a guide to take me into the "Special Protection Area" for just a few Zloty. I was to be back there at 6am for an 8Km walk into the forest. 8Km, with my back?! I had serious doubts about my ability to do this, but thought it best to see how I felt in the morning.

In search of a youth hostel that I'd seen signposted earlier, I rode out of the Palace Park through the impressive wooden arch. Signs for Bed & Breakfast were everywhere: accommodation would have been no trouble. Youth hostels these days have computers for hire or even free use and I needed one to update the blog. I found the hostel tucked around some back streets, surrounded by the babble of young travellers hanging out on patches of grass or sitting astride the low walls. Inside, next to the reception desk were two ancient PCs, their screens ominously dark and blank. I paid less than a pound for a no-limit session on one of the PCs and sat down to switch it on. Almost immediately, twenty mosquitoes rallied around the monitor as it flickered into grey life: the little buggers were everywhere! I killed nineteen, but the one that got away must have gone to get his mates because another twenty appeared within minutes. I carried on typing and uploading photos until it became unbearable, then I realised the front door was constantly being left open by the chilled-out youngsters. I was far from chilling in the War of The Mozzies and I developed a deep resentment every time the door was left open: type blog, kill mozzie, type blog, get up, kill mozzie, close door, sit down, kill three mozzies, type blog, upload photo, type blog, close door, kill mozzie, close door...

"Oh for fuck's sake shut the door!" I bellowed after one gaggle of girls drifted out, casually leaving the door wide open for another battalion of mozzies to enter the fray.

I got a note on my blog from my sister in law:

22nd May
Robbie, I've just spent ages going through last weeks papers... We've got a pair of Purple Herons nesting in Dungeness. Apparently a first time for the UK. Local police have been drafted in to keep a watchful eye on the comings and goings! If all goes well, the RSPB are going to set up a viewing station. The chicks are due to hatch in June. So I was very interested to see your Purple Heron! Can't save the paper cutting though – it's gone!! Tracey

27 May
Hi Tracey – Just seen this comment. What news for birders! I had no idea. Yes, it would be first time nesting (they turn up as rarities sometimes, but not breeding, though I bet they have tried or even succeeded in the past cos it's the sort of thing that gets "suppressed" – that's birder lingo for kept secret!). Somehow, I think you'll be having a "Purple Heron" visit from us!! Cheers. R

This may not sound that significant considering that I was thousands of miles away on my trip, but it was the first time Purple Heron had ever bred in Britain (it was a fair rarity, even as just a visitor) and secondly, my sister in law (who isn't a birder) had been to see it! So here I was in far flung, unspoilt Eastern Europe, bottling out of birding and losing my belief, while my sister in law was seeing firsts for the UK. It was an uncomfortable feeling, but it was good for me: things had to change.

I spent so long on the blog and the mozzie hunt, it was dark outside by the time I rode back to the visitor centre. The arched gatehouse entrance was now severely closed with large wooden doors; not even enough room to squeeze the bike down the side. I was stuck – until a guard appeared from inside the cubicle on the right-hand side of the arch. He motioned that I should take a long way round to the back of the centre. With no map and in the pitch black, I turned round, hoping that the route would be obvious. There was a tiny sign a few streets further on: "Palacowy". It still didn't register that this meant "Palace", but I knew it had something to do with the visitor centre, so I turned right. Immediately the "road" degenerated into something not unlike no man's land of the First World War trenches: deep holes and undulating mounds where a track should have been. Swerving and dipping, this was proper off-roading – but I didn't have an off-road bike – and all the panniers were still on. I spent most of the time standing on the foot rests to let the bike rock underneath me rather than have it buck me around too much. It took a great act of faith or just blind hope to keep going; everything about it said this couldn't really, seriously, be the back entrance to the centre, but I persevered until, after about a mile, the winding, bucking track eventually opened out and smoothed into a wide gateway on the other side of the park. The lights of the visitor centre guided me along footpaths back to where I had previously parked the bike.

Over a cup of tea in the swish restaurant, I left a dictaphone message:

"I think I deserve a medal. Message to Iain: this is like Long Way Round!"

The message went on to bemoan how much of biking in Eastern Europe had been this way:

"I should have brought an off-road bike. There is so much of this: rutted bumpy roads – even the tarred ones."

By the time I got back, it was too late for dinner. I moaned into the dictaphone:

"I blame the blog. It takes far too long to do it on unfamiliar PCs. Especially uploading all those individual photos,"

Eventually, I stopped complaining into the machine and enjoyed the refreshing cup of tea; except for all the mozzies – again! Yes, once more, everybody who came into the restaurant left the door open and let swarms of them in.

A group of drunk women on a nearby table were laughing so much, I thought one of them was going to pass out. This sort of raucous normality felt a little surreal after the nightmare ride to get back here; it should have led to a deserted log cabin or a cave, not this modern, brightly lit scene of hilarity. Despite the joy of killing a few hundred more mozzies, and watching this woman give herself a laughter induced aneurysm, I headed off for an early night: up at 05.00 next morning to meet my guide at 06.00.

Irek was a student ecologist at some university in Poland. His English was very hesitant, but good enough, despite a very thick Polish accent, and he was extremely quiet and mild mannered. I didn't dislike him, but I felt a little uncomfortable in the silences. He tended to act as if he was in a church; with extreme reverence for the cathedral that was Bialowieza Forest. Turns out this was entirely appropriate: the place was like a natural cathedral and walking round it with someone like Irek was exactly right.

After approaching through an open, but uncultivated meadow with tall grasses, orchids and the buzzing of insects, we entered the dappled gloom of the forest. Despite being dull and damp, the atmosphere was one of exuberant life as sunlight broke through in misty shafts. The trees seemed endless, both upwards to the enriching sunlight and sideways into a disappearing expanse of undergrowth and shrub. Our path meandered deeper into the forest; a real sense of passing into another time or another world. The hype about it being primeval and ancient was no hype: this place really was untouched, in its fantastic decay and regeneration. Irek explained the philosophy of leaving everything to nature. Fallen trees were left where they landed, across paths, against other trees or simply lying on the forest floor. They would provide a habitat for other organisms and rot away after a few decades, passing their rich resources back to the soil. It made me realise how different our ancient woodland is in the UK: most of it managed to the nth degree and cleared to keep it safe and accessible. Rotting wood in our forests is left in neat piles, having been dragged out of harm's way. Maybe we are missing a trick: leave the dead trees where they are?

The Polish attitude towards Bialowieza Forest is one of "leave it alone, let nature take its course". This flies in the face of most conservation wisdom here in the West. We believe so much damage has been done that we need to actively manage nature reserves and other sites to improve them for wildlife. Maybe both are true. Bialowieza is so big, so ancient and so untouched that it can remain environmentally healthy with no human intervention. On the other hand, in more developed regions where habitats have been destroyed, reduced or radically altered, the only way of restoring and maintaining a "natural" system is to manage it. I've always been uncomfortable with this, but ecologists believe that our wild areas would simply run down to some lowest common denominator and collapse under the weight of introduced species, climate change, pollution and a host of other threats. Without management, they claim, we would have a much less diverse natural environment and certainly nothing like that which we have lost. I'm not so sure: given time, I wonder if some of our wild places would not be best left alone – like Bialowieza (Discuss!).

Irek stopped as a burst of song issued from a nearby clearing. Although he wasn't a bird expert, he knew this one well enough:

"Red-breasted Flycatcher!"

Such a sweet song; like a cross between an energetic Chiffchaff and a Willow Warbler. The little bird, a juvenile, popped up onto a branch just a few feet above our heads, cocked his black and white tail and carried on singing. Despite being fairly plain; white below and grey above with a faint hint of orange near his neck, his body language and his whole demeanour ("jiz" to a birder) was feisty and confident. This little chap ("R.B. Flicker" to UK birders) charmed the pants off me and I could have stayed listening to him for ages. However, he seemed to suddenly clock us and, with a little buzzing call, he took off, displaying white side tail feathers mixed with black in a chequered pattern, very like a Wheatear[55].

The bird song in these woods echoed like in a church, some familiar like the loud burst from a Chaffinch or a Wren, some unfamiliar like an alarm call from an unidentified species. The overall effect was like an orchestra. The closest I could come to it was dawn chorus in a wood at home at five in the morning. Here, it was a constant backdrop and the sound seemed to be contained by the damp cool air as if we were in a small room.

"Red Banded Pol-ee-pore foongus," said Irek, pointing to a bracket fungus growing on the side of a dead tree. It was the size of a car tyre with a dull red band around the edge. It looked like half an umbrella stuck to the tree.

"Bird's Nest Orchid," was the next plant of interest from Irek as we strolled on.

[55]To UK birders, the black inverted "T" shape in the tail is so characteristic of Wheatears, it was almost a shock as the little flycatcher took off, unexpectedly showing the same pattern.

"Eet ees paraseetic on the roots of thees treess. No Chlorofeel. No leafs," he said.

The plant was a drab brown thing, but it had the flower spike of an orchid. It had no leaves and not a hint of green (no Chlorofeel!). I had never heard of a parasitic orchid before, but was fascinated to see it growing by getting its nutrients direct from the tree roots: more like a fungus than a flowering plant.

We stopped at an opening where Irek clearly always delivered his next speech:

"Thees ees special airea: here you see the wet meecro 'abitat." He pointed to some trees growing out of little conical mounds surrounded by water. Of all the places we passed through, this was the one that really made the forest seem otherworldly. It reminded me of the marshy world in The Empire Strikes Back, where Luke Skywalker first meets Yoda: essentially a shallow lake, with small islands of moss and other vegetation scattered across it. The water almost surrounded us and from each island, no more than a metre or two across, a tree sprouted, rising slim and elegant in search of light.

"Een thees wet plaices, there ees Black Alder, but on the islands, eet ees Spruce. Thees ees becawse they are growing on dead tree under the wawter, and other plants grow too. Then the island comes and the spruce can grow out of the wawter"

"Ah, yes," I said, the penny dropping, "It's a kind of succession"

"Yes!" said Irek, surprised that I knew this and, I suspect, relieved that he didn't have to go on with the speech any further.

I explained my background in Biology and education and we talked a bit about how this wonderful habitat came about. He told me that there would be Black Alder growing if it was like other woodlands, but because it is so old and untouched, this process has been allowed to continue for the last 7000 years – and probably for eons before that. I took lots of photos of this serene, weird and special place. I could have stayed there for ages; in fact, Irek was quite happy to linger too. I got the impression that he stayed longer than usual because of how captivated I was by it all. Irek suited this place: he was a quiet, serene man, in no hurry.

The air smelled heavy with wild garlic in places where patches of its white flower carpeted the forest floor. We walked past endless trees cloaked and dripping with mosses and lichens like I've never seen: they must have been there for centuries to become so adorned. As we rounded a sharp bend in the path, a flash of black and white caught my eye as it flew onto a low dead tree trunk in front of us. I knew it was a woodpecker and Irek stiffened with binoculars to his eyes. We both saw it together

"Three-toed Woodpecker?" I asked in an excited, urgent whisper

"Yes, yes!" exclaimed Irek.

"Oh my God Irek," I hissed in an excited whisper, "I have waited so long for this. I never thought I'd see one, not even here"

This should have been a major "Fuck, fuck, fuck!" moment, but I couldn't risk offending or embarrassing the mild-mannered Irek and I didn't want to come across as an oaf, in this of all places. Instead, I whispered it to myself over and over:

"Oh fuck, fuck, fuck, fuck, fuck: a fucking Three-toed fucking Woodpecker! Fuck, fuck, fuck" (I can be very eloquent!).

I should explain: this woodpecker is not the rarest in Europe (that dubious honour belongs to the White-backed Woodpecker, which Roy Adams had shown us so easily and unceremoniously in the Bukk Hills of Hungary), but Three-toed is not at all easy to find. It is very much a species of Northern Scandinavia, breeding east across into Russia/Siberia and beyond. There are some isolated populations in the Alps and in the Carpathians, like the mountains I had walked in around Zarnesti in Romania, but I doubt if I really had much chance of seeing one there, especially on my rather pathetic birding walk from Gigi Popa's place. Here in Poland, they were right on the western edge of their Russian range, which according to the maps, starts in Belarus. I should have had no expectation of seeing one of these, except that Gerard Gorman's book, *Birding in Eastern Europe*, has Three-toed Woodpecker on the front cover, and he lists it for several sites; a very good bird in anyone's book and one of the least likely of all my target species. Even Irek was amazed and excited at this unusual encounter.

The bird was so close – and confiding – as he clung and hopped his way along the dead tree trunk just a few yards from us. After soaking up the joy of this encounter through the Red Spots, I slowly got out the 'scope. The woodpecker filled the field of view and I could even zoom in on its yellow crown. I took an obscene number of photos of this little beauty; not that it sparkled with colour or anything so obvious, but its black and white striped head and general humbug plumage was captivating – and so different to all the other woodpeckers I had seen so far.

We watched the little woodpecker for at least fifteen minutes before he flew off. I could have left Bialowieza happy after that, but there was more to come. Further on, Irek stopped at a nest hole: clearly, one he knew and stopped at as a matter of routine on these walks. Within minutes, another woodpecker appeared right next to the hole, did the usual check around, then plunged inside. I recognised it straight away, having seen a few on my travels:

"Middle Spotted?"

"Yes, thees nest has been very acteef in the last days"

The scope and camera were still out and I managed a few photos of the bird at the hole and emerging a few minutes later. The photos I was taking looked good on the camera, but on later viewing, the challenging conditions for photography became apparent: the wood was so dark, the images were either dull or grainy and, being highly magnified through the 'scope[56], they were often not very sharp. Nevertheless, I was dead chuffed to get any pictures of some of these birds. The Middle Spot was a handsome black and white bird, like the larger Greater Spotted

---

[56]Taking photos through the telescope makes things even darker and I had no "digiscoping" adapter for the camera; holding my bog-standard digital camera up against the eyepiece made my photography very hit-and-miss.

Woodpecker that we get commonly in the UK, but with a whiter face, pale red on his cap and a flush of pink under his tail.

In a particularly dark part of the forest, Irek pointed silently into the gloom. I couldn't see what we were looking at, but began to hope that it was one of the extremely elusive Bison. He said something, which I missed, so was none the wiser, but eventually, I could see a wooden cross surrounded by a low, rough wooden fence almost overgrown with tangled weeds, then closer to us, a bronze plaque. Bialowieza was used by the Nazis as a hiding place for bodies; a mass grave of Polish civilian resistance fighters murdered by the Gestapo from 1941 to 1944. We stood silent for a protracted few minutes. Rarely does the sad history of a place fill the air of the present day the way that spot did for me then.

The walk with Irek had brought us round in a circle, back to the open, sun-drenched meadow. I was sad to be heading back to the Palace visitor centre. I think Irek had been pleasantly surprised to have someone so enthusiastic and appreciative of something he valued so much. He bid me a warm farewell at the door to the centre and I dragged myself inside, realising that I had done a lot of walking on the sore back, the distraction of the forest and its inhabitants acting as an analgesic.

Breakfast! Coffee! My walk with Irek had started so early that, although long, it had only taken me to 9.30. I felt I deserved a proper sit-down meal this time and I was in no rush.

Down in the rather swish restaurant where hilarity had filled the large L-shaped room the previous night, it was quiet and calm. I sat on a plush red chair and ordered a full cooked breakfast (or the closest you can get in Poland: basically eggs with tomatoes and bacon). I had orange juice, coffee and toast, and I watched the TV screen, which was showing more images of rising flood waters in both city and countryside. Over a second coffee, I wrote my notes: all about Bialowieza forest, Flycatchers, Woodpeckers and trees growing out of islands in the water.

The Biebrza Marshes were only two and a half hours ride away and that much closer to Lithuania. I debated about cutting things short; maybe leaving Biebrza for another time – a reason to return if you like. If I went to Biebrza, it would be my final birding hot spot. Like the Hortobagy in Hungary, the Danube Delta in Romania and Bialowieza here in Poland, Biebrza was a legend to me. I was concerned that I wouldn't do it justice with my bad back, and general weariness from all the rain and floods. I consulted Tim: Biebrza was only a two-hour ride away. In decision-making mode, and over another coffee in the comfortable surroundings of the restaurant, I phoned Ieva in Lithuania to make arrangements for meeting and going to Wilma's grave:

"Hi Ieva, it's Robert."

"Ah, Robert! Where are you?"

"I'm in Poland, not far from Bialystok."

"I can't believe you are here! When are you coming to Kaunas? How is your trip?"

"It has been great Ieva. An amazing adventure. I have one more place to go then I can meet you. I have a ferry booked from Klaipeda on Thursday quite late, at 5.30pm. Will you be free on Wednesday or Thursday morning?"

"Yes, I'll be here. So will Emilija. We are looking forward to seeing you. I never thought you would come here!"

"Ok. Could we meet around 12.00 on Wednesday?"

"Yes, yes. I will tell Emilija and Alma – that is Wilma's sister: she wants to meet you."

"I'm looking forward to it too. It will be nice to see you again. Ok Ieva, I've got to go now. See you soon."

"See you on Wednesday Robert, bye."

Having such a domestic conversation with someone I knew and these arrangements marking the final leg of my journey, I came off the phone feeling strange. It was all falling into place now and it helped me to decide on Biebrza: I had today and the next day to get there, then Wednesday morning to ride to Kaunas and meet Ieva. I could stay over somewhere and do some birding in Biebrza. I couldn't just bypass it; not coming this close.

The journey to Biebrza isn't even a blur, it's a total blank. The only landmark I have is the town of Monki, very close to Biebrza itself, and I only remember the name because it sounds like Monkey (yes, I'm that good!). I covered the miles fast, doing a lot of overtaking, with trucks moving over to let me past. At one point, a line of cars lay ahead. I flicked the indicator to overtake, checked the mirror and zipped out – right in front of a blue Chrysler car which had appeared from behind. The driver hadn't paid any attention to my signal and he seemed not to have given me any room at all: it was an aggressive act. I caught sight of him just in time to move back a little as he shot past just a few centimetres from my handlebars, so close I could see the dirt on his door and a cobweb on his wing mirror. He was clearly trying to force himself past. Perhaps he felt I was going too fast or was unhappy about my previous overtaking manoeuvres, but his way of showing it was unacceptable to me: a biker is so vulnerable to the slightest impact, he had seriously endangered my life (*Cars 9; Bikes 7*). I was livid and set off in pursuit to make my feelings felt. He was racing me – or trying to. In a veil of road rage, I chased after him, knowing the bike was way quicker than his car (*Cars 9; Bikes 8*). When I finally got into a position to overtake him, I pulled alongside him doing about 70mph and shook my fist at him then sped off. What a child! In my defence, I was angered, not by his overtaking or racing, but by how he had risked my safety, even my life.

Not sure how far I had to go to the visitor centre at Biebrza, I stopped at an "Orlen" services in Monki. I had decided that I liked these clean red and white services in Poland and sought them out in favour of other, less corporate joints, which were often a little seedy. Orlens were crisp and new, clean and bright and I liked the coffee. The Monki Orlen (what a name!) was full, so I had to sit outside (which I'm not fond of). Almost as soon as I sat down, a bloke approached, striding across the car park with a big smile and his hand stretched out.

"Hello. I am Eric."

I shook his hand. He had an American drawl, but a strong Polish accent to his fluent English.

"You are riding very fast my friend. Where are you going?" he asked, pointing to the bike with all its gear piled up. I got the feeling that he was less than impressed at my bike riding and I wondered if this was his way of having a little go, after the near accident I'd just had: perhaps he had witnessed it and thought I was at fault. Maybe I was.

I ignored this conjecture and told him all about my trip. He became extremely animated.

"Oh man! I would love to do that. Wow, that's great. That's a good thing, man!"

Eric had a flashy air about him. He was scruffily dressed in a cool, Easy Rider (without the bike) style, with his shades and a black Stetson hat.

"Yeah, I'd love to do that, it must be great, but bikes scare me, man. I couldn't do it. I rode a bike a bit, years ago, but it scared me, man. You should watch your speed around here though."

"Yes, I was going a bit fast. I hate being behind cars and trucks. It's the potholes," I explained, "you can't see them coming if you're following a car. Trucks are even worse. I always overtake if I can; to get a clear view of the road ahead of me, you see?"

Eric nodded sagely, appreciating my reasoning.

"Sure, sure. But watch out for the cops, that's all I'm saying, man. They'll slap a fine on you. They're all over here and they're bored, you know?"

I nodded sagely, appreciating his reasoning.

Eric danced around a bit, repeating how he would love to do what I was doing and how I was so brave 'n all. He was high on something, definitely high. We shook hands and I set off, grateful to be shot of hyper-Eric.

The Orlen services in Monki were just a few kilometres from the Biebrza centre, which was pleasantly tucked away in some woods. Tim got a little confused trying to find the side track that switched back off the main road, following it a short distance along a railway line. Past a tall lookout tower, I found the park visitor centre: another large new building, like the one at

Bialowieza, with an accommodation block, an interpretation centre and a small museum of local wildlife (dubiously presenting stuffed birds and mammals of the area). It was all very professionally done and wardens were there to greet you. Because of the language issue, I waited for a volunteer warden who spoke English. His name was Artur, a young guy in his early twenties and one of the nicest, most helpful people I'd met on the whole trip. Everything was "Yes, can do". He even helped me carry the bike luggage up the three flights of stairs to the little suite of rooms.

"Artur, I need to find a guide to help me find some birds. Do you know anyone?"

"Yes, we have a list of local people who can go out with you – but it is the weekend. I don't know who will be free. You can phone them. I give you the list"

The rooms were like spacious student accommodation. I had a kitchen with a fridge and a separate shower and toilet. I felt so good about the place, I decided to stay two nights to do Biebrza justice.

Once back in the centre reception, Artur produced the list of guides on which he had numbered the five best to try. As Artur was leaving for the evening I set about phoning them. Nightmare! With every one, I felt I should ask if it was ok to speak English. This got extremely cumbersome: one or two couldn't speak English and ended the conversation with a mumble, others spoke English and didn't see the need to be asked.

"Yes, of course, I speak English!" came a couple of responses, followed by "No I am not free to guide you, sorry"

Others were a little less brusque, but still not available. I had exhausted Artur's recommended highlights and tried some others until a female voice said,

"No, I'm not free tomorrow, but if you want, I am going out this evening with an American man. You can join us"

Despite feeling tired, I jumped at the chance: being a weekend, this might be my only option. I scribbled down

Katarzyna's details. I was to meet her in Goniadz, just up the road, at her residential garage where I could leave the bike.

I heated up the last space meal (chicken dopeaza) in the kitchen, washed it down with a cup of tea and shovelled down a yoghurt in a rush to get to Goniadz in time. With no luggage, the bike felt light and responsive. I flew the 6 km to the block of flats where Katarzyna lived. As I pulled in next to the flats, a car drew up and a tiny young woman dressed in combat fatigues got out in a whirl of boots, zips, press studs and hair. Kasha was a buzzing knot of energy. She was also unexpectedly attractive: a foot taller and she could have been a model on a photo-shoot for female military uniforms.

"Hi. With the bike, I guess you are Robert. I am Kate," she said rather brusquely.

Katarzyna had become Kasha, Kasha had become Kate.

"Hello, Kate. Thanks for doing this at such short notice."

"That's ok. If I wasn't out with John, the American guy, I couldn't do it. You are lucky." I was indeed.

"Is it ok with him if I tag along? How much will it be?"

"I checked with him. It's ok. You don't have to pay for just this evening; John has booked two days guiding."

This was unbelievably generous – of both of them. Kate could easily have pocketed some extra dosh from me, and John might have wanted a contribution since he was no longer getting one-to-one guiding. I felt a little uncomfortable about it, as if I was scrounging.

Kate busied herself around in her garage, giving me boxes of stuff to put in her car for a wildlife talk she was giving somewhere the next morning. Finally, she handed me an animal skull.

"Do you know what animal that is?"

The most obvious feature of the skull was a pair of huge brown teeth curving out of its upper jaw and round in front of the mouth: some enormous gnawing animal. I set it on the bonnet of her car to have a look at and take a few photos.

"Is it a beaver?"

"Very good. Yes, we have them a lot here in Biebrza"

"Very impressive – with the teeth!"

"Ok Robert, let's go. We have to pick up John. He wants to see Aquatic Warbler this evening, but I hope we see more for you too. Can you get your bike in the garage ok?"

There was a metal rod in the floor that formed a base for the door to shut against. Not expecting such an uncompromising bump, it almost bucked me off as I rode the bike over. I worried that it could be very difficult to get the bike out over that on our return.

Kate sat, diminutive in the driver's seat, with her mane of grey-brown hair tumbling over her shoulders. She really was a lovely looking woman and yet she had (or she had cultivated) a macho, outdoor-adventurer air; almost suspicious and stand-offish. She certainly didn't play on her femininity and there was no joking around. Perhaps she had to act this way to be taken seriously in her job and maybe to avoid being hit on constantly, or perhaps this was just how she was. I liked her, but I was wary: familiarity didn't seem appropriate.

We picked up John from his B&B accommodation and sped off in search of Aquatic Warbler. John was a portly American in his mid-seventies; a gentle, quiet type who, although he talked a lot, was calm and easy to be around. Kate had been guiding him around Biebrza for the last couple of days and he was on friendly terms with her. She treated him as if he was her granddad: a little condescendingly, but in a nice way. We talked about John's European birding trip, my bike journey and the birds we wanted to see.

"Do you have target birds here Robert?" asked John.

"Well, yes, the usual ones for Biebrza. I expect Kate is fed up with people asking to see the same ones but, I'd like to see Great Snipe, Greater Spotted Eagle, Citrine Wagtail, Scarlet Rosefinch, and Aquatic Warbler. Bluethroat would be nice because I couldn't find any in Hungary"

"The eagle is a possibility," said Kate, "They are around, but not guaranteed. The Great Snipe lek has been flooded, but you could see one or two around. The others you will see. Aquatic Warbler – here tonight!" Kate was bullish.

I was disappointed to hear about the Great Snipe: if there is one bird people come here to see, that's it. In common with some other species like Black Grouse and Ruff, Great Snipe perform a mating display called a lek, where males get together in a competitive group to display to females. It is an experience most birders have on their bucket list. Great Snipe are also very rare and only found in the Baltic countries, Northern Scandinavia, Russia and here in Poland. Kate was fairly definite that the famous lek was literally a washout: a further victim of the recent floods.

"You have to go there at sunset and wait for a long time. Sometimes we need lights to see them. It is not worth trying all that until the water levels go down. Sorry"

Just as she said this, she slammed on the brakes, forced the car into reverse and backed onto the side of the road.

"Through those bushes. Look!"

Kate got out of the car and started to set up her telescope and tripod which, when assembled, looked bigger than her. The way she had stopped the car, I was sure she must have seen a Great Snipe but, through the binoculars, I could see this big grey shadow moving in amongst the tall marshy grass of a wet meadow. It resolved into the shape of a large mammal with its head down in the grass stems.

"Do you know what that is?" Kate asked.

Silence. It looked just like a big cow – until it lifted its head.

"Elk!" I exclaimed, unprepared for this big, wild mammal.

Its strange, elongated nose and lumpy forehead were unmistakeable once it raised its head out of the long grass.

"Yes, *Alces alces*. That is a male. Can you see the small antlers? He is growing new ones for this year."

I got my 'scope out and took a few misty, distant record shots of this magnificent animal. I hadn't checked up on general wildlife much and had no idea that Elk[57] were here.

"Are there a lot here, Kate?" I asked.

[57]European or Eurasian Elk are the same as North American Moose (barring sub-species differences). Confusingly, North America also has an "Elk" which is more like a large Red Deer.

"There are about half a million in Europe," she replied, "Most are in Sweden and Finland. Poland has three thousand only. Biebrza is the largest population in Poland: about seven hundred."

I think that was her way of saying we were lucky to see one.

Back in the car, Kate drove further along the "Tsar's road", a dead straight route which cuts through the park, but its surface was like that of the moon. I was glad not to be riding the bike over this cheese grater. John was fairly quiet (unusual for a yank!), but he chatted away about birds and showed some interest in my bike trip and the birds I'd seen.

As we pulled in at a large lay-by with a few other cars, John collared Kate as she put on her walking boots:

"Oh Kate, I must ask you about a bird I saw near the house yesterday evening. Pine Grosbeak."

"Pine Grosbeak!" I exclaimed, "wow John, good bird, didn't think they were round here, are they, Kate?"

Kate was diplomatic:

"Unlikely John, not a bird of Poland."

But I could tell from her demeanour, she meant, "Not a cat's chance in Hell mate!"

John insisted:

"Oh yes, definitely a Pine Grosbeak."

Now, being from the States, John should know a Pine Grosbeak when he sees one (in fact he more or less said as much). Kate had no problem politely dismissing it as nonsense, but I couldn't help thinking that maybe this guy had seen a real rarity for Poland and maybe we ought to let him show us. Kate was having none of it: out of John's earshot, she told me John was in fact a bit of an old duffer.

"John is lovely, but he's not quite, how you say... with it?"

"Away with the fairies?" I suggested.

"What!?" Kate said with a broad smile on her face, "you say that in English?"

"Yes, it means living in a bit of a fantasy world"

"Away with fairies," Kate repeated, "I like that."

"Away with THE fairies, is better," I said.

We giggled a little childishly, then Kate snapped back into guide mode, closing the chink in her armour, possibly out of consideration for John. She strode off in her combat gear, ready to do battle, hefting her telescope and tripod as if it was a shotgun and we were off hunting. In a way, we were.

"Savi's," she said, pointing into the reed bed to our left.

We were on a substantial and fairly new boardwalk, built to carry us a couple of feet above the standing water of the marshy reed bed below. The thin trilling of Kate's Savi's Warbler weakly penetrated the air around us until I heard another singing nearby, but this one sounded different.

"Is that a Grasshopper Warbler, Kate?" I asked, "I've never heard them both together."

"Yes, well done; his one is the Savi's and that one is the Grasshopper."

"I can't hear either," said John, a bit pitifully, and I felt sorry for him as he explained that he just couldn't hear much birdsong any more.

We hear Grasshopper Warblers reeling their eponymous trill in a few marshy areas of the UK, but Savi's is a bit of a rarity. The two have an extremely similar continuous buzzing song, a bit like a grasshopper, and the only way to learn them is to hear them together; not really possible at home. I was chuffed to be able to do it here – and get it right!

We ambled along the boardwalk, picking up Whiskered Terns, White-winged Black Terns, Reed Buntings, Reed and Great Reed Warblers, a distant Marsh Harrier and more Savi's Warblers. Cranes were bugling somewhere in the marsh, their far-carrying trumpet calls providing a perfect, haunting atmosphere to this place. The board-walk ended abruptly in a wide, circular platform where several binocular-encrusted birders stood scanning the expanse of marsh and the odd bush that projected from the sea of reeds. It was a cool, calm and clear evening, so quiet, every avian chirp could be heard. Snipe were drumming as they tumbled in the sky, their outer tail feathers making a weird pulsing, primeval hum, and the trumpeting music of those cranes filled the air as the light began to fade.

"We are a bit late, but we will look for Aquatics from here," said Kate, settling down with her telescope.

"Looking for Aquatics" from that particular spot was fine by me! As she chatted to the other birders in Polish, arms were outstretched and sweeping to indicate where one or two birds had been seen recently. I set up my 'scope and had a look too. A White Stork flew over us.

"None showing just now," said Kate, "but they are calling and have been up on that smaller bush there." She pointed to a middle distance shrub growing all on its own, in a flat plain of wafting reed stems. It was getting darker by the minute. A slightly hesitant, squeaky call sounded plaintively from very nearby. No one batted an eyelid; a common bird then, but not familiar to me, except something rang bells from hunting for this thing before – in Hungary with Roy Adams.

"Bluethroat?" I said, a bit hesitantly.

"Yes," said Kate, still intent on finding Aquatic Warbler for us.

That was the second time I'd heard and failed to see Bluethroat, but if they were common here, I might have a better chance the next day.

It was getting more and more gloomy. A big orange sun was setting behind the only tree on the horizon, a tall spindly bush really, but it made a great photo.

Getting bored, I spent my time taking some pics of it through the 'scope.

Kate's tenacity was amazing. Like other guides I've been with, she was far keener to get the bird than me; I'd have given up half an hour earlier.

"Aquatic! In the 'scope," said Kate after another five minutes.

Both John and I had a good look. John could only just make out a bird, but eventually, and better through my own scope after the little bird had moved to the top of the bush, I got a decent if distant view. For a European warbler, they are striking, with a heavily striped head (not unlike Sedge Warbler, which is common in the UK) and bold cream coloured streaks in the wings. Aquatic Warblers are birds in trouble: the International Union for Conservation of Nature, the main body responsible for monitoring the status and threats to birds of the world, has classified it as "vulnerable", and Birdlife International has said the following:

"Since 1970, [Aquatic Warbler] is likely to have declined significantly as a result of the destruction of 80-90% of its habitat in the river systems of upper Pripyat, Yaselda (Belarus) and Biebrza/Narew (Poland). These systems hold approximately 75% of the European population. Owing to extensive conservation projects, the decline has been stopped in its central European strongholds in eastern Poland, Belarus and Ukraine, but continues in the Pomeranian population of north-west Poland and north-east Germany. In Hungary, the population collapsed in 2002-2007. The tiny Siberian population is on the brink of extinction and has probably already disappeared, in which case the species has become a European endemic breeder. Recent work has suggested the species may have suffered disproportionately from radiation following the Chernobyl disaster, though the reasons for this are unclear."

Biebrza, therefore, is about the only place *in the world*, where a casual visitor has any realistic chance of seeing one. Watching this little chap, and recalling how rare they are, I was ashamed not to have had more of Kate's tenacity; she would have done this many times (it was her job, after all), but John and I needed to get them here or the likelihood was, never again in our lives. With this in mind, and giving myself a good talking to, I watched the little bird for another fifteen minutes until it really was too dark to see anything.

"We must go, Robert," said Kate.

"Kate," I said, "that was fantastic. Thanks so much."

She could see I felt emotional about it and she accepted a hug, which I don't think was quite her usual style. I guess I had given her the reward she hopes for in her job; someone who is blown away by what she has to show them. John was more reticent; he was a lot older than us and he was clearly getting tired, as well as suffering from a bit of arthritis. He loved being here and giving it a go, but seeing everything was a luxury he couldn't expect.

"I can't get to see all the birds the way I used to," he said, "but I feel privileged just to be here at my age."

This confirmed there and then the value and urgency of doing my bike trip the way I had. I was in my early fifties and John could only have been fifteen years older; a salutary lesson in getting on with it while you can.

As we dropped John off, I thanked him for letting me gatecrash his evening with Kate. We returned to my bike, which I got out of Kate's garage over that metal rod, only with a lot of puffing and panting in the dark. Kate helped with a few shoves and we ended up giggling again at the absurdity of it. I decided that her brusque military air was just a defence mechanism; she took the giggles far too easily! Still grinning, we shook hands. She gave me some final advice for birding the next day then it came time to part.

"Can I buy you a drink Kate, as a thank you for this wonderful evening?" I asked.

"No, that is all right. I am glad you enjoyed it so much. I have a very early start tomorrow – you rememebr my talk, with the beaver? I must go to bed now. Thank you anyway. Good luck on the rest of your trip. I hope you see Bluethroat tomorrow – you will!"

We parted with the usual continental kiss to both cheeks and I rode off into the night.

Next day was very strange. After the late birding with Kate and John, which had come straight after the bike ride from Bialowieza, I was paralysed with tiredness and my back was as bad as it had been at any time. I stayed in bed until gone 10am. It is difficult to explain the shock this would cause to many birders;

"What! You were in the middle of the Biebrza Marshes... in May... in the morning... and *didn't* get up to go birding before breakfast?!"

Well... no! But that voice wasn't only coming from the spirit of all those birders out there, it was coming from inside me too; I was just too knackered to care. Even worse, I whiled away the day, putting off any birding as if it was a chore like painting a fence. I busied around, having breakfast, checking the bike a little and finding a bank. It was as if I were two Robs at once; one who was content to just amble about, not pushing his complaining body, and the other who was spluttering inside with outrage and incomprehension ("Get off your arse and go birding – you're wasting the day. You might never come back here. This is *Biebrza Marshes* for God's sake!"). The first Rob won; I just couldn't summon up the energy to get out there again.

I made a call to Emilija in Lithuania to arrange a meeting. Apart from ferries home, her mother's grave was the final goal of my trip and in many ways the true end of it all. I also wanted to meet Ieva who I had only known through Wilma and hadn't seen for a long time.

"Emilija?" I said into the phone

"Robert? You are here?" Emilija replied

"I'm still in Poland, at Biebrza."

"Where is that?"

Constantly taken aback that these amazing places aren't known by nearly everyone, I said,

"It's a big nature reserve near Grajevo. Not far from the border. I'm planning to get to Kaunas tomorrow, late morning."

"Oh, okay. Can you find the university in the centre of town? I can meet you there at about 1. pm."

"I think so. I have satnav, but tell me the street name just in case."

I got all the details and we said goodbye. Once again, it felt very strange to be talking like this, making an everyday arrangement to meet in a city where I had never been before, so far from home, but with someone I already knew. I had become so used to everything and everybody I encountered being new to me.

Eventually, by 3pm (a ridiculous time to *start* birding!), I was out on another boardwalk, looking for Kate's suggestions from the previous evening. My target birds were; Bluethroat (at least), Scarlet Rosefinch, Citrine Wagtail and Greater Spotted Eagle. I was also hoping to fluke a Great Snipe. Nearly all of this seemed highly unlikely as I left the bike in a roadside lay-by not far from the centre. The place was hiving with people. It was a Sunday and this was a weekend playground for many Poles. An open, flooded river plain lay to the right of the boardwalk with recently coppiced willows screening the left side. Tall young willow shoots, forced into rapid growth by the coppicing, wafted airily near my left shoulder.

"*BREEEOOOMM!*"

"*NEEEYAAOWWW!*"

"*EEEYEEYEEYOOOMM!*"

Three motorbikes buzzed loudly past on the other side of this tranquil hedge, like giant, angry wasps. They were the sort of lightweight, nasal trail bikes beloved by so many teenage males. This was a nail in the coffin for birding at Biebrza. Torn between incredulity that these bikes could be allowed in a place like this (so close to the marsh) and disappointment at myself for having left it so late to come out here, I walked on, feeling more and more that this was a final birding death throe rather than a spectacular finale. Thankfully it all quietened down further along the boardwalk towards a big wooden observation tower. I forced myself into serious birding mode. It was the perfect place for it; marshy, with lots of open water, scrubby for birds to flit around in and open all around for skyward or distant views of raptors. Biebrza really is one of *the* best sites in Europe to come birding. If I had come here at the beginning of the trip, I would be buzzing with excitement, everything feeling new; the air, the temperature, the vegetation and, of course, nearly every bird.

Three species of tern were ever present, screaming as they dipped and twisted, elegant as big white swallows. I reached the observation tower and spent a pleasant hour watching whatever flew, swam, paddled or walked by; Purple Heron, Spoonbill, Penduline Tit, Meadow Pipit, Whinchat, Lesser Whitethroat, more terns and a distant view of a White-tailed Eagle.

From the tower, the boardwalk continued for a few hundred yards before giving way to a hard path. It eventually led to another area full of people; mown grassy flats for picnics, and ponds with "out of bounds" signs which were being ignored by some Sausages who climbed a fence to go for a family paddle (no doubt, seriously destroying the habitat of some rare amphibian that only occurred in that one pond, here in Biebrza).

Thinking I'd got a young Citrine Wagtail (would-be Trip Tick) sitting in a low leafy tree, I put up with all the people for long enough to get some decent photos through the 'scope; I could ID it later. It didn't feel like there was anywhere else to go from here.

Heading back to the bike really would be the beginning of the end as far as birding was concerned. Sure, I might see a few more on my way back, but from there, I wouldn't be going anywhere new. I felt sad and suddenly tired at the thought;

"I'd like to go home now." I said out loud. Maybe that wagtail, Citrine or otherwise, was a bird too far.

I made myself stay a while to make sure I wasn't rushing away from this wonderful place a bit too quickly. On the distant horizon, across vast reedbeds and marshes, another (or the same?) White-tailed Eagle appeared. Just as I focused through the 'scope, a big brown bird dive-bombed it – another eagle! All I noted was "all brown" and "a bit smaller"; extremely frustrating because I might well have been looking at *Greater* Spotted Eagle – a bird that only occurs in this part of Europe (Poland and the Baltic states).

Things were feeling a little ragged at the edges now. I headed back along the boardwalk, more certain than ever that this was it for birding;, but there was just one more little frisson of excitement to come. Not far from the observation tower, I stopped to check out a few Little Brown Jobs (birders can rarely just walk away). One, in particular, did not want to play ball; a little grey-brown thing kept flitting up the tall reed stems, singing a song I'd heard before on this trip – in fact, I'd heard it the previous evening with Kate and John. It kept its back towards me as it sang; grey-brown and little else. Through the scope, I could see dull rust coloured patches on its outer tail feathers. I knew what that meant, but it wouldn't turn round for me to confirm its identity. After long minutes the bird eventually jumped 180 degrees round its reed stem, as easy as you please, revealing in the 'scope a riot of colour as it burst out a volley of song. Around its throat, as I'd suspected and hoped, were bands of shining blue, rust, white and black with a bold white spot in the centre. At last; a Bluethroat (Tick! – No 243) and this one was the white-spotted variety of Central Europe, which I had never seen before. A perky relative of Robin and Nightingale, we occasionally get red-spotted Bluethroat as a rare visitor from Scandinavia to the UK. This was to be the last new bird of my trip . I failed to see the other Biebrza specialities that I'd hoped for, but at least white-spotted Bluethroat was a cracking bird to end on; a blaze of colour and song – definitely *not* a bird too far.

Chapter 13 – A Grave Tale

With Claire almost finished her degree and Iain just about to start his, we put the house in Harrow up for sale over the summer just to test the market. While away on our annual sojourn in the Far North, we start getting offers. The unexpected speed of our house sale only contributes to my feelings that life is sweeping me along a little out of control. Rather than being absorbed in the usual return to a new academic year at work, I am preoccupied with sorting out where and how we will live.

We get a map of Britain and go through all our moving options from Scotland to North Wales, and Northumberland to Suffolk. In the end, I remind myself and Anne how much I loved the Suffolk countryside from my days working in Cambridge and we take a couple of trips driving around the county, looking at houses and getting a feel for things. It's like Escape to the Country, without the help of the BBC! A move to Suffolk is not only sensible, being still fairly close to family and friends, but it is far enough from London to get away from the gridlock and stress of city life, to a place where maybe I can find the peace and time to look after Anne-and find a life for myself at the same time.

We move to near Bury St Edmunds in the middle of October, two months before I am due to finish work. Iain has gone to start his first year at University from his home in Harrow, which now belongs to someone else! I feel very unhappy that he won't be able to come back to the place he calls home; instead, he has to trek all the way to Suffolk from Oxford to a new house that he can surely never think of as home. I worry that, if things don't work out in the rarefied atmosphere of Oxford's dreaming spires, he will feel lost. Thankfully, all seems to go well on that front – or Iain hides well any sense of abandonment (sorry Iain; it was a gamble we had to take).

The new house is in the middle of nowhere, in a strange row of ten bungalows all on their own, a mile down a dead end single track lane. It's perfect! And the perfect time for my bike trip; Claire and Iain can be at home between terms (in Claire's case, at the end of her degree) and Anne isn't so bad that they can't look after her. They may not be so free to help in my absence once they leave home to work or travel; it is now or never. I plan and I organise; all the logistics, all the equipment and by no means least, care for Anne for two months. Finally, the date is set for April 12th of the following year, leaving on a ferry from Portsmouth to Santander in northern Spain.

*

My return to the Biebrza centre was weary, but in a way, oddly settled. I was happy that the birding was over. No more hunting, no more "will I, won't I". After another welcome night in the centre, I said a fond goodbye to Artur and headed off via Grajevo and Augustow for Lithuania – and the final stage of the whole trip.

I left Biebrza after an abortive attempt to adjust the bike chain. On most bikes, the drive chain is a set of interlocking links and rivets which drive the rear wheel on a ring of sprockets, very similar to that on a push-bike. It has to take considerably more pounding though and the force required to drive a heavy bike causes the chain to stretch. Here in northern Poland, after nearly six thousand miles, it was flapping around a bit too much and the rear wheel needed nudging back a little to tighten it. I had the tools, but not the strength to get the wheel nuts off; my back was having none of it. The distance I now had to cover was relatively small and anyway, you are supposed to have some slack in the chain, or so I told myself! I decided to leave it, rather than find a garage and wait around for it to be done.

Heading into Lithuania, the border was another redundant affair; a desolate expanse of tarmac with no one on it. Presumably, these vast concourses are legacies from communism and the Cold War when the border was a holding place to check every person, vehicle, horse, cart or goat that tried to get in or out. They must have been forbidding places to wait in endless queues. Now they just felt pointlessly empty and deserted. A single, lonely looking guard glanced at my vignette to let me through. I exchanged my Polish Zloti into Lithuanian Lei and headed off for some petrol.

The A5 towards Kaunas was uneventful – apart from the fuel stop along the way. As I stood beside the bike, injecting petrol into the big silver tank, a distant quiet murmur slowly built and turned into a deafening rumble from all sides; two groups of Hell's Angels met in a pincer movement to park all along the access road within the petrol station. It was like a military coup. There must have been about thirty of them, and their presence was palpable, verging on threatening. Two, in particular, made me feel extremely nervous; they were at the pumps closest to me and followed me into the shop. As a sort of safety release, I chose to defuse the tension by asking them how far I had to go to Kaunas then Klaipeda for the ferry. Being a biker, I thought I might make a connection with them ("Oh, you are a travelling on your own. How brave of you. We only feel safe in big, intimidating groups.")

They weren't interested. I was the wrong sort of biker – a wuss in their eyes, no doubt! One did gruffly ask the other how far, and I got a dismissive, unsmiling guess in reply.

I hung around to see how all this worked and I watched as they took over the place. Looking a little more carefully at some of them, hidden behind dark glasses and the Angels Chapter uniforms of Latvia and Lithuania, more than a few were middle-aged, fat guys who probably went home to their mothers or the wife and kids and to work in the office next day. Their acceptably mean-looking bikes were clearly the only ticket needed to join this army. For most of them, I concluded, it was all about the bikes; Harleys mostly, with crazy modifications that made them look like battle vehicles. Nearly all were painted black, with high handlebars, chopper style seats and enormous, loud engines and exhausts. One machine was a Triumph 2300 Rocket III, with an engine from a car, I swear![58]

I was a little disappointed at how these Angels were living up to their historical reputation. I had heard many times that nowadays, Angels Chapters are just friendly, charity-giving groups of lifestyle freaks. Here, they strutted around and generally imposed with an intimidating air, giving no quarter to anyone else. Apart from that, I suppose they behaved themselves, but I was sure that any over-familiarity would have been met with a four-letter version of "go away", and the slightest provocation would've led to all-out war.

Like a battalion getting ready to move, they fired up their various bikes. A low rumble filled the air and vibrated the ground as they rejoined the highway in two groups. A large Transit van support vehicle followed them out; this explained how they could travel with so little luggage. Wimps!

Kaunas looked like a major city, with a wide river and a long sweeping bridge taking busy traffic into the town. It had lots of open water and green spaces around the centre and seemed like a pleasant place to live. I went straight to the meeting point with Emilija, sent her a text to say exactly where I was and waited. Again, I felt oddly out of place, in the middle of a busy city, leaning against the bike on a paved concourse outside the large university building with students milling around. The bike, the luggage and my travel-worn attire, as well as my general hobo disposition, did not fit in here. I got a few stares, but as in most cities, the engrossed masses tend to be oblivious to the individual. I waited.

Emilija duly appeared, smiling and a little surprised at my whole appearance.

"Wow! You look like you have travelled a long way! I never thought you would actually do it. Look at you and this bike – so cool!"

She was young.

---

[58]Currently, at 2294 cc, the Rocket III has the biggest engine of any production motorcycle – bigger than that of most cars on the road!

"Well, Emilija, I'm tired now and have hurt my back, but this is journey's end. I've been heading here for the last seven weeks. How are you?... and Ieva?... and her mum?"

"All good, thanks. You will meet them all. Let's go to Ieva's flat now. I walk and you can follow on your bike?"

"Ok. Is it far?"

"No. Just a few blocks."

We waited for Ieva, having a cup of tea in her spacious apartment within a beautiful big old (19th century?) building. Everything ordinary and civilised like that struck me as odd; I was so conscious of it all. This grand inside space felt strange after so long on the road and all those wild places. Zarnesti, Trigrad, Tarvisio and Loporzano all came flooding back and I even found it strange to just sit down indoors and chat. Somehow, this wasn't how it was supposed to be.

Ieva arrived, a smiling waif of a girl, she blew away all those thoughts. I had met her some years before in London where she had visited us with Wilma and I had taken to her straight away. It was so good to see her again. She looked older, but still very youthful and she dressed with great style; like Wilma, she was an artist.

"You have a great place here Ieva," I told her, looking around, and could see that it was only partly redecorated.

"Yes, it is good, but there is a lot to do. We were going to do it all, but I have split up with my partner and it has all stopped."

I could tell it was a difficult subject for her, and one she'd had enough of, without having to explain it all to a relative stranger. A little late in the day, I gave her a warm hug which she returned with a welcoming kiss on the cheek.

"So lovely to see you again," she said, "I didn't think you would do it. So many people make plans and don't do them. I am envious of you. What are you going to do now?"

"Well, I need to find a hotel – do you know one? I want to go to Wilma's grave and I'd like to meet Alma finally. But I don't have long. I have a ferry booked for tomorrow from Klaipeda, so I can't stay long in Kaunas"

"Oh, you will have no time at all. You won't go to Vilnius or do some touring of Lithuania? You have come so far."

"I know Ieva. I have just run out of time. I had to book the ferry to make sure I could get home. I've also hurt my back and am very tired after such a long trip."

This was the first of several embarrassing moments where I felt I was making a faux pas. To come here in Wilma's memory, to meet long lost friends again and her sister for the first time, and not stay a little to see their country, was perhaps a bit like a slap in the face for them. No one said anything remotely like that, but nearly everyone I met seemed disappointed at my rushing through their homeland.

The only place Ieva and Emilija knew of was a central business hotel, but the last thing I wanted to do was haggle over prices or location so I plumped for it regardless. The Reval Hotel Neris was the swishest hotel I'd stayed in; full of business people, snappily dressed in suits. Then there was me!

The bike had gone in the hotel's underground car park, where I met Emilija again, just outside the roller shutter door. As if from a dark cave, I appeared on the bike, ready to go to Wilma's grave. She had borrowed a helmet so she could ride pillion with me, but I could tell she wasn't very into all this.

"I don't go to Mum's grave," she said, a little dismissively, "I don't really see the point. I prefer to remember her when she was alive."

This left me a little deflated, though I feel exactly the same about graves at home (even my own mother's way up North in Scotland), but I wasn't going to be put off after coming all this way.

"I know what you mean Emily," I said, "but I didn't see your mum again after leaving her at the airport all those years ago. She was so upset and frightened, I will never forget it. I just need to say goodbye... sort of."

Emily nodded with a little sad resignation. Maybe there was more to not visiting her mum's grave than just "not seeing the point".

With the luggage left back at the hotel and Emilija on the back of the bike, we sped off. I didn't tell her that I'd never had someone riding pillion before. So much easier than you might think, it changed the riding slightly, but the only awkward thing was judging speed; I rode far too fast. Maybe it was the weight distribution or maybe she was lighter than my luggage had been,, but the bike seemed to move so much quicker than before. The front of Emilija's helmet kept bashing into the back of mine as she directed me through the outskirts of Kaunas to the cemetery. After a couple of miles, I got the hang of it and was riding a bit more smoothly as we entered the cemetery gates.

A stall-holder sold me some flowers; another awkward moment with Emilija. She really was not into all this, but she maybe felt some pressure to join in. She took me to the family grave where Wilma was buried. I just stood for a while, but was aware of Emilija's discomfort and it got in the way of any deep reflection on my part. Maybe just as well; after all that journey to get here and remembering Wilma as I do, I'm sure I'd have worked up to some gushing sentiment if I had been alone.

The headstone read "Markaucku seima". Emilija explained this was a family grave and individuals weren't mentioned separately. At the bottom of the gravestone were words which, in my hastily scrawled notes, look like "Liudi artimeiji". I failed to ask Emilija for a translation, but I later found that "Luidi" means uniquely beautiful and "seima", music. Uniquely beautiful music will do me as my memory of dear Wilma.

In the evening we all met for dinner at a trendy rooftop restaurant where we were given blankets for our knees. I met Wilma's sister, Alma, and a few people who had known Wilma and her connection with me. Alma's English was hesitant but, with a little translation and non-verbal communication, we had a meeting of spirits.

Wilma had left London years before. I will never forget taking her to Luton airport and watching her go through customs in floods of frightened tears; she knew she would never come back and I knew why she was so upset. Her cancer had left her horribly bloated with oedema; she could hardly walk and she had lost all her hair. She would have arrived back here in Kaunas, meeting Alma in this frightening condition. Alma and the rest of Wilma's family then had to watch her die.

To say there was an unspoken connection between Alma and me would be a huge understatement. I could tell from her eyes that I represented a part of Wilma that she never knew, a part that was finally here in front of her, in flesh and blood. Our meeting was as significant for her as it was for me; possibly a painful reminder of those sad times. But, for the rest of the evening, the banter amongst the young people and the clumsy translations between Alma and myself made the time pass easily.

The subject of my brief time in Lithuania came up again and the result was an invite to Alma's flat for breakfast with her, Ieva and Emilija. I accepted, despite feeling really nervous that I might miss the ferry by not getting away in time in the morning. I had most of the next day to ride the 140 miles to Klaipeda, but I was a little paranoid about getting a bike breakdown on the very last leg. It almost happened too.

Before going to bed in the Reval Hotel Neris, I decided to send Claire a text to confirm my plans;

Hi Claire. In Kaunas with Wilma's family. Planning to get the ferry you booked tomorrow from Klaipeda to Kiel in Germany, then Esbjerg to Harwich and home. All going ok. Hope all ok with Mum. See you soon. Dad x

Alma's flat was interesting to visit; Ieva got us a taxi next morning to an austerely grey housing block that looked like so much of the social housing erected in the sixties and seventies by governments across the Soviet Block. The walls, floors, partitions and stairwells were solid concrete slabs. When Alma explained that people bought these flats now because the structure was so good, I believed it. It wasn't pretty on the outside, but inside, Alma had transformed the place into a lovely home. They had bought it as a family and were making the most of it. There was a topsy-turvy sense to the arrangements here; Ieva was Alma's daughter, but she lived in the town centre, while Emilija shared the flat with Alma, her aunt – and there were no men on the scene at all. Wilma had broken up with her husband some time before she came to London and Alma seemed to have separated from her guy too. This left an all-girl group, living and looking after themselves.

Breakfast was cosy and welcome. Once more, it seemed strange to be in a domestic setting with people I knew instead of in some café on the road, on my own and surrounded by strangers. Alma got out some childhood photos of Wilma and their family and we reminisced.

"This is of you and your family with Wilma?" said Alma, producing a little clutch of photos that I had taken and given to Wilma years before.

"Yes, yes!" I said, "we all went to a big house called Littlecote. This is Wilma rolling down the grass with Claire and Iain. They were having fun. And this is Wilma helping Anne to walk with her stick."

I scribbled a note on the back of the photos, saying where they were taken and "Happy Days with Wilma. Gone, but not forgotten." Ieva translated and passed on her mum's reply;

"Mum says she has often imagined you and Anne from these photos and has always wanted to meet you. It means so much to her that you have come here all this way."

Alma said more to Ieva.

"... and she wants to thank you for everything you did for her sister all those years ago."

Alma was nodding, tears rolling down her cheeks. I reached out and held her, on the point of tears myself. What I couldn't feel at the cemetery, I felt now.

We looked at a few more photos and bizarrely, someone put on some music and we danced; Ieva with Emilija and Alma with me. Maybe this was a Lithuanian custom, but I never asked.

Soon Ieva had to go and I had to go with her. I said some very heartfelt goodbyes and she took me back to the hotel. More goodbyes saw Ieva disappear and I was on my own again.

A text came in from my daughter;

That's all correct EXCEPT 27TH IS TODAY! GET ON THE FERRY! XX (unless you sent that yday – weds – & I only just got it, in which case all ok!)

I had a frantic moment thinking I'd made some cock-up with the dates or in communicating them with Claire, then I remembered that I'd sent my text the previous evening, and today was indeed the 27th, the day of my ferry. This heart-in-mouth moment only fuelled my artificial and unnecessary sense of urgency.

Now I had to check out of the hotel, extract my bike from the underground garage and get to Klaipeda. It started raining again, as it had off and on for weeks. I was determined not to get wet feet again, so I set about tying plastic bags around the lower part of my boots. A few miles out of Kaunas, one bag had already shredded, doing nothing to stem the ingress of water. The other, a much more heavy duty job, was intact and proving the theory quite well until it too came loose and disappeared in the air flow; wet feet it was then.

In my unreasonable and unnecessary rush to get to the ferry (I had hours before the sailing), I decided not to waste time filling up with petrol. This was the main road across the centre of Lithuania to its main port and I assumed there would be a petrol station within twenty or thirty miles. After forty miles, still no petrol. One or two were signposted, but they were at some distance from this main road. I pulled in at another, to find that it only did paraffin, diesel and LPG. What?! No petrol?

The further I went the more worried I got. With something like ninety miles to go, I would run out well before Klaipeda. There had to be petrol somewhere on this road. At a mind-boggling 45 miles since leaving Kaunas, I saw a miserly sign to some service station set well off the route. I had to take a chance, hope it wasn't too far and that it had petrol, not kerosene, coal or plutonium. The place was little more than a shack, but it did have a pump that produced petrol. Thank God. I couldn't get over the lack of fuel stops on a major route like this. I felt that I'd had a close shave on the home straight, and all I wanted now was to get to Klaipeda for the ferry.

Tim abandoned me at the last minute as we approached the port; he knew nothing of the commercial terminal where the ferry would be sailing from, and his little video screen became a sea of nothing with little biker-man lost in the middle of it. I followed a lorry, more in hope than judgement, but it worked. Despite a circuitous route that I would never have found (along a perimeter fence and over freight railway lines) we got to the right terminal with no setbacks. The ferry didn't sail until 5pm. I had a couple of hours to spare, but was happy to just wait until they'd let us on board. Parking the bike, I chatted to my fellow prospective passengers: a German couple who were driving a Red Cross lorry back from delivering aid to Kosovo and a quiet Dutch bloke who was a biker with a BMW F 650, the bike I almost bought for the trip.

Unlike the ferry from Portsmouth, the deck hands did not usher us away from the bikes so they could lash them down properly; we had to do that ourselves, sandwiched between lorries and vans. The Dutch guy was the only other biker so we worked together.

I was so glad to have some long hours trapped on the ferry, to just sit and relax, sleep, and catch up with my notes. With the exhaustion of two months on the road, this was exactly what I needed. Over dinner, I met up with Roald, the Dutch biker and we talked (rather I talked!) about our common interests; bikes, guitarists and guitars. He was almost painfully quiet – or shy. But I was unstoppable. Poor bloke! I talk a lot at the best of times, but after so much isolation, and despite the brief time with friends in Kaunas, I couldn't help, but fill his silences with chatter.

"You're a pilot! Excellent – how did that come about?"

If Roald found my gabble irritating, he didn't let on.

"I am used to moving around." he said. "so it seemed a good thing to do. I was born in Africa, moved to Italy, then Holland and then to the USA to train as a pilot."

"So you don't think of anywhere as home?" I asked.

"Probably Holland, but I am based around Riga in Latvia now. I work for Baltic Air."

Roald was so unassuming, he didn't realise that his was an interesting life compared to many. He was very self-effacing about being a pilot.

"It's not as glamorous as people think," he said, "I don't get paid much, not much holiday and the hours can be long, away from home."

"I've heard that about commercial pilots. Would it be better working for the bigger airlines?"

"In some ways, but there is a lot of pressure there. It is also more like being a robot, not a pilot. With Baltic, I fly smaller aircraft and go different routes. There is more variety."

"So you're on holiday now?"

"Yes, just a short vacation, biking to Denmark. I am looking for a left-handed guitar." he said, changing the subject.

We talked guitars, guitarists and then bikes. I told him about my close shave with a buying a BMW F650 like his.

"I have just bought this bike," he said, "I like it, but I'm not an experienced biker."

I gabbled on about my trip, why I was doing it and a little about why I was here in Lithuania. Looking back, I hope he found some of my chatter half as interesting as I had found his few words. A few days later, I discovered that he went onto my blog, left a little message and donated £50 to my online fundraising for the MS Therapy Centre. Thanks Roald!

When it came to bedtime, I discovered that Roald didn't have a berth; he was trying to kip in the darkened lounge with a load of others strewn across the floor. I agonised over offering him the second bed in my cabin, but it felt too familiar and, sorry to say, I didn't want him thinking it was some sort of pick-up (I wasn't sure I had mentioned my wife and family in all the chat). Back in the cabin, I agonised some more and almost went back to find him, but in the end my stuff was everywhere, my back was seizing up and, unfairly (having inflicted my yakking on him), I wanted a bit of time to myself. I needed to write some notes and phone home.

"I'm on the ferry in Klaipeda." I said to Anne on the mobile.

"Did you have a good time?"

"Yes, but it's been long. I'm looking forward to getting home now. Emily took me to Wilma's grave yesterday and I met Ieva again with Wilma's sister, Alma."

"Oh well, I'm glad your back is getting better."

This was said in an icy tone, showing no interest in those people whom she knew, including Wilma. I knew the story now; Anne's hackles were up, she was feeling every bit as abandoned and resentful as before, possibly more. I bristled myself, in return.

"My back is not better. I never said that, but how are things at home? Is Claire around?"

The phone went quiet.

"Hi Dad. You on the ferry?" came Claire's voice, "you gave me a heart attack with that text!"

"Yes, I'm on the ferry. Thanks for doing all the booking. Texts were a bit out of synch; don't know what happened there, sorry."

We had a chat about things at home and some of my experiences. Anne didn't come back on the line.

Next morning, the ferry pulled into Kiel in northern Germany. I had a two hour ride north into Denmark for a second ferry from Esbjerg next day across the North Sea to Harwich, a mere fifty miles from home.

All things in Kiel and through most of Germany were so much more developed and urban than nearly everywhere else I had been. A café I stopped at was clean and neat to the point of being clinical. It was good though; comfortable and easy (Western life in a nutshell?), and maybe the reason why we are so reluctant in the West to relinquish our home comforts, which we now believe are "essentials". But who am I to preach, with my love of Kaffee und Kuchen!

The German autobahn experience (no speed limit) was one I could have done without. On a bike, with vehicles right on your elbow, speeds in excess of 100mph are just scary. Even with the power and acceleration of my bike, I found it nerve-wracking to pull out in order to overtake a lorry. A car which looked like a distant dot in the mirror would be right next to me in a flash. I had to be so much more focused and committed in making moves on this road. It was so tiring, I was glad to pull off the autobahn onto a smaller road, heading for Kolding and hopefully a hotel that would be less expensive than those a little further on in Esbjerg – wrong!

Why I didn't ride on to Esbjerg I don't know, but I stuck with Kolding, a medium-sized seaport town halfway up the east side of Denmark, and ended up in a very expensive chalet hotel. With the trip all but over, I was a bit gung-ho with the cash. How much could I possibly spend in the last couple of days? The answer is – a lot! Denmark is one of the most expensive places I have ever been to. Compared to the countries I had been travelling in, the cost of things was just ludicrous. In Esbjerg next day, for example, I spent over £5 in Danish Krone on one cup of coffee. I didn't feel I could afford to have anything to eat; I could get some cheap grub on the ferry and would need to fill the time anyway while sailing.

Esbjerg was lovely though, with its pretty cobbled square, outside cafes and old streets with lots of small artisan shops. I even found a café with internet access and, for some reason, the kindly patron lady wouldn't take any money for use of the computer nor for the coffee which she offered without request. She was just about to close when I arrived, so she locked us in as she put her feet up after a long day, insisting pleasantly that I stay as long as I needed to. I could say she set all this up as an opportunistic seduction leading to tumultuous sex on the coffee tables but, in the absence of sex (tumultuous or otherwise!), it seems she simply couldn't be bothered opening up the till again to charge me for the coffee. Or maybe she just liked bikers.

"Do you speak English?" I asked another shopkeeper further down the street.

"Of course!" was the slightly indignant reply. Everybody spoke English here – impeccable English. Even round a table at the £5-a-cup café, Danish people were talking in English, as if dropping into a local accent, rather than another language. As always, when faced with this Scandinavian linguistic prowess, it made me feel unsophisticated and backward on behalf of myself and my country-folk; we are so inward looking in Britain. Why can't we teach our kids to speak at least one foreign language half decently?

I wanted the ferry home to last forever. I needed a lot of mental preparation for my return and I was aware that my weeks of not caring for anyone, but myself were over. I was also dreading the homecoming, considering Anne's obvious and repeated resentment at my absence. This was compounded by another phone call to home. It started off all friendly. Anne even sounded genuinely glad that I'd be back home soon, but like all the other calls, it deteriorated until finally she said, "If we're not in when you get home, we'll have gone shopping."

Sure, go shopping so the house is like a morgue when I get back! Maybe I'll meet you and go round Sainsbury's as a homecoming. I still wonder if, after an absence of two months on the trip of a lifetime, this wasn't perfectly reasonable. No, it bloody wasn't! But Anne was just expressing her deep sense of abandonment again. I knew that, and I could understand it. She had never really accepted, at any point, that I needed to make this journey, how much it meant to me or how damaging it would have been if I *hadn't* done it.

I set the alarm for a ridiculous six o'clock wake up. It was all part of wanting to stretch out this last bit of freedom; for the last time trapped on a boat with only my thoughts, cups of coffee, the odd meal and fellow passengers to chat to. I mused on one of the unique aspects of my trip; trying to decide if biking and birding make a successful combination. Well, in as much as it meant I had spent nearly two months doing both (double value, so to speak), it was a great success. On the other hand, there were many ways in which one compromised the other. Biking meant being constantly aware of the valuable equipment I had with me; I could rarely leave it somewhere on the bike and just go for a walk. Equally, birding almost exclusively determined the route and it restricted the freedom I might have had to choose the best biking routes and distances. A car would also have been more sensible in many ways, but then that wasn't the point. I concluded that yes, you can go birding on a bike and enjoy both. Anyway, *Cars 9; Bikes 8*-it's more or less a draw!

Harwich came into view all too soon, but by then even I had had enough of ferries. I was itching to get off the boat and get on the bike for the last time. It was so strange to be doing this in such familiar surroundings; riding on the left, noticing our quaint road signs, the style of English towns and villages and just how clean and green everything was. I used to wonder in what way Britain feels foreign to visitors. I could never quite step out of the ingrained familiarity to see it through a visitor's eyes, as anything other than – familiar. This was the first time I had ever been able to look in from the outside, with fresh, foreign eyes... and it was wonderful. Suffolk, at least, was a beautiful patchwork of green lanes, hedges, fields and tidy villages-with proper pavements! It was all surprisingly neat and clean with welcoming old pubs and thatched cottages (lots of them, where people actually lived), many painted that Suffolk Pink – or Dulux Gaudy Pink, in some cases – which is so characteristic of where I now live. I realised how much of both the countryside and the built areas of Europe are parched, dusty and uncared for, or just plain run down. Britain is still a rich, developed nation with a culture and countryside that is largely protected and lived in. It is changing, of course; we have lost so much of our native wildlife and their habitats, and there are many, many pockets of neglect and deprivation, especially in our cities. But I now saw why people would want to come to Britain. As I rode the last few miles along those rich country lanes, I was choked by the gentle, understated beauty of the place in which I lived.

I was home.

THE END

Appendix – The Bird List

Quail
Pheasant
Greylag Goose
Mute Swan
Shelduck
Ruddy Shelduck
Gadwall
Wigeon
Mallard
Shoveler
Garganey
Teal
Red-crested Pochard
Pochard
Ferruginous Duck
Tufted Duck
Goldeneye
Little Grebe
Red-necked Grebe
Great Crested Grebe
Black Stork
White Stork
Glossy Ibis
Spoonbill
Bittern
Little Bittern
Black-crowned Night Heron
Squacco Heron
Cattle Egret
Grey Heron
Purple Heron
Great Egret
Little Egret
Great White Pelican
Dalmatian Pelican
Gannet
Pygmy Cormorant

Great Cormorant
Lesser Kestrel
Common Kestrel
Red-footed Falcon
Hobby
Saker Falcon
Peregrine Falcon
Red Kite
Black Kite
White-tailed Sea Eagle
Lammergeier
Egyptian Vulture
Griffon Vulture
Black vulture
Short-toed Eagle
Western Marsh Harrier
Montagu's Harrier
Levant Sparrowhawk
Sparrowhawk
Goshawk
Buzzard
Long-legged Buzzard
Rough-legged Buzzard
Lesser Spotted Eagle
Eastern Imperial Eagle
Golden Eagle
Bonelli's Eagle
Booted Eagle
Great Bustard
Little Bustard
Water Rail
Moorhen
Coot
Common Crane
Black-winged Stilt
Lapwing
Ringed Plover

Little Ringed Plover
Common Snipe
Black-tailed Godwit
Bar-tailed Godwit
Whimbrel
Curlew
Spotted Redshank
Common Redshank
Marsh Sandpiper
Greenshank
Wood Sandpiper
Common Sandpiper
Curlew Sandpiper
Dunlin
Ruff
Collared Pratincole
Great Black-backed Gull
Common Gull
Herring Gull
Yellow-legged Gull
Lesser Black-backed Gull
Great Black-headed Gull
Common Black-headed Gull
Little Gull
Caspian Tern
Common Tern
Little Tern
Whiskered Tern
White-winged Black Tern
Black Tern
Pin-tailed Sandgrouse
Black-bellied Sandgrouse
Rock Dove
Stock Dove
Woodpigeon
European Turtle Dove
Eurasian Collared Dove
Great Spotted Cuckoo
Common Cuckoo
Barn Owl

Scops Owl
Tawny Owl
Little Owl
Short-eared Owl
Alpine Swift
Common Swift
European Roller
Common Kingfisher
European Bee-eater
Hoopoe
Wryneck
Lesser Spotted Woodpecker
Middle Spotted Woodpecker
White-backed Woodpecker
Syrian Woodpecker
Great Spotted Woodpecker
Three-toed Woodpecker
Black Woodpecker
Green Woodpecker
Grey-headed Woodpecker
Lesser Grey Shrike
Red-backed Shrike
Woodchat Shrike
Golden Oriole
Jay
Azure-winged Magpie
Common Magpie
Red-billed Chough
Jackdaw
Rook
Carrion Crow
Raven
Great Tit
Blue Tit
Coal Tit
Penduline Tit
Sand Martin
Barn Swallow
Crag Martin
House Martin

Red-rumped Swallow
Long-tailed Tit
Calandra Lark
Greater Short-toed Lark
DuPont's Lark
Crested Lark
Thekla Lark
Woodlark
Skylark
Cetti's Warbler
Grasshopper Warbler
River Warbler
Savi's Warbler
Great Reed Warbler
Aquatic Warbler
Sedge Warbler
Paddyfield Warbler
Reed Warbler
Marsh Warbler
Olivaceous Warbler
Icterine Warbler
Willow Warbler
Common Chiffchaff
Blackcap
Garden Warbler
Barred Warbler
Lesser Whitethroat
Orphean Warbler
Greater Whitethroat
Spectacled Warbler
Subalpine Warbler
Sardinian Warbler
Bearded Tit
Goldcrest
Wren
Nuthatch
Wallcreeper
Treecreeper
Short-toed Treecreeper
European Starling

Spotless Starling
Blackbird
Song Thrush
Mistle Thrush
Fieldfare
European Robin
Bluethroat
Thrush Nightingale
Common Nightingale
Black Redstart
Common Redstart
Whinchat
Common Stonechat
Isabelline Wheatear
Northern Wheatear
Pied Wheatear
Black-eared Wheatear
Black Wheatear
Common Rock Thrush
Blue Rock Thrush
Spotted Flycatcher
Pied Flycatcher
Collared Flycatcher
Semi-collared Flycatcher
Red-breasted Flycatcher
White-throated Dipper
House Sparrow
Spanish Sparrow
Tree Sparrow
Rock Sparrow
Dunnock
Yellow Wagtail
Grey Wagtail
White Wagtail
Tawny Pipit
Meadow Pipit
Chaffinch
Serin
Greenfinch
Goldfinch

Common Linnet
Bullfinch
Hawfinch
Corn Bunting
Yellowhammer

Western Rock Bunting
Ortolan Bunting
Black-headed Bunting
Reed Bunting

Printed in Poland
by Amazon Fulfillment
Poland Sp. z o.o., Wrocław